UNDERSTANDING OURSELVES AND OTHERS

Understanding
Ourselves
and
Others

KURT HAAS

Professor, Behavior Science Division
State University College
New Paltz, New York

Prentice-Hall, Inc., Englewood Cliffs, New Jersey

PRENTICE-HALL PSYCHOLOGY SERIES
Richard S. Lazarus, editor

PRENTICE-HALL INTERNATIONAL, INC., London
PRENTICE-HALL OF AUSTRALIA PTY., LTD., Sydney
PRENTICE-HALL OF CANADA, LTD., Toronto
PRENTICE-HALL OF INDIA (PRIVATE) LTD., New Delhi
PRENTICE-HALL OF JAPAN, INC., Tokyo

© 1965 by PRENTICE-HALL, INC.
Englewood Cliffs, N. J.

Library of Congress Catalog Card No.: 65–12483

Printed in the United States of America
93606—C

PREFACE

One of the characteristics that distinguish man from other animals is his intense interest in understanding himself and others. Today, many specialists concern themselves with probing the actions of men. In addition, each one of us, whether trained or not, has his own views of human beings and interpretations of their personality. It is the purpose of this book to provide some of the information uncovered by psychologists, psychiatrists, and other scientists so that we may better understand ourselves and intelligently perceive the behavior of others.

The organization of this book is intended, first, to help the reader understand the roots and many ramifications of human behavior, and then to introduce him to the techniques used to evaluate personality and treat its disorders. After an introduction to the methods and principles of the psychologist, Part One sets forth the developmental processes, the major environmental and inherent determinants, that shape personality. Part Two is concerned with the description and

v

measurement of various aspects of human behavior, and Parts Three and Four describe adjustive processes, abnormal conditions, and treatment techniques. The closing chapter addresses the reader directly, and suggests a personal orientation intended to help maximize mental health potentials.

Within the parts, each chapter is prepared so that the reader gets sufficiently detailed factual information to enable him to grasp the meaning of psychological studies while he learns to understand the actions of men. Whenever relevant and feasible, the chapters include the results of current research and extensive samples and illustrations. In several instances case histories, drawn directly from identified professional sources, are given in their entirety. Although the cases are especially selected for the chapters in which they appear, they can also provide excellent sources for discussions of motivation, adjustment processes, and psychological diagnoses and treatment.

This book might be useful to any of several groups of readers.

1. For students in courses in personality, adjustment, human relations, mental hygiene, or related areas—whether offered in psychology or other disciplines—the book may serve as a text.

2. For students in modified or shortened courses introducing the psychological, behavioral, and social sciences, the book may provide a text, or supplement, that discusses those areas usually of greatest interest.

Kurt Haas

ACKNOWLEDGMENTS

The preparation of this book was assisted by many persons whose work is gratefully acknowledged in the Reference section and on the pages on which their contributions appear. Thanks are due to associates and colleagues who generously provided case history material that is not otherwise identified.

Special thanks are due Miss Lenora King, who assisted in typing during the several stages of the preparation of the manuscript. I am indebted also to several reviewers, to Dr. Richard S. Lazarus, of the University of California, and Mr. Roger T. Holloway, Prentice-Hall editor, for their suggestions, which helped shape the direction of the book. Especial gratitude is owed Mr. Cecil Yarbrough, Special Projects editor, for his patient and creative editing.

Very special appreciation is owed my wife, Adelaide N. Haas, for her aid in preparing the entire manuscript and especially for her contributions to Chapter Fourteen.

CONTENTS

ix

UNDERSTANDING OURSELVES AND OTHERS

Psychology:

The Science of

Human Behavior

O N E

How the Facts of Psychology Become Fables
The Subject Matter of Psychology—The Study of Human Behavior
Understanding Multiple Cause and Cause and Effect
Causality and Responsibility
Individual and Group Prejudices that Impede Understanding
of Normal and Abnormal Behavior

1

Psychology is an exciting and in many ways brilliant new science. It is a vigorous and expanding enterprise that, through its efforts to evaluate and guide normal as well as abnormal behavior, intimately touches the lives of everyone. Since nearly all of us are interested in probing and helping ourselves and those close to us, psychological information is avidly sought. We want to understand psychology, to know why we and others act and feel as we do and whether our thoughts and emotions are shared by the people around us.

In response to the widespread curiosity about human behavior, magazines, newspapers, television, and motion pictures are filled with articles and stories that seek to translate the facts of psychology into everyday language. Too frequently, however, they oversimplify, misinterpret, and create fables. Thus, despite the attention given psychological phenomena in all communication and entertainment media, little information of real worth is produced. Few who have not actually been patients have an accurate idea of the complexities of psychotherapy. Despite the fact that concepts like introversion, neurosis, and IQ have crept into everyday conversation, their valid use and meaning eludes most persons.

FACT INTO FABLE

False notions about psychology abound. Some people expect psychologists to be mystics or eccentrics. Others think they possess techniques that enable them to probe the very deepest and hidden recesses of personality and at a glance reveal all there is to know about a person. Or they may expect psychologists, by a few well chosen words or hypnotic passes, to free them from inferiority feeling, the habit of smoking, or enuresis. These mistaken ideas are relied upon by many incompetents who announce themselves as "psychologists" and feed on the ignorance and gullibility of the distressed. Such scientifically untrained people often publicize their supposed skills in reading character from handwriting or bumps on the head and advertise their imagined ability to "cure" all sorts of "nervous" conditions. There are other self-styled psychologists whose lack of training or qualification is more difficult to detect. Many "psychoquacks" call themselves—as legitimately trained psychologists might—therapists, counselors, or marriage consultants and boast "degrees" from mail-order schools that provide elaborately impressive but meaningless documents—for a steep price.

Psychologists are scientists, trained as other specialists are, in reputable universities (see Chapter Sixteen). Their skills enable them to assuage a great deal of human distress and to investigate many of the perplexities of behavior. Unfortunately for too many people whose comprehension is limited, the legitimate, actually intriguing, facts of psychology are not so attractive as the misinformation and fables that have become associated with it. The uninformed unknowingly avoid qualified practitioners and seek out dramatic but invalid remedies and spellbinding orators. The latter, despite their claims, are unable to help any patient recover.

The process of converting psychological fact into fable is only partly the result of popularization. Misinformation is produced also because the science of behavior is new and its subject matter, humanity, is elusive and complex. Although a great deal has been learned, many psychological observations represent educated guesses or are fairly preliminary estimates. But since too many people are unable to think in terms of probabilities and qualifications, they change the statements of psychologists into supposed immutable truths.

In a well-conducted experiment, C. W. Simon and W. H. Emmons found that some learning could take place during what outwardly resembled sleep. But the important fact about their findings was that, according to EEG measures of depth of sleep, learning took place while the subjects were not deeply asleep. The little learning that did occur was during the drowsy state between wakefulness and sleep. There really was no learning during sleep itself. Simon and Emmons concluded, "Results support the hypothesis that learning during sleep is unlikely." [1] Imagine the way this experiment might be reported in many newspapers or magizines:

LEARN WHILE YOU SLEEP

Two RAND Corporation psychologists have just proved that people need not waste all their time in bed. They can learn while they are asleep. Fascinating facts such as "What kind of store did U. S. Grant work in before the war?" (answer: hardware) were fed by tape recordings to twenty-one volunteers while they were asleep. Despite the fact that heavy snorers were among the subjects, the napping students managed to learn.

Such combinations of misleading explanation and insufficient understanding, plus the penchant for magazines and movies to fix on the sensational and to glamorize, lead many to expect too much of psychology. Frequently, when actual contact is made, the difference

---

[1] Simon and Emmons, 1956. (This notation refers to the article of that year listed in the References that follow the text.)

between the all-powerful image and the reality of psychology is enough to produce cynicism and disappointment. Psychology is then unjustly accused of being a jumble of meaningless advice, common sense, and clichés. In truth, however, psychology, despite its limitations and disregarding the extravagances of popular claims, can and does make a real and meaningful contribution to human well-being.

If an attempt is made to understand the facts of psychology rather than remain content with popular misconceptions, certain pet notions and well-worn, somewhat lazy habits of thinking must be discarded. In the following pages some of the most common impediments to understanding contemporary psychology will be examined so that they may no longer act as stumbling blocks to a comprehension of the facts of normal and abnormal behavior.

THE SCIENCE OF BEHAVIOR AND "MIND"

Psychologists today are not students of the mind. It is true that psychology originated as, and that the word itself means, the study of the mind. For centuries psychologists were scholars who philosophized and speculated about the human mind and spirit. As recently as the beginning of the twentieth century the famous Harvard psychologist E. B. Titchener attempted to develop a scientific approach to the study of mind. He called his technique *introspection*. The method of introspection consisted of an observer carefully analyzing his thinking processes in order to arrive at the so-called mental elements that were thought to constitute the building blocks of all experience. The trained introspector might, for example, carefully describe all the sensations he experienced while smoking a cigarette or looking at a picture. This approach quickly proved too narrow, for little is revealed about the complexities of thought and action just by searching for the hypothetical building blocks that make up the human repertoire.

The study of the mind was taken in another direction by Sigmund Freud. In the early 1900's he began to report on his technique of psycho- (or mind) analysis. Freud was faced with the fact that although he had convenient psychiatric labels for his patients, he knew little about the causes of mental disorders. After experimenting with a number of means designed to discover more about human beings, Freud hit upon the method of *free association*. Free association consisted simply of having the patient report completely whatever thoughts and ideas came to him. The subject was instructed not to inhibit his responses in any way but to reveal whatever came to mind, no matter how silly or undesirable it might seem. Using his patients' free-flowing thoughts, Freud was able to gain monumental insights into the origins of much human behavior. Quite incidentally, he discovered that his investigatory technique, *psychoanalysis*, had therapeutic effects, and he soon used it to help patients readjust (see Chapter Fifteen).

Today, psychologists recognize the value of analysis as a technique for helping to understand human beings. But psychologists now place

Fig. 1-1 Infant monkeys in social playroom situation. Although human subjects are ordinarily the object of psychological research, much can frequently be learned about behavior by careful study of animals. These monkeys are being tested and observed to determine the development of play under various conditions of social and mothering experience. Photo by Sponholz. Courtesy of Dr. H. F. Harlow, University of Wisconsin.

most emphasis on the study of observable human behavior (see Fig. 1-1). Further, they no longer consider themselves students of the mind. Whatever is meant by *mind* is so beclouded by mystical and philosophical overtones that the word has little descriptive value for scientists. Psychologists *describe and probe human behavior.* Whereas mind implies something inscrutable, behavior is a quantity that can be observed and measured. Psychologists try to learn whatever they can about human thoughts and feelings by carefully measuring and analyzing conduct. To evaluate, for example, the effect of overindulgent parents on growing children, the investigator diligently inspects, possibly measuring with psychological tests, the behavior of father, mother, and child. Or a psychologist interested in the value of different types of therapy might contrast the effects of group therapy, psychodrama, play therapy, and other techniques on similarly diagnosed patients. Whatever the interest of the researcher and whether his techniques consist of simple survey questionnaires, clinical analysis, or complicated laboratory investigations, the psychologist today, as the following quotation points out, focuses on *measurable behavior* so that he can identify the basic facts governing human action.

The Scientific Task of the Psychologist

1. Gathering Facts

The first big task of psychology is to gather information about man and his behavior. Psychology relies heavily upon two basic approaches in making its observations and gathering needed data: the *clinical* and *experimental.*

The clinical method involves the intensive study of the personality make-up of a given individual. Various techniques may be employed here, including psychological tests, dream analysis, developmental records, and personal interviews. In addition to yielding information about the personality traits and adjustment problems of particular individuals, the clinical method —by collecting and analyzing data on a great many individuals—has contributed substantially to our understanding of human behavior in general.

The experimental method involves the formulation and carefully controlled testing of hypotheses about specific aspects of behavior. The experimental psychologist may design an experiment, for example, to investigate the effects of anxiety on man's ability to solve problems. As with the clinical method, a wide range of techniques and tools may be utilized, ranging from mechanical measuring devices to psychological tests to opinion surveys. The crucial feature of the experimental method, however, is that the investigator tries to design his experiment in such a way as to hold constant all conditions or variables except one independent variable (e.g., anxiety), which is allowed to change systematically so that its effects upon a *dependent variable* (e.g., performance in solving problems) can be studied.

If more than one variable were allowed to change (e.g., level of fatigue as well as level of anxiety), it would be impossible for the experimenter to determine which of these variables—or what combination of them—was responsible for whatever variations occurred in the subject's performance.

2. *Formulating Principles*

Facts, to be useful, must be not only gathered but interpreted. Thus the scientist tries to integrate his data into meaningful principles which, in turn, can be systematically related to one another in a theoretical framework that will explain all the known facts.

Since facts owe no prior allegiance to any scientist, they can sometimes be interpreted in several different ways. This is especially true in a relatively new science such as psychology, where data are far from complete. Thus we find considerable differences in the theoretical positions of such "schools" of psychologists as the behaviorists and psychoanalysts. But even though current theories of human behavior must be regarded as highly tentative, they are of inestimable value in helping psychologists to organize their thinking about the facts now available and to design additional research that may support or correct their present conclusions. Every theory is potentially useful so long as it is held open to question and is used as a stepping stone to additional knowledge. Indeed, the progress of psychology as a science may well be accelerated by having different groups of psychologists work on the same central problem—a comprehensive understanding of man's structure and functioning—from complementary or even contradictory points of view.

3. *Applying the Findings*

It is apparent that scientific facts and principles are of little value unless they can eventually be given some practical application. For a long time most psychologists were reluctant to go beyond the theoretical level in discussing their findings for fear of making premature applications and falling into the same booby traps as many of the popular books on "right thinking" and "personality adjustment." As modern psychology has amassed a growing body of experimental support for its findings, however, it has begun to take a much more active role in disseminating its conclusions and applying them to human problems. While caution is still very necessary, it has become increasingly apparent that man cannot afford to wait until psychology has turned in its final report.[2]

SINGLE CAUSE

If human behavior is to be understood, a persistent way of thinking that must be modified is the lazy inclination to reason in terms of

[2] James C. Coleman, *Personality Dynamics and Effective Behavior* (Chicago: Scott, Foresman and Company, 1960), pp. 18–19. Copyright © 1960 by Scott, Foresman and Company. Reprinted by permission.

single causes. What is *the cause* of juvenile crime? *The cause,* someone may assert, is "broken homes." What is the cause of divorce, psychoses, or homosexuality? Too frequently, an alleged expert is ready to cite a single cause. Allied to these queries are the questions adults often pose psychologists. "How," they ask, "can negativism or 'being a worry-wart' be cured?" Implicit in the queries is the assumption that there is just *one* clear and distinct cause of behavior and conversely that there is, therefore, *one* neat and proven answer for each of mankind's ills.

Human behavior is rarely, if ever, explained by a single cause and seldom, therefore, remediable through a universal solution. For a long time it was believed that mental illness was due to sexual excess. As a consequence, psychotically disturbed patients were subjected to a wide variety of thoughtless, even ludicrous, treatments designed to re-strain their biological appetites. For decades, too, parents were cau-tioned to watch their children carefully to prevent what was actually innocent childish sexual interest, lest it lead to mental deterioration. In fact, as recently as the 1940's, the Boy Scout manual cautioned that masturbation would lead to emotional disorder. An equally inaccurate variant of this single-cause explanation of psychiatric disturbance is current. Today, many otherwise educated adults believe that good mental health practice implies that sexual inhibition is harmful. Based largely on newspaper and magazine misrepresentations, they believe that excessive sexual restraint produces mental illness. In actuality, of course, neither sexual overindulgence nor deprivation, in and of itself, causes psychosis or neurosis. Abnormal behavior, as well as all normal conduct, is produced by an overwhelming and subtly related *combina-tion* of environmental circumstances and personal factors. The follow-ing record enumerates a few of the many factors that caused just a single behavioral incident.

Observable Behavior

Larry L. was apprehended by the police, after a short chase, in the car he had stolen about one hour before.

Known Causes

1. Unlocked expensive auto was parked near Larry's high school.
2. While working in a garage, Larry learned to start cars without a key.
3. Some of Larry's friends had cars, and some boasted of stealing autos and returning them before owner became aware of theft.
4. Automobiles were admired by Larry's family for their status value.
5. Larry wanted to "show off" to girl who had recently "snubbed" him.
6. Larry had strong sexual needs but seemed unable to express them ade-quately or to find satisfactory outlets.

7. Larry felt inferior, being smaller than average.
8. Larry was youngest of a family of four and had learned to fight for attention.
9. Both of Larry's parents seemed indirectly to encourage him to act impulsively. His family, generally, seemed unrestrained.
10. Temper tantrums, poor emotional control, hostility to authority seemed to be central in Larry's personality.
11. Larry's paternal grandmother had been in a mental hospital at various periods of her life.
12. Larry's father seemed "nervous" like his own mother and had periods of excessive drinking.
13. Discipline in Larry's high school was very weak. Students did not have much respect for teachers or property.
14. Larry had low, slightly below average IQ, but was forced to compete with students of average intelligence.

Psychologists, when attempting to describe behavior, say that all human wants and actions are multidetermined. This means that all conduct, no matter how simple it may appear, is determined by a multiplicity of causes. To begin with, two closely related sets of causal factors always have to be considered: the individual himself and the environment in which he lives. Thus, for example, someone may have all the potentials for becoming an anxiety neurotic; but if he lives in unusually placid and comfortable circumstances, his neurosis may never become apparent. It is because of this interaction between environment and self that stressful conditions frequently produce emotional disorder. During wartime, for example, many soldiers are discharged with "war neurosis" or "combat fatigue." The obvious conclusion is that their disorder is due to the dangers of warfare. More accurately put, however, it should be said that the psychiatric breakdown was *precipitated* by the rigors of combat. The soldier who becomes deranged does so because, personally *predisposed* toward abnormality, he interacted with an environment uniquely designed to aggravate and accelerate his psychological weaknesses.

HIDDEN CAUSES OF BEHAVIOR

Behavior is determined not only by several causal factors acting in concert but also by determinants that are not immediately apparent. It is easy to understand that a scientific observer may not know all the causes of a single act, but even the person himself may not be fully aware of all the reasons for his behavior. Psychoanalysts have demonstrated that people are frequently unaware, or only partially conscious, of their own desires and goals. Many basic psychological needs, such as those for security, social approval, love, and others, may be operative on a relatively *unconscious* level. People may get married, join prestigious clubs, and involve themselves in any number of activities for reasons of which they are not completely conscious. Most people are able to produce seemingly sensible explanations of their behavior, but their real reasons are not always disclosed. A mother may overprotect and "spoil" her child not because she is as attached to him as she claims, but actually because she is compensating for unconscious resentments toward motherhood. Psychoanalysts point out that the failure to take unconscious motivation into consideration is probably the cause of more inadequacies in the understanding of human conduct than any other one thing.

That some behavior may be motivated by circumstances of which the person is not aware does not mean that "the unconscious" is an entity unto itself. One may hear "His hostility toward others comes from his unconscious." This statement assumes that in every human being there is a kind of organ called the "unconscious" that may serve as a source of behavior. This is, of course, not true. To call an act or motive unconscious merely means that the origins or causes are not immediately apparent. Instead of saying "His hostility comes from his unconscious," the correct statement would be "He is unconscious (or not fully aware) of how hostile he is toward others."

We can illustrate to ourselves the degree to which many of our own attitudes and characteristics are not fully known to us by reading the following list of traits. At first glance, nearly all of us will deny that the characteristics egocentricity and deceitfulness truly describe our own personality. But if we pause and think about some of the techniques we use to get along with others, we may slowly become aware that some of the personality descriptions actually apply to us.

Common Sources of Difficulty in Interpersonal Relationships [3]

Egocentricity.   A concern with one's own interests to the extent of being insensitive to the welfare and rights of others. The egocentric individual is incapable of establishing anything but the most superficial relationships.

Deceitfulness.   A tendency, often accompanying egocentricity, to take an exploitive approach to interpersonal relationships. Sometimes deceit extends to outright lying and stealing, but more commonly it shows itself in the efforts of an "operator" to manipulate people and situations to his own advantage.

[3] James C. Coleman, *Personality Dynamics and Effective Behavior* (Chicago: Scott, Foresman and Company, 1960), p. 357. Copyright © 1960 by Scott, Foresman and Company. Reprinted by permission.

Overconformity. An emphasis on getting along with others at the expense of personal integrity, often accompanied by a tendency to be overawed by the authority of those whose good opinion seems important—and, in turn, to be authoritarian and hostile toward those considered inferior.

Rebelliousness. A tendency to rebel against all authority and to become hostile and uncooperative at the slightest suggestion of being "bossed." Sometimes rebelliousness takes the form of flouting all of society's mores and manners in an ill-conceived attempt to assert one's independence.

Overdependency. A tendency to lean excessively upon others for either material aid or emotional support and to rely upon them for making one's decisions. The overdependent person contributes little or nothing to a relationship and usually loses his self-respect as well as the respect of the other person. Occasionally, underlying feelings of dependency are concealed by an exaggerated show of independence (e.g., refusing to become "indebted" to anyone) which is equally destructive of close relationships.

Hostility. A tendency, usually associated with authority problems, to be antagonistic and suspicious toward other people. When hostility is openly expressed, it creates immediate problems in a relationship. Equally harmful in the long run, however, are such covert expressions of hostility as being gossipy or overly competitive.

Inferiority feelings. A basic lack of self-confidence or self-esteem which may be expressed either in oversensitivity to "threat" or in exaggerated efforts to prove one's own adequacy and worth by such techniques as boasting, showing off, and being hypercritical of other people.

Emotional insulation. An inability to make the necessary emotional investment in a relationship, for fear of being hurt.

Human behavior is the result of many causes, some observable, many subtle and obscure, and very many below the level of awareness. Almost without exception, therefore, a characteristic such as hysteria, alcoholism, or low IQ is never fully explained in terms of a single cause. The causes of human behavior that have been uncovered must always be viewed with caution, since what is known is likely to be only an incomplete representation of all possible determinants.

CAUSE AND EFFECT

One of the most perplexing difficulties in describing cause plagues not only psychologists but other scientists as well. It is commonly held that two events occurring in succession or in close temporal sequence must be causally related. Thus for many years high-school and college students were erroneously taught that mental deficiency and a wide variety of psychological disorders ranging from insanity to alcoholism were inherited. One of the supposedly most convincing bits of evidence was produced by a psychologist named Goddard. Dr.

Goddard uncovered the history of a family that he called, for the sake of anonymity, the Kallikaks, living in the Philadelphia–New Jersey area. The Kallikak family was noted for two branches: one full of good and noteworthy citizens and the other abounding in social and psychological misfits. Through a hazy chain of circumstantial evidence, the good Kallikaks were traced back to a set of virtuous parents, and the bad to disordered forebears. The genealogy supposedly demonstrated that both wholesome and inadequate stock continues to produce, through ensuing generations, desirable or undesirable members. Psychological health and deficiency were attributed to heredity. It is recognized today, of course, that among many other serious flaws in his research, Dr. Goddard did not at all consider the causal effects of environment. It is true that neurotic parents tend to produce neurotic children. But this need not be due to hereditary deficiency; it may be attributable to the faulty environment that is usually provided by emotionally disturbed parents.

In almost every case, causal confusion is woven together with faulty research design. A classic example of inadequate experimental methodology followed by erroneous conclusions occurred in the highly influential work of Dr. Clara Davis. In her well-known experiment, virtually unchallenged since it was conducted over thirty years ago, children were tested for their ability to select their own diets. To probe their aptitude, Dr. Davis provided infants and youngsters with the opportunity to select food freely and eat it in any quantity. As expected, over a period of time the food chosen represented a well-balanced diet, and the participants thrived. This proved to Dr. Davis, and to countless "authorities" since, that the body is wise and reliable. It will correctly dictate its needs if we listen to it. "What else," it was asked, "could have produced the healthy intake of food, but that the children were allowed to select freely?"

Yet this well-publicized and influential experiment, dutifully reported in Dr. Spock's otherwise excellent book on baby and child care, did not prove that free selection results in nutritional balance. Just two of the many errors will be cited. First, the children had a choice of only desirable foods. There was no opportunity to ingest sand or cotton candy. Second, the experimenter did not determine whether a completely random or chance selection of foods might not have produced the same results. In short, that two events appeared to follow in order—free selection and balanced food intake—is no proof that the causal relationship asserted actually existed. In almost all instances, cause and effect must be carefully examined, since even experts may be misled by spurious relationships.

CAUSATION AND RESPONSIBILITY—A NOTE OF CAUTION

Much of human personality and behavior is determined by the example provided by parents and environmental conditions. An adolescent who becomes a delinquent may have been virtually forced to adopt criminal codes of behavior by the callous neglect of his family and the pressures of his surroundings. It is sometimes argued, therefore, that parents should be punished for the transgressions of their children. Perhaps they should be. Nevertheless, as individuals, lawbreakers themselves—and nobody else—still need to be held accountable if the ethical structure of our society is to be maintained. An errant adolescent could argue that his delinquency is not his own fault, but due to his deficient upbringing; therefore, his parents should be summoned to the courts. If the parents actually appeared before the judge, they could point out that though they admittedly gave their teen-ager a poor home, it was not really their fault. They owed their own shortcomings to their parents, who provided an inadequate standard for them. This kind of argument leads logically to an infinite regress, resulting in the continual shifting of responsibility. It may not be entirely just, but if propriety is to be maintained and we are to govern ourselves by law, then responsibility must be assigned.

Many professionals whose work brings them into contact with psychology and other behavior sciences confuse causality and responsibility. Once they learn that deviant behavior may in part be causally traced to failures within the home, they believe it follows logically that all personal responsibility disappears. Parents, violent movies, and much of our exaggerated emphasis on sex and acquisition doubtless contribute greatly to all kinds of aberrations—criminal and otherwise. It would, understandably, be desirable if the influence of many of the most destructive aspects of our culture could be curbed. But partly explaining antisocial acts in terms of family, neighborhood, and environment does not erase personal responsibility for one's conduct. Even a soldier who, under orders from a superior, perpetrates atrocities is, by international law, held accountable for his behavior.

Human beings possess the capacity to weigh alternatives, although often the most disadvantaged individuals clearly have few avenues open to them. Nevertheless, choice is available to nearly all. Were this not so, then many of the most eminent human beings who enriched the lives of all mankind would never have been able to prevail against the handicaps with which their backgrounds encumbered them. In short, much of what people are and do is attributable to their upbringing and the influence of the culture in which they lived; but ultimately, they alone are responsible for their actions and should be rewarded or punished accordingly.

PREJUDICIAL THINKING

There are a number of reasons why causal oversimplifications and errors persist in the attempt to understand and describe human behavior. One of the most common reasons why only fragments of complex behavioral descriptions are retained is simply prejudice. The distorted thinking produced by bias can be illustrated by a lecturer who gave a thorough yet easily understood talk on schizophrenia. In his hour-long discussion he mentioned several factors leading to schizophrenia; unloving parents, heredity, the stresses of modern-day living, overproductive imaginations, and others. Immediately following the talk, a large group of students and adults was asked to describe, in writing, what the speaker had said. Most of them listed only a single cause for schizophrenia. A few mentioned two or more causes, but only a few were able to relate that the speaker enumerated a number of reasons that interact *possibly* to produce the psychotic disturbance.

When the written statements of the listeners were carefully examined to determine why they had remembered one particular cause of schizophrenia, the results were quite revealing. The audience tended to pick out of the entire lecture that which neatly fit their preconceived notions. People who, for one reason or another, liked to believe that schizophrenia is inherited were certain to remember this, above all else. Others, probably bearing a grudge against their parents, remembered that the speaker said schizophrenia was "caused" by cold and unloving fathers and mothers.

The errors of prejudice have been illustrated also, by a well-known sociological experiment (Allport and Postman).[4] Groups of people were very briefly shown a picture of a white and a Negro man standing opposite one another. The two men were in what might have been a train or subway car with few other people around. The important point was that the *white* man was holding in his hand something that could be taken for an old-fashioned barber's razor. As might be guessed, when the audience was asked to recall it, many of them were able to "remember" the razor—but now in the hands of the Negro. Prejudices seem to dictate that if a white and a Negro are seen together and the razor is in the white man's hand, it has to be transferred to the hands of the Negro. Furthermore, the people who

4 Names in parentheses refer to authors of works listed in the References that follow the text.

stated that the Negro had the razor did not express any doubt. They were certain. After all, they argued, they had just seen the picture and could "clearly remember" the Negro "threatening" the white with the razor.

It has long been apparent that human beings see and hear largely what they are prepared to see and hear. Memory provides the recollections that are *wanted*. New learning about human behavior can take place only when biased thinking is carefully guarded against.

GROUP THINKING

Although prejudices distort what is thought to have been seen and remembered, the feelings of the associated group play an important role, also. Psychologists have demonstrated this in a number of ways. In one interesting experiment subjects were brought into a darkened room with just one pinpoint of light on the ceiling. Staring at such a tiny light, most people believe that the light moves or wavers a bit, although it is actually stationary. One can now show how group judgments will influence an individual's decisions. An innocent subject is put in a room with three other people who have agreed beforehand to say that the light is moving in counterclockwise circles. Almost invariably, the subject, not in on the plot, agrees. Or another group will state that the light is moving up and down. Again the subject agrees. This can be done indefinitely with the light said to be moving in any number of directions; again most subjects will agree. And not only will they agree, they will unhesitatingly assert that the light is, without a doubt, moving in the directions the other, pre-agreed people have said it moved. Furthermore, one can interrupt the experiment and show the innocent subject that the light could not possibly move. Still he will argue that it did move and that he knows it for a fact (Sherif).

In this way too, most people are ready to assert what their group, the people they call their friends and fellows, would have them see and believe. It is a rare individual who can see beyond the collective biases of his associates and give evidence of an original and meaningful position. It is a currently popular notion among many professionals, for example, that delinquent criminals are best rehabilitated by being permitted to "act out," and by full "acceptance." The result is that many institutions designed to retain legal offenders are virtually without any meaningful treatment procedures. Juvenile delinquents, it is assumed, will soon return to normal if they are unrestrained, no matter what they do, and given extra care. The ineffectiveness of such rehabilitative efforts is demonstrated by the majority of children who, after being discharged from such institutions, are soon incarcerated again, having committed worse crimes. Delinquency is a complex phenomenon consisting of many different variations that cannot be simply treated according to some current professional prejudices (Cloward and Ohlin). Nevertheless, because certain professional groups hold freedom and acceptance as a requisite belief concerning rehabilitation, despite their uselessness, it continues. Professionals are not immune to parroting each other as a substitute for individual thinking.

Because of group pressure, the urge to conform to those with whom individuals identify, people select from the mass of information available the few tidbits that support their collective notions. One need not be surprised, therefore, that on some issues one social worker sounds like any other, elementary school teachers are indistinguishable from one another, or one corporation executive is interchangeable with any one of dozens of other businessmen. There are very few Democrats, union members, physicians, or Republicans who, individually, have thoroughly digested or thought out for themselves the beliefs and perceptions that their group has prescribed for them. But if effective understanding of human needs and feelings is to be attained, many group, preconceived notions will have to be discarded.

THE LIMITS OF PSYCHOLOGY

A last, though by no means final reason for being misled in understanding human behavior is that, as mentioned before, all of us expect and have been promised too much. Psychology and all of the other sciences that deal with behavior are still very young. Only in the last several decades have vigorous experimental efforts been made to document and explicate the vastness of human conduct. The more scientists learn about the world of man, the more astounded they are by the infinitude of behavior not yet even approached. This is far different from the armchair speculators who preceded scientific psychology and often asserted that their grasp of life was complete as they expounded colorful but limited theories.

In order to understand the needs and actions of man we must rid ourselves of oversimplified and biased concepts of human behavior. We cannot expect the complex and subtle causes of conduct to be neatly revealed to us. No authority or expert is able to provide easy maxims to guide human beings. For the present, and doubtless for decades to come, psychology will be clouded with uncertainties. The process of learning about human behavior must be accompanied by a critical appreciation of our own limitations and our tendencies to glide into slipshod and prejudical thinking patterns. Yet, even with all these hindrances and cautions, it is undeniable that the attempt to understand the workings of human beings can be thoroughly satisfying and enriching.

FOR REVIEW AND DISCUSSION

1. Although psychologists, like other well-trained scientists, exercise great care in their investigations and reports, psychological facts often become "fables." Why is psychological research often misinterpreted? How can we guard ourselves from misinterpretations and distorted opinions?

2. Why is psychology defined as the study of human behavior? Why do psychologists stress that they deal with behavior rather than "mind"? What is the "scientific task of the psychologist"?

3. How is human behavior "multidetermined"? Are all persons aware of all of the causes of their own behavior? If one event follows another, is the first necessarily the cause of the second? Why is it often difficult to distinguish cause and effect?

4. Doug has a record of minor juvenile offenses and recently stole an automobile. His lawyer has been able to demonstrate that his delinquency was caused by inadequate parents, poor environment, and other serious background deficiencies. Who is responsible for Doug's crimes? Should Doug's parents be punished?

5. What is a prejudice? What are some prejudices that might interfere with our understanding of our own behavior and that of others? Can prejudices be overcome? Is it possible to be entirely free of false notions and assumptions?

From

Birth

to

Marriage

Infancy and

Childhood

T W O

From the moment a child is conceived, the environment in which he lives and all the genetic capacities he possesses interact to produce a complete human being. Whether the skills he is born with are shaped into useful tools or squandered recklessly depends largely upon the milieu and family in which he finds himself. There is little that can be done about the traits a child inherits or acquires by birth. The family and social environment in which a child is reared, however, can be powerfully shaped by human determination and action.

BEFORE-BIRTH INFLUENCES

Life begins at conception. While the human organism is developing in the uterus, the effects of environment are first experienced. Thus children from well-nourished, healthy mothers are provided with a favorable uterine milieu. They are likely, as a consequence, to be born more easily and be more robust than children from nutritionally deprived parents. There is a world of difference, however, between the scientific statement that the prebirth environment may affect the developing fetus and the old wives' tales that assert babies can be influenced by experiences mothers have while pregnant. Superstition, for example, attributes birth marks to pregnant women's being frightened by animals. Or, it is asserted that if mothers read meritorious literature or immerse themselves in worthwhile music and art, their children, yet unborn, will assimilate the cultural benefits of their efforts. Such superstitious beliefs have not been substantiated. But it has been shown that a wide variety of conditions help determine intra-uterine development.

Certain diseases in the mother during particular stages of pregnancy may have physically and mentally damaging effects on the babies they are carrying. German measles, malaria, tuberculosis, and syphilis, among others, may possibly produce cleft palate, mental retardation, or other organic damage. In addition, some drugs and chemicals, including quinine, barbiturates, alcohol, and nicotine, may in certain quantities affect fetal welfare. The extremely harmful effects of one medication were only recently documented. Through the efforts of a number of European and American physicians it was learned in 1962 that a sudden increase in a severe congenital deformity—babies born with stunted arms and legs as well as other disfigurements—was due to a relatively new drug, thalidomide, taken by pregnant women. Unfortunately, as is often the case, many children were born grossly handicapped before it was realized how destructive the medication was to intra-uterine development.

Severe emotional experiences should, according to superstition, affect the welfare of the baby about to be born. There may be a grain of truth in this contention. Mothers who have *intense* and *highly* prolonged periods of extraordinary stress *may* produce children a little less stable and healthy than calm mothers. Apparently, severe distress, while itself not directly affecting the intra-uterine organism, may damage the mother's health. Because of their overwrought emotional state mothers may eat less, sleep poorly, and become generally mal-nourished and run down. Since mothers in poor physical condition have more birth difficulties than healthy mothers, it is possible that extreme emotion by adversely affecting their health indirectly in-fluences the well-being of the intra-uterine organism.

Many other prebirth conditions may impair the welfare of embryo and fetus. Certain blood differences (Rh factor) as well as other internal chemical incompatibilities infrequently cause birth difficulties. Xrays, radium, and other radioactive substances may result in genetic as well as fetal damage and are usually avoided during certain stages of pregnancy. Radioactivity inherent in the atmosphere and that brought about by nuclear explosions, of course, cannot be avoided, and exposure to fall-out and radiation is suspected of being potentially quite damaging to reproductive cells and intra-uterine organisms. There is considerable debate, however, as to how many hundreds or thousands of infants throughout the world may be damaged by current levels of radioactivity (Stern).

MATURATION

The early months after a child is born are marked by rapid be-havioral changes. Not all children, of course, develop at exactly the same rate. Nor does somewhat slower or more rapid development imply that the child is either intellectually slow or advanced. Most of the skills that emerge during the early years of growth are called maturational because they develop mainly through physical maturing or growth. Learning as such is not necessary in order for the ability to emerge. Thus at ten months babies may creep and at fifteen months they may walk. Both skills are the result of physical growth (see Fig. 2-1). Despite what many parents believe, it is not necessary to "teach" a child to walk. Under the usual environmental circumstances, this, like other maturational skills, simply emerges. Attempting to teach a child to walk or creep before he is physically ready will not accelerate development. In fact, attempts at teaching may actually retard the emergence of a skill, because the child may develop anxieties

0 months
Fetal posture

1 month
Chin up

2 months
Chest up

3 months
Reach and miss

4 months
Sit with support

5 months
Sit on lap, grasp object

6 months
Sit on high chair, grasp dangling object

7 months
Sit alone

8 months
Stand with help

9 months
Stand holding furniture

10 months
Creep

11 months
Walk when led

12 months
Pull to stand by furniture

13 months
Climb stair steps

14 months
Stand alone

15 months
Walk alone

Fig. 2-1 Emergence of early motor skills. Redrawn from Clifford T. Morgan, *Introduction to Psychology*, 2nd ed. (New York: McGraw-Hill Book Company, 1961), p. 57. Reproduced by permission.

and hesitancies about something that should instead come quite freely.

Misunderstanding of maturation is particularly apparent in the area of toilet training. American parents are especially concerned about bowel and bladder functions and frequently attempt to force children to exercise toilet controls of which they are not capable. The neurological sensitivities and muscular controls necessary for toilet training develop slowly and, like all other maturational processes, cannot be speeded up by argument or persuasion. In fact, as is the case with other maturational skills such as crawling and walking, toilet training may be seriously delayed or impaired if extreme pressure is focused on it.

As the child grows older, maturational skills gradually play a less important role in determining behavior. Much of the activity of a child after he is two or three years of age is heavily influenced by experience. Whether or not a three-year-old inquires about the origin of babies, as most do, depends to a great extent on the relation he has established with his parents and the degree to which his curiosity has been aroused. Whether the five- or ten-year-old is aggressive or shy, or whether he exercises his physical endowment to become a tennis player or ballerina, depends more on his environmental experiences than on maturation.

The following list of developmental norms [1] gives approximate ages at which most children begin to perform certain activities. Individual variations of several weeks or months are common and normal. Note that most of the activities toward the bottom of the list are results of environment rather than maturation.

Birth. Head, arms, fingers, and legs move randomly, without control. Sucks, burps, cries, coughs, grunts, and sneezes. Usually sleeps about 18 or more hours a day. Average weight about $7\frac{1}{2}$ pounds. Length about 19 inches. Smell, taste, temperature, and pressure senses fairly well developed. Needs to be fed every 3 or 4 hours.

Four weeks. Can pursue object with eyes. Can hold head erect when in a prone position.

Twelve weeks. Eyes focus fully on objects, but may still be poorly coordinated. Hearing is acute. Able to turn self from side to back. May reach for objects, but usually appears to miss.

Sixteen weeks. Can pull self to sitting position and remain with some support. Plays with and sucks fingers. Weight double that at birth. Laughs aloud.

Six months. First teeth appear. Sits briefly. Grasps objects placed before him and puts them in mouth. Transfers objects from one hand to the other. Makes many vowel sounds. Can move feet to mouth when lying on back. Pats mirror image.

[1] Based on information reported by Hurlock, Ilg and Ames, and Pressey and Kuhlen.

Ten months. Pulls self to standing position. Creeps on hands and knees. Pokes at small objects with extended forefinger. May be able to vocalize "mama," "dada," and one other "word."

One year. Helps slightly when being changed or dressed. Can walk with one hand held. Can pull self up holding to playpen or furniture. Birth weight trebled. Plays peek-a-boo. "Plays" at talking. Has 4 to 6 teeth.

Fifteen months. Walks alone. Can say 4 to 6 words. Uses jargon. Can play "games" like offering toy to mother but taking it back again.

Eighteen months. May be negativistic, can be very jealous. Walks well. Can seat self in a small chair or climb into adult chair. Can say 10 words. Looks at pictures in a book. Feeds self, often spilling contents. May have some toilet regularity. Thumb sucking sometimes at a maximum.

Two years. Many fears. Walks up and down stairs alone. Turns pages of a book singly. Speaks in 3-word sentences. Knows 300 words. Sometimes verbalizes toilet needs. Refers to self by name.

Three years. Interested in babies and their origin. Can ride a tricycle. Uses plurals in speech. Feeds self with little spilling. Toilet trained. Can put on own shoes.

Four years. Can throw ball, turn on television set. Can count 3 objects. Can wash and dry face and hands, brush teeth. Dresses and undresses self if supervised. Plays cooperatively with other children.

Five years. Knows 2,000 words. Can count 10 objects correctly. Can tell how many fingers on each hand. Can name colors correctly. Ready for kindergarten or school.

CHILD-REARING PRACTICES THEN AND NOW

Throughout the history of the human race, some parents have been kind, affectionate, and understanding to their children, and others have been harsh, rejecting, and hostile. But superimposed on individual parental feelings are the socially prescribed ways of child rearing. All societies devote considerable time and effort to the rearing and training of the generation to come. The African Masai teaches his child fearlessness and dignity in ways most Americans might find reprehensible. The Samoan mother weans her child by putting pepper on her nipples. Parents, whether they are individually good or bad to their children, also act toward them in the ways designated by their own culture. Our own child-rearing practices, like those of other societies, are composed both of our individual feelings toward our children and the techniques prescribed by our own social identifications.

In the United States, culturally prescribed child-rearing philosophies and practices have changed frequently. Just as fashions determine the length of skirts or the number of jacket buttons, so also do current modes and fads influence how a child is brought up and trained. In the 1920's and 30's the emphasis was on strictness, precise scheduling, and early bowel and bladder training. One mother recalled the advice she was given by her physician in 1926:

Well, first of all they kept me and the baby in the hospital over two weeks. I had to stay in bed nearly all that time, although both the baby and I were perfectly healthy and it was a normal birth. I rarely ever saw him, either. Hygiene and cleanliness was emphasized above everything else— everybody wore surgical masks all the time.

Before I left the hospital with the baby I got a schedule from my doctor. It read like a railroad timetable: 6 A.M. milk, 6:20 burp; 7:15 change diapers, 8 A.M. twenty-minute nap. Every minute was scheduled, and I was warned not to depart from the schedule because it might spoil the baby.

Toilet training was very strict. I was supposed to begin at six months —put him over the potty, insert suppositories to encourage the movement. Some doctors had the mothers begin earlier. Just when you were supposed to do it was also tightly scheduled. The instructions I got from the doctor also said I should give strict punishment. If I saw the baby touch his genitals, while changing diapers, for example, I was supposed to punish him severely and immediately.

The fashions in child rearing seem to have swung slowly to the opposite extreme. In the last decade or two, probably in reaction to the strict, authoritative discipline of forty years ago, "permissive" and "demand" have become popular child-rearing slogans. Children are supposedly best able to set their own pace. Infants should be fed when they are hungry, bowel-trained when they indicate they want to be, and their "natural" inclinations should not be interfered with lest they develop "neurosis." The notion has grown that unless the child is permitted whatever he wants he will feel inhibited, and that inhibition will lead to neurosis. The situation was caricatured in a cartoon in which a despairing "modern" mother says to her husband, after seeing that their child has crayoned over all their living-room walls, "I don't care if it does inhibit him, I'm going to wallop him."

Most mothers, of course—in the 1930's or in the 1960's—do not go to the extremes dictated by the child-rearing fashions of the times. But they are influenced by the prevailing trends. Dr. Urie Bronfenbrenner, Cornell University psychologist, has pointed out how contemporary child-rearing practices are different from those of three decades ago. Today's parents are much more permissive. They allow infants and children to explore and experiment much more freely than was permitted in former days. Punishment is less common. Children are viewed with more sympathetic tolerance and allowed to indulge more of their immature whims. Discipline also is much less physical and more likely to be indirect. That is, punishment frequently consists of reasoning and deprivation of privileges rather than spanking.

CHILD-REARING PRACTICES—SOCIAL AND ETHNOID DIFFERENCES

It has long been popularly held that middle-class children are reared in distinctly different ways from lower-class offspring. In addition, Negro, Jewish, and Catholic families supposedly have rather unique ways of training and child rearing. Although there are some differences among American groups, by and large child-rearing practices and philosophies are becoming fairly similar among all segments of our population. Negro middle-class parents more closely resemble white middle-class ones than they do lower-class Negro fathers and mothers. Catholic lower-class child-rearing techniques have much more in common with lower-class Protestant methods than they do with middle-class Catholic ones. If there are meaningful differences in child-rearing techniques, they are differences between American socio-economic groups rather than between ethnoid or religious segments. And the child-rearing and other differences that do exist among middle-, lower-, and upper-class families frequently merge in a rapidly changing pattern and are thus fairly elusive (Davis and Havighurst; Bronfenbrenner). Some of the more frequent and fairly persistent social class attitudes and differences are reported in Table 2-1.

CURRENT AMERICAN CHILD-TRAINING PRACTICES

How do contemporary American parents train their children? Are children still spanked? One of the best answers is provided by the voluminous study by three psychologists, Drs. Robert Sears, Eleanor Maccoby, and Harry Levin. They investigated how 379 American mothers brought up their children from birth to kindergarten. Each mother was extensively interviewed and encouraged to talk fully about her methods and viewpoints concerning the rearing of children.

Discipline

Nearly all mothers in the Sears survey use physical punishment to help discipline their children. But only about a fifth slap or spank

Table 2-1 SOCIAL CLASS INFLUENCES ON CHILD-REARING PRACTICES—DIFFERING ATTITUDES AT VARIOUS SOCIOECONOMIC LEVELS

Upper	Middle	Lower
	Attitudes toward family	
Family tightly knit; emphasis on maintaining family name and prestige.	Considerable emphasis on independence; family ties often less close and less permanent than at upper levels.	Family less closely knit than average family in higher socioeconomic groups and homes more apt to be broken.
	Attitudes toward education	
Emphasis on quality of education and prestige of schools; training for high-level administration rather than financial gain.	Great emphasis on grades and concern about failure; education seen as the road to advancement and security.	Family's needs often given priority over child's education; school usually regarded as unpleasant; low premium put on good grades.
	Attitudes toward aggression and destruction	
Value of property stressed; destruction and fighting discouraged.	Value of property stressed; guilt and anxiety over open expression of anger, but "fighting back" sometimes encouraged at school age.	Children often permitted or encouraged to settle differences by fighting; physical prowess valued; less emphasis on value of property.
	Attitudes toward sex	
Inhibition of sexual behavior during early years but considerable freedom by later adolescence.	Severe inhibition in early years, with accompanying anxiety over sexual impulses; adolescent sexual activity usually limited to petting and masturbation.	Sex accepted as matter of course; tendency to early sexual experience, often regarded by boys as proof of masculinity; petting and masturbation often regarded as perversion.
	Attitudes toward recreation	
Relatively exclusive sports common, like golf, sailing, horseback riding; strong tendency to participate in community activities; reading and TV viewing common.	Considerable emphasis on social skills like dancing, ping-pong, tennis; tendency to join organized community activities; reading and TV viewing common.	Basketball, softball, boxing popular; little reading; TV viewing common.

Source: James C. Coleman, Personality Dynamics and Effective Behavior (Chicago: Scott, Foresman and Company, 1960), p. 62. © 1960 by Scott, Foresman and Company. Reprinted by permission.

very frequently or severely. Most mothers, about two-thirds, spank only occasionally. More popular than corporal punishment is deprivation of privilege. Denying special "treats"—television, ice cream, etc.—as a form of discipline is used by nearly all parents and employed very extensively by nearly a third.

Another favored method of discipline is for mothers to threaten not to love their children, or to act as if they no longer care about

them. Although mothers do not readily admit they use such in-
timidating techniques, there is evidence that probably all at one time
or another use some variant of withdrawal of affection. The following
is a statement by one mother who withholds love as a punitive
weapon. "Most of the time I say to him, Tommy, now stop it. You're
a bad boy when you do something like that. And Mommy doesn't
like bad boys. And he'll turn around and ask me if I love him. I'll
say, Yes, I love you, but I don't like you. He tries to figure that
one out, but he can't." (Sears, *et al.*, p. 343.)

Another mother described her techniques as follows:

INTERVIEWER.   When you are scolding her, what else might you say?

MOTHER.   It's hard to think.

INTERVIEWER.   Do you warn her about what you might do if she doesn't
behave?

MOTHER.   Yes, in fact I've used an awful threat with her at times, not
recently but when she'd say that she didn't like me, I wasn't a nice mommy,
she wished she could live with Gertrude or something like that. I'd say: "Yes,
you go ahead, I don't have to keep you either, Carol; I'm going to bring you
back to Dr. Phillips and he can find another mommy for you." She almost
got hysterical then; she really believed that I was going to take her back to
the hospital and she would be sent to another mommy. [Sears, *et al.*, p. 343.]

Mothers also resort to positive approaches to child training. More
than half frequently use reasoning, explaining why certain behavior
is desirable or undesirable. Rewards for good conduct are also much
in use. Incentives for good behavior are reported by nearly half of
all parents. They may vary from an occasional cookie to actual
monetary prizes. Some mothers, Sears, Maccoby, and Levin reported,
have elaborate reward systems. One parent interviewed used a star
system. The children had a list of things they were supposed to do,
such as brush their teeth, wash their faces, and make their beds. For
each successfully completed activity they got a star. At the end of
the month the child with the greatest number of stars was given a
fifty-cent prize.

Another positive approach to child training is the use of models.
Some parents hold up older siblings, themselves, or other relatives as
examples for the child to follow. Nearly three-fourths of mothers occasionally or frequently point to someone whom they hope their child
will emulate. A very few parents, however, oppose this kind of discipline, for they feel it is wrong to compare children to other children
or older people. Discipline techniques currently used by American
mothers are summarized in Table 2-2.

Table 2-2 DISCIPLINE TECHNIQUES USED BY PARENTS

Type	Per cent using technique
Physical Punishment	
Rarely or never	48
Fairly frequently	44
Withdrawal of love	
Rarely or never	26
Moderately or fairly frequently	24
Extent of use not known	50
Rewards for good behavior	
Rarely or never	30
Sometimes or fairly often	43
Frequently to regularly	25
Deprivation of privilege	
Rarely or never	15
Occasionally to sometimes	51
Frequently	14
Reasoning	
Rarely or never	20
Some use	36
Considerable	19
Praise	
Rarely or never	27
Moderately to frequently	69

Source: Data based on Sears, et al.

NEGATIVISM

Many discipline problems arise from what is frequently called negativism. Almost as soon as a child learns to say "No" at about fifteen months, the prerogative to dissent is exercised. The sixteen- or eighteen-month-old child wants to feel independent once in a while. When he is offered milk, though he actually wants to drink it, he loudly enunciates "No!" There are, after all, almost no other ways available for the young child to assert his own status. The only way he can demonstrate that he too is a full human being is simply to say or do the opposite of what his parent wishes.

Negativism, refusing parental wishes just for the refusal's own sake, may last well into the third, fourth, or fifth year of childhood. Usually, however, by the time the child is six or seven he has learned to discriminate between refusals that are worthwhile and those that are not necessary; and some children learn the difference as early as their third or fourth year. Probably those children who have been given most reassurance of their independent worth are likelier to give up sheer negativism before others. The last to give up negativism may well be those children severely punished for their refusals and obstinacy.

EFFECTIVENESS OF PUNISHMENT AND REWARD

Do punishment and reward work equally well? The answer depends upon what is being punished or rewarded and who is doing the disciplining. Punishment that is immediate, for short-term goals, may be quite effective. A very young child can be prevented from touching a hot stove or sticking his finger into the back of a television set by a firm and consistent "No" sometimes coupled with a spank or slap. But punishment, particularly harsh discipline, is not only generally ineffective but aggravates many of the problems it was intended to solve. Attempting to toilet train a child by severe beatings or solve food preferences by continual spanking actually will make toilet functions more complicated and produce eating problems much more severe than initial finickiness. Coupled with this is the fact that the effects of punishment differ depending upon whether the parents are warm and accepting or rejecting and hostile toward their children. Fundamentally unaffectionate parents are likely to find that punishment results in more problems than it solves. In contrast, loving fathers and mothers can exert even the sternest discipline with surprising effectiveness. Over-all, however, with few exceptions *severe* punitive techniques, especially when directed against events largely out of the child's control, lead only to an enlargement of difficulties. Sears, Maccoby, and Levin put it:

> The evidence for this conclusion is overwhelming. The unhappy effects of punishment have run like a dismal thread through our findings. Mothers who punished toilet accidents severely ended up with bed-wetting children. Mothers who punished dependency to get rid of it had more dependent children than mothers who did not punish. Mothers who punished aggressive behavior severely had more aggressive children than mothers who punished lightly. They also had more dependent children. Harsh physical punishment was associated with high childhood aggressiveness and with the development of feeding problems. [Sears, *et al.,* p. 484.]

TECHNIQUES RECOMMENDED BY PSYCHOLOGISTS

Not infrequently psychologists are quoted in newspapers or magazines as opposing this or that kind of discipline or advocating some particular kind of training. Severe punishment and hostile parents are known to have detrimental effects. But outside of these extremes, there is no reliable evidence that any of the usual child-rearing procedures are superior to others. Some psychologists seem to be as much influenced by contemporary fads as the most uninformed and slavish adherent of every miniscule swing in feminine fashions. Thus psychologists can be found who expound permissiveness today as loudly as their forebears advocated strictness thirty or forty years ago. Fortunately, however, the loving and sensitive relationship maintained by good parents and children is seldom damaged by techniques momentarily recommended by supposed experts.

There are no reasonable techniques of discipline or reward that are in themselves harmful or especially worthwhile. Wise, psychologically healthy parents use those methods that are in keeping with their own inclinations and that make them most comfortable. Parents who are sensitively attuned to their own children and sincerely regard them with respect and affection can use spankings or a system of stars for good behavior, so long as the methods they employ are effective and do not create undue anxiety. Parents who really have little regard or love for their offspring frequently attempt to make up for their own lack of feeling by avidly reading advice on how to bring up children. Though they attempt to substitute "expert" recommendations for their own shortcomings, no special child-rearing method will compensate for their inability to love and understand their children. Such inadequate adults need psychotherapeutic help and care so that they may learn to become more willing parents. The only advice any psychologist or other child specialist should really give is: avoid extreme punishment, recognize the capabilities of your children, hold them to their responsibilities, and train them in any way, as long as you love and respect them.

LOVE AND ACCEPTANCE OF CHILDREN

Not all parents really want and love all their children. Of course, all parents, even the very best, are occasionally fed up with their children's antics and feel that, in the words of one good mother, "I could cheerfully wring her neck." But some parents are fairly negative toward their children most, if not all, of the time. To begin with, about one in four pregnant mothers is dissatisfied that a child is on its way. But not all mothers remain displeased. After birth, many seem to be won over by the delightful helplessness and dependence of their baby. Many find themselves full of new feelings of warmth and affection that some can only describe as "being a mother": "I didn't think I would feel that way. I'd read all those descriptions about how terrible those newborn babies look. But I loved her from the minute I saw her. She's so helpless and cuddly; you just want to hover around her and take care of her. And she looks at you and she knows you're her mother."

It is difficult to ascertain what proportion of mothers and fathers actively reject their own children. It is likely, however, that possibly one out of ten parents is less than delighted with the responsibilities of parenthood. Yet, it is not easy to discern immediately whether a parent is unaccepting of his children. Adults do not readily announce that they irrevocably hate their offspring. To complicate matters further, most hostile parents feel guilty about their negative feelings toward their children and try to hide their emotions both from others and themselves. In an effort to obscure and compensate for his rejecting attitude, the unloving parent frequently overindulges or "spoils" his children. He seems to give them everything they want, and of course they continue to want more. Other rejecting parents may seem to overprotect their children or even to be overly affectionate toward them. But frequently, underlying these seemingly acceptable attitudes are fundamental feelings of nonacceptance and hostility.

Parental attitudes toward children are believed by Sears and his associates to be of central importance in determining a child's behavior and personality. Mothers who are cold, unaccepting, and unloving tend to have children who develop many problems—particularly feeding difficulties and bedwetting. The loving, accepting mother, on the other hand, has far fewer difficulties with her child.

A warm mother spends more time with her child. She offers him more rewards . . . and gives more guidance. He develops stronger expectancies of her reciprocal affection, and thus is more highly motivated to learn how to behave as she wants him to. He becomes more susceptible to control by her, for he has more to gain and more to lose. It seems likely, too, that he gets proportionately more satisfaction and less frustration from his growing desire for affection. [It is possible that] children of warm mothers mature more rapidly, in their social behavior, than those of cold mothers. [Sears, et al., pp. 483–84.]

A summary of some of the factors that Sears and his associates found to be important in determining family atmosphere [2] is listed below.

2 Sears, et al., pp. 472ff.

Permissiveness-strictness. Low-permissive, strict parents are quick to punish physically, intolerant of sex play and immodesty, and demand quiet, obedience, good manners and high performance in school. High-permissive, low-strictness parents put few restrictions on children, tolerate dependence and immodesty, and demand less immediate obedience.

General family adjustment. The well-adjusted families are defined by mothers who agree with husbands about child rearing, are free of anxiety, satisfied with their lives, enjoy their children, and have feelings of esteem and strong affection.

Warmth of mother-child relationship. Warm mothers spend much time interacting affectionately with infants, accept dependency, and tend to use reasoning as a method of training.

Child-training orientation. Mothers who exhibit a high and positive degree of this trait demand a continued and satisfactory progress of their child to maturity. These mothers are confident and view their children as people who must be taught many things.

Aggressiveness and punitiveness. Mothers who are high in this characteristic encourage their children to be aggressive toward other children but tend to punish aggression when it is directed toward themselves.

PERMISSIVE OR STRICT DISCIPLINE?

For the last two decades much has been written about the virtues of permissiveness. Parents are urged to let their children "find themselves" by being freed of adult restrictions. The permissive home in which a child grows up unrestricted, allowed to do as he pleases, is frequently equated with the American democratic way of life. Strictly disciplined homes, in which children are "seen but not heard," are called authoritarian, and made to resemble European dictatorship. Some psychologists have been especially prominent in their attempt to label home situation in political terms and thus confuse the whole question of family environment and personality.

Much of the information concerning the effects of discipline versus permissiveness has been unsystematically obtained by biased individual observation. Some of the conclusions regarding the effects of home environment have been the results of observing disturbed families and calling them discipline or authority oriented and contrasting these with well-adjusted families, which are labeled permissive. Dr. Goodwin Watson has devoted considerable time to investigating the discipline- and permissiveness-centered home. The first condition Dr. Watson set was that all the families studied provide healthy, normal environments. He rejected all homes in which there were serious distortions in family functioning.

Forty-four children brought up in good, loving, but strictly disciplined homes were compared with 34 children from the same community and also brought up in good, loving homes but with an extraordinary degree of permissiveness. Two periods of psychological testing, supplemented (in 38 cases) by teacher ratings, have yielded measures of nine dimensions of personality. . . . None of the personality differences applies to all cases; some children from strict and some from permissive homes may be found at every level on every characteristic tested.

As far as Dr. Watson was able to determine, whether a home tended toward the permissiveness or the discipline orientation did not have any discernible effect on any particular traits found in the children. Apparently the well-being and growth of children is not adversely or beneficially affected by their being reared in either one or the other home atmosphere.

Another point should be made. *Permissive* and *disciplined* are partly misnomers. Both types of homes set certain rules. Children are not allowed in either atmosphere to endanger their lives and safety. In both family orientations children are made aware of their limits. The differences between discipline- and permissiveness-centered homes are undoubtedly distinctions only in terms of a few degrees. The permissive home tends to have fewer rules, use punishment less, and respond more to the children's demands. The disciplined home respects the needs of its children, but there are more rules for conduct. Propriety is expected earlier. There may be more punishment than in the permissive home. It is likely, however, that, except for the unfortunate labels, permissive and disciplined homes are much alike. Certainly the well-adjusted *permissive* home is much more like the well-adjusted *disciplined* home than it is like the psychologically distraught permissive family.

THE GANG AGE

During late childhood, the years six to twelve, children tend to cluster in gangs. They develop strong allegiances to particular groups of playmates and make their interests coincide with those of their peers. It is during this period that children develop the games, jokes, and rituals that are uniquely a part of childhood. Instead of playing adult games like tennis or softball, they prefer their own amusements such as hide-and-seek, tag, or house. Similarly, they quickly discover a reservoir of quips, puzzles, and puns. Moron and knock-knock jokes are passed around, elaborated, and perpetuated for generations of children to share. In all ways during this period, children develop a culture and way of life that is distinctly their own and separate from the adult world.

In their efforts to liberate themselves from parents, children may become highly secretive and think of their playmates as part of a conspiratorial society. They are aligned, alone, both against parents and older and younger children. The continuing intensive and clandestine association between gang-age children leads to the development of rituals and ceremonies not unlike those found in older secret groups. Some children have a hidden clubhouse or meeting place. Others develop signals, signs, and passwords to identify themselves. Some even devise initiation rituals.

> PSYCHOLOGIST. What do you have to do to be a member of your club?
> CHILD. You have to do three things. First you gotta swear not to tell the secret hideout—where it is, and then you must get a secret code ring from Captain Kazoo by sending in the boxtop. Then you have to buy an orange crush and everybody has to drink from the bottle.

Many intitiation rituals are not so mild as this. Although the children's gang is in no sense delinquent, some groups insist on filching an article from parents or a store. Other initiation rites that have been reported range from having children eat cooked cold spaghetti that they are told is worms to hitting or pulling the hair of a favored little girl enemy.

Gang-age children want to be left to their own devices. They frequently reassure adults that they can take care of themselves and set their own standards of conduct. In fact, a rough legal code does result as a consequence of the efforts of six- to twelve-year-olds. The essential legal morality of this age group seems to center about the concept of fairness. Children and adults believed to have acted unjustly are denounced as unfair. Arguments during games revolve about the issue of what is fair and not fair. There are, of course, subsidiary rules, such as not hitting those with glasses, or those smaller than yourself, or hitting "below the belt." It is especially difficult for adults to accept another important gang-age ethic—that of not being a "tattle" or "stool pigeon." Children, convinced of the unimpeachable morality of not telling about the activities of another, may go to surprising lengths not to have to reveal information about their associates or activities.

In the close company engendered by the gang age, children discuss and experiment with many of the biological details of life. Jokes about sexual and digestive functions are common. Many of the jokes, however, make little sense to adults, since the punch line, if there is one, often depends simply on the enunciation of a supposed "dirty" word. Typically, too, children are more closedmouthed about their quasi-sexual activities than most other concerns. It is rare, for example, that a gang-age child will reveal the amount of misinformation he has developed in the course of his associations with equally interested but ignorant children of the same age.

The concern and anxiety children frequently have about bodily functions often expresses itself in rather unique, sometimes amusing ways. Certain essentially neutral words, for example, may be alleged to have some underlying biological connotations. One teacher of eleven-year-olds reported that the word *it* apparently had a secret meaning for a group of her pupils. She sent them into embarrassed and suppressed merriment when reprimanding a careless student doing a construction project by loudly announced "I'll show you how to do it." The teacher became aware thereafter that conspicuously using *it* in a sentence always initiated giggles.

The gang-age child is highly conscious of his sexual affiliation and is very wary lest he be apprehended fraternizing with the opposite sex. Boys are probably more hostile to girls than girls are to boys. In fact, girls frequently make efforts to inveigle boys into playing games with them. A boy may be needed to fill a role in the game of house or to carry out some other vital game function. On the other hand, boys will rarely if ever invite a girl to participate in a game with them. If a girl is accepted, she has to be at least as "tough" and athletically able, if not more so, than the boys she wishes to join. Girls, in desperate need of a boy to play some game with them, sometimes resort to clever coercive ruses. They may, for example, continue to harass a group of boys and leave only if one consents to play house with them. Or an intrepid girl may follow boys to their secret hide-out and threaten to divulge its location unless they acquiesce in her wishes. It is likely that many of the techniques the two sexes eventually use to get along with each other are rooted in this period of their childhood.

Probably all children throughout the world, during the six-to-twelve-year age period associate in loosely knit gangs. American children call their unique game cops and robbers or cowboys and Indians. In another culture the activities, concerns, and games of gang-agers may be exactly the same, though they may call their games Zulu versus Hottentot. The desire of six- to twelve-year-olds to cluster together seems to be a universal need of human children and many other mammals as well. It is a way to step from childhood into adult independence. The transition is made easier by relying upon the security and protection of other children before the bold separation from adult domination is completed. In primitive societies the gang age ends with puberty, and full adult responsibilities begin. In our own culture adolescence, a sort of semichild status, continues the process of achieving independence gradually.

It appears to be a current impression, probably derived from the publicity and attention focused on juvenile delinquency, that there is something destructive or criminal about children's gangs. The two should not, however, be confused. The gang-age period, roughly from six to twelve, is an expected and worldwide developmental stage. Children who belong to such gangs are not corrupted by their experience but rather helped to grow. Nearly all adults now in their forties, fifties, and beyond, can recall, probably with delight, their own childhood gangs and the firm commitments that they inspired. This is not so for adults who have grown up within the last two decades. Since the end of World War II adults have actively attempted to regulate and disintegrate the child's world of games, rituals, and allegiances. Elementary-school children are taught tennis or golf, which are adult games. Children are sent to playgrounds and closely supervised. Commercial appeals from movies or television motivate parents to costume their child according to currently popular fads. Fathers are told to be "pals" to their boys, and mothers are encouraged to act like "sis." Children are supervised, tutored, regulated, and regimented so that little opportunity is available for them to find solace among others of their own age.

It is neither necessary nor desirable for adults to interfere with the normal group associations that form during childhood. Children's gangs do not lead to delinquent gangs. Persuasive evidence even suggests that the innocent friendship clusters of childhood may actually lead away from the destructive groups associated with adolescent delinquency. In fact, many of the rules of normal social living are learned through early gang associations. Children learn to share and cooperate. They become aware of what it means to have their opinions and feelings honored and develop an understanding for the meaning of trust, truth, and justice. All these skills and important social attainments are learned easily in healthy gang associations. Taught through the efforts of adults, however, many of these precepts become merely peculiar-sounding words and suspicious types of preaching. Children's gangs are healthy, expected developmental phenonmena that allow the child both to become an independent human being and learn many of the social skills necessary for healthful living.

During the first dozen years of the child's life, his personality is molded. The attributes he was born with, the atmosphere and examples provided by his parental home, the children with whom he associates in his gang, and the whole world in which he lives combine to help shape the person he is. These early years, if healthy and satisfying, can leave the child with strength that will help him meet many of the most serious challenges of adolescence and adulthood. If, however, the individual is weakened by unfortunate parental attitudes and circumstances, he is easily overpowered by the new problems he meets as he continues to grow. The part that parents play in shaping their children is limited. They can do little or nothing about the child's innate endowment. Nor can they significantly alter the influences that companions, entertainment, neighborhood, and school will have. But if they provide their child with a truly worthy example, an accepting home and family, and modify their discipline with affection and understanding, they will have contributed greatly to their child's total well-being.

FOR REVIEW AND DISCUSSION

1. Do environmental influences begin at birth or at conception? How can the intra-uterine environment affect the unborn human organism? What are some common superstitions about prebirth influences?
2. What is maturation? Do maturational skills play their most important role relatively early or late in the child's development? Can a primarily maturational skill be appreciably speeded up by intensive training?
3. What are some currently popular child-rearing ideas or practices? Are children reared somewhat differently today from the way they were several decades ago? How do middle-class practices differ from lower-class ones? What social, national, or other ethnoid differences may influence child-rearing attitudes? What techniques are suggested by psychologists? How important are love and acceptance in raising children?
4. What is the "gang age"? What does the child learn in the gang? Are children destined to become delinquent because of belonging to a children's gang? Are children's gangs more or less common today and more or less accepted now than they were several decades ago?

The Adolescent

Years

T H R E E

Throughout much of the world childhood ends and adulthood starts at the beginning of the second decade of life. In our own and other advanced technological societies, adulthood is deferred until a person reaches his twenties. During the last several generations, this interim level has been marked by us as a separate stage of growth called adolescence. Recognizing the teen-age years as a distinct developmental phase is relatively new. Our society's high standard of living and need for prolonged education both permit and necessitate that adolescents remain aloof from many adult responsibilities. At the same time, realizing they are no longer young children, adolescents increasingly demand adult privileges. But since those between twelve and twenty have only recently been accorded separate maturational status, there are few precedents or traditions that can help determine appropriate adolescent roles. It does not follow, however, that adolescence is more unusual than most other periods. It is a part of the process of growth and change that, with its recurring dilemmas, is characteristic of all human life.

PHYSICAL DEVELOPMENT

Adolescence begins with immense physical changes. The body grows with new, if uneven, rapidity. Sexual interests and physical characteristics are invigorated. Changes in bearing, conduct, and outlook swiftly follow. The physical development that begins the teen-age years is well described in a Children's Bureau pamphlet, *The Adolescent in Your Family.*

Girls who are well nourished and in good physical condition, whose homes and living conditions are above average, tend to mature somewhat earlier than those in less favorable surroundings. Also, a moderate climate favors earlier maturation than either a very hot or a very cold climate.

The largest number of girls first menstruate when 13, although a good many do so at 12. An occasional girl has her first menstrual period as early as 9 or 10. Very few girls begin to menstruate more than 2 years before or 5 years after the average age of 13. It is a rare girl who has not menstruated by the time she is 16. However, there is nothing abnormal in such comparatively late maturation, or in its early arrival at 10 or 11. About 3 percent of girls begin to menstruate before 11, and another 3 percent after 15.

For a while, menstrual periods are usually irregular, with wide gaps between. From this, and other evidence, it is concluded that the appearance of menstruation does not necessarily mean the girl is sexually mature, in the sense of ovulating (producing eggs) and being able to bear a child. Conception extremely rarely occurs during the first year of menstruation. The length of time the menstrual flow lasts is different in different individuals. In younger girls it may last a day or so longer than the 4 and one half days which is an average to be expected of young adult women. Some girls, onces the menses are established, menstruate a little oftener than every 28 days, some a little less often. Few have an absolutely regular cycle, now or later.

In addition to the appearance of menstruation, related, or secondary, sex characteristics show up. Among them are the development of the breasts, and a gradual rounding of the figure into curves that mark the departure from little-girlhood. Along with these is rapid growth of the sex organs—the vagina, uterus, fallopian tubes and the ovaries that will produce eggs throughout the child-bearing years.

The structural changes that indicate the end of childhood are less apparent in boys.

In the boy outward bodily changes, such as the appearance of pubic hair, are usually relied on to mark his passage into adolescence, for he has no special function, like menstruation, whose appearance can easily be dated. The finding of sperm cells in the urine would be conclusive evidence of a boy's sexual maturity. But the time when this occurs is hard to determine without the bother of frequent examination, so other signs are counted on: the need for shaving, the lowering of the voice, which comes late in the period of pubescence, often in the fifteenth year, the broadening and thickening of neck and shoulders, and the increased growth of the genital organs.

The largest group of boys can be expected to reach puberty at about 14 or 15, which is a year or 2 earlier than would have been the case 50 years ago. They will have begun their spurt in height about 6 months earlier than their pubescent gain in weight. By 13 and one half, about 35 percent of boys will be going through the changes that lead to sexual maturation; at 15 and one half, 60 percent of boys will have passed into adolescence, and by 17 and one half years, over 90 percent will have done so.

In both girls and boys, the approach of adolescence is marked by the appearance and development of hair in the pubic region. Though that is one of the less important happenings of the period, "puberty" takes its name from it, probably because it is so easily observable a change. Fine and uncolored at first, this pubic hair is later succeeded by coarser, darker hair which becomes kinky. While the pubic hair is growing denser, hair begins to appear in the armpits.

In the boy, hair also begins soon after to appear on the face, where it first occurs as down on the upper lip, and gradually spreads and coarsens, until shaving becomes necessary. Not until much later in adolescence does hair begin to come on the chest, and this is much more marked in some boys than others.

The hairline on a boy's forehead often undergoes a change during adolescence. Where it formed a curve in childhood, two indentations begin to show up, so that the hairline appears to be receding a little at the sides of the forehead.[1]

Although many young teen-age boys and girls worry about the changes taking place within them, they do not readily admit their concern. This was illustrated when a psychologist talked to a large social club composed of fourteen- to sixteen-year-old boys. After a short speech concerning some of the sexual and societal problems of growing, he called for questions. Since none of the adolescents raised their hands to make a query, the psychologist suggested they write their questions on slips of paper and pass them in to him. Few written interrogations were forthcoming. As a last resort the speaker asked the boys to submit questions they believed bothered *other* teen-agers. The response to this request was overwhelming. Dozens of questions ranging from "dating" etiquette to sexual deviation poured in. Each boy, of course, while naïvely believing that his questions described someone else's curiosity and concern, was actually recording his own uncertainties.

Their new physical capacities make many teen-agers acutely aware of their bodies. Crooked teeth, moles, need for eyeglasses, or other imperfections real and imagined may become serious sources of concern. Similarly, the irregularities of early menstrual flows may cause considerable anxiety among some girls. In boys, the freshly discovered erotic excitability, frequent erections, seminal emissions, and other sexual signs may become the focus for long-lasting worry. Fortunately, for most adolescents, reassurance coupled with forthright information that the changes and desires are an expected part of becoming an adult serves to lessen tensions.

THE ADOLESCENT'S DILEMMA

Throughout the world in many rural and tribal societies childhood ends and adulthood begins with the physical changes of puberty. The history of our own culture demonstrates that twelve-, thirteen-, and fourteen-year-olds were once considered adults. Shakespeare's Romeo

1 Pp. 18–19. Reprinted by permission, courtesy of the Director, Division of Reports, Children's Bureau, Welfare Administration, Department of Health, Education, and Welfare.

and Juliet were in their early teens when they initiated their tragic love affair. In Renaissance Europe many not much beyond the age of fourteen assumed the mature responsibilities imposed by maintaining a wife and earning a livelihood. Currently, many religious denominations maintain traditions that admit young adolescents to full adult status. In Judaism, for example, qualified boys are admitted to membership in the congregation when they reach the age of thirteen. In most creeds, ranging from Christianity to relatively "primitive" beliefs, the confirmation of young men or women as adults nearly always takes place during the beginning of the second decade of life. Historically, it was well recognized that, in terms of the example provided by other mammals, the ability to reproduce is nature's signal of adulthood.

In the United States and other developed nations, the biological signs of maturity are largely ignored. Children are not accorded adult status when their bodies suddenly change to prepare for reproduction. The fourteen-year-old who is functionally an adult is treated as a child. Certainly he is not supposed to evidence his procreative urges in any but the most indirect ways. The result is that the adolescent faces a dilemma. He is physically fully capable of the role of a mature member of his species, yet he is denied the privileges accorded those who are different from him only by being a few years older.

The adolescent's uncertain status was described by Dr. Kinsey and his associates, who wrote that our society

specifies the right of the married adult to have regular intercourse, but it makes no provision whatsoever for the approximately 40 percent of the population which is sexually mature but unmarried. Many youths and older unmarried females and males are seriously disturbed because the only source of sexual outlet available to them are either legally or socially disapproved. Most unmarried males, and not a few of the unmarried females, would like to know how to resolve this conflict between their physiologic capacities and the legal and social codes.

In addition, Kinsey points out, not only is the adolescent sexually equivalent to an adult, but as if to compound the dilemma, his sexual energies far surpass those of older people.

In actuality, the teen-age and twenty-year-old males respond more frequently than most older males; their responses are, on the whole, more intense than those of older males; and, in spite of their difficulty in finding socio-sexual outlets, they reach orgasm more frequently than most older males. Among unmarried males the frequency of orgasm is at a maximum somewhere

between the ages of sixteen and eighteen. Similarly, among married males
there is no age group in which sexual activity is, on an average, more frequent
than it is among the males in their late teens and early twenties. The attempt
to ignore and suppress the physiologic needs of the sexually most capable
segment of the population has led to more complications than most persons
are willing to recognize. [Kinsey, *et al.*, 1953, p. 13.]

Like any other group that is denied outlet, teen-agers, as Kinsey
has suggested, develop problems both for themselves and for others.
Our culture tells the adolescent that he is in an in-between stage: not
a child anymore but definitely not an adult. His own reason informs
him, however, that he is as capable and motivated as those who are
older. But what privileges are to be granted during the teen-age
years? Most adults are as confused as adolescents themselves. Should
teen-agers be subject to a curfew? If so, what hour? Should "necking"
be encouraged as a healthy outlet or discouraged because it might
lead to further erotic involvement? Adults reach different conclusions.
While some colleges chaperon their dorms with police intensity,
others permit boys and girls to visit each other in their rooms.

Adolescents share not only many of the sexual needs of adults but
many of their emotions as well. The psychological make-up of teen-
agers is highly similar to that found in people many years their senior.
This is little recognized, however, so that many adolescent feelings
are mistakenly labeled immature or unrealistic. It may well be that
much of the affect seen during the teen years is unstable, but this
alone, of course, does not distinguish it from adult responses. Even
if satisfactory criteria of maturity were available, it is likely that
not very many in either the younger or older age groups would
qualify as fully emotionally "adult." Yet adolescent emotions may
strike many adults as "childish" because they frequently appear to
center about seemingly unimportant events. How can a fourteen-year-
old girl become so distressed about a particular dress, or a sixteen-
year-old suitor have such intense feelings that he elopes? The failure
of many adults to understand the reactions of their rapidly growing
children doubtless contributes considerably to conflict within families.
There is nothing innately more immature about an intense longing
for an automobile at the age of seventeen than there is about wanting
a prestigious set of golf clubs at forty-five. The needs of adolescents
differ in content and mode of expression from those felt at age thirty
just as the needs of thirty-year-olds differ from those felt at age sixty.

The adolescent's dilemma is created by the fact that while he is
physically and emotionally qualified for adulthood he is disfranchised
from participation in an adult-dominated world. In many states mar-

riage must wait till the twenty-first birthday. Alcoholic beverages, signing most legal contracts to buy or sell, and voting are denied to teen-agers nearly all over the United States. Yet many who reach age fourteen (and even twelve) in various parts of this country are allowed to leave school and assume full job responsibilities. As a consequence, the adolescent, in order to work out his proper place in society is called upon to enact many different, even conflicting roles. For most adults and in most situations he must play the dependent child. On occasion, however, he is forced to act as, and fully expected to be, the adult he essentially is.

Al, sixteen years old, was referred to the clinic by the local police. He came from a middle-class, apparently well-adjusted family. He was the youngest of three children and complained that his parents and older siblings treated him as a baby. Although legally eligible at sixteen, he had not been permitted to drive the family car because his father felt he was "just a kid." In actuality, Al is nearly six feet tall and well proportioned. Al mentioned that his parents plan "nearly everything" for him. They prescribed his high-school curriculum, have planned his college, and frequently, without his knowledge, consult his teachers. Nevertheless, Al states that his parents treat him well and that he gets along with them "nicely."

Al is "going steady" with a neighborhood girl. The girl's parents supervise their behavior very closely, though Al reported he and she had been able to "get away with a few things" occasionally. Al seems to understand his sexual needs fairly well but believes that his own and his girl friend's parents have a distorted idea of their sexual requirements.

Al and his girl friend have discussed marriage but know both sets of parents to be adamantly opposed. Al's parents want him to attend and complete college and be in his middle twenties before starting a family. His girl friend Nancy's parents also want their daughter to obtain a college education and wait till she is at least twenty-one before marriage.

Al and Nancy had a disagreement concerning the ethical limits they had imposed upon their own sexual conduct. Al felt that Nancy was unreasonably "puritan." He described the argument they had and reiterated how he was especially irritated by Nancy's conviction that they were "just kids" and should not "go too far." Al said he was "sick and tired" of being treated like a "baby" by everyone and decided he would do something that would result in his being treated like a man. He had read that the merchant marine hired sixteen-year-olds, so he impulsively decided to run away to sea. Gathering some money early one Saturday morning, he took a stand on an expressway to hitchhike to New York City, 700 miles away. Since hitchhiking was illegal, he was quickly apprehended by the police. Although merely reprimanded by the officer for hitchhiking on an expressway, Al reported that he "blubbered like a baby" and told the police all of his plans to run away. His crying in front of the officers humiliated Al because he said that though he was usually treated like a child, when he actually acted like one, "everyone" told him he was a man of sixteen and that he should act his age.

Adolescents are not only caught in the dilemma of possessing most adult capabilities while being denied many adult privileges; they also face another conflict. Since the time when the parents of today's adolescents were teen-agers, there have been marked social changes. The values that parents cherished as youngsters may not be relevant to children growing up today. When the parents were young, it is likely that smoking, boy-girl relationships, and other signs of maturity were reserved for late adolescents or young adults. Today dating begins as early as thirteen years of age. Many are smoking openly at fifteen. Parents find it hard to revise their own standards and frequently tend to think of current adolescent practices as undesirable or even immoral. As a result, the behavior of teen-agers is judged by one set of standards by their parents and by another group of values by the adolescents themselves and their young friends.

All the kids my age are dating and staying out till one or two [at night], but my mother keeps telling me that's not the way they did things when she was my age. So I keep telling her that that was a lot of years ago and the kids do things differently today. And she don't believe me. If I don't do what the other kids do they think I'm just out of it, and if I do then my mother lets me have it. So I don't know what to do.

THE PROFESSIONAL TEEN-AGER

Adolescents are confronted with the dilemma of being virtually adults, yet in most instances being treated like children. But neither role, that of dependent youngster or of autonomous adult, is fully available to them. One way in which adolescents escape from the ambiguity of their status is by helping create and escaping into a new role—that of the "teen-ager." Adults, recognizing an easy resolution of the uncertain position of twelve- to twenty-year-olds, have helped form the teen-age image. In addition, experts ranging from businessmen to journalists supply styles of dress, language, and etiquette that are reputedly typical. The world of the teen-ager thus projected is ostensibly populated by long-legged, gawky, sex-conscious human beings capable of few thoughts beyond what will replace the currently favored dance craze. Interspersed with endless telephone conversations are alleged refrigerator-raiding forays resulting in continual bizarre eating. Though many adolescents find this conception of their existence repellent, they have little choice but to enter into the make-believe world of the mythical teen-ager.

> I don't go for all this teen bit. The cookie party, or the beer, the big deal about the Prom. You got to have the latest disc that some singer put out or be drooling for a ragtop [convertible]. But you have no choice. You don't want them to treat you like a kid—they won't let you do half the things you want to—so you make it big with the "I'm a teen-ager." You become sort of a pro at it after a while—the professional teen-ager.

The artificial world of the teen-ager is not a creation that can be traced to any specific source. The current style of life of many adolescents results from and combines many elements within our complex culture. Several commercial enterprises, for example, find perpetuating and exploiting the manufactured teen-age role profitable. By aiming directly for the patronage of teen-agers, movies with their lurid sexual and aggressive themes consistently exaggerate and thus distort the adolescent's own emerging interests. The popular songs that reiterate the glory and despair of romanticized love reinforce the most deformed picture of relations between the sexes. Responsible adults, too—often teachers, ministers, and others—view with benevolent tolerance and thus implicitly encourage adolescents to enact their fraudulent, stereotyped roles. The synthetically created teen-age world serves too many masters—adolescents themselves, parents, as well as significant segments of our total economy—to be easily modified.

Besides banding together in the current teen-age fashion because it solves many aspects of the dilemma created by their uncertain adult-child status, adolescents are drawn to one another because, surprisingly often, they are literally abandoned by their parents. Even mothers and fathers who have been fairly adequate when their children were five and ten years of age may feel their task is ended when their offspring become thirteen or fourteen. The adolescnt devoid of parental interest and example has little choice but to enter into the mythical existence created for him.

Becoming a professional teen-ager, that is, adopting the behavior we have come to believe characteristic during the teen years, results in a noteworthy loss both for the adolescent and for his society. Adolescents can be remarkably sensitive and idealistic individuals. But instead of supplying the creative sparks that the young have typically contributed to their nations, many become members of a huge conformity-bound mass. The adolescent himself suffers irreparable loss when he abandons his identity to assume the part of a teen-ager. It is during the years after puberty and before the twenties that firm commitments to serious study or dedication to ambitious life goals are made. Few adolescents who are sidetracked by the lures of the deceptive teen-age world are provided a second chance to reshape their futures. By forcing adolescents to adopt the shallow role of teen-ager, by denying them access to the adult world, many of the most valuable qualities that such youngsters possess are irrevocably lost.

No serious authority argues that fifteen-year-olds in our own country should, like those in less developed societies, exercise all adult roles. Our own culture is by this time far too complex to permit a child of fifteen all the functions of a twenty-five-year-old. But instead of denying adolescents total entry into the adult world, instead of relegating them into an artificially created teen-age milieu, we could bring teen-agers slowly and carefully to full senior status. When the thirteen-year-old boy or girl, quickly becoming biologically mature, seeks the attention and understanding of parents, he is entitled to be allowed to make the first tentative steps toward adulthood. All too often, of course, he is denied either sympathy or acceptance. The adolescent wants to become a member of adult society gradually. Allowing him to do so will doubtless necessitate changes both in the way adults and adolescents now act and in their expectations of one another.

ATTITUDES TOWARD THE OPPOSITE SEX

Adolescent boys and girls, like many adults, tend to view each other with a mixture of desire, trepidation, and hostility. The opposite sex is sought after, but also feared. Some adolescents' ambivalent feelings are so distressing that they effectively isolate themselves from sociosexual contact and thus seriously impair their chances for establishing satisfactory marriages. On the other hand, many adolescents seem to compensate for their sexual uncertainties by cultivating an impressive succession of romances.

Adolescent males are prodded by the cultural stereotype of the teen-age boy to act aggressively and exploitively. Fathers even encourage their sons to take every heterosexual advantage. In many instances it is considered a prerequisite of masculinity to be able to boast of a significant number of female conquests. At the same time, females are persuaded that their role is to uphold traditional virtues. If they have sexual desires, they must turn them into romantic yearnings and fix them on males—such as movie stars—whom they will never meet.

Many girls have to take out their romantic yearnings on boys they see, but never meet—admiring from afar. The passionate and mass devotion of bobby-soxers to a current movie star or TV crooner affords a safe way of providing someone to dream about. This is the age when almost any male figure, if personable enough, whether a clerk in the neighborhood drugstore, the tenor in the church choir, or even a high-school teacher may be the object of a romantic devotion of which he, happily in most cases, remains completely unaware. One pudgy girl whom the boys at school ignored exerted herself every morning for months to reach the bus early enough to get the seat behind the driver. As she could get little conversation out of him, she had to discharge her feelings by gazing at the back of his head. The qualities that have begun to take shape in the mind of the love-dreaming girl must find expression in a person, no matter how little the real person may match up with the imagined charms. [Children's Bureau, 1955, p. 66.]

Adolescent males and females bring conflicting attitudes toward each other into their relationship. The boy is oriented toward sexual exploitation while the girl yearns for romance. These differing expectations, plus the traditional misunderstandings that occur between sexes, make most teen-age boy-girl friendships highly unstable. Frequent shifts in partners are common and expected. Changing boy or girl friends for the flimsiest sounding reasons—"His car was two years newer"—is an everyday occurrence. Were it not for the well-defined ritual of dating (see Chapter Five), which clearly details the exact nature of boy-girl contact, it is possible that the misunderstandings and conflicts between adolescent boys and girls might be great enough to keep them almost irreconcilably apart. Dating provides girls an opportunity for romantic fantasy, while giving boys an opportunity for sexual exploration. Dating at the same time allows males and females to be in the company of one another and requires very little personal interaction.

I like dating, especially with another couple. I can't talk to girls—maybe I'm shy, or there's nothing much to say. On a date you pick her up and you got maybe fifteen minutes before you get to a movie. Then you don't have to say nothing at all during the movie, but you might neck there and things like that. When you get out of the movie you might eat something and you just eat and don't have to say much, and here and there you kill a half hour and get them home. All together you have less than forty-five minutes you're supposed to talk. It isn't hard just to kill those forty-five minutes. But like if you go to a dance you're standing around for hours, supposed to say things. That kills me. I can't do that.

DISCIPLINING ADOLESCENTS

Adolescents in our society cannot be treated as full adults, yet they cannot be expected willingly to submit to the authority exercised over a child, since they are no longer dependent children. The threats, rewards, and physical punishments that may have proven practical discipline for seven-year-olds are powerless when the age of seventeen has been reached. Parents who are aware of the new status of their grown children find that explanation and reason become increasingly effective ways to motivate them. Since the teen-age years are a period not only of rapid physical awakening but also of moral and ethical understanding, adolescents are probably more responsive to logical persuasion than is any other age group.

The family milieu in which a child grows up is always an important determinant of behavior. Since children learn to think and act largely through parental example, what parents actually *do,* rather than say, significantly shapes the activities of all youngsters. Perhaps adolescents more vividly than children of any other age group demonstrate the effects of parental example. Teen-agers who come from firm, affectionate homes in which ethical standards have been practiced rather than preached will probably pass through their adolescent years with a minimum of conflict and distress (Britton and Winans). Those children who are reared in families in which chronic tensions and deficient codes of civilized living are commonplace will doubtless suffer from—and create most of—the disturbances associated with this period. Adolescents, just like adults, behave in accordance with the standards they have witnessed. It it thus not surprising that a promiscuous parent finds advocating virtue to her fifteen-year-old daughter ineffective. A fifteen-year-old girl, physically more mature than most girls her age, was brought to a mental health clinic by her mother. The mother said she had found out that her daughter had a "sex life" and wanted the clinic to "straighten her out," because "beating her up" and all the "discipline in the whole world that I tried wasn't helping any." The following is the girl's description of her background.

My mother was always working on some man. When she was divorced from my father she had a job as a manicurist. She used to tell me how she was working on this one customer that she knew had money. Then she got him and they were married. I was about five years old. He stayed about a year and then he ran away. They had wild arguments. He didn't have any money. He just boasted all the time. I don't think he had a job. She kept on working. After that we lived alone till I was about ten. She had a lot of boyfriends and used to tell me how it was hard to get them to marry her because of me. Some of them used to stay overnight and even hang around for a few weeks.

She married Nick [the present husband] when I was ten. He drinks— she does too now—and they get along, sort of. He's stayed longer than any one else. He's nothing as fathers go; I don't have much to do with him. He's not got much interest in me either, I think. They do yell at each other, and she has walked out a few times, but they get along. She buys me what I want. She's always saying how lucky I am to have such a good mother that will work so hard for me. She says she's done everything she has just to take care of me. Then she gets excited and calls me an ingrate and a snot. She's always saying how I've never seen anything but the best at home—that they're God-fearing, honest, hard-working people. She says that I ought to learn by her example.

I wasn't doing very much really—to get that excited about. Just a bunch of the kids I knew. We'd go for a drive. Some of the kids would play around a little. [The girl has been involved in a group participating in promiscuous intercourse with one another.] You get that way. It is just a way of keeping some of the boys interested in you.

Descriptions of the backgrounds of healthy adolescents, not involved in sexual or other delinquencies, are less dramatic than the story told by this girl. Inherent in nearly all statements from wholesome teen-agers are indications of the degree to which parental example and family tradition have shaped their lives (see Table 3-1). Adolescents, like other children and many adults as well, have the ability to detect what is real and what attitudes are "put on" for their benefit. One famous adolescent, J. D. Salinger's Holden Caulfield, points out how he detests "phonyism." His search, like that of many adolescents, is for the true and real with which he can identify. The preachers, with their "holy Joe" voices, as Holden puts it, do little to convince adolescents. Instead, they frequently turn them away in disgust.

It is an axiom of most child-treatment centers that youngsters cannot be treated alone. Parents must be part of the therapy. Adolescents are partly what they are because of the emotional climate of their parents' own standards—or lack of them. To change an adolescent or any child, the parents must change radically.

Adolescents are biologically and psychologically relatively adult, but in our own culture they are viewed as being in the process of

Table 3-1   FACTORS IDENTIFYING POTENTIAL JUVENILE OFFENDERS

Predictive factors	Percentage incidence of delinquents
Discipline of boy by father	
Firm but kindly	9.3
Lax	59.8
Overstrict or erratic	72.5
Supervision of boy by mother	
Suitable	9.9
Fair	57.5
Unsuitable	83.5
Affection of father for boy	
Warm (including over-protective)	33.6
Indifferent or hostile	86.2
Cohesiveness of family	
Marked	20.6
Some	61.3
None	96.9

Source: After S. Glueck and Eleanor Glueck, Predicting Delinquency and Crime (Cambridge: Harvard University Press, 1959), p. 28. Reported by Calvin, et al.

changing from dependent childhood to independent maturity. Teen-agers, therefore, though they possess adult capacities, are permitted few of the prerogatives of those ten or more years older. Since they are neither part of the world of children nor part of adult society, adolescents develop strong allegiances to their peer group. Their own age-mates become a dominant force in their lives and create, with the calculated help of many segments of our culture, a unique teen-age environment. The mythical teen world characterized by conformity, popular songs, movies, and dance crazes is artificial, but it provides at least some measure of acceptance for most adolescents.

Complicating the problem of finding his appropriate role is the fact that the adolescent's parents have little understanding of his dilemma. Since the teen-agers' parents were young, swift social changes have occurred, altering many of the values that guided children growing up three or four decades ago. The fact that parents find it hard to revise their own standards adds to the likelihood of conflicts about boy and girl friends, money, automobiles, and countless other details.

The problems of adolescence cannot be characterized as either more or less serious than those that occur during any age period marked by rapid changes. Most adolescents themselves are neither delinquents nor psychological problems. They manage to live with their multiple and ambiguous obligations and make the best of them. Those adolescents who do have severe difficulties and strike out at others usually come from backgrounds and parents that have ineffectively guided them toward maturity. Well-adjusted adolescents commonly come from families that have been firm and affectionate and have provided a responsible example by their own conduct. Though teen-agers possess most of the needs of those older than themselves, our society cannot realistically permit them to share all adult obligations and prerogatives. Nevertheless, as they mature and leave their childhood years, adolescents must gradually be accorded the status and autonomy of men and women.

FOR REVIEW AND DISCUSSION

1. What physical changes typically accompany adolescence in boys and girls? How can young adolescents be reassured about the changes that are taking place in their bodies and minds?

2. What is the "adolescent's dilemma"? How can the adolescent be helped to adjust to the fact that his desires and capabilities exceed his privileges? What is the "professional teen-ager"? How does the professional teen-ager solve the adolescent dilemma?

3. How do the sexual attitudes of many teen-age boys differ from those held by most teen-age girls? Why are boys commonly oriented toward sexual exploitation while girls yearn for romance?

4. What are effective ways of disciplining teen-agers? Why do parents have to practice what they preach? Why do some adolescents adopt the values of their peer group and attempt to live by these standards rather than those offered by their parents, religion, and other social norms?

Sexual

Development and

Behavior

FOUR

Sexual activities begin during early childhood and continue through-out life. During the tenth to fourteenth year of growth, however, there comes a sudden spurt in physical development, and sexual drives are accelerated. Yet children are surprisingly active even before puberty. Nearly all youngsters are involved, to varying degrees, in several kinds of sexual expression—alone, with their own, or with the opposite sex. Kinsey (1948) reports that as early as his seventh year one out of five boys has engaged in sexual experimentation. Closer to puberty, by age twelve, almost a third have participated in play with the same sex, a fifth in heterosexual activities, and one in eight has attempted coitus. Neither childhood nor extreme old age, contrary to usual belief, is entirely free of sexual enterprise.

CHILDHOOD SEXUAL ACTIVITY

Children may experiment sexually in ways that often seem peculiar or repulsive to adults. But much of their experimentation is not sexual in the sense that adults interpret erotic appetites. Children are curious about everything that surrounds them. They are particularly interested in exploring those parts of one another's bodies whose function appears to be an especially challenging mystery. In addition, children learn largely by imitating adults, and part of their "sexual" activity is an attempt to simulate adults' erotic interests. Believing it a sign of maturity, they may copy "necking" or "petting," though it provides them no real satisfaction. Sexual curiosity and imitative needs are most commonly expressed through games and play. Children seeking ways to satisfy their sexual energies sometimes incorporate into their rough-and-tumble chase and tag games some of the elements of erotic pursuit. Or they may unite their secretive rituals, originally used to assert independence, with sexual exploration. Stimulated by curiosity and adult example (including sexual scenes in movies, on television, etc.), children quickly learn to combine many of their previously untouched childhood activities with sexual experimentation.

Billy, age nine, was one of three boys and two girls who had been playing sexual games. According to Billy, the games involved a wide range of activities, frequently beginning with the boys exhibiting their genitals in the presence of one or two girls. These occasions were accompanied by "horsing around" attempts at disrobing the girls. Billy described having once tried genital juxtaposition that superficially resembled intercourse with one of the girls. On other occasions two or three of the boys mutually stimulated sexual tumescence. The games continued for about one year before Billy confided them to his mother and was brought to a psychiatrist.

The psychiatrist had a complete diagnostic study carried out and had several interviews with Billy and his parents. According to the psychiatrist and psychological test evidence, Billy was not emotionally disturbed. He seemed within normal limits in all ways.

Billy's parents were advised to actively discourage the continuance of sexual games but not to use unreasonable force or terrifying threats. It was suggested that the parents forbid the activities in the same way that they might forbid any other childish indulgence that was potentially harmful or disturbing to society.

Billy's parents reported that "after a good talking to" and the psychiatric visits, the sexual games did not continue. They believed he "got the point" that the activities were highly disapproved and should be stopped.

In our own society, childhood sexual activity is actively discouraged. Children are urged to wait until adolescence to begin demonstrations of erotic interest. In contrast, among some of the Melanesian Islanders in the South Pacific the sexual curiosities of early youth are recognized and accepted. The Melanesians argue that no possible harm can come from childish sex play, since children are incapable of reproducing. Adolescents, on the other hand, are not allowed to mingle hetero-sexually unless supervised, since their strong erotic inclinations may result in unwanted births. It is reported that Melanesians are "shocked" when informed that custom in the United States is the reverse of theirs. Many cultures, in fact, find it difficult to understand why through our emphasis on dating and by providing facilities such as cars and youth centers we stimulate unmarried youngsters to become sexually involved.

Does childhood sexual experience disturb future adjustment? The studies by Kinsey (1948, 1953) and others suggest that the extent and type of activity in childhood is not, commonly, an effective predictor of later sexual well-being. Thus, if childhood sexual activity is realistically regarded for what it is—curiosity, imitation, and ex-perimentation—and appropriately treated, there is no reason to believe that it should disturb normal sexual development.

ADOLESCENT SEXUAL ACTIVITY

The physical and psychological sexual capacities of adolescence lead to the beginning of adult-type sexual behavior. At first most adolescents experiment with self-stimulatory techniques. Nearly all boys and more than 60 per cent of girls masturbate with regularity for at least some period of adolescence. Many of the boys and a few of the girls will continue masturbation until and even after marriage.

Another swiftly developing sexual outlet for teen-agers is petting. Petting has referred to a number of different types of sexual contact. As used here and in most contemporary sources, petting means heterosexual manipulation of breasts, penis, and other erotic body regions and is thus a variant of masturbation. By the end of adolescence, nearly all have petted. For many, in fact, it becomes a major diversion and chief sexual outlet. About a fourth of those petting frequently use this technique to reach sexual climax.

The number of partners used for petting is frequently very great. Among some teen-agers it is "expected" that all dates lead to some petting or "heavy necking." Undoubtedly, the increasing tendency for adolescent youngsters to "go steady" contributes also to the frequency of petting. Constant association develops opportunities and intimacies that more casual dating does not. One fourteen-year-old girl described her feelings in this way.

They were all going steady, so when I moved and started school here I had to go steady too. It's the only way you could get a date. I mean if you weren't going steady they'd think there was something wrong with you.

Well no, my parents didn't like it. I didn't either. I wasn't raised that way. I used to go out with this boy all the time, so I'd have a steady.

We were always together; after school he'd hang around the house.

I'd see him three or four times a week—we ate together in school, we was always holding hands, kissing, and that, you know. The first time we did anything like that was when he and I were at this party. He wanted me to sneak off into another room; he was real excited and started fooling around real hard. I didn't want him to but he said that everyone did it; and I guess he's right. All the kids are like that in this school. You're supposed to do it since you're going steady.

Adolescents may also have copulatory experience. Half of all girls and eight out of ten boys have had intercourse before marriage. But unlike petting, which frequently involves many partners, premarital coitus is usually limited to a very few companions. Most commonly, in fact, intercourse takes place only with the future spouse. The high incidence of coital experience before marriage is, therefore, somewhat misleading. A large portion of the contact is limited to just one partner—namely, the intended husband or wife. Figure 4-1 shows the percentage of adolescents who engage in various kinds of sexual activity, according to the Kinsey reports.

Sexual climax, or orgasm, is first experienced by most adolescent males during their fifteenth year. The major source of orgasm for

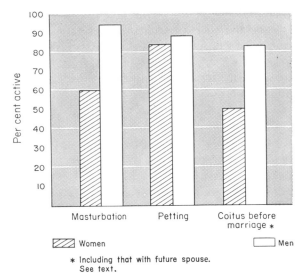

Fig. 4-1 Sexual activity during adolescence. Based on data of Kinsey, et al., 1953.

teen-age males is masturbation. Adolescent girls are also introduced to orgasm mainly through masturbation, although coitus and petting are close seconds. Most girls experience their first climax somewhat later than boys. Girls also have a lower frequency of orgasmic experience. By age twenty only about one woman in two has actually reached sexual climax (see Fig. 4-2).

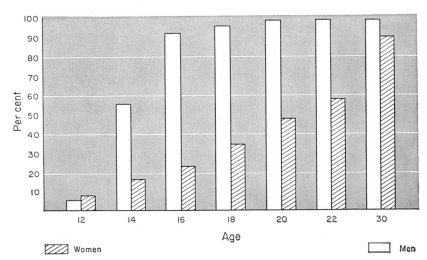

Fig. 4-2 Those who have experienced orgasm (cumulated percentage at each age). Based on data of Kinsey, et al., 1953.

Adolescence is a period of relatively intense sexual activity (see Chapter Three), since physical capacities are near a peak. For many adolescents, however, and adults as well, sexual experiences satisfy needs other than purely physical ones. Some girls make themselves sexually accessible in order to ensure themselves dates. Boys may amass sexual conquests to assure themselves of their adequacy both as males and as adults. Further, some adolescent sexual activity may owe its origin solely to the fact that teen-agers believe this kind of behavior is expected of them. The statistics concerning petting, masturbation, and premarital coitus have been so well publicized that many come to the erroneous conclusion that "everyone does it." Of course this is not true. More than 40 per cent of girls do not masturbate. Seventy-five per cent of adolescents do not habitually pet to climax, and fewer than one in five teen-agers have intercourse before marriage with any but the intended spouse.

MALE AND FEMALE SEXUAL DIFFERENCES— CAPACITIES AND ATTITUDES

There are a number of consistent differences in the sexual attitudes and the responsiveness of males and females. From childhood to old age the sexual predilections and activities of men and women are guided by their individual biological and cultural heritage. In our own, and in most societies, men are expected to initiate and direct sexual activity. Men are supposed to pursue and females to provoke the chase. Undoubtedly the near-universality of the male as aggressor and female as enticer indicates the partly biological origin of the male and female roles.

Female sexuality is usually initiated very slowly. From childhood on, girls seem to maintain some interest in boys—which is commonly not reciprocated. At the beginning of menstruation the heterosexual interest of girls appears to be gradually strengthened. In contrast, puberty produces a much more sudden budding of sexual interest for boys. As a consequence, sexual interest and activity is much stronger among young adolescent males than among young adolescent females.

During adulthood, men can be aroused by a wide variety of stimuli only tangentially related to sexual functioning. Display of the female form in person or through pictures, scents, clothing, and erotic literature excite a male. Women are not usually sexually aroused by comparable items. But female adolescents and some adults too are provoked to romantic reverie and infrequently sexually aroused by certain stories, movies, and the like.

The genital areas of men and women are differently responsive to sexual stimulation. Male genitalia are because of their neural and vascular abundance highly responsive to various kinds of physical stimulation. The vagina, however, is less well supplied with nerve endings and hence somewhat less sensitive to manipulation. On the other hand, while most male sexual excitation is limited to the genitalia themselves, the female may be responsive in other anatomical regions, ranging from the clitoris to the axillary surface. These physical differences between adult men and women lead to dissimilar kinds of sexual receptivity and orgasm. For men, after increasing sexual excitation orgasm is sudden, complete, and accompanied by the discharge of sperm. For some women sexual climax is quite similar to the process found in men. But many women experience orgasm in terms of progression to a peak of physical sensation that subsides relatively slowly. Another dissimilarity between men and women is that for males orgasm accompanies nearly every copulation. Typically, too, males experience a single climax. Although some normal women may not reach climax with every sexual contact, others may have several orgasms during coitus.

The innate structural and functional differences that exist between the sexes are maximized by the way in which the two groups are reared. In our own society boys and girls are taught from their earliest years the different standards they are to expect from one another and mutually exercise. Girls are dressed in "frilly" clothes, encouraged to be "ladylike," sweet, and passive. Boys are urged to be tough, physically active, and aggressive. Girls are told to let boys open doors for them, carry their books, and call them for dates, while boys are instructed to protect girls, present invitations to them, and act as their escorts. Even during childhood, while proper social roles are being assimilated, different codes of sexual behavior are inculcated. Girls are made aware that it is they who exercise control over sexual conduct. The sexual contact that does take place is dependent, they are informed, on "how far they will *let* a boy go." At the same time boys are encouraged to be assertive and attempt whatever they can "get away with." As a consequence, the inborn sexual differences of men and women are multiplied by society. Male and female grow up possessing not only relatively distinct sexual capacities but fairly different sexual attitudes.

SEXUAL FUNCTION IN MARRIAGE

The sexual function of marriage is highly emphasized by our culture. Through an avalanche of articles, particularly in "women's" magazines, and a plethora of books advising erotic techniques, the role of sex in marriage has probably been exaggerated beyond all proportion. Unsatisfactory sexual relations may superficially appear to be an underlying source of discord and divorce, but the evidence discussed in Chapter Five suggests that marital sexual problems are most likely just a reflection of deeper individual and personality failings. In most instances sexual practices cannot themselves be held responsible for either a happy or an unhappy family.

The standards of sexual practice exercised by individual couples vary widely. One husband and wife may believe particular precopulatory tactile, visual, oral, and other activity a vital necessity. Another pair may regard as undesirable anything but direct intromission. In addition, for a few couples some aspects of the premarital sexual activity may survive wedlock. Behavior ranging from masturbation to promiscuity to homosexuality may continue for some time after marriage or even coexist with marital coitus.

The sexual function of marriage is defined by society and culture. All groups, with the exception of rare ascetics such as the Shakers, countenance and encourage coitus in marriage. (Since they forbade married copulation, the Shakers, of course, have died out.) Though coitus is universally accepted, additional qualifications are placed on married sexual behavior by law, religion, and custom. Many states have statutes defining allowable married sexual practice. Thus in some areas oral techniques may violate legal prescriptions. Religion and custom also influence the forms of sexual contact. Standard middle-class American practice, for example, defines as acceptable only a few coital positions. In accordance with approved practice in our society, unlike the techniques practiced by others, in nearly two-thirds of all coitus the woman is supine while the man is over her. In fact, many sexual practices that couples consider distinctly their own can frequently be shown to reflect primarily the unspoken suggestions of the people and groups with whom they identify.

Psychologists, marriage experts, and other social scientists often describe "normal" married sexual practice. Several decades ago these authorities viewed all sexual contact hesitantly and advocated extreme modesty and restraint. Today's marriage specialists and authors of marriage essays seem to have approached the opposite extreme. One current writer states that anything, literally anything, that occurs in heterosexual contact is not only normal but desirable. In contrast to the conservatism of a generation or two ago, most contemporary books and articles clearly describe the tiniest minutiae of sexual stimulation. By their detailed discussions they imply that any sexual contact not embellished or prolonged as they have described is unfortunately inadequate.

Sexual practices are extensively molded by social and cultural circumstances. Whether an adult is a high-school or a college graduate makes a significant difference in sexual preference and experience. Kinsey (1948) reported that by age twenty-four about two-thirds of single male college graduates had copulatory contact. Among non-college males, however, the frequency of premarital coitus was nearly nine out of ten. Similar differences exist between college and non-college males in a wide variety of sexual activites. The college-educated customarily elaborate and prolong petting and coital foreplay, while the less educated tend to view these embellishments with aversion. Similarly, middle- and upper-class adults, though initially quite inhibited, gradually vary and maximize sexual contacts in ways that lower-class people deem undesirable.

The degree of sexual expression is related to religious factors also. Those who are highly devout—Protestants, Jews, and Catholics—have fewer and more confined sexual experiences than relative nonobservers. Sexual behavior, like nearly all human conduct, is modified by each individual's class, gender, religious affiliation, and background. The specifics of sexual experience cannot be prescribed for any couple. What is acceptable to one pair may be highly offensive to another. Further, marital adjustment is not dependent upon the type of sexual activity practiced. It is unjustified, therefore, for supposed authorities, doubtless middle-class college graduates who share the biases of their fellow group members, to argue that couples are inhibited or headed for marital disaster because their religious convictions, education, or social class dissuade them from certain practices.

One couple, married twenty-three years, attended a lecture given by an eminent marriage adviser. They were sufficiently disturbed by the speaker's suggestions to seek another professional opinion and consulted a psychologist. There was no doubt that the pair's marriage, and their family of five children, were far better adjusted and happier than most.

My wife and I are both members of the . . . faith. We don't believe many of the things that Dr. T said. We've been happily married for 23 years. We've discussed sex, pretty frankly too, and both feel that some things he was saying are not part of our moral teaching. He made fun of people who wouldn't do things like that—he said they were too inhibited. Well we don't think we are. We believe what our [faith] teaches us. I think what he believes may be all right for him and maybe others, but I don't see why he has to try to force his views on others. We don't. Every couple has to work out their own way and look for guidance in the things they believe. When a doctor who is as well known as he is tells you things you should or shouldn't believe, it's enough to make you stop and wonder about yourself.

No specific kind of marital sexual technique is likely to lead to emotional disorder. But severe conflicts over a particular practice may well lead to tensions and disturbances. The only suggestion an authority may fairly make is that married couples act sexually the way their upbringing, faith, and experience have taught them to function and that they discuss frankly with one another, or with a trained professional, their own areas of disagreement.

PROBLEMS OF SEXUAL FUNCTIONING

Psychiatrically, sexual practice is abnormal if, in the absence of mitigating circumstances, it consistently deviates from the ultimate end of voluntary adult heterosexual coitus. Thus voyeurism, homosexuality, bestiality, and other such deviations are considered pathological. Practices such as petting and masturbation are usually held acceptable, however, since, though they may not meet all criteria of normality, they are commonly coital preliminaries or substitutes. The severe disturbances of sexual development are discussed in Chapter Twelve. The following sections describe some of the sexual problems that may be associated with normal sexual functioning.

Impotence

Impotence is a term that applies only to males. It refers to a consistent lack of interest in sexual experience or a physical inability to gratify aroused desires. Impotence is sometimes used specifically to describe the inability to obtain or maintain an erection. In some cases impotence is due to temporary fatigue or illness. In rare cases it may be attributable to physical disorder. Most commonly, however, in men under sixty years of age, it is psychological in origin.

In some cases impotence is provoked by deep-seated fears and conflicts concerning marriage or sexual functioning. These are usually responsive to psychotherapeutic treatment. In many instances, however, impotence is initiated simply by inexperience and fears concerning sexual abilities. Many men seem to believe that they need to be instantly responsive to sexual stimulation and become fearful when their reactions seem slow. Sometimes a vicious cycle is created when the male anxiously watches for signs of hesitation within himself. This careful self-inspection makes him even less responsive, which makes him more tense, and finally culminates in impotence. In most of these situations sexual malfunction is alleviated by reassurance and frank discussion between husband and wife.

Frigidity

Frigidity is a term that applies to women. It describes the inability to become sexually aroused or experience orgasm. Some authorities have contended that almost a third of all women are frigid. This is probably based on a faulty understanding of the nature of sexual excitation in females. Not all women experience orgasm in the way that men do. Many women do not have a focalized climax, but may instead feel erotic sensations gradually heightening and then diminishing. Further, although there may not be any orgasmic response, women may nevertheless find coitus sensually satisfying. Nearly all wives report they have periods when they do not experience anything equivalent to orgasm. For some, these periods may be caused or aggravated by illness, tension, or marital disputes. Many of the conditions that produce impotence in men may cause frigidity in women. In most cases frigidity that is appropriately diagnosed and medically or psychologically treated gradually improves markedly. Most cases of frigidity are, however, probably never brought to the attention of a specialist. They too may improve greatly after several years of marriage, when sexual and marital harmony increases. The incidence of true and lasting frigidity is probably quite low.

Excessive Sexual Appetite

Satyriasis in men and *nymphomania* in women refer to excessive sexual appetites. Most married couples in their thirties and forties have from two to twenty copulatory experiences per month. It is very difficult, therefore, to decide what constitutes excessive sexual appetite (see Table 4-1). There are intense and wide individual differences. One wife may consider a husband who desires coitus daily as excessively demanding. Another spouse may consider contact every day strictly what is to be expected.

In some cases excessive sexual demands are symptoms of more extensive and serious psychological disturbances. In most cases, however, excessive sexual demands are excessive just from the point of view of a spouse who wants considerably less experience than the other spouse desires. In instances of this type, if the couple is otherwise well matched,

Table 4-1 MEDIAN NUMBER OF TIMES PER MONTH ORGASM * IS EXPERIENCED AMONG SEXUALLY ACTIVE INDIVIDUALS

	Late adolescence		Early thirties	
	Per cent active	Orgasms	Per cent active	Orgasms
Single females	22	2	70	2
Married females	78	9	94	6
Single males	95	9	99	6
Married males	100	13	100	8

Source: Data based on Kinsey, et al., 1948, 1953.
* By all methods, including coitus, petting, masturbation, etc.

the frequency of contact desired is eventually compromised to their mutual satisfaction.

The story of the nymphomaniacal girl whose appetite is highly pronounced, and whose beauty commensurately provocative, is a carefully nurtured adolescent myth. One variation of this theme is that the girl is forced by her own craving to turn to prostitution. If fiction supports the theme of the insatiable, beautiful prostitute, the facts of life are unromantically different. In one study of sexually promiscuous girls in San Francisco, for example (Lion, *et al.*), most were not particularly attractive and 60 per cent were relatively frigid.

AGING AND SEXUAL ACTIVITY

It is popularly believed that with advancing age interest in sex declines. Men are supposed to become impotent and women to lose erotic sensitivity. These opinions are reinforced in our culture by regarding any sexual interest in a fifty- or sixty-year-old with suspicion. As is true with many other normal functions and privileges throughout life, sexual interests are regarded as proper only in the young.

During their forties or fifties most women gradually cease to menstruate. After menses end, reproduction, except in rare cases, is no longer possible. There is no necessary loss of interest in sexual activity commensurate with menopause, though some women report they experience a lessening of desire. At the opposite extreme are women in whom menopause heightens sexual inclination and responsiveness. One explanation may be that the possibility of giving birth has had sexually inhibiting effects. Physicians and other authorities have attempted to ascertain whether men undergo a change comparable to menopause. There is no conclusive evidence that there is at any point in a human male's development any sudden cessation of physical functioning equivalent to menopause.

In general, sexual interest and desire do not decline with age. Evidence gathered by Kinsey (1948) shows the aged have sexual needs and seek erotic outlets just as do younger people. Investigations of the sexual functioning of older people revealed that when adequate opportunities and good health exist, sexual expression continues. More than three-fourths of fifty- and sixty-year-old couples maintain sexual relations, although intercourse is less frequent. Furthermore, impotence—a male's inability to achieve orgasm—was experienced by little more than one in five males at age sixty. By seventy years of age, more than 70 per cent of men were still potent. Even by age eighty, a fourth of all men were still capable of sexual climax. Kinsey and his fellow writers believe that impotence is actually not an inevitable part of aging. If a person is healthy and is not conditioned by society to believe he is sexually incompetent, he may continue to be potent as long as he lives.

The maintenance of sexual interest with advancing age is often coupled with decreasing opportunities for expression. Men may find their wives unreceptive, or a spouse may be widowed by the death of a partner. The aged are also confronted with unfavorable social attitudes toward any display of sexual interest on their part. Many an aged person feels torn by feelings of shame and guilt concerning some of the erotic desires he maintains.

Having few sources of sexual satisfaction available, the older person may try to satisfy his sexual needs in a wide variety of compensatory ways. These can range from attending burlesque theaters, where a "bald-headed row" is a common sight, to infatuations with youngsters of the opposite sex. On the other hand, some older men spurn what they consider inferior substitutes and openly state their intention of wanting to make love to all the women they encounter, feeling their "age" entitles them to boldness. Or if he has the necessary attractive resources, an aged citizen may marry a woman forty years or more his junior. An older woman, too, may become infatuated with a man young enough to be her grandson, and in rare circumstances be able to consummate her desires or even marry him.

For many women and men normal sexual interests and erotic capabilities continue into extreme old age. For a few people of advanced years, however, aging seems to bring on several signs of sexual deviation. Senile changes in the brain may cause a general decrease in intellectual functioning and have marked disinhibitory effects. Older people afflicted with structural brain damage may begin to exhibit themselves, fondle children, and engage in other acts indicative of their loss of control over many of their impulses.

A European once noted that he had always believed that no matter what was said about it or however much attention was paid it, sex was so overwhelmingly important that its role could not possibly be overemphasized. But after living here, he pointed out that we in the United States had accomplished the impossible. There may be much truth in this probably apochryphal story. Sex is the obvious ingredient of nearly all entertainment media, much of advertising and business appeals, and lectures by all sorts of experts and authorities. With less attention paid it, sex might well, like any other developmental characteristic, assume its rightful place in the hierarchy of human needs and pleasures. Sexual energies directed ultimately toward reproduction are part of the biological inheritance of human beings. They develop as the organism matures (somewhat differently in men and women) and remain with human beings for most, if not all, of their lives.

FOR REVIEW AND DISCUSSION

1. Though children may experiment sexually, their activities are not fully "sexual" in the way adults define erotic activity. How do children's sexual needs and activities differ from those of adolescents and adults? What motives may impel children to engage in activities that adults consider erotic?

2. What needs besides outright physiological ones may motivate adolescent sexual behavior? Do you believe teen-agers are more sexually active today than there were several decades ago? Are standards of acceptable sexual conduct changing?

3. What are some of the differences between adult men and women in physical capacity and psychological outlook with regard to sex? Is any single set of rules for marital sexual practice of proven superiority over others? What are some of the background factors that affect sexual practices and attitudes?

4. Define impotence, frigidity, and excessive sexual appetite. What effect does aging have on sexual capabilities and activities? Do you believe sex is overemphasized or too much discussed and written about in our society?

Dating, Love, Marriage, and Divorce

F I V E

Dating and Mate Selection

Love and Courtship

Predicting Marriage Success and Failure

Factors that Produce Marital Happiness

Marriage Counseling

Divorce

One out of every four Americans is married by age nineteen. Eventually 95 per cent of all men and women will wed (see Table 5-1), and many will consider the joining their most marvelous attainment. But marriage is a complex involvement. Despite the fact that our entertainment media demonstrate with simplified romantic concoction boy-girl chases ending in idealized marriage, nearly all husbands and wives have serious adjustments to make. Getting married is frequently recommended as a way of solving old problems or legitimizing

Table 5-1 MARRIAGE PROSPECTS OF SINGLE MEN AND WOMEN

Age	Approximate per cent reaching age that will marry	
	Women	Men
15	93	92
18	93	92
21	90	92
24	80	85
26	70	85
30	50	70
35	30	45
40	20	30
50	5	10
60	1	3

Source: Data based on U.S. Bureau of the Census, Statistical Abstract.

adolescent sexual inclinations. But rather than providing solutions for pre-existing difficulties, marriage invariably creates new dilemmas. What differences exist between those who use the puzzles of living together to create a firmer bond and those whose marriage disintegrates? Whether marriages ultimately succeed is attributable to many causes, beginning with the selective processes that result in the choice of a mate and the decision to wed.

DATING AND MATE SELECTION

People begin to "date" today at somewhere between twelve and fourteen years of age. Active daters may average three, four, or more engagements a week throughout much of their adolescence. On the other hand, between 10 and 30 per cent of all adolescents rarely or almost never date during their teen-age years (Hurlock). Dating usually consists simply of a boy-girl couple going to some activity.

But first dates frequently consist of foursomes, two pairs of boys and girls going out together. Double dating is popular because there is less chance of not finding anything to talk about or of becoming sexually involved. Dating is the American prelude to marriage. It enables people to select and become acquainted with possible spouses. To some extent the dating process as a way of meeting potential mates has been curtailed, however, by the rising trend of "going steady." While the objective of dating is to widen one's aquaintance and social (tangentially, sexual) experience, the effect of going steady is to limit friendship.

It is an interesting exercise to ask adolescents how they choose a "date." Several studies in which this has been done have glowingly reported that adolescents are not the shallow, hedonistic creatures they superficially appear. The alleged profound values adolescents possess are substantiated by citing the attributes teen-agers *say* they look for in a date. In a survey made by the author, teen-age girls *said* they select dates on the following basis, in order of preference:

1. A friendly personality
2. Intelligence
3. A sense of humor
4. Gentlemanly and courteous manners
5. Serious attitudes toward life
6. Cleanliness and good looks

In order of preference boys *said* they select dates on the following basis:

1. A "nice" personality
2. Interesting to talk to
3. A sense of humor
4. Understanding and sympathetic
5. Fun to be with
6. Attractive

Judging from the seeming maturity that adolescents express in typical surveys one might expect that all American marriages are close to perfection. This, we know, is hardly the case. Adolescent date and, eventually, mate selections are frequently based on the most marginal attractions. One seventeen-year-old explained the difference between his stated date preferences and his actual criteria.

Well, when we filled out that form on what you look for in a date you put down all the nice things that you're supposed to. But if you ask me, most of the fellows will take out someone they think is special good-looking or someone they can play around with. And somebody that you're glad to be seen with—that'll make the others jealous. This girl told me what they look for in a fellow are four things: a convertible, a convertible, a convertible, and a convertible.

Dating is supposed to blend into courtship and eventuate in the selection of a mate. Kerckhoff and Davis investigated some of the steps involved in choosing a spouse. They demonstrated that, at their best, dating and courtship have a "filtering" function. At first partners are chosen on the basis of variables such as religion and socioeconomic class. Thus, most boys and girls, recognizing that present dates are future mates, only go out with those with similar religious affiliation and social standing. After some time, when all those not socially appropriate have been eliminated, agreement on personal values becomes a selective factor. Couples now explore how they feel about topics such as occupation, education, sex, and parental relationships. The last filtering factor is called need complementarity. This means that as a final step the potential husband and wife explore the extent to which they are able to satisfy each other's psychological needs (Stuart). One could more romantically, perhaps, describe the various filtering stages as the process of "falling in love." It is the period when couples progressively examine each other's background and personality and become increasingly attracted and attached as they recognize the compatibility of their attitudes and motives.

Very often, however, instead of serving as an initial step in the process of mate selection, dating is misleading. For many teen-agers the prestige and sexual exploitation sought on dates are the sole criteria for filtering choices. Though qualities such as emotional stability and dependability are important in marriage, daters may never reach the stage in their relationship with each other where they are able to assess whether their partners possess such traits. Instead, they may slide into marriage knowing only that their companion dances well, is sexually accessible, and is a lot of "fun." For many teen-agers, dating may be a false lead to marriage, since the criteria of a "good" date are not necessarily the same as those that make a suitable husband or wife.

COURTSHIP AND LOVE

The casual trading of friends and acquaintances and the trying out of new partners that characterize dating are gradually replaced by courtship. Eventually a casual date or chance acquaintance leads to the development of a romantic interest and a "love affair" culminating in engagement and marriage. It is difficult to pinpoint the average age when serious marriage commitments are made. Some young adolescents "go steady" soon after they begin dating and eventually marry the person with whom they have been associated throughout their growing years. More typically, however, it is not till the later years—seventeen to the early twenties—when dating relationships become courtships leading to marriage.

Most people think of courtship as the process of cementing and deepening bonds of love. Just what is meant by love is difficult to describe, for the word has been applied to so many situations. Love, used to define the attachment between boy and girl, connotes an intense emotional involvement. The love attachment motivates extreme possessive needs and often distorts realistic perceptions. Some teen-agers and adults try to distinguish between love and what they call infatuation. Whether there is any real difference probably depends more upon the circumstances than on the intensity of feeling. When a teen-ager idealizes and becomes enamored of one who is regarded as an unsuitable partner, say a forty-year-old, the emotion is frequently regarded as an infatuation. Similarly, when love feelings are quickly dissipated or when the suitor is distracted by a rival, the emotion is also called infatuation.

Crushes and infatuated attachments seem to characterize some part of adolescence for many youngsters, but are seen more typically in girls.

They are so common among girls that they must fill some natural and quite normal need, surely. The devotion sometimes shown to a teacher, as transient as it is passionate, illustrates the need adolescents have for embodying an ideal. To search for someone who seems to be all that one would like to become typifies youth's reaching out toward the future. Finding someone to admire and to copy, whether among heroines in books, among actresses, or in real life, is part of the search toward finding oneself.

Once in a while a crush tells us more than this about a girl. Looked at closely, an exaggerated attachment sometimes reveals that a girl is being starved for love. Perhaps she has a mother who has not known how to interpret her daughter's changing needs. Or perhaps her mother has never understood her the way she did a brother or sister. A crush can easily be taken very seriously when a girl has no mother. Or, a girl who is very much in need of admiration or affection can be flattered by another's kindness into believing it means more than it does.

Occasionally a girl seems to pick out another girl to receive her devotion because she is afraid of being unattractive to boys. Her outpouring of love for someone of her own sex may be an unconscious effort to deny her growing interest in boys. Still another possibility is that a girl who doesn't seem to be outgrowing the normal crushes we expect in the teens may be seeking to make up for something that is lacking in her. Thus an intensely feminine girl may pick out one who has more so-called masculine traits than she has, or the other way round. To seek these differences in persons of her own sex may mean that she needs help in learning how to make friends with the opposite sex.

Among girls whose parents are not keeping them dependent, at a level of emotional immaturity, and who have had plenty of chances for natural expression of affection, the crush stage is just another phase to be passed through, much as they earlier went through one of devotion to "series" stories. [Children's Bureau, 1955, p. 49.]

Many adolescents have several love affairs or infatuations with different partners before making a final mate selection. Frequently the unsuccessful affair is terminated by one or the other partner or with mutual consent. But sometimes, parental or other pressures are brought to bear in order to dissolve the relationship. How do couples react to the dissolution of love affairs? Kirkpatrick and Caplow questioned college students regarding their response to the collapse of a love affair. About half of the students reported that they had suffered no significant emotional trauma and that they had very quickly readjusted. But about 10 per cent felt seriously disturbed by the break-up and took a year or more to adjust. The authors also found that substantial portions of all love affairs were characterized by emotional ups and downs. A fourth of all couples reported jealousies, serious conflicts concerning friends, and disagreements concerning the future. It is possible that the greater the number of love affairs and of disagreements during courtship, the poorer are the chances for marital happiness.

When courtship with one partner endures long enough, personal and socially recognized expectations develop that marriage will ensue. Not infrequently it is the latter fact, social expectation, which by itself ensures that marriage actually does take place. Some couples may lose interest in each other as they become more intimately acquainted through courtship and no longer desire marriage. Nevertheless, the fact that their relationship and engagement have been publicized and that "everyone" expects their marriage may persuade them to wed, somewhat against their own better judgments.

When engagement has been announced, the courtship process begins in earnest. Most engagements last between six months and a year, thus giving couples a little time to explore one another's needs, potentials, and shortcomings. The engagement period usually stimulates increased sexual and emotional intimacy and is viewed as a period of preparation for marriage and of testing social and personal compatibility. The length of engagement, incidentally, except for extremes such as only a few days or many years, does not seem to be related to the chances for marital success.

PREDICTING MARITAL HAPPINESS

One of the most comprehensive and well thought out studies designed to determine whether marital happiness can be predicted was conducted by Stanford University psychologist L. M. Terman and his associates (1938). For their project, the psychologists tested and interviewed several thousand subjects and followed their progress. After intensive analysis of the data, they came to many surprising conclusions. Some characteristics long thought to be important in determining happiness were found to be not at all closely related to the success of marriage. Factors such as amount of income, differences in age, and schooling had little or no value in predicting failure or success. This does not mean, of course, that they were unimportant in individual cases. What is meant is that by themselves certain levels of income or schooling do not indicate that a couple will necessarily be happy or unhappy. Not as surprising were the factors that were found to predict marital happiness. The most important predictor was the happiness of the parents. Spouses who came from happy homes themselves had an excellent chance of happy marriage. Those who came from disturbed parental homes had a very poor chance of establishing a happy family. Some of Terman's results are summarized below.

The presence of the following indicates a *strong* probability of happy marriage:
>   Marriage of parents largely a happy one
>   Happiness during childhood
>   Firm and consistent discipline during childhood

The presence of the following is *frequently* predictive of happy marriage:
>   Intelligence and mental ability of couple about equal
>   Good affectional attachment of couple to own parents

The presence of the following is *slightly* predictive of *unhappy* marriage:
>   Premarital attitude of disgust at sex
>   Strong conflicts with own parents
>   Punishment during childhood characterized by severity and frequency

The following have little or no value in predicting whether marriage will be happy or unhappy:
>   Age at marriage
>   Adequacy of sex instruction
>   Length of acquaintance preceding marriage
>   Amount of "petting" before marriage

According to current thinking, sexual techniques after marriage are decisive in determining adjustment. When Terman investigated the relative importance of sexual factors in marriage, he found that some sexual practices—such as the type of sexual techniques employed and whether contraceptives were used—were little related to marital happiness. On the other hand, whether the wife had the capacity to achieve sexual orgasm was slightly correlated with marriage success. Wives who rarely or never reached sexual climax were a little less likely to have happy marriages than those who frequently or regularly had orgasm. Some of the sexual factors and their relative importance for marital happiness are listed below.

The following have *little* or *no* relationship to marital happiness:
    Use of contraceptives
    Varieties and types of sexual techniques
    Differences between how often intercourse is desired and actual number
    of times it occurs
The following are *moderately* related to marital happiness:
    Relative similarity of sexual drive for husband and wife
    Intercourse not refused too frequently
    Wife's capacity to reach orgasm most of the time
    Wife not particularly prudish

Terman determined that marital happiness was far less dependent on sexual factors as a whole than on family background. Emotionally well-suited couples have an easy tolerance for sexual frustration. They work out any difficulties they are experiencing. But mutually hostile husbands and wives use sexual disagreements as weapons against each other. In fact, since marriage involves many sexual and emotional adjustments for everyone, it provides fertile ground for argument. All couples have serious disagreements concerning sexual rights, money matters, and children. Those couples whose relationship is firm and affectionate are able to resolve their difficulties. But couples whose marriages are weak, immature, and ill-conceived in the first place soon find "issues" to argue about and progressively build into causes for separation and divorce.

Happily married couples tend not only to come from happy backgrounds themselves but also to possess many similar personality characteristics. Terman and his associates investigated the personality of happy and unhappy spouses. Although they used rather precise methods in evaluating personality and marital accord, their findings can be summarized in general terms.

Happily married wives tend to be kindly toward others and expect kindness in return. They are not easily offended and do not look upon social relationships as rivalry situations. They are cooperative, are not annoyed by advice, and do not object to taking a subordinate role to others. They are methodical in their work and careful with regard to money. They have a decidedly optimistic outlook on life.

Unhappily married wives are tense and have frequent ups and downs in mood. They have feelings of hostility and inferiority and aggressively attempt to atone for them. They are irritable and dictatorial. They are impatient, fitful workers and are unmethodical. Often they develop highly individualistic artistic and other kinds of interests, adopt radical notions, and join radical groups.

Happily married men are emotionally stable and cooperative and look at others, including their wives, as full equals. They are somewhat extroverted socially, have relatively great initiative, and work with care and diligence. They tend to be conservative, favorably disposed toward religion, and to uphold sexual and other moral conventions.

Unhappily married men are moody and tend to be neurotic. They are ill at ease in company and tend to feel insecure. Frequently they attempt to be very domineering and to like situations in which they can feel superior. They tend to be careless in their work and with money and to indulge themselves excessively.

Whether a marriage will be happy or unhappy depends to a large extent upon the characteristics of the couple who have entered into it. The same personality, attitudes, and habits that made an individual happy and able to work out a beneficent relationship with life before marriage will tend to make him similarly successful after finding a mate. Terman put it, "In other words, we believe that a large proportion of incompatible marriages are so because of a predisposition to unhappiness in one or both of the spouses." (Terman, 1938, p. 110.)

MARRIAGE COUNSELING

The folklore on marital discord suggests that "problems" concerning sex, companionship, mothers-in-law, and money are important sources of marital difficulty. Some marriage "counselors," "experts," and newspaper advisers therefore persuade couples to "talk things over," while other self-appointed authorities advise complaining spouses to take revenge. The following letter, sent to two newspaper advisers, elicited opposite answers.

Problem

My husband and I have been married six months. He isn't paying me much attention any more. He goes out with the boys two or three times a week, drinks a lot, bowls, and spends a lot of money. Last week he spent half his pay check. On nights when he is home he isn't much company and won't tell what he's done on his nights out. I miss him and feel like a

Lonely Working Girl Again
A.R.L.

Answers

Dear A.R.L.,

Husbands are entitled to a little time with their friends. You should learn to share his interests with him. Learn to bowl, and talk about the things that he likes to talk about. That way you'll find that he spends more time at home and shares more with you.

Miss Truelove Counselor

Dear Lonely Working Girl Again,

Show the lug where to get off. You can be independent just like he is. Take the other half of the pay check and go out and have yourself a good time. That will make him come crawling back to you.

Miss Heartpatch Adviser

Just what is wrong with newspaper advice? The main failure of all such attempts is that they conceptualize unhappy marriage in terms of specific problems. But marriages are not made happy or unhappy by any particular dilemma. Just the reverse is true. The happy marriage creates few disagreements. The unhappy marriage produces a continual round of difficulties. Thus, discords in marriage cannot be resolved by generously offered but essentially meaningless advice. The only way to truly reconcile a marriage is to attack the roots that are continually responsible for marital quandaries.

The underlying characteristics that result in marital discord can be altered. In recent years many couples have consulted therapists or marriage clinics looking for solutions to their problems. Since personality shortcomings are nearly always responsible for poor marriage adjustments, it is frequently necessary that either one or both of the pair undergo a relatively complete course of psychotherapy.

Mr. K. came to a mental health clinic seeking help in attempting to bring back his wife who had taken the children and fled to her parents' home. Mr. K. said that their problem was that his wife was a sloppy housewife and that he would get "good and mad" at her. On one occasion he admitted striking her. His wife had run away before, but he had prevailed upon her and her parents to have her rejoin him. Additional questioning of Mr. K. elicited the information that he "drank too much" on occasion. Mr. K. also contended that his wife was cold and sexually unresponsive. He said he could not understand his wife's attitude and that she clung too much to her parents. He also complained that she did not know how to "stretch" his pay check and always "bothered" him about money.

Considerable effort was necessary to obtain the wife's consent to visit the clinic. Several letters were written, and two visits by a local welfare worker were necessary before the wife consented to speak with the clinician.

Mrs. K. stated that her husband squandered money on alcohol, consumed too much, was careless and slovenly in his habits. and made the house a "mess." "I couldn't be picking up after him all the time." Because of the nature of his work his hours were somewhat irregular, and Mrs. K. complained that Mr. K. "hung around" and "bothered me while I was trying to get the work done, or take care of the kids." Mrs. K. also complained that Mr. K. made "funny" sexual demands. Mrs. K. stated that her husband wanted her to disrobe completely and "sort of wrestle on the bed." Mrs. K. felt that his approach was crude and tasteless. She said she was motivated to leave Mr. K. by a "knock-down-drag-out fight" about sex and money.

The psychologist who interviewed and examined Mr. and Mrs. K. reported that both were quite unprepared for many of the compromises and responsibilities of marriage. They were relatively hostile and suspicious persons. In addition, Mr. K. was extremely dependent and expected Mrs. K. to play a rather protective role. Mrs. K., in turn, was quite reserved and felt it difficult to express any love or give affection. The therapist wrote that "while it might be possible to keep this marriage together a while longer by appealing to the couple's own enlightened self-interest and by authoritative persuasion, the marriage could not easily be made a successful one." Long-term therapy for both husband and wife was recommended.

Marital tensions, if they are to be successfully resolved, usually require prolonged therapy with both husband and wife. Realistically, however, this kind of intensive treatment is not readily available, and, as a result, many well-trained marriage counselors and psychologists attempt to exercise a sort of arbitrating function between disputing husband and wife. The therapist, by listening to both sides, encouraging full expression, and making some suggestions, is often able to help the couple overcome temporary marital failures and help sustain the relationship a while longer. Although the therapist recognizes that by mediating he is not attacking the roots of the disorder, he hopes that his objective intervention will allow the inharmonious couple to stay together a few more weeks or months. During this time some of their own more mature tendencies may, perhaps, help them reconcile their differences.

Many marriages are kept together by limited therapeutic intervention or by other means, including religious counseling and the pressure of children, friends, and relatives. Not all marriages that remain intact through these means, obviously, are happy or provide a healthy environment for children. But surprisingly many husbands and wives bound together in these ways become reconciled. After several years their marriage may work itself out quite amicably to the benefit of the couple, their children, and society.

DIVORCE

Whether a couple is happily married is important not only to the pair but to all of society. The mismatched, poorly adjusted couple may produce children who, through their own disturbed personalities, reflect their parents' predicament. The children of unhappy marriages, whether or not the union breaks up in desertion or divorce, frequently become a burden to society and must be cared for and protected. The unhappy marriage infects others, as it were, since the dissolution of a family involves other people.

Decades ago the problems that now exist within marriage were probably just as common, but divorce was less frequent. There are many reasons why divorce has risen in the last several years. A rise in real income and female job opportunity makes husbands more able to undertake the financing of a separation and wives able to earn their own living. And divorce is today much more socially acceptable than it was one or two generations ago. Though divorce is really an admission of personal failings and poor judgment, little stigma results from breaking the bonds of marriage and family.

In 1900 for every hundred couples married only seven were divorced. This more than tripled by 1950 so that for every four couples wed one was divorced. Since the 1950's, however, the rate appears to be leveling out at about one in four or five (see Fig. 5-1).

But a note of caution concerning divorce rates needs to be introduced. The well-known statistic of one in four can make marriage breakups seem misleadingly commonplace. Divorce is actually still quite rare. The ratio one in four is obtained by noting the number of marriages that take place in each year and contrasting these with the number of divorces for the same period. This kind of comparison can distort the actual divorce ratio because there are a few men and women who pile up divorces for themselves. The divorced husband or wife has a much greater chance of divorcing again than he had originally. In fact, the probability of more divorces increases con-

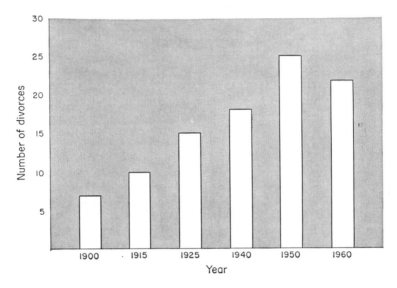

Fig. 5-1 Divorces per hundred couples. Based on reports of the Public Health Service, Department of Health, Education, and Welfare.

sistently after each divorce. Thus a relatively small, much married group spuriously inflates divorce figures. One way in which a truer picture could be obtained might be to compare the number of divorces with the number of existing marriages. Data drawn from the Census Bureau report in 1959 show that in each year throughout the Fifties only nine divorces took place for every thousand marriages. This means that in any single year only about one out of a hundred married couples dissolve their relationship.

Over-all divorce rates need to be qualified by a number of additional variables. Teen-age marriages are broken twice as often as are the ones of those who get married in their twenties. Further, the rate of divorce decreases for nearly every year a couple has been married. Thus, husbands and wives married ten years are half as likely to split up as those married five years. After twenty-five years of marriage, less than one in a thousand couples divorce. Divorce is also closely related to religious affiliation. Catholic and Jewish couples show the lowest rate of divorce and separation. In contrast, marriages where one or both members are without formal religious affiliation have a very high incidence (see Fig. 5-2). Similarly, there is a wide difference in the frequency with which childless families and families with offspring dissolve their union. During the first twenty years of marriage couples without children have a divorce rate two to three times as high as couples with children (Jacobson).

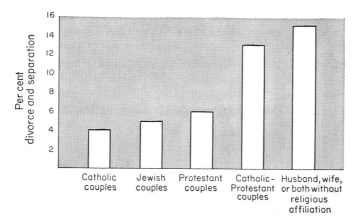

Fig. 5-2 Divorce, separation, and religious affiliation. Based in part on Landis, 1949.

How divorce or separation affects children is difficult to evaluate. In some instances it appears that almost any kind of environment would be preferable to the traumatic home climate created by a bitterly opposed couple. Landis (1960), investigating the effects of divorce, reported that when children believed their home a fairly stable and happy one break-up was psychologically quite damaging. Those children who saw themselves in unhappy, conflicting family situations, however, did not suffer when divorce took place. Since most divorce is preceded by obvious family conflict, it is possible that initially most children are less harmed by family dissolution than by the continuation of the tensions that caused the split.

After a family unit is willingly broken, most children live with just one parent—usually the mother. The presence of only one parent may be disturbing to quite a few children, especially in their early years. But since the explosions within the marriage have commonly been intense before the break-up of the family, living with a single parent or a remarried one is frequently the lesser of two evils.

Few experiences in the lives of human beings are as exciting or potentially as rewarding as the process of selecting a marriage partner. For many persons the events leading to marriage stand out as the high point of a lifetime. This is perhaps as it should be. A well-matched, happy couple produces well-adjusted, psychologically sound children and creatively contributes to the welfare of all. Marriages torn by tension and despair may dissolve, result in traumatized offspring, and burden society. Family relationships that are affectionate and healthy can be a human being's single greatest source of happiness, security, and comfort.

FOR REVIEW AND DISCUSSION

1. What are the differences between what many adolescents say they want in a date and what they actually desire?

   Dating is the American prelude to courtship and marriage. What other ways have been used to help adolescents find future marital partners? What is the "filtering function" of dating? How does courtship differ from dating? What are the advantages and disadvantages of dating over other mate-selecting procedures?

2. What are some of the factors that tend to produce a successful, happy marriage? What characteristics are likely to lead to marital failure? How many adolescents realistically prepare themselves for marriage? Why does simple newspaper-column advice do little to remedy faulty marriage? Is psychotherapy for both partners in an unhappy marriage always necessary?

3. Is divorce increasing? What are some of the factors that are likely to lead to divorce? Does religious affiliation affect divorce? Do you feel it more harmful for children to live in a seriously discordant atmosphere or to live in a home broken by divorce?

Personality, Potential, and

PART TWO

Their

Measurement

Motivation,

Learning, and

Personality

87

All organisms have a variety of inborn and acquired needs. They must eat, eliminate, sleep, and satisfy many other vital and learned demands. When these needs are not met, the organism is driven to activity until his want is satisfied. A rat deprived of food for several hours wanders restlessly about his environment, like a famished adolescent, poking into everything in order to locate something edible.

An unsatisfied drive not only energizes—pushes the organism to act—but also alerts the individual to stimuli that may satisfy his motivational deficiency. Drives function as *sensitizers,* making the rat or the human being keenly perceptive of situations that may reduce his needs. The hungry automobile driver rapidly becomes aware of signs pointing to restaurants, while his differently motivated son notices every imported vehicle they pass on the highway.

The sensitizing function of motives also means that individuals may misperceive their own milieu. A drive may be so intense that it causes people to look for satisfaction in ways that appear quite remote. Those with extremely strong needs for sexual experience, money, or affection, for example, seem particularly ready to "see" opportunities for relieving their desires in situations that may strike others as quite unlikely. Their highly intensified motivation impels them to misinterpret common environmental cues much in the way the lost wanderer in a desert sees an imaginary oasis.

DESCRIBING MOTIVES

Motives are frequently explained in terms of *drive* and *need,* and classified according to their origin. *Need* refers to a lack of something the organism wants or requires—from financial success to a glass of water. *Drive,* usually used synonymously with *motive,* refers to the impetus to behavior that the need produces.

Physiological Needs

Among the obvious physiological deficiences that produce drives are hunger, thirst, cold, fatigue, and other tissue needs. Many physiologically based motives are best described in terms of the body's tendency to maintain an internal balance—a process called *homeostasis.* It is essential for the individual's survival when tissues dehydrate, blood pressure falls, or other deficiencies threaten the body's intactness, that the body regulate itself to restore its life-sustaining balance.

Not all physiologically based needs are homeostatic or "life-preserving" in the way that hunger is. Sexual motives are physically rooted, though in human beings they seem infinitely capable of modification by learning and experience. Other drives that may be modified by experience may have a physiological basis, although their satisfaction may not appear vital to the survival of the organism. Among such drives maternal behavior, the need to take care of one's young; activity and manipulative drives; curiosity; and fear have been suggested to have physical origins (Morgan).

Psychological Needs

The difficulties of pinpointing and agreeing on the nature of the needs that are primarily physiological in origin are small compared to the disagreements about which motives are based on experience or learning. The nature of acquired motives varies from society to society and group to group. Our own culture stresses achievement needs, while the warlike Comanche Indians valued fierceness and combativeness. Motives vary from individual to individual, because each has grown up in a particular family atmosphere that may have reinforced one or another aspect of behavior. Most psychologists, however, have agreed that a few acquired drives seem nearly universal in our culture: needs for achievement, affiliation, prestige, security, and social approval probably operate in most individuals.

The Hierarchy of Motives

A useful way of conceiving of motivation is to recognize that some needs take precedence over others. A. H. Maslow has suggested that the basic, physiological needs are more potent than any others. He conceives of drives in terms of a progressive steplike arrangement. Before moving up to each successive motivational level, one must satisfy the needs immediately below (see Fig. 6-1).

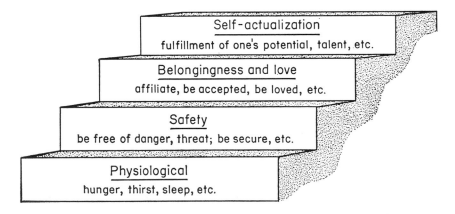

Fig. 6-1 The hierarchy of motives. Based on Maslow.

Emotions as Motivators

Emotions may serve as motives. Fear, anger, and other unpleasant feelings act as drives because they are tension states that seek to be relieved. Pleasant emotions such as joy and affection function as motivators, since they instigate behavior intended to seek their arousal.

Anxiety is a special kind of fear believed to be of fundamental importance in determining behavior. While ordinary fear is related to a specific situation, anxiety is felt as a vague apprehension not associated with particular objects or events. Anxiety attains its significance as a motivating emotion because, according to many contemporary psychotherapists (e.g., Urban and Ford), it is the core of pathological processes. Anxiety-prone persons are unable to engage in most of the usual activities of contemporary adult life without feeling intensively and continually afraid. Since their ordinary actions are not adequate to reduce their intense and chronic forebodings, they involuntarily adopt defensive techniques that may eventuate in neurosis or other personality disorders (Chapter Ten).

Negative feelings characterized by hostility and aggression are as important as anxiety in the development of personality (Horney). Sigmund Freud believed that man is born with destructive, hostile needs and emotions that he called *thanatos*. In every man, Freud wrote, the aggressive and destructive urges continually seek for expression—and often slip out in little, disguised ways. The manner in which a man breaks a used match, laughs when he accidentally drops a dish, or happily goes hunting might be cited by Freudians as suggestions of the innate destructive feelings of men.

Today it is believed that aggressive and hostile attitudes are more likely to be the results of experience than inborn. Particular attention has been paid to the frustration-aggression sequence. When obstacles are put in the way of motivated acts, aggressive and hostile behavior is likely to result. Children brought into a psychology laboratory that has several attractive toys behind a fence, just out of their reach, soon begin to inquire about the playthings. When told they may keep whatever they are able to secure, they devise numberless clever ways to fish out the toys. Unfortunately, the psychologists have engineered things to make retrieving the toys *seem* possible although it is virtually impossible. As the children become increasingly frustrated, they react. Many—though not all—bang angrily at the fence, fight with one another, kick whatever is in reach (including the psychologist), and generally demonstrate their aggressive emotions (Maier).

Because the aggressive feelings accompanying frustration are discomforting, the frustration-aggression sequence often serves as a drive leading to new behavior. Occasionally, as with many other drives, aggressive motives accumulate. Thus, while an individual may seem to explode over a trivial incident, in reality he may have been "saving up" his aggressive feelings to release them only when the frustrating incidents reached a point no longer tolerable.

Consciousness and Interaction of Drives

We must not think of behavior as being commonly energized by a single, clearly defined motive; nor should we suppose that we are completely aware of the needs on which our actions are based. Human behavior is determined by a subtle and intricately related complex of motives derived from both physiological and acquired needs. We are seldom fully aware of the nature of all the drives and emotions that impel us to act. Just how interwoven and subtle our needs are can be ascertained by examining a seemingly simple act. We are hungry, enter a restaurant, and order a cheese sandwich. It seems that this is a simple response to a physiological need—hunger. But it is not. We did not order a hamburger or tuna fish because of dietary and taste preferences. We chose this restaurant rather than another because it is said to have more reasonable prices. If we really examine our own motives, we may remember that this diner is where a certain attractive waitress is employed. Moreover, this restaurant attracts many white collar employees, whereas another one we passed serves mainly factory workers. Though we may believe we understand our motives in going to a specific restaurant, attending a given college, or marrying a particular person, it is unlikely that we fully understand the many needs we are satisfying by our actions.

Many of the impulses that drive us without our being aware of them—called unconscious motives by psychoanalysts—are believed to partly reveal themselves in dreams, absent-minded mannerisms, and slips in speech and thought (see Chapter Fourteen). It is in fact an essential tenet of psychoanalysis that in order to rehabilitate patients their unconscious drives must be uncovered.

Summary

Behavior is produced by needs—both physiological and psychological. Emotions may also motivate behavior: we act both to arouse pleasant emotions and to relieve the tension caused by unpleasant ones. Here are some commonly identified motives, classified according to their origin. The categories are not exclusive.

Primarily Physiological
    Hunger-thirst
    Sleep-elimination
    Warmth-cold
    Sex
    Activity

Primarily Psychological
    Achievement
    Independence
    Change
    Dominance
    Affiliation

Motives of Uncertain Physiological-Psychological Roots
    Maternal drives
    Curiosity
    Manipulation
    Affectional needs
    Sexual needs

Primarily Emotionally Based
    Anxiety, fear
    Aggression, anger, hostility, disgust
    Joy, pleasure, thrill, elation
    Affection, love
    Envy

LEARNING AND CONDITIONING

Learning brings about an alteration in an individual's way of perceiving or responding as a result of experience. Thus, we say that an individual has learned when his perceptions of his surroundings or his responses to environment have changed because of his experience. Men possess few, if any, innate behavioral patterns. Nearly all they do and strive for is influenced by what they have learned. Though all men share basic needs—such as those based on physiological demands —the ways in which these are satisfied vary immensely from individual to individual and culture to culture. Each has learned fairly distinct ways of satisfying its desires.

Classic Conditioning

One of the first steps toward understanding how organisms learn resulted from the work of a Russian scientist, Pavlov, in the early part of this century. Pavlov, a Nobel Prize physiologist, discovered the nature of the conditioned response quite accidentally. While experimenting with digestive processes in dogs, he noticed that his animals began to salivate before the food was actually placed in their mouths. In fact, since the food was usually brought to the dogs by an assistant, just hearing the helper's footsteps approaching the laboratory started the salivary-digestive processes (see Fig. 6-2).

Realizing the importance of his accidental observation, the investigator carefully studied the anticipatory salivatory response. Initially, the dog salivated only when the meat powder was placed on his tongue. Pavlov labeled this reflexive salivation at the taste of food

Fig. 6-2 Dog in experimental stand similar to that used by Pavlov to investigate classic conditioning. From Warner Brown and Howard C. Gilhousen, *College Psychology* (Englewood Cliffs, N.J.: Prentice-Hall, Inc., 1950).

the *unconditioned response*. The food was called the *unconditioned stimulus*. In the next phase of his experiment, Pavlov consistently preceded the presentation of the meat with the sound of a bell. Soon the dog was observed to salivate whenever the bell was sounded—whether or not the meat appeared. The dog now exhibited a *conditioned response*—that is, he salivated whenever the bell was rung. The bell, a previously *neutral stimulus*—one that had aroused no salivation response in the dog—had become a *conditioning* or *conditioned stimulus,* through consistent association with the meat.

Following the preliminary investigations, it became apparent that a wide range of learning phenomena could be produced by manipulating the conditioned and unconditioned stimuli and responses (CS, US, CR, UR). Each time the scientists gave the dog meat after ringing the bell, they *reinforced* the conditioned response. Salivation (CR) persisted whenever the bell (CS) was sounded, even when the food (US) was only given to the dog periodically—the dog did not have to be reinforced every time. But when the reinforcement with food was completely discontinued, salivation in response to the bell alone (CS) soon ceased. The response was said to be *extinguished.*

Since the early conditioning experiments of Pavlov, much more has been learned about conditioning. The phenomenon of *generalization* has been observed. An animal taught to respond to a bell, for example, will also react to a buzzer, gong, chime, or any other stimulus resembling the original one. In addition, it has been found that one conditioned response may be used to elicit another. If the dog originally conditioned to salivate at the sound of a bell is exposed to the bell paired with a flashing red light—without being reinforced—it will learn to give the conditioned response to the light alone. This is called *higher order conditioning*. With care and diligence, animals (and human beings as well) may be trained to respond to two, three, or more levels or orders of conditioning.

Much human behavior is learned through classic conditioning. A child given a slap and told "No" when he does something dangerous soon learns the meaning of the word. Some neurotic symptoms—particularly those we call *phobias* or persistent, irrational fears—may be understood in terms of a conditioning sequence. In the following example one can identify conditioning, generalization, and higher order learning.

An otherwise normal girl said that she had always been terribly frightened by automobiles, trains, and other means of travel. She could recall that as a young child she had to be taken to a baby sitter daily because her mother worked. While she did not fear the car as such, she was terribly frightened of the sitter, who seemed to be a harsh and punitive woman. At first, she cried only as they neared the baby sitter's house; but soon she was frightened as soon as her mother placed her in the car for the trip. Before long she habitually cried, vomited, and was intensely frightened of the automobile alone.

After some time, as she grew, the girl reported growing less frightened of the baby sitter but continuing to be scared of the car. Worse yet, her fear of the car seemed to spread so that she became afraid of other conveyances and destinations to which she was frequently driven.

Instrumental Conditioning

A hungry animal placed in a box that contains a single lever eventually, in the course of randomly moving about, brushes against the lever and thus actuates a mechanism that pops a pellet of food into the box. Before too long the animal appears to learn that in order to obtain food he merely needs to push the lever. Another example of instrumental learning is seen when an animal placed on an electrified grid slowly learns that by touching two knobs he can turn off the shock. *Instrumental conditioning* describes the process whereby an animal or a person learns how to act upon his environment to satisfy some need or drive.

Dr. B. F. Skinner, Harvard psychologist, has intensively investigated instrumental learning. Through his work and that of others it has been shown that reinforcement, extinction, generalization, and higher order conditioning can be applied to instrumental conditioning—in the same way they were applied to classic conditioning.

Animal trainers frequently rely upon instrumental learning. They may teach an elephant to waltz around in circles by using instrumental methods. Every time the elephant makes a desired turn, he gets a peanut—but if he moves in a wrong direction, he is prodded by an electrically charged stick. By reinforcing those variations in the animal's behavior that he desires, and by attempting to extinguish unwanted sequences, the animal trainer shapes the behavioral sequence that he wants.

Much human learning is essentially instrumental in nature. We withdraw and stay away from situations that cause us pain. A baby burnt by a stove may diligently avoid that object as well as other large white-enameled pieces like the refrigerator and washing machine. Similarly, those acts that are successful seem to persist. The neurotic who is burdened with rituals and compulsions (Chapter Ten) may originally have found that his seemingly senseless acts actually reduced his anxiety. Thus, his behavior persists. In learning to speak, instrumental conditioning is also apparent: when a child wants a cookie he must make the right noises for others to understand him and reinforce his vocalizations.

The Varieties of Learning and Awareness

Human learning cannot be entirely accounted for by even the most thorough expositions of classic and instrumental conditioning. Much of human learning is *perceptual*. We learn how stimuli are related to one another, to responses and outcomes, just by seeing or hearing about them or without otherwise directly participating. Or we may simply copy what we see others do. In fact, imitation is one of the chief means through which children learn. Some learning is *conceptual* in nature. We look at one situation and, seeing its essential similarities to another, transfer a whole variety of responses drawn from many different sources.

Then, too, much learning takes place without our voluntary participation. Learning without awareness was demonstrated in the following experiment reported by Haas. Subjects were asked to read aloud and complete three hundred incomplete sentences like the following: My mother_____; In the morning_____; I think women are_____. Every time a subject completed a sentence with a positive tone (My mother is a wonderful person; in the morning I feel great), the experimenter simply said, "Hmmhmm."

The results of the experiment demonstrated that in contrast with a control group not reinforced—no "Hmmhmm"—the frequency of "positively toned" responses continually increased for the experimental subjects. What's more, not one of over fifty participants realized that he was being conditioned, or that he was increasingly giving positive responses.

Application of Information about Learning

Psychologists have uncovered a great deal of information about human learning and its practical applications. The following rules may prove useful.

1. Learning will be most rapid and retention strongest if students are informed of the results of their work.
2. Meaningful material, or topics that can be related to previously learned matter, is more easily learned and longer retained.
3. Distributed rather than massed practice (cramming) is generally more conducive to retention (See Fig. 6-3).

Fig. 6-3 Cramming for the final. How much will this student learn in the next few hours? Will he retain it? See text. Photo courtesy of State University College, New Paltz, New York.

4. Frequently, whole learning—attempting to grasp the entire material as a unit—is better than trying to learn part by part. This is not always true, however, since some information is more easily mastered in segments.

5. In order to facilitate the learning of many materials, each segment should be designed so that it is related to other learning to come, if possible.

6. With some exceptions, reward rather than punishment is believed to facilitate learning. Reward strengthens the reinforced behavior, but punishment may not weaken or extinguish behavior not desired.

7. Learning under emotional stress is handicapped. People appear to learn best when they are relatively free of extreme pressure, worry, anxiety, or the need to achieve. A moderate to high degree of motivation is essential, however, to effective learning.

THE FORMATION OF PERSONALITY

In growing up, children select from their surrounding and, in turn, are literally captured by aspects of their milieu that mold them. They learn to like and imitate certain qualities of their homes, families, and friends and to dislike others. They accept and depend on some adults and children and shun those they do not need or want. Since each of us is somehow unique at birth and each grows up in surroundings that are somehow special, we develop individual sets of motives and responses. The particular characteristics, needs, likes, dislikes, reactions, and responses that have become typical of an individual constitute his *personality*.

Important as learning from family and environment is in determining personality, heredity and physical makeup also play a part in the development of particular traits. At birth, children may already be disposed toward the emergence of certain kinds of reactions. Every mother who has had several children knows how distinctly the personalities of even tiny infants manifest themselves. During the first year of life definite characteristics seem to appear. Some babies are placid, relaxed, and accepting, while others show they are easily upset, sensitive, and finicky. Several investigations have been directed at establishing whether these early signs of individual personality remain, and to what extent they help determine future development.

One of the most interesting demonstrations is the result of the independent work of two psychologists, Mary Shirley and Patricia Neilon. Over thirty years ago, Dr. Shirley investigated the behavior of infants so that she could determine whether babies possessed a nucleus of personality that persisted. She carefully observed children ranging in age from just a few weeks to several years, and was forced to conclude that many of the personality traits she had noted at birth remained with the child as he grew. Part of Dr. Shirley's work consisted of writing very detailed personality sketches for each of her infants. If Shirley's conclusion—that personality is partly present at birth—is accurate, then her infant personality descriptions should still have been accurate years later when the children were full-grown. Whether the personality sketches were still descriptive, hence whether traits present at birth persist, was investigated by another psychologist, Patricia Neilon. In 1948, fifteen years after Shirley wrote her descriptions, Neilon located most of the original subjects. Without reading what Shirley had written many years earlier about each subject, Neilon investigated the adolescents and wrote a complete character sketch for each. The two sets of results, the infant and the teen-age observations for each child, were then handed to psychologically trained judges for matching. The judges were highly accurate in matching the two sets of personality reports. It appeared that the personality signs evident so many years before, during infancy, were conspicuous enough in later life to be identifying characteristics.

Since the studies by Shirley and Neilon, other investigators have established the importance of early, relatively innate factors in determining personality (e.g., Escalona). Though some people change considerably as they get older, most individuals possess a personality core around which other identifiable traits develop as they learn to deal with their environment.

For many years it was popularly debated whether "learning" or "heredity" played the more important role in the formation of human behavior. Many "environmentalists" contended that a child could be molded into anything from a beggar to a genius just by manipulating what he learned. Debates on the relative importance of acquired and inborn traits are rare today. It is recognized that both types of traits function in all people. Even the drive to sleep, which would seem to have a pure physiological basis, is modified by experience. Apparently, nearly all inborn characteristics are shaped by learning, and what is learned is in turn influenced by innate capabilities.

Personality, then, is determined by a multitude of factors. Coleman, in his *Personality Dynamics and Effective Behavior,* includes a useful list of some of the key influences in personality development, together with some of their possible results when they are favorable and when they are unfavorable. Heredity, and many varieties of experience are important in the shaping of who we are. Coleman's list is reprinted here as Table 6-1.

Table 6-1 KEY INFLUENCES IN DEVELOPMENT OF PERSONALITY

Common Results If Favorable	Possible Results If Unfavorable
Heredity and constitution	
High capacity for achievement; adequate physical and intellectual resources; resiliency.	Restricted capacity for achievement; difficulty in solving life problems; predisposition to illness.
Mothering in infancy	
Physical well-being; feelings of security and self-acceptance; ability to move ahead with developmental tasks.	Poor physical and psychological development; listlessness; feelings of insecurity; high mortality rate in infancy.
Physical care	
Good health; physical and psychological efficiency.	Retarded or stunted growth; poor resistance to illness; lowered efficiency in all areas.
Love and acceptance	
Self-acceptance and self-confidence; trust in others; ability to tolerate failure and disappointment; ability to form warm and open relationships with others.	Feelings of insecurity and inadequacy; withdrawal or retaliation, with accompanying behavior problems; low tolerance for stress; inability to give and receive love.
Protection	
Feeling of adequacy; gradual assumption of responsible self-direction, commensurate with level of maturity.	Overprotection: passivity and dependency; egocentricity; often rebelliousness. Underprotection: failure to develop feelings of adequacy and/or responsibility to others.
Opportunity and stimulation	
Curiosity; eagerness to learn and to expand horizons.	Intellectual apathy and provincialism; minimal intellectual growth.
Structuring and discipline	
Clear values and ethical concepts; strong inner controls; confidence in ability to handle situations.	Confused concepts of right and wrong, of acceptable and unacceptable behavior; weak inner controls.
Guidance and assistance	
Adequate competencies; integrated values; reliable frame of reference; ability to meet developmental tasks.	Continued reliance on trial and error; important gaps in learning; identification with faulty models.
Success and recognition	
Self-confidence; ability to make best use of learning potential; desire for further achievement; ability to tolerate failure and use it constructively.	Too much failure: feelings of inadequacy; impaired learning ability. Too easy success: unsureness about actual competency; unrealistic aspirations: low tolerance for failure.
Frustration and trauma	
Success in handling moderate stress increases self-confidence and ability to tolerate and handle frustrations.	Feelings of insecurity and inadequacy; withdrawal to avoid further hurt; special vulnerability to later stress.

Source: James C. Coleman, Personality Dynamics and Effective Behavior (Chicago: Scott, Foresman and Company, 1960), p. 105. Copyright © 1960 by Scott, Foresman and Company. Reprinted by permission.

DESCRIBING PERSONALITY

The temptation to describe personality in terms of types has always lured scientists as well as laymen. The twofold typology offered by the Swiss psychoanalyst Carl G. Jung is commonly encountered. He suggested that people might be described in terms of their introversive and extroversive tendencies.

Extrovert. Tends to be socially aggressive, outgoing, self-expressive, and dependent on others for personal-affectional satisfaction.

Introvert. Tends to be socially withdrawn, isolated, reflective, contemplative, and dependent upon himself for personal satisfactions.

More recently, a Harvard social scientist, David Riesman, has offered personality descriptions that include a threefold classification of inner-directed, other-directed, and tradition-directed types.

Inner-directed. Tends to be self-reliant; behavior based on his own values; guides himself by his own beliefs.

Other-directed. Tends to rely on others; behavior based on what he perceives others expect; guides himself by the beliefs and practices of others.

Tradition-directed. Tends to rely on traditional standards and guides.

Though many type descriptions of personality are offered, few account for the subtle variations that actually exist among people.

One of the best worked out, though controversial, typologies resulted from the work of two psychologists, Drs. W. H. Sheldon and S. S. Stevens. They attempted to allow for individual variation within a type by describing not so much exact types as a wide number of components that combine in varying degrees to constitute a type. In addition, they attempted to demonstrate how their personality types are closely related to physical structure.

Sheldon and Stevens found that people may be generally described physically in three ways—as endo-, ecto-, or mesomorphs—on the basis of body build, distribution of fat, and prominence of bones. They theorized that there may be a correlation between the three body types and three personality types—viscero-, cerebro-, and somatotonia—that they described in terms of temperament, sociability, and energy (see Fig. 6-4). Sheldon and Stevens recognized that most people do not fit one of their constructs exactly, but possess the body and personality traits in various degrees. They developed a seven point scale to show the degree that any individual exhibits each trait. Thus, precise measurements of a person found to be nearly a pure mesomorph might read: mesomorph 5, ectomorph 1, and endomorph 2. Someone who is a mixture of nearly all types would probably be

4-3-5. The greater the degree of any one physical component in a person, the more likely he is to exhibit the traits of the associated personality type. Thus someone who is meso- 3, ecto- 6, and endo- 1 should have most of the characteristics described by cerebrotonia.

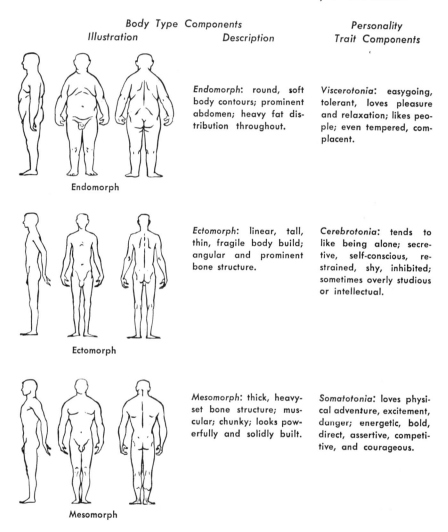

| | Body Type Components | Personality |
| Illustration | Description | Trait Components |

Endomorph

Endomorph: round, soft body contours; prominent abdomen; heavy fat distribution throughout.

Viscerotonia: easygoing, tolerant, loves pleasure and relaxation; likes people; even tempered, complacent.

Ectomorph

Ectomorph: linear, tall, thin, fragile body build; angular and prominent bone structure.

Cerebrotonia: tends to like being alone; secretive, self-conscious, restrained, shy, inhibited; sometimes overly studious or intellectual.

Mesomorph

Mesomorph: thick, heavy-set bone structure; muscular; chunky; looks powerfully and solidly built.

Somatotonia: loves physical adventure, excitement, danger; energetic, bold, direct, assertive, competitive, and courageous.

Fig. 6-4 Body type and associated personality trait components (according to Sheldon and Stevens). Illustrations redrawn from Clifford T. Morgan, *Introduction to Psychology*, 2nd ed. (New York: McGraw-Hill Book Company, 1961), p. 495.

Many psychologists, dissatisfied with the rough categorization implied by type descriptions of personality, have attempted to delineate the essential traits that determine human behavior. Some, like Edwards (see Chapter Seven), have detailed the needs that may describe an individual's personality. A person with a high need for achievement, low esteem motivation, and low heterosexual drive is very much different from one low in the first and high in the last two. Other psychologists have attempted to describe personality in terms of the traits that typify behavior. R. B. Cattell, using the refined techniques of modern statistics, has been able to isolate several of the fundamental descriptive dimensions that may be used to describe personality. He feels that such traits as schizothymia, dominance, and others represent the fundamental ways in which personality may be described:

Gregariousness.   Sociability, need to interact with others.
Impulsiveness.   Tendency to act quickly, rashly, without thinking.
Dominance.   Self-assertion, aggressiveness, confidence.
Schizothymia.   Reserve, quietness, withdrawal.
Autonomy.   Strong need for independence, desire to be left alone.
Deference.   Self-subordination, liking to follow a leader.
Orderliness.   Need for logical and clean arrangements, neatness.
Socialization.   Tendency to adhere to norms, do what is expected.

THE CONCEPTS OF ROLE AND SELF

Personality is the end product of a wide diversity of determinants. It is shaped by innate and inherited dispositions and is continually modified by new learning by the individual. Personality is further altered by the group and culture in which the person finds himself and the role that he is forced to play. Whatever our individual personality, when certain roles are thrust upon us we shape our behavior—usually without being aware we are doing so—to meet the new expectations. Although a twenty-seven-year-old woman is physically one person, her roles as mother, wife, or school teacher each demand different attitudes and behavior, and so reshape her actions to suit each situation. Similarly, all human beings find themselves being molded by the groups and situations in which they find themselves and notice that their behavior shifts to suit each occasion.

"But which is the real me?" a confused student may ask. The questioner is puzzled by the fact that personality is an infinitely subtle and fluid combination of inborn and learned determinants that are further modified by the demands of milieu, social position, and obligations. He is perhaps further disturbed by the many ways that typologies, trait descriptions, and other rationales are used to describe personality. One solution to understanding personality in an integrated way has come about through conceiving of personal functioning in terms of the concept of *self*.

As the infant emerges from his helplessness and dependency on those about him, he slowly grows aware of the parts and characteristics that are part of himself and those that belong to others or to the world around him. The parts of the body closest to him, which hurt or tingle or feel cold or warm, are his. The pangs he experiences indicate that he is hungry. As he continues to grow, he recognizes his clothes, his room, house, town, and world. He develops, in short, an organized *concept of self*.

The individual learns that he is a unit and strives to preserve himself as such. He recognizes many of his own needs and realizes that the world regards and treats him in certain ways. He may obtain a confident, approving view of himself, as most healthy individuals do, or he may learn to regard himself with reproach and severity. Once the individual formulates his self-image, he acts accordingly. He wants to maintain the view he has of himself. Much the way the homeostatic mechanism regulates innate motives and drives, the self, so to speak, seeks and rejects experience to maintain a harmonious existence.

Client-centered psychotherapy, initiated by Carl Rogers (Chapter Sixteen), approaches the reconstruction of personality in terms of the concept of self. The Rogerian believes that as the individual grows, he attaches many characteristics and values to his concept of self that may actually hamper his further development. By exploring his client's feelings about himself, the Rogers-oriented therapist hopes to be able to free the individual's self concept from hopeless restraints and produce a more confident, integrated, and capable self-image.

A vast and unceasing array of factors determines what we are; they influence development from the moment of conception, nine months before birth, and continue throughout life. A multiplicity of learned and acquired drives, many below the level of awareness, continually alert us to special aspects of our environment and energetically push us toward satisfaction. Through the several ways in which we learn, ranging from classic and instrumental conditioning to the subtleties of perceptual learning, the experiences we encounter become a part of our total being. Ultimately, everything we have inherited, encountered, and learned shapes for us a pattern of behavior—a personality—that guides us through the challenges of living.

FOR REVIEW AND DISCUSSION

1. What are motives? What are the sensitizing and energizing functions of motives? Define drive, need, psychological motives, physiological needs, general drives, and motive hierarchy. How many emotions act as motivators? What are "unconscious" drives?

2. Define classic conditioning, unconditioned response, reinforcement, extinction, generalization, instrumental conditioning, and higher order conditioning.

3. How is behavior learned by methods other than the simple conditioning and instrumental processes? Which methods do you think are most important? Why? What are some practical ways in which we may help ourselves learn?

4. What do psychologists mean by *personality?* How are attributes that constitute personality determined? What are some of the ways in which personality has been described? Are there essential differences between Jung's personality descriptions and those used by Sheldon and Stevens?

5. What is the "self"? How is this a useful concept in describing personality? Define role, typology, inner-directed, ectomorph, viscerotonia, and introversion.

Using

and Abusing

Psychological Tests

SEVEN

Psychologists have developed tests that can measure intelligence, assess personality, and help predict success in school and work. Some of the devices used to appraise human behavior and potential are easily understood. Thus, intelligence examinations require the solution of a variety of problems of increasing levels of difficulty. Tests designed to survey the abilities of engineers consist of mathematical and scientific questions. But the contents of many other psychological devices make little sense to nonprofessionals. They do not understand how significant cues about character and mental health can be obtained by asking subjects to describe Rorschach ink blots or to tell stories in response to TAT pictures. In the following pages some of the tests used to gauge aptitudes, interests, and personality will be described. Intelligence and its evaluation are explained in Chapter Eight.

UNDERSTANDING TESTS

Tests are extremely useful to psychologists and other trained specialists. They allow experts to examine hundreds of people simultaneously. College freshmen are usually given a wide range of aptitude and personality tests when they begin their university education. In this way counselors can pick out those weak in certain subjects or those with emotional handicaps. Without tests, all the students might have to be interviewed individually to determine which of them need special aid. Testing is a valuable timesaver. It also permits professionals to compare one person with very many others. A psychologist may be able to interview only a relatively small number of clients during his own career. But every examiner has available the scores of literally thousands of people on many dozens of tests. By comparing a specific score with the scores of the group with whom the test was originally devised and verified—the *norms*—test interpreters are better able to understand the results of any single performance.

Not all tests are equally worthwhile. Some, though diligently constructed, are inconsistent and do not appraise what they are supposed to. The adequacy of tests is described by their *reliability* and *validity*. Reliability refers to the evenness with which a test measures. A test that cannot be relied upon to give the same results upon repeated measurement is like a scale with defective springs. One moment the broken scale indicates a person's weight as 138, and the next it reads 110 pounds. An undependable test, like an irregular scale, is useless.

The second vital test component, validity, refers to the test's ability to measure what it says it does. An aptitude exam allegedly probing intelligence must be shown actually to measure that component. Too frequently a test built to gauge intellect actually appraises the quality and quantity of a person's education. Though schooling is certainly related to intelligence, it is not synonymous with it. A test falsely influenced by scholastic background when it is supposedly surveying intelligence is invalid.

Tests are not just haphazardly thrown together and used on innocent persons, and decisions about the validity and reliability of tests are not arbitrary. The process of test construction and the assessment of test strengths and weaknesses involve hundreds of human subjects, complex statistical procedures, and continual sifting and refinement of thousands of potential test items. The end result of many months, sometimes years, of such effort is a *standardized* instrument whose accuracy and dependability have been calculated. Because of the labors that precede the launching of an examination, the psychologist knows not just whether an instrument is consistent and truthful, but the actual numerical degree of its validity and reliability. An experienced tester is aware, for example, that the reliability of certain MMPI scales is .8 and that the validity ranges from .4 to .7 (on a scale of .0 to 1.0).

So-called tests of personality and intelligence are common in some newspapers and magazines. Fortunately, most people who take these "tests" recognize that they are only for amusement and have no real diagnostic or descriptive value. Unlike authentic psychological examinations meeting all the specifications of a scientifically created instrument, tests that appear in popular reading material are simply made up by clever writers. It is likely that if newspaper-type tests were to be critically evaluated, their validity and reliability would be mathematically zero.

Presently, no tests of intelligence, personality, or aptitude are perfectly reliable or valid. All tests have a degree of infidelity. But psychologists know the quantity of error inherent in an examination and are able to exercise proper precautions in interpreting test scores. Untrained people who do not know how to assess and compensate for deficiencies in validity and reliability are frequently responsible for reaching the most farfetched, even harmful, conclusions.

Since no test is perfect, psychologists almost always use a group or *battery* of tests. In this way the errors in any one evaluation can be understood and counterbalanced by using another. The thorough examiner also attempts to find out as much as he can about his subject's background and experiences. Very often, similar test results have to be interpreted quite differently because of major differences in the history and circumstances of the people taking the test.

The following list summarizes some terms used to describe tests and their characteristics:

Types of Tests

Personality.   Measure emotional and mental well-being and the functioning of personality. May be specifically designed to measure any of several aspects of behavior.

Ability (aptitude).   Measure *potential* skills. An aptitude test may be given college students to determine how well they would do in particular curriculums.

Achievement.   Measure how much a person has learned. Before hiring, a large engineering firm might give an engineering achievement test to assess whether the candidate has learned enough to be useful to it.

Interest inventories.   Measure only the degree of interest (not ability and not achievement) that a person has in a particular career or vocation.

Characteristics of Good Tests

Validity.   The accuracy with which a test measures what it is intended to measure. Not all tests measure what they profess. They are therefore not valid.

Reliability.   The degree to which repeated measurements with the same test, or with equivalent forms of the examination, give essentially the same results. Some tests are so inconsistent that their results are meaningless.

Norms.   Test results can be interpreted only by comparing the specific score obtained with the scores of the group with whom the test was originally devised and verified. Good tests have large and representative populations that serve as a normative sample (basis for comparison).

Standardization.   Valid and reliable tests are accurate only when they are administered and interpreted exactly as intended. The process of testing and scoring for all good tests is standardized so that meaningful results will emerge.

OBJECTIVE PERSONALITY TESTS

Personality tests are of two main types. The most common type, frequently used to examine large groups as well as individuals, is the *objective* inventory. The second type is the *projective* test. Projective tests are usually given individually. Unlike multiple-choice questionnaires, projectives do not consist of questions that have to be answered "yes, no, true, false, sometimes." Instead, they require that subjects use their imagination to describe an ambiguous stimulus or to make up a story about some picture or scene. Both objective questionnaire and projective tests have special uses and unique strengths and weaknesses. Some psychologists become quite expert with a particular technique and can glean information from an MMPI or Rorschach that surprises even their professional colleagues.

Minnesota Multiphasic Personality Inventory (MMPI)

The MMPI is one of the most carefully constructed objective personality questionnaires. The test consists of over five hundred questions to be answered true or false. It was developed by Dr. S. R. Hathaway, a psychologist, and Dr. J. C. McKinley, a psychiatrist, associated with the University of Minnesota. The MMPI assesses many different phases of personality. It is especially useful in detecting mental disorder, although it is also employed for other purposes. The MMPI appraises the degree to which a person is depressed, whether his thinking is disturbed, and whether he has hypochondriacal symptoms, phobias, and other "nervous" manifestations.

An advantageous feature of the MMPI, much to the dismay of test fakers, is a series of "control" scales. More than 10 per cent of MMPI questions are subtly designed to evaluate the degree to which a person is deliberately making himself look worse or better. One of the problems of psychological testing is that the people examined frequently slant their answers to cover up their failings or, in some situations, to exaggerate their difficulties. On the MMPI, however, a malingerer seeking a psychiatric discharge from the service or a highly disturbed adult trying to hide his emotional disorder may have the extent to which they are lying on the test detected. By carefully analyzing the result of the questions that comprise the control scales and comparing them with predetermined standards, psychologists are able to estimate the truthfulness of the persons examined.

Empirical validity. A common misconception about the questionnaire personality inventory is that the test's accuracy is dependent on the subject's understanding of himself. A question such as "I tend to harbor grudges against people" apparently requires that the person examined have real insight into his personality. Or "I frequently believe that I'm going to have a nervous breakdown" seems to rely upon how individuals variously interpret the key word, *frequently.* However, most personality tests are constructed to take into account the fact that subjects have varying degrees of self-understanding and that they interpret many words differently. The relationship between what is said on the test and what subjects actually do is not always expected to be a literal one. Subjects who say certain things on tests tend to have certain feelings and do certain things in life.

The question "I am easily awakened by noise"[1] appears on the MMPI. What does it measure? In the literal sense, superficially, it assesses nothing very significant. However, it has been determined by empirical investigation that people who answer "Yes" to this and certain other questions are probably depressed. It is possible that two people being examined on the test are equally easily awakened. Careful pretest procedures have shown, however, that regardless of the facts concerning the depth of their sleep, the one subject who *says* "Yes" to the question is statistically more likely to be depressed than the one who answers "No."

Edwards Personal Preference Schedule (EPPS)

The MMPI is primarily intended to uncover psychiatric illness. The Edwards Personal Preference Schedule is designed to detect variations in normal personality. The EPPS measures the strength of fifteen basic motives or needs. The method for doing this is quite simple. Subjects are forced to choose one statement from each of 225 pairs of statements. Each pair of statements weighs one motive against another. Eventually, all fifteen motives measured on the Edwards are compared with one another so that their relative strength can be assessed. The Edwards is like the MMPI in that it attempts to detect and compensate for subjects who distort and slant their answers.

Here are three sample pairs of statements from the Edwards Personal Preference Schedule.[2]

1. A. I like to help my friends when they are in trouble.
   B. I like to do my very best in whatever I undertake.
2. A. I like to find out what great men have thought about various problems in which I am interested.
   B. I would like to accomplish something of great significance.
3. A. Any written work that I do I like to have precise, neat, and well organized.
   B. I would like to be a recognized authority in some job, profession, or field of specialization.

Only a qualified analyst for the Edwards test could draw your personality profile, of course. But by applying the general standards used by the test analysts, we can at least say that the choice of state-

---

[1] These items from the MMPI are reprinted by permission. Copyright 1943 by the University of Minnesota. Published by The Psychological Corporation. All rights reserved.

[2] Reprinted by permission. Copyright 1953 by The Psychological Corporation, New York, N. Y. All rights reserved.

ment A in the first pair above would register a tendency toward the need for nurturance, whereas selection of statement B would suggest a need for achievement. In the second pair, statement A might be interpreted as a response to the deference need, and statement B another sign of the achievement need. Statement A of the third pair could be viewed as an indication of the need for order, and statement B still another manifestation of achievement need.

The test profile of "Mona McDougal" in Fig. 7-1 shows how an EPPS might be interpreted. The vertical column of three-letter words is the code for the fifteen personality needs measured on the Edwards test: achievement, deference, order, exhibition, autonomy, affiliation, intraception, succorance, dominance, abasement, nurturance, change, endurance, heterosexuality, and aggression.

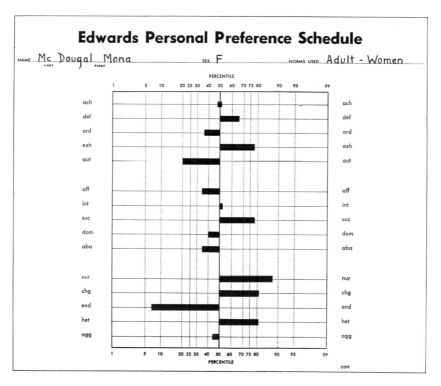

Fig. 7-1 Test profile of Mona McDougal. Reproduced by permission. Copyright 1959 by The Psychological Corporation, New York, N.Y. All rights reserved.

Mona's profile displays a significant deviation from the norm for adult women in the area of endurance. Preferences for the statements suggested below would be interpreted as endurance needs on the EPPS:

> Endurance: To keep at a job until it is finished, to complete any job undertaken, to work hard at a task, to keep at a puzzle or problem until it is solved, to work at a single job before taking on others, to stay up late working in order to get a job done, to put in long hours of work without distraction, to stick at a problem even though it may seem as if no progress is being made, to avoid being interrupted while at work.[3]

The fact that Mona's endurance score is below the tenth percentile suggests that she probably is not able to persevere or stick to a task.

Mona McDougal's need for autonomy is quite low (twentieth percentile), while her need for succorance is high (eightieth percentile). Statements used by the Edwards testers to describe these needs are:

> Autonomy: To be able to come and go as desired, to say what one thinks about things, to be independent of others in making decisions, to feel free to do what one wants, to do things that are unconventional, to avoid situations where one is expected to conform, to do things without regard to what others may think, to criticize those in positions of authority, to avoid responsibilities and obligations.

> Succorance: To have others provide help when in trouble, to seek encouragement from others, to have others be kindly, to have others be sympathetic and understanding about personal problems, to receive a great deal of affection from others, to have others do favors cheerfully, to be helped by others when depressed, to have others feel sorry when one is sick, to have a fuss made over one when hurt.[4]

Mona's profile indicates that she is a fairly dependent person who is unable to do things through her own initiative but needs the protection and support of others. Several other motives stand out and hint at the complex pattern of her personality.

California Psychological Inventory

A relatively recent personality test, the California Psychological Inventory appears to be a promising instrument. Like the EPPS, the inventory is designed primarily for use with "normal" subjects, rather than with psychiatrically disturbed ones. The test seems to

---

[3] Reprinted by permission. Copyright 1959 by The Psychological Corporation, New York, N. Y. All rights reserved.

[4] Ibid.

measure various aspects of personality and character that are important in social living and everyday interaction. Ten true-or-false items from the test are given here.[5]

1. I sometimes pretend to know more than I really do.
2. It's no use worrying my head about public affairs; I can't do anything about them anyhow.
3. As a child I used to be able to go to my parents with my problems.
4. I think I would like the work of a school teacher.
5. Women should not be allowed to drink in cocktail bars.
6. Most people would tell a lie if they could gain by it.
7. Every family owes it to the city to keep their sidewalks cleared in the winter and their lawn mowed in the summer.
8. I usually take an active part in the entertainment at parties.
9. I think I would enjoy having authority over other people.
10. I hate to be interrupted when I am working on something.

The results of the California Psychological Inventory are "profiled" in order to determine the relative strengths of particular characteristics (see Figs. 7-2, 7-3, and 7-4). Notice that the profile of an eighteen-year-old male (Fig. 7-2) reaches a peak at self-acceptance

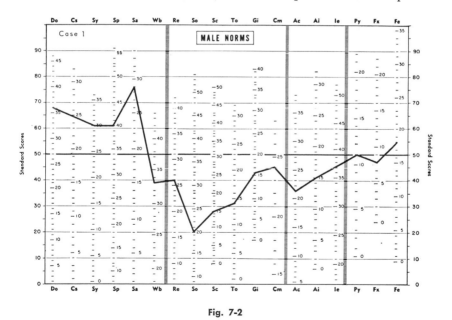

Fig. 7-2

[5] These items, together with Figs. 7-2, 7-3, and 7-4 and the analysis of them in the text, are all reprinted by special permission from the California Psychological Inventory, by Harrison G. Gough. Copyright 1956. Published by Consulting Psychologists Press, Inc., Palo Alto, California.

(Sa) and a low point at socialization (So). The purpose of the CPI's self-acceptance index is "to assess factors such as sense of personal worth, self-acceptance, and capacity for independent thinking and action." High scorers in this area tend to be seen as "intelligent, out-spoken, sharp-witted, demanding, aggressive, and self-centered; as being persuasive and verbally fluent; and as possessing self-confidence and self-assurance."

The socialization scale is designed "to indicate the degree of social maturity, integrity, and rectitude which the individual has attained." Low scorers on this scale (e.g., the eighteen-year-old boy in Fig. 7-2) tend to be seen as "defensive, demanding, opinionated, resent-ful, stubborn, headstrong, rebellious, and unpredictable; as being guileful and deceitful in dealing with others; and as given to excess, exhibition, and ostentation in their behavior."

Now read the CPI interpretation of the profile and compare it with the opinion held by the boy's high-school principal. Remember that the final interpretation of each profile must be based on all of the characteristics measured, not simply on peaks and lows.

Case 1: Male, Age 18

This profile [Fig. 7-2] is marked by a general elevation of those scales having to do with poise, ascendancy, and self-assurance, and a general lower-ing of those indicative of socialization, maturity, and sense of responsibility. These trends are highlighted by the elevation on the self-acceptance scale and the low point on the measure of socialization. In order to arrive at an interpretation beyond what is already suggested by the listing of high and low scales, the descriptive words and phrases for each scale should be con-sulted.

From a reading of these interpretational guides, a picture of this boy can be evolved. Our expectation is that he would be assertive, socially forward, probably self-centered and overbearing, rebellious, impulsive, undependable, and overconcerned with personal gain and pleasure. Because of his very considerable social skills he might function adequately, in the sense of attain-ing his own ends and objectives; yet, his deficiencies in the area of respon-sibility and interpersonal maturity seem almost certainly to destine him for social friction and difficulty. *(Note: This boy was one of the three in his class of over 400 high school students who was identified by the principal as a "serious disciplinary problem.")*

Now look at Fig. 7-3. It is quite evident that the seventeen-year-old girl whose profile appears there has feelings of self-acceptance that are different from those of the boy in Fig. 7-2. This girl also registered a low score in capacity for status (Cs), a scale designed "to serve as an index of an individual's capacity for status (not his actual or achieved status)." According to the CPI, low scorers in this area tend to be seen as "apathetic, shy, conventional, dull, mild, simple, and slow; as being stereotyped in thinking; restricted in outlook and interests; and as being uneasy and awkward in new or unfamiliar social situations."

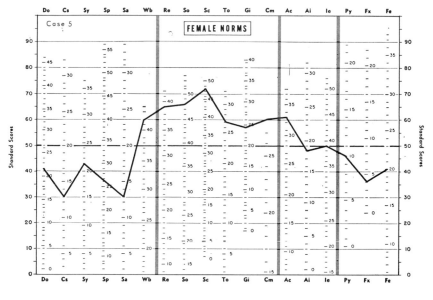

Fig. 7-3

On the other hand, the girl's profile rises sharply in the areas of socialization (where the boy in the previous case reached his low) and self-control (Sc). The latter scale is intended "to assess the degree and adequacy of self-regulation and self-control and freedom from impulsivity and self-centeredness." Here is how high scorers in self-control tend to be seen: "calm, patient, practical, slow, self-denying, inhibited, thoughtful, and deliberate; as being strict and thorough in their own work and in their expectations for others; and as being honest and conscientious."

After examining these and other prominent features of the profile in Fig. 7-3, the CPI analysts reached the following conclusions. Again, compare these profile interpretations with the subject's school performance.

Case 5: Female, Age 17

The scores on this profile [Fig. 7-3] are quite low in the first cluster, those measures assessing self-assurance, self-confidence, and capacity for leadership. However, in the group of scales having to do with dependability, self-restraint, and conformity to social expectations, the scores are quite high. If we again have recourse to the interpretational section for information on the three most significant deviations (the high score on Sc, and low scores on Cs and Sa), we get a picture of an individual who is patient, strict and thorough in her work, quiet, conventional, honest, conscientious, perhaps submissive, and somewhat given to feelings of guilt and unworthiness. Attention might also be paid to the difference between the two achievement scales (Ac [achievement via conformance] and Ai [achievement via independence]); this discrepancy suggests that whereas achievement via conformance can be predicted, only moderate attainment can be expected in situations demanding independent action and thought. The low scores in the area of social poise [Sp] and initiative [Do], when viewed against the backdrop of her exceptional level of responsibility [Re] and integrity [So], point to some specific improvements which a counseling and guidance program might seek to realize. *(Note: This girl was nominated by her high school principal as one of three "outstanding citizens" in her class of 200.)*

Figure 7-4 shows the profile of a twenty-three-year-old female clearly unlike either of the two subjects previously discussed. Although she has high scores in social presence (Sp) and flexibility (Fx), she also shows a marked low in communality (Cm). The latter scale tries "to indicate the degree to which an individual's reactions and responses correspond to the modal ('common') pattern established for the inventory." By her low score in communality this woman seems to place herself with those who tend to be seen as "impatient, changeable, complicated, imaginative, disorderly, nervous, restless, and confused; as being guileful and deceitful; inattentive and forgetful; and as having internal conflicts and problems."

But that is only one score in the woman's profile. Consider also her high rating in flexibility, which suggests that she is seen as "insightful, informal, adventurous, confident, humorous, rebellious, idealistic, assertive, and egoistic; as being sarcastic and cynical; and as highly concerned with personal pleasure and diversion." Remember also that she has high scores in social presence (and thus tends to be seen as "clever, enthusiastic, imaginative, quick, informal, spontaneous, and talkative; as being active and vigorous; and as having an expressive, ebullient nature") and on achievement via independence (hence tends to be seen as "mature, forceful, strong, dominant, demanding, and foresighted; as being independent and self-reliant; and as having superior intellectual ability and judgment"). What do CPI analysts make of these seemingly conflicting scores?

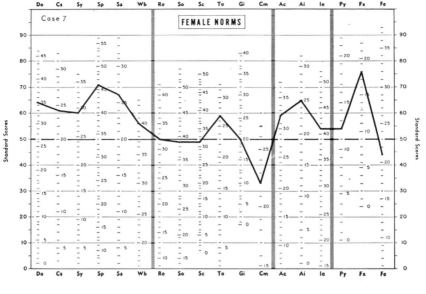

Fig. 7-4

Case 7: Female, Age 23

This profile [Fig. 7-4] shows several marked deviations both above and below the average. On the plus side the key scales are those for social presence (Sp), self-acceptance (Sa), and flexibility (Fx). From the earlier description of the scales we can abstract the characteristics seemingly common to all three; the result includes such traits as: cleverness, enthusiasm, intelligence, informality, verve and expressiveness, self-confidence, and self-assurance. The next highest scales, Do [dominance], Sc [capacity for status], Sy [sociability], and Ai [achievement via independence] serve to emphasize these trends. The one low score is on the Cm (communality) scale. This scale reveals the degree to which an individual's responses to the inventory correspond to the modal pattern established by all persons. If the remainder of this profile were less favorable than it is, the low score on Cm would be a negative sign. In the present context, however, it should probably be interpreted as an indication of uniqueness; this woman is an independent-minded individual, with a somewhat different outlook and set of views from others. She is not, neverthe-less, at odds with others or out-of-step socially. On the contrary, she is an effective, outgoing, flexible, and resourceful person, convincing and decisive in manner while at the same time able to adapt easily to others. *(Note: Case 7 was one of 60 airline hostesses tested in a research survey. Her job effectiveness rating was the highest one obtained in the sample of 60 hostesses.)*

PROJECTIVE PERSONALITY TESTS

Projective tests do not require that specific questions be answered. Instead, subjects are asked to describe what they see or to make up a story about a relatively neutral stimulus presented them.

Rorschach Ink Blot Test

The Rorschach Ink Blot test is one of the least structured and most ambiguous projective tests. The Rorschach consists simply of ten ink blots originally selected by a Swiss psychiatrist, Herman Rorschach, in 1918. He found them useful in helping to diagnose the personality disorders of some of his patients. The technique has become immensely popular all over the world. Nearly all clinical psychologists in the United States use the ink blots to help them reach diagnostic conclusions.

What can a psychologist tell about a person from his response to the ten Rorschach cards? The question is not easily answered. The Rorschach is a highly debatable instrument, as are most projective techniques. Many psychologists feel that it offers little and that it is a scientific anachronism. There is considerable evidence that many diagnostic conclusions based simply on Rorschach testing may be quite erroneous. Nevertheless, the Rorschach is still extensively used. Some practicing clinical psychologists contend that because it is a highly personal technique, its effectiveness cannot be evaluated in the same way as that of an objective questionnaire test.

With experience, a trained Rorschach clinician can often tell a good bit about the emotional well-being of the person to whom he has administered a test. Most people think that the clinician "interprets" what the subject says he sees. In fact, although the content of what is perceived is important, the way in which something is viewed and described can be more helpful in arriving at a diagnosis.

The Rorschach is analyzed in several steps (Klopfer, *et al.*). First a score is assigned for the location of a response. What part or parts of the ink blot are used in the subject's description? Location is scored W if the whole ink blot is used; if a large detail makes up the percept, the score is D; small detail is scored d. There are many other types of location scores depending upon the parts of the ink blots used.

The second step in Rorschach analysis is finding out what properties of the ink blot made it appear the way it did. The subject may report seeing something because the shape of the blot reminded him of the way it looked. That would be scored F, to signify that form determined the percept. Perhaps something about the blot suggested human beings engaged in some kind of action. This would be scored M, for human movement. Many other aspects of the blot may stimulate a perception. The way in which the ink blot is shaded, colored, the perspective it gives, etc., are all scored if they helped determine what the subject saw on the card.

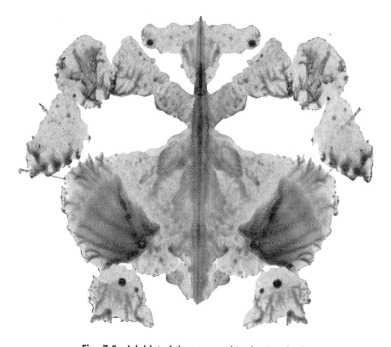

Fig. 7-5 Ink blot of the type used in the Rorschach.

In Figure 7-5 a Rorschach-like ink blot is reproduced. Many different things can be seen. The following is, in part, an example of how one subject's responses might be scored. (The parenthetical remarks are the psychologist's.)

It looks like a woman in a hoop skirt doing a dance. (Where is that?) The whole thing here. (Describe it.) She's wearing a long, fluffy-type hat; she's got her arms up and is waving feathers or fans which are hanging down. She's got a big hoop skirt and it trails down in funny ways. *Scoring: Location, W (whole); determinant, M (human movement).*

If you turn the whole ink blot upside down, then right on top here on the right and left it looks like it could be the face of a cat or kitten. There are two. One on each side. (Describe it.) These round dots look like the eyes, the ears are here on top; the whole thing is just shaped like a kitten's head and face. *Scoring: Location, D (large detail); determinant, F (form).*

After the psychologist has scored the Rorschach for location, determinant, and several other factors, he considers all of his evidence together to reach conclusions. Each score by itself or in combination with others may give the clinician a hint about his subject's personality. If a psychologist administered all ten Rorschach cards and received a total of perhaps thirty responses without observing any M involvement, he might suspect a number of personality deficiencies. The absence of M, or an extremely low number of such responses, *may* in combination with other evidence suggest low intelligence, lack of self-control, and a relatively low opinion of the self. The careful examiner, however, always arrives at tentative conclusions about his subject on the basis of the Rorschach, and then attempts to verify them using other techniques. Frequently the initial assumptions made on the basis of Rorschach testing turn out not to be accurate.

Thematic Apperception Test (TAT)

Another projective technique, rather different from the Rorschach, is the Thematic Apperception Test. The TAT, as it is usually called, was devised by a Harvard University psychologist, Dr. H. A. Murray, and his colleagues in the 1930's. The TAT consists of twenty different pictures, which serve as stimuli about which subjects make up stories. It is a lengthy test, and many psychologists do not use all twenty of the pictures, or break the testing into two or even three sessions.

Stories about the TAT pictures may be scored in many different ways. Some psychologists make a careful analysis and count of the words that testees use. Most clinicians, however, use a less formal approach in deciphering the meaning of the stories. They base their interpretations on the assumption that a person's responses to the pictures are dictated by his own feelings and experiences. The person, it is thought, projects himself into the picture and identifies with a character just as he might imaginatively take the place of an actor when he sees a movie. Thus, the clinician is particularly interested in the subject's plot and theme. Is the story filled with conflicts and hostilities that might reflect the patient's own feelings? Are the traits imputed to the characters in the story possibly representative of the examinee's own personality?

The following two stories and a brief analytic statement are based on the TAT-like picture reproduced as Fig. 7-6. Again, parenthetical remarks are the psychologist's.

Fig. 7-6 Projective picture similar to those that appear on the Thematic Apperception Test. Subjects are instructed to make up a complete story to fit the picture. Photo courtesy of NaCamU Studio.

This girl is in a mental hospital. She's pretty depressed. She's thinking about something. (What is she thinking about?) She's got her children on her mind. She feels bad that she wasn't strong enough to take care of them. She's ashamed because she became mentally ill. (Go on.) Well, she's never been very strong. She's always been afraid that some day she would break down. And now she has. (What happens?) Well, maybe she gets better eventually and goes back to her family.

In interpreting this picture the psychologist might hypothesize that the subject seems worried about his own mental health and whether he can bear up under the stresses of his life. Of course, no trained professional would ever attempt to reach a conclusion about personality on the basis of just one picture. As with the Rorschach, once the examiner has obtained a few hints about his subjects on the basis of the TAT, he checks his speculations against other evidence so that he can confirm or reject his original ideas.

Another subject interpreted the picture in Fig. 7-6 as follows:

> This girl is being punished by her parents. She has gotten into some kind of trouble and she's moping in a corner. Maybe her father beat her up. (Why was she punished?) She stayed out too late. She's with this boy that she's crazy about and they just didn't realize how fast time was passing. Her father don't like the boy anyhow. (Why not?) He's not got much education. He quit high school and her father wants her to marry somebody from college. (How do things end?) Well, she runs away with the boy. Her father really explodes when he finds out. (How does he find out?) She calls him and lets him have it right over the phone.

On the basis of this card the psychologist might tentatively feel that the patient telling the story had strong hostile feelings toward her own father or toward both parents. She appears to be harboring aggressive feelings and permitting them to escape through the story. These, and many other assumptions that an examiner might make on the basis of this single TAT response, would have to be carefully compared with information derived from other stories that the subject relates, as well as with all her other tests, in order to determine what her personality and emotional life are actually like.

Incomplete Sentences Test

Another projective test is the Incomplete Sentences Test, devised by Dr. J. B. Rotter. As the name of the test implies, subjects are asked to finish incomplete sentences. Just as in the TAT, interpretation is based on the assumption that they will indirectly reveal their own feelings, conflicts and motivations by the way they finish the sentences. Three items from the Rotter test for the high-school level are given below.[6]

Complete these sentences to express *your real feelings*. Try to do every one. Be sure to make a complete sentence.

1.   I like   .   .   .   .

2.   The happiest time   .   .   .   .

3.   I want to know   .   .   .   .

Other Tests

There are several other projective tests. The Blacky Pictures, originated by Dr. Blum, is a special test used mainly with children. The stimuli consist of a set of cartoons about a small dog, Blacky, and his canine relatives. The Children's Apperception Test (CAT) by Dr. Bellak is also specially useful with children. It consists of animals enacting human-type roles and situations. The Make a Picture Story Test (MAPS), another projective technique, is shown in Fig. 7-7.

Fig. 7-7 The Make a Picture Story Test (MAPS) is a projective technique. Subjects are instructed to arrange the characters and the scene in any way they desire and to make up an accompanying story. Photo courtesy of The Psychological Corporation, New York, N.Y.

Some projective tests require subjects to draw, as well as to tell stories about specific stimuli. The House-Tree-Person (HTP) by Dr. Buck requires that subjects draw a house, a tree, and a person. Many examiners then ask subjects to talk about what they have drawn. Another well-known drawing technique is the Bender-Gestalt, formulated by Dr. Lauretta Bender. This test requires that subjects reproduce some simple geometric figures set before them.

One of the most colorful and controversial of projective tests is the Szondi, named after a Hungarian psychiatrist. It was brought to the attention of American psychologists in the 1930's. The test consists of photographs of patients suffering from various psychiatric disturbances. Subjects are asked to indicate their preferences among the photos. The test is complicated, since it requires countless rearrangements and assessments of preferences.

The names Rorschach and TAT have become household words in our society. But the student should realize that the personality tests described in detail in this chapter are only the more popular methods. The testing field has mushroomed to meet the demands of many different institutions often dealing with people from special backgrounds. There is no universal personality test. A glance at the list of variations below will give a hint at the multiplicity of testing methods.

Projective

Machover Draw-a-Person Test.   The subject draws a person and may be asked to describe his sketch. (Karen Machover, author; published by Charles C Thomas, Publisher, 1949.)

Rosenzweig Picture-Frustration Test.   Consists of cartoons depicting discomfiting situations (e.g., a waiter spilling soup on a patron). The subject is asked to indicate what the cartoon character might say in response to the situation. (Saul Rosenzweig, author and publisher; St. Louis, Missouri, 1949.)

Symonds Picture Story Test.   Pictures similar to those of the TAT, but specifically designed for children and adolescents. The subject is asked to make up stories about the scenes depicted. (P. M. Symonds, author; published by the Bureau of Publication, Teachers College, Columbia University, 1948.)

Thompson Modification of the Thematic Apperception Test.   Pictures similar to the TAT set, but the people appear Negroid. The test is specifically designed for use with Negro subjects. (C. E. Thompson, author; published by Harvard University Press, 1949.)

Objective

California Test of Personality.   Specially designed versions may be used with young children, and forms for testing adults are also available. The test measures the presence of nervous symptoms, antisocial tendencies, feelings of belonging, etc. (L. P. Thorpe, W. W. Clark, and E. W. Tiegs, authors; published by the California Test Bureau, 1942–53.)

Guilford-Zimmerman Temperament Survey.   Measures traits of temperament such as objectivity, thoughtfulness, and ascendance. (J. P. Guilford and H. G. Zimmerman, authors; published by the Sheridan Supply Company, 1949.)

The Personality Inventory.   Measures neurotic tendency, introversion-extroversion, self-sufficiency, etc. (R. G. Bernreuter, author; published by Consulting Psychologists Press, Inc., 1931–38.)

The Value of Projective Techniques

The value of projective techniques is highly debatable even among psychologists. Evidence supporting the diagnostic effectiveness of projective devices is very shaky. But not all projective tests are alike. Some tests—the Szondi, for example—are probably interesting but useless. The Rorschach and a few others, on the other hand, continue occasionally to find support in well-conducted research (Koppitz; Renner, et al.). In the hands of skilled examiners some projectives can often be extremely helpful in providing a revealing sample of a patient's behavior.

INTEREST TESTS

Two of the important determiners of success in any field of endeavor are aptitude and interest. Aptitude refers to the amount of ability a person possesses to carry out the demands made by a job and to his potential to undertake successfully the training for it. Interest refers to the extent to which the person's likes and dislikes will make a job palatable. Aptitude and interest are not necessarily related. A student may want very much to be an engineer, share many of the interests of engineers, but have little aptitude for mathematics or fine drawing. The reverse may also be true. A medical school graduate may discover that while he has the knowledge and skills of a physician, he lacks the interests common among physicians. Thus, the British author W. Somerset Maugham found his preferences leading him to literature rather than to the medical career for which he had been trained.

Tests to measure vocational interest ask people about personal preferences and activities. Subjects indicate their likes and dislikes for certain types of activities. Some of the kinds of questions that might appear on interest exams are reproduced below.

I. Check which activity you like most (+) and which liked least (−).

( ) a. Hunt rabbits
( ) b. Go ice-skating
( ) c. Browse in a book store

II. Circle whether you would like (L), dislike (D), or be indifferent to (I) the following.

1. Acting   L I D
2. Reading   L I D
3. Dancing   L I D
4. Tennis   L I D
5. Picnicking   L I D

The items above are the type that appear on the two best-known interest tests, the Strong Vocational Interest Blank and the Kuder

Preference Record. These tests measure interest in nearly fifty separate careers and over a dozen occupational groups. The following is a partial list of job interests measured by one or the other of these tests.

Accountant	Farmer	Office worker
Advertising man	Forester	Pharmacist
Artist	Housewife	Physician
Buyer	High-school teacher	Policeman
Chemist	Lawyer	Psychologist
Dentist	Librarian	Social worker
Dietician	Minister	Stenographer
Elementary-school teacher	Musician	Veterinarian
Engineer	Nurse	

Interest tests cannot tell people who are in a muddle what occupation they *should* follow. They are useful in helping determine whether a specific person's interests coincide with the occupation for which he hopes to prepare himself. Thus, if a person believes he wants to be a teacher and the tests indicate he shares few likes and dislikes with teachers, it might be worthwhile for him to consider changing his vocational objectives. Sometimes interest patterns about which the subject was quite unaware emerge. These newly discovered patterns may successfully redirect him in his vocational quests.

Interest patterns are by no means rigidly bound to specific vocations. People who take interest tests should understand this fact and should weigh carefully all available information before coming to a decision. For the neophyte in an occupation, similarity of interests with others in the field, as opposed to dissimilarity, assures a much higher likelihood of success. Nevertheless, in all occupations there are people whose likes are quite different from those of the majority. There are highly successful and affluent engineers whose interest scores in engineering are quite low. There are scientists whose preference patterns are closer to those of an artist or writer than to those of a chemist or physicist—and they may be wholly satisfied with their work. Interest tests must never be interpreted simply at face value. They are sensitive instruments. In the hands of experts and in combination with other data they can be used to help people determine their occupational goals.

GOOD TESTS AND BAD

Some tests are good, in the sense that their reliability, validity, assets, and limitations are known. Some tests are bad because they do not really measure anything. Some good tests are misused. The evaluation of any single test or group of instruments must be left to a specialist. Whether a particular test is appropriate or inappropriate, worthwhile or worthless, cannot be stated here. Cronbach explained,

> One cannot identify one group of tests as good and recommend it for use. For every type of decision and for every type of psychological information, there are many techniques and many specific instruments. The instruments differ in practicality, in the degree of training required to use them, in the variety of information they obtain, and in fidelity. The instrument that works best for one tester will not be best for another tester making the same decision. Tests must be chosen by a highly qualified professional worker who has a thorough understanding of the institution and persons he serves.[7]

USING AND ABUSING TESTS

All psychological tests are designed to be used by experts only. Unfortunately they are used too often by people who are simply not trained to understand the weaknesses and special problems inherent in all examinations and who are thus likely to draw false conclusions. Scoring most tests and assigning such labels as "domineering" "aggressive," and "anxious" to certain types of scores is a simple clerical job. The simplicity of this task is misleading, however. *The scoring and diagnostic categories of most tests cannot be accepted at face value.* In addition, the meaning of any single test must always be derived from the relationships emerging from several tests administered to the subject and the subject's own background. It would be very easy, for example, to misinterpret TAT stories filled with disease, death, and gore, if the examiner were not aware that the subject was a medical student in the midst of a strenuous pathology course.

Schools, industries, and other institutions too often fasten upon one or another psychological examination and administer it to all students, employees, or applicants. On occasion, in qualified hands, such personality testing is worthwhile. Too often, however, partially informed or even totally untrained people reach all sorts of unjust and bizarre conclusions on the basis of what they have read in the test manual or otherwise believe the test "proves."

Mrs. N., an educational supervisor, took a summer course in which the Rorschach test was mentioned. Thereafter she instituted a new program in the schools she supervised. She administered the Rorschach examination to two

[7] L. J. Cronbach, *Essentials of Psychological Testing*, 2nd ed. (New York: Harper & Row, Publishers, 1960), p. 607.

hundred first- and second-grade children. Thirty-six children showed "signs" that their "ego structure" was weak and that they would eventually have a "mental breakdown." Those thirty-six children were then moved to special classrooms, where extraordinary techniques were used in an effort to forestall impending breakdown.

Mrs. N. and countless other well-intentioned self-appointed experts did not know that no single test or single group of techniques can reliably forecast who will be mentally disturbed. In addition, even telling who is presently emotionally defective is, to all intents and purposes, virtually impossible on the basis of just one or even two tests. But like others who appoint themselves experts with one or another test, Mrs. N. will not easily be convinced of the futility and potential harmfulness of her amateur meddling. Thousands of school children have already been dubbed "emotionally disturbed" on the basis of the flimsiest and most unscientific use of tests. Countless thousands more will undoubtedly be subjected to all kinds of indignities that will surely produce disturbances in even the initially sanest of children. Here lies the real tragedy. Once a child acquires the label "disturbed," he is accorded special treatment all the time. Is it surprising that even the initially most stable child becomes upset by this process? Mrs. N. and her misguided colleagues eventually find their initial diagnoses "justified." Things turn out just as they had expected —after six years of special classes the child labeled "potentially disturbed" develops into an "educational problem."

Mr. R. is a personnel manager. He uses a "test" produced by a publisher whose intentions are highly suspect. Very likely the test has not been scientifically constructed or validated. Mr. R. has his secretaries administer and score the test, which asks more than 300 questions. Afterward, various elaborate charts and tables are drawn up purportedly to gauge anxiety, aggressiveness, intelligence, creativity, "stick-to-it-iveness," etc. All job applicants who do not have certain score levels are automatically not hired. Mr. R., feeling quite the scientist (his use of tests has gotten him a huge merit raise) contends that his testing program saves his company huge sums of money. Now that tests are used, only 34 per cent of all those hired after testing are let go or leave spontaneously. When asked how many men were lost yearly before the testing program, Mr. R. replies that he does not know since no records were kept at that time. One may suspect, however, that before the testing program began the rate was below the current astonishingly high turnover rate. Mr. R. probably has not improved selection with his nonsensical tests. He has certainly demonstrated his own inefficiency by not knowing the pretest turnover; consequently, he fails to see how invalid his testing procedures are.

It cannot be emphasized too strongly that tests are continually abused. They are used by people whose training, despite their own pretenses, does not enable them to administer tests with the necessary precision and caution. Some of the worst offenders are professionals whose background included some psychology or testing courses. They feel themselves well equipped to dazzle their colleagues with jargon that sounds profound while they actually know very little. The words of Alexander Pope, that a little learning is a dangerous thing, are particularly applicable.

Whereas the psychologist can qualify scores as demanded by their invalidity and unreliability, few laymen have this training. They frequently overrate the power of psychological tools and misinterpret test reports. Both clients and such professional workers as teachers, physicians, and social workers may place false reliance on test data. Even when the tester's report is carefully qualified, the person receiving the report is likely to remember only portions of it. A parent, learning that a child's IQ is 87, may forget the tester's cautions about what the test does and does not measure, the possibility of growth or decline in IQ, and the approximate nature of predictions from it. Instead, the figure itself may be carried sharply in mind for years and used as a basis for rejecting the child or for making significant decisions.

Gross fallacies are often present in lay thinking about tests. There is the ever present belief that the IQ measures native intelligence. There is the misquotation that any child of IQ 140 is a genius. Percentiles are misread as percents. Norms—what the average sixth-grader does do—are misinterpreted as standards—what every sixth-grader should do. Most psychologists now make it a practice never to give any client or co-worker a test score unless he can interpret that score so that the person will understand it.[8]

Much criticism is directed at psychological tests and testing. Testers are accused of indiscriminately labeling children, inaccurately designating people emotionally disturbed, and destroying sensible personnel recruitment procedures. These charges are equivalent to indictments of cocaine plants for causing dope addiction. In the hands of an M.D. an injection of cocaine can ease pain and heal. But the physician has little control over addicts who use dangerous drugs to satisfy distorted craving. In the same way an examination is a valuable tool when administered by a skilled psychologist who is aware of the weaknesses and dangers inherent in all tests. When the untutored experiment with and interpret tests, lack of training causes them to make the most glaring errors. They invariably rely solely on the test manual and

[8] L. J. Cronbach, *Essentials of Psychological Testing* (New York: Harper & Row, Publishers, 1949), p. 357.

echo the generalizations that appear there. This is a blatant mistake, for all interpretations must be guided by knowledge of the extent to which the particular test is inaccurate and the unique circumstances of the individual who has taken the exam. Incompetent testers are responsible for many of the glaring injustices of which tests are frequently accused. Tests are like a powerful chemical—neither good nor bad—until in the hands of an expert they become instruments that can help and guide human behavior.

Psychological tests administered and interpreted by the few who are qualified have made a significant contribution to human endeavor, ranging from selecting job applicants to assessing mental health. The systematic evaluation of man's capabilities and resources is, in fact, one of psychology's proudest achievements.

All in all, psychological testing is an accomplishment its developers may well boast of. Errors of measurement have been reduced year by year, and the significance of tests has been increased, until today all facets of American society feel the impact of the testing movement. The school has perhaps been most radically affected. But industry, marriage, governmental policy, and character-building agencies have all been studied or directly improved by means of tests. Testers are daily making the lives of people better by guiding a man into a suitable lifework, by placing an adolescent under therapy which will avert mental disorder, or by detecting causes of a failure in school which could turn a child into a beaten individual. Methods are now available which, if used carefully by responsible testers, can unearth the talents in the population and can identify personality aberrations which would cause those talents to be wasted. Building on these techniques, we are in a position to capitalize as never before on the richness of human resources.[9]

FOR REVIEW AND DISCUSSION

1. Why are newspaper "personality tests" invalid? Are any tests perfectly reliable or valid? Why do psychologists usually administer a test battery rather than a single test? What are the characteristics of a good test? Define norms, standardization, achievement test, and aptitude test.

2. What are some differences between objective and projective personality tests? What do the MMPI "control" scales measure? What does the Edwards Personal Preference Inventory measure?

3. What are some advantages of the Rorschach and TAT over objective tests like the MMPI? Why is the worth of projective techniques highly debatable?

9 Cronbach, *Essentials of Psychological Testing*, 2nd ed., p. 607.

4. What do interest tests measure? Does a high score in a special interest category (e.g., physician) ensure that the testee has either the ability or the motivation necessary to learn the profession? Are the interests of all those in the same profession exactly alike, as measured by tests like the Strong and Kuder?

5. What is a good test? How are good tests abused? Why can't the scoring and diagnostic categories of most tests be accepted at face value? What are the qualifications of a competent psychological examiner?

Intelligence,

IQ, and

Human Ability

E I G H T

Nearly every American has taken an intelligence test, and although he is anxious to "know his IQ," he usually misunderstands and is puzzled by these tests and their results. Not all tests that measure intelligence are labeled "intelligence test." Many so-called tests of *aptitude, verbal reasoning,* or *quantitative reasoning* may actually be measures of mental ability. Moreover, there are so many forms and varieties of tests that it is not infrequent for a person to do well on one measure of intellectual capacity and relatively poorly on another. IQ scores may vary not only with the type of test used, but with the time and circumstances as well: a given person's performance on the same test may be quite different on two separate occasions some time apart. Test scores may be influenced by factors that do not seem to be related to intelligence at all. A person's school background, his socio-economic and cultural heritage, and many personal circumstances may produce falsely high or low intelligence test scores. The instability of IQ scores and their extreme susceptibility to all kinds of individual and social circumstances can be understood if the distinction between IQ and intelligence is recognized.

WHAT INTELLIGENCE IS

It is difficult to describe intelligence. In mock despair some psychologists have facetiously suggested that "Intelligence is what intelligence tests measure." Through this humorous definition the experts point to the fact that they have not been able to determine the exact attributes that make up the characteristic commonly referred to as intelligence. Nevertheless, it is recognized that when intelligence is described, such qualities as the ability to reason, learn, plan ahead, and remember are jointly involved. Psychologists still ask precisely what role each ability plays and what interaction takes place.

Intelligence may be assumed to be a physical attribute very much like basic bone structure, eye color, or blood type. The conditions in the brain and higher centers of the central nervous system that determine intelligence are not known. It has been hypothesized, however, that intelligence is related to the quantity or quality of gray cells in the brain matter, to the extent to which convolutions or folds have developed around the brain, or to the character of certain chemical and synaptic mediators. The size of the brain or of the head is not related to intelligence. If brain size were important, elephants and certain types of cranially enlarged mental defectives would be far superior to most human beings.

Since the conditions that determine intelligence are probably structural parts of the organism, they, like comparable physical traits, are hereditary. This does not mean that bright parents are guaranteed bright children; it does indicate that the intelligence of parents and offspring is likely to be very similar. In fact, like all hereditary attributes, intelligence is most similar among those closely related, and least similar for those distantly related. Figure 8-1 shows the correlation between intelligence measured by tests with near and distant blood relationships. Although we know that environmental factors influence IQ scores so that they may not reflect native intelligence, the inclusion of identical and fraternal twins with other siblings in this study would seem to bring to a minimum the possible differences of environment acting on the test subjects.

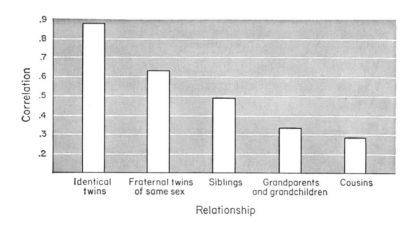

Fig. 8-1 Family resemblance in intelligence: correlation of intelligence test scores with degree of blood relationship. Based on data of Burt and Howard; McNemar; and Newman, *et al.*

Although intelligence is a physical attribute, the once common belief that it needs to be "exercised" is without basis. Not too long ago children were encouraged to study Latin or geometry because these subjects allegedly strengthened their intellectual abilities. Languages and mathematical subjects are valuable in and of themselves but neither they nor anything else can invigorate intelligence. The central nervous system cells that determine intellectual ability are not like muscle tissue. Muscle is strengthened by use and and atrophies with disuse. Brain tissue is not appreciably changed by intellectual use or damaged by laziness.

IQ AND THE MEASUREMENT OF INTELLIGENCE

Intelligence refers to the fact that people are *innately* different in abilities such as reasoning, understanding, learning, and remembering. But no technique now exists that would permit scientists to peek inside an individual's head and count cells, measure conductivity, or evaluate whatever parts of the brain may function to determine intelligence. Since there is no direct way of assessing intelligence, intellectual ability is evaluated in terms of its hypothesized results. That is, since intelligence involves the ability to learn, someone with more such ability is assumed to have learned more. If intelligence involves the ability to understand, then this aptitude should be measurable in terms of the complexity of understanding possible. *Intelligence is therefore measured by administering tests that make use of the abilities to learn, reason, and remember. The results of these tests are called, largely for historical reasons, IQ scores. (IQ* is an abbreviation for *Intelligence Quotient.*) It can now be seen why IQ scores are only roughly synonymous with intelligence. *Intelligence refers to an inborn, inherited attribute, while IQ refers to an indirect measure of the probable results of this native ability.*

IQ is derived from a test score as will be explained later in this chapter. Intelligence, the inherent native ability, is only one factor that determines the test score. IQ scores are heavily influenced, also, by the quality of a person's education. Two people of equal native intelligence, may obtain radically different IQ scores solely because their school backgrounds were quite different. Psychologists have shown in several studies that children coming from poorer school systems (i.e., overcrowded, incompetently staffed, etc.) obtain much lower IQ scores than children from good or average schools. But since native intelligence cannot be damaged by lack of use, children from deficient school systems who are put into better institutions show rapid IQ score increases. One investigator, Otto Klineberg, reported that Negro children who moved to New York City schools from inadequate southern schools at first obtained much lower IQ scores than New Yorkers. But the longer the Negro children remained in their new schools, the higher their IQ scores became. Intelligence test scores may frequently be increased through an enriched school curriculum, or through certain types of drills in subjects like vocabulary.

Motivation and general health also play important roles in determining IQ scores. The poorly motivated child or the person forced to take a test against his will or when he is frightened or not feeling his best will obtain lower scores than he otherwise would.

When untrained people administer and interpret examinations, the resulting intelligence scores are likely to be greatly distorted. Intelligence tests are carefully constructed to be handled by experts. Testers who are not specially trained may give tests not particularly suited to the person they wish to evaluate, or they may inadequately challenge or ineptly instruct their subjects. Specially qualified test administrators understand the limitations and special conditions of their own instruments. Tests themselves vary in accuracy. A qualified examiner will draw more meaningful conclusions about the IQ he obtains for a subject.

Table 8-1   INFLUENCES ON INTELLIGENCE AND IQ

Factor	Intelligence	IQ
Physical damage to brain	May be lowered	May be lowered
Poor schooling	Unaffected	Lowered
Poor environment	Unaffected	Lowered
Incompetent examiner	Unaffected	May be raised or lowered
Subject ill	Unaffected	May be lowered
Wrong test used	Unaffected	May be raised or lowered
Special training (vocabulary or reading)	Unaffected	Raised
Nursery school attendance	Unaffected	Raised
Coaching on how to take tests	Unaffected	Raised
Eating special "brain" foods or vitamins	Unaffected	Unaffected

Intelligence test scores are therefore a joint product of many factors—native intelligence is just one of the variables that determine IQ. The final IQ or intelligence test score reflects inborn intelligence that has been influenced by quality of education, competence of the examiner, the adequacy of the test, and numerous other personal and testing circumstances. Thus, IQ varies with quality of education, whereas native intelligence remains constant. Parents who do not understand this frequently seek special training for their children in hopes that it will give them a higher IQ. They do not realize that changes in IQ induced by whatever means cannot indicate any corresponding change in inherent intelligence. Intelligence is a physical attribute and is not affected by altering education, examiner competence, or test adequacy—although changing these can certainly change IQ. Table 8-1 lists ten factors that might seem to influence intelligence. Compare the real effect each factor has on IQ with its effect on native intelligence.

Scientifically constructed IQ tests should not be confused with the amusing but nonsensical "intelligence tests" that frequently appear in newspapers and magazines. Newspaper readers may be challenged and entertained by questions produced by popular writers, but they are not really measuring intellectual ability. A valid test involves the combined efforts of literally dozens of experts and thousands of subjects. Before a test becomes a test, it must be shown to measure with accuracy and to be related to what it purports to evaluate (see Chapter Six). For example, the work on the 1960 revision of the Stanford-Binet Scale actually began ten years earlier. Nearly five thousand representative subjects from many parts of the United States were pretested, and the results were carefully examined, modified, and rearranged *before* the Stanford-Binet was ready to be used to test intelligence.

THE COMPUTATION OF IQ

Intelligence Quotient was originally obtained by dividing the subject's mental age (MA) by his chronological age (CA) and multiplying the result by 100. The *mental age* concept was devised by Binet and Simon. Children who could successfully complete tests typically passed by seven-year-olds but could go no higher were said to have a mental age of seven. If a child's *chronological* or *actual age* were also seven, his IQ would be 100. The formula for computing IQ follows:

$$IQ = 100 \times \frac{MA}{CA}$$

Thus, a child who was chronologically six years old but could complete tests up to the nine-year level (MA of 9) would have an IQ of 150.

The best intelligence tests no longer derive IQ by dividing mental age by chronological age. Such division is now understood to be based on so many erroneous assumptions that the resulting IQ's are seriously misleading. However, mental age as a descriptive category retains some usefulness in helping teachers and parents understand the relative level of intellectual functioning of their children.

IQ today is commonly calculated by comparing a subject's score with the scores of others of the same age. This is known as *deviation IQ*. The more an individual's score deviates from—rises above or falls below—the average score for his age group, the higher or lower will be the assigned IQ.

COMMON IQ TESTS

The Stanford-Binet

Probably the best-known test of intelligence is the Stanford-Binet. Its renown is well justified, since the Stanford-Binet is not only the forerunner of nearly all existing intelligence tests, but also very likely one of the very best techniques now available for evaluating the intelligence of children. The test came into being at the beginning of the twentieth century in Paris, through the efforts of the French psychologist Binet and his collaborator, a psychiatrist named Simon. Its fame soon brought it to the United States, where it has been translated and updated several times. The latest complete revision of the examination was published in 1960. It is the work of Drs. Terman and Merril of Stanford University (hence the name Stanford-Binet).

The Stanford-Binet is called an *age scale* because it is divided into age groups. For example, the average six-year-old has to define six selected words and be able to solve problems like "What is the difference between a Fish and a Cat?" or "A bird sings; a dog . . .?" Six-year-olds who pass all tests up to and including the six-year level but none beyond are said to have a mental age of six and an IQ of 100. If they pass all tests up to eight- or ten-year levels, they have a mental age of eight or ten and an IQ of up to 170.

Here are examples of questions posed by the Stanford-Binet type of intelligence test. Mental age level is given in parentheses for each test item.

Building (2-year).   Builds tower of four or more blocks in imitation of examiner's block tower.

Copying (3-year).   Correctly draws a reasonable circle.

Comprehension (4-year).   Answers two questions correctly. "Why do we have houses?" "Why do we have books?"

Differences (6-year).   Answers questions such as "What is the difference between a Fish and a Cat?"

Reversing digits (9-year).   Able to repeat in reverse order four digits he has just heard.

Abstract words (12-year).   Able to define three abstract words (e.g., sympathy, inquisitive, fact).

Vocabulary (average adult).   Able to define twenty words correctly from a list of words of increasing difficulty (e.g., orange, paragraph, digit, maudlin).

Proverbs (superior adult III).   Able to explain two rather difficult proverbs. An example: If you have a reputation for coming early, you can never come late.

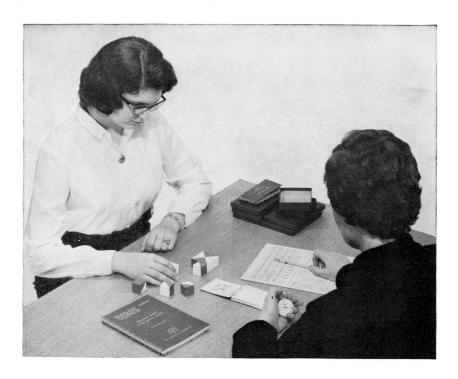

Fig. 8-2 The Block Design Subtest from the Wechsler Adult Intelligence Scale (WAIS). Photo courtesy of The Psychological Corporation, New York, N.Y.

The Wechsler Tests

The Wechsler Intelligence Scales are actually an entire test group. These tests have been assembled under the direction of Dr. David Wechsler of Bellevue Hospital in New York City. They consist of separate test batteries for children and for adults, each broken into two parts: performance and verbal. The verbal tests are made up of vocabulary definitions, abstract reasoning ("How are a mouse and a rose alike?"), and current information ("Name one justice of the Supreme Court"), for example. The performance scale consists of tests wherein subjects have to arrange blocks into certain designs (see Fig. 8-2), arrange cartoon strips into proper sequence, and assemble pictures from jigsaw puzzle pieces. In this way intellectual abilities such as reasoning and learning may be measured not only verbally but in ways that do not require word explanations. Thus those who are quite bright but are not able to demonstrate this except by using their hands to manipulate designs and make logical arrangements are given a chance to show their capacity. When a child is poorly schooled, he will be less likely to be at a disadvantage on performance tasks.

Group Tests

A wide variety of other intelligence tests are mainly given simultaneously to large groups. Tests like the Otis, ACE, California Test of Mental Maturity, Kuhlman-Anderson, and a number of others are designed primarily to be given to large groups of children for screening purposes. The accuracy of these tests is limited. They are intended only to select children who may have special intellectual problems so that they can be more validly examined with a more precise test like the individually administered Stanford-Binet or Wechsler-Bellevue. The group tests are not intended to replace individual exams. Unfortunately, many schools place undue emphasis and reliance on the very rough scores obtained on group tests, and through them parents fall into the same errors. Too frequently, children are even skipped ahead, promoted, or left behind on the basis of a group test result. That this is a great injustice becomes apparent when one realizes not only how difficult and indirect measures of intelligence are in the first place, but how especially inaccurate group test results may be.

Group tests of intelligence usually rely heavily on the child's or adult's ability to follow written instructions. One group test item reads, "Which of the following four materials is most likely to be damaged by moisture—cotton, paper, aluminum, nylon?" It is apparent that while ostensibly evaluating intellectual ability, this question, like many others, calls for highly developed reading and vocabulary skills. A very bright person who has had little opportunity to learn to read or who was otherwise culturally limited would obtain a falsely low IQ score on such an exam. Because IQ scores are so highly influenced by cultural, educational, and related factors, tests have been devised that attempt to minimize the effect of differences in training or background. These tests, so-called *culture-free* examinations, are not altogether uncontaminated by biases, but they are frequently useful in obtaining a more meaningful IQ score than can be obtained from the Wechsler or Stanford-Binet tests. One instrument that attempts to limit the influences of schooling is the Chicago Non-Verbal Examination. This test makes extensive use of pictures that the subject has to arrange or interpret in some manner. Words are diligently avoided. Some of the sample items introducing tests on the "Chicago" are reproduced in Fig. 8-3.

THE MEANING OF IQ SCORES

Largely in order to help explain the meaning of intelligence test scores, psychologists have adopted a scale of scores that approximates

Test 1

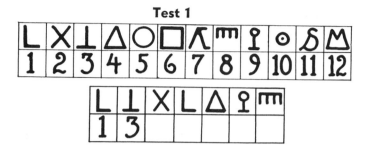

Test 6

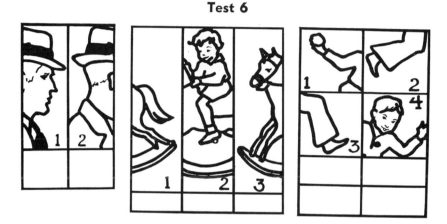

Test 8

Fig. 8-3 Sample items from the Chicago Non-verbal Examination. Reproduced by permission. Copyright 1936 by Andrew W. Brown and Seymour P. Stein. Published by The Psychological Corporation. All rights reserved.

those shown in Table 8-2. The table (8-2) illustrates that IQ scores are very rough measurements indeed. Someone with an IQ of 95 has essentially the same score as another person with 105. Despite the ten-point difference in score, little if any difference in intelligence is indicated. IQ tests are not like thermometers. A temperature of 99° F is normal, while only three degrees higher indicates fever. Thermometers measure temperature intervals with precision, while IQ tests

Table 8-2   MEANING AND DISTRIBUTION OF IQ SCORES

IQ Scores	Description	Per cent in category
Under 70	Retarded	2
70 to 80	Borderline	7
80 to 90	Dull normal	16
90 to 110	Normal or average	50
110 to 120	Bright normal	16
120 to 130	Superior	7
Over 130	Very superior	2

measure only relative rank. It might be better to say that someone's score is normal or above normal, rather than to give an exact number. Even when test conditions are excellent, the numbers reported as IQ test scores must be understood as approximations that may readily change as much as five, ten, or even more points (Bradway and Thompson).

IQ DIFFERENCES, SEX, RACE, AND RELIGION

Few topics will provoke as much discussion among psychologists, scientists, and laymen as whether or not there are meaningful intellectual differences between men and women, Negroes and whites, or Jews, Catholics, and Protestants. Unfortunately, strongly held opinions have frequently been substituted for documented fact. In truth, there is no evidence available today that will conclusively prove either that there are or that there are not definitive over-all intellectual differences between various groups.

Women tend to get higher scores than men on tasks involving the ability to define words and to use language and aesthetic skills. Men and boys tend to do better on items measuring mechanical skills, reasoning, and mathematical abilities. As a consequence of these fairly consistent differences between men and women in special abilities, IQ test differences often result. The Stanford-Binet test tends to be saturated with verbal items and is therefore biased in favor of girls. The Selective Service Qualification Examination and other tests heavily loaded with mechanical and mathematical problems are biased in favor of the traits in which men excel. We must know more about how to make up good intelligence tests before we can sensibly study any differences in intelligence between the sexes.

The difficulties involved in measuring intellectual differences between men and women are minor compared to the problems raised by the question of racial and religious IQ differences. The racial intelligence debate may owe its origin to events of a half century ago. During World War I an early intelligence test, the Army Alpha, was administered to millions of men as they were processed for the armed forces. Analysis of the Army Alpha showed that Negro servicemen obtained lower mean intelligence scores than white soldiers. In the intervening fifty years, there has been a continual outpouring of studies and opinions evaluating Negro and white intelligence. One major fact has seemed to stand out: in most instances Negro and white test comparisons have been in favor of whites. Dr. Otto Klineberg, an expert on racial differences, assisted by Dr. Kenneth Clark, himself a Negro and University of Minnesota psychologist, reviewed more than twenty-seven racial intelligence studies (1963). They concluded that whereas the average IQ for whites is about 100, an "IQ of 86 represented the approximate Negro median."

Originally, much of the evidence for lower Negro IQ rested solely on comparisons of scores between white and Negro school-agers. For example, in the 1930's Klineberg tested white and Negro school children and found Negro students performing significantly less well than white. Studies of this kind were questioned, however, because it is known that a large variety of environmental factors may affect IQ. In fact, Klineberg himself demonstrated how erroneous conclusions could be drawn from his study. He compared the scores of four hundred Negro boys who had moved to New York City with those of three hundred who had been born and reared there. Those who had been in New York two years or less had scores markedly below those born in the city. But the longer the child lived in New York, the higher his IQ became and the closer it approached that of native residents. Through this study it became apparent that IQ scores may reflect differences in schooling and other cultural opportunities.

Because IQ's are so easily influenced by educational and socioeconomic conditions, one could endlessly pile up tests that show Negroes do less well than whites. Negroes are on the average less well schooled, their median income and class standing is below that of whites, and they are openly and subtly discriminated against. All these factors are reflected in impaired intelligence test performance. Negroes, however, are not alone. All other groups that are at an environmental disadvantage do poorly on tests. In some deprived areas farm children score about ten points lower than city children. Many other groups, ranging from the hill folk in the Kentucky area to certain groups of Eastern European immigrants living on both the East and West Coasts, tend to do poorly on tests. In every instance educational facilities and sociocultural opportunities can be demonstrated to be markedly inadequate.

IQ scores are invariably depressed when inequities deny full environmental opportunities. For this reason recent efforts to evaluate Negro and white differences have attempted to "equate" educational and social backgrounds. In one such study by H. A. Tanser, Canadian Negroes living in Kent County, Ontario were tested. The Negroes in Kent had lived there since before the Civil War. The first settlements dated back as early as 1812. According to Tanser, the Negroes in Kent were accepted, went to good schools, and were on a level with the white population in regard to every political and social advantage. Surely these Negroes, it has been argued, having the same opportunities and advantages as the whites, should do just as well on IQ tests, unless they are really inferior. Tanser found Negroes consistently below whites. The average white scores tended to be around 104, while Negro scores were in the low 90's. But how equal were the white and Negro groups? Some statistics are of interest. School attendance for Negroes was markedly below that of whites. Family incomes for Negroes were similarly depressed. The socioeconomic status of the Negro families was much further down the scale than it was for the whites.

A much better designed study of racial intelligence was conducted in the 1950's by Dr. Frank C. J. McGurk, Villanova University professor. He studied over four hundred white and Negro high-school youths. New Jersey and Pennsylvania students from both races were matched for age, high-school curriculum, social level, economic background, and other relevant variables. McGurk reported that Negroes did less well than whites on the intelligence test administered. Negro students socioeconomically higher were even more distinctly different from their white socioeconomic equals.

The question one must now ask about Negro and white intelligence is not whether tests demonstrate consistent differences, since they undeniably do. In the majority of instances Negro intelligence test performance, even when educational and other environmental conditions have apparently been equated, is significantly below that of whites. The puzzle that needs to be explained is how can one account for this difference. Is the Negro-white IQ difference suggestive of an innate biological discrepancy? Or is the IQ distinction based on the mechanism of the highly complex process of intelligence testing itself?

The evidence supporting the biological intellectual inferiority of Negroes would be persuasive if the present tests actually measured intelligence. They do measure some facets of intelligence well enough for most ordinary purposes. But those intellectual aspects that are measured are unfortunately and unavoidably those most easily affected by educational and environmental restrictions and frustrations. The items on tests and their basis for administration represent primarily the language and culture of American public schools. Children from partly unassimilated groups or from groups that do not share in every way the culture of the white majority are seriously handicapped on all such tests. Minority-group children even in the same school may view the school experience entirely differently from the way native white children do. To the average middle-class white child, school may be a challenge or a bother. To a Negro it is more likely to be, partially, a threat and a frustration. Because of the inequities he knows he is and will be subject to, school often represents a discomforting source of anxiety for the Negro child.

The tests measuring intelligence are largely validated and standardized with white students. As a consequence, they assume a kind of "hurry up" achievement orientation not shared by all cultures. One examiner testing southwestern American Indians reported that she failed entirely to get across to her children that there were strict time limits placed on many of the intelligence tasks. The American Indian elementary students had not learned to hurry and were not about to work swiftly just for the sake of a test and a suspect white examiner. Of course their IQ scores suffered considerably.

In view of the inadequacies of intelligence tests, it is clear why studies that have asserted they matched educational and cultural circumstances for the Negro and white testees actually have failed to do so. Merely ensuring that Negro and white school children come from the same economic background or attend the same grade in school is not a true matching. One would hardly contend that a Mississippi Negro storekeeper with a good annual income can give his child the same psychologically healthy environment and opportunities that a comparable white shopowner could give his offspring. We are not able today in the United States to equate environment and the opportunities it offers for Negroes and whites. One instance of how misleading attempts at equating environment could be was pointed out by Otto Klineberg. In the Tanser Canadian study mentioned before, both races were said to enjoy equal advantages. Klineberg lived in Canada for the first twenty-five years of his life and was acquainted with old Negro communities. He says that outwardly Negroes were admittedly well off and seemingly enjoyed all the privileges of citizenship. Nevertheless, Klineberg is forced to admit "emphatically" that they did not live under conditions of complete equality and that their environment was not free of constraining and frustrating prejudices.

If the effects of environment and lack of equality are so stifling, then those instances in which minority groups enjoy greater freedom should result in higher IQ. For example, American Indians tend to score nearly twenty points below whites. But Indian children placed in white foster homes relatively early in life, after several years have IQ's of about 102. The Osage Indians, enriched by oil discoveries, have IQ's similar to those of whites. They, of course, enjoy a social status, education, and economic level clearly on a par with if not way beyond that of white Americans. The same is true for Negroes who live in situations that provide greater freedom. Comparison of northern and southern Negroes in the armed forces and in colleges clearly demonstrates that northerners obtain significantly higher mental test scores. Incidentally, several studies have shown that if white and Negro from North and South are ranked on the basis of intelligence test scores, the order would be embarrassing to some elements of our society. From highest IQ to lowest, a sequence frequently found is northern white, northern Negro, southern white, and southern Negro. *If* one were to accept the argument that lower IQ scores indicate true intellectual inferiority, then one would be forced to conclude logically that southern whites are on the average inferior to northern Negroes.

Although major attention has focused on Negroes, they are not unique in their lower test performance. If we were to believe that IQ scores reflect true intellectual differences, then the white American majority would not find itself on top. In many studies, Americans of Chinese and Japanese origin have been found superior to white citizens.

A very important point frequently overlooked in the discussion of Negro and white intelligence is the definition of race. What is a Negro? Can one tell a Negro by skin color, hair, shape of head, and other physical characteristics? It is generally assumed that a certain shade of darkness, hair texture, and other characteristics combine to suggest the racial label *Negro*. But eight of every ten American Negroes, if not more, have some white ancestry. It is known that thousands of Negroes yearly literally give up their identity and blend into the community as whites. If being a Negro produces lower intelligence, then the more "purely" an individual is racially Negro the lower should be his intelligence. Conversely, the more white has been mixed into the racial composition of a Negro, the higher should be his IQ. There is, of course, no substantial evidence indicating that degree of racial purity is correlated with IQ. The very lack of such evidence suggests that the somewhat arbitrary decision on the part of the white majority to treat certain peoples differently—rather than racial makeup—is what produces intelligence test differences.

Perhaps the most telling blow at the contention that Negroes have lower scores is struck by evidence produced by those who themselves contend Negroes do less well on tests. McGurk, in his study discussed earlier, notes that though Negroes do less well, the "curve" of Negro and white intelligence overlaps. This alludes to the fact that the spread of scores resulting from any intelligence test can be distributed on a bell-shaped curve. The scores at the extremes of the curve, the very lowest and highest scores, are obtained by the fewest people. Most people receive scores plotted along the middle of the continuum. In nearly all studies that have demonstrated that Negroes obtain lower scores, it has been implicit that the overwhelming majority of Negro and white scores are the same. An analysis of the distribution curves of IQ scores for both races indicates that about 80 to 90 per cent of Negroes and whites obtain similar IQ scores. When nine out of every ten Negroes have the same score as whites, the race as a whole cannot be said to be inferior.

Dr. J. B. Miner of the University of Oregon described the conditions necessary for fair intellectual comparisons in his book *Intelligence in the United States*. He wrote,

It would be necessary to equate Negro and white groups on all aspects of environmental stimulus potential that might be related to performance on the measuring instrument. In addition, and this is perhaps the crucial factor, motivation to develop learning sets would have to be controlled. The children, white and Negro would have to attend the same schools for the same number of days a year and come from the same or practically identical homes. The teachers and parents not only would have to assure an equally rich environment for the white and Negro children but also would have to instill the same degree of motivation to make use of this environmental stimulus potential. The factor that is most difficult to deal with is probably that of motivation. Negroes do not have the same expectations of achievement as whites have, not even at the same socio-economic level. They expect to be restricted to certain occupations and to be deprived of many cultural advantages that are open to whites. It seems highly probable that Negroes, therefore, are not even motivated to make full use of such environmental opportunities as are offered.

Negroes are probably innately as intelligent as any other group of Americans. It is the social and psychological climate created by the endless varieties of discrimination practiced in our country that must bear the responsibility for test score differences. In short, while at present there are consistent IQ score differences between several American groups it is also true that there are immeasurable differences in schooling, motivation, and environment between these very same groups. The differences in IQ score obtained are thus likely to be a result of several cultural factors rather than actual innate intellectual variations.

IQ AND SUCCESS

Intelligence tests were first devised to help predict success in school. They are still most widely used to help place individuals in proper scholastic programs or to help them reach decisions concerning the nature of their educational capabilities. The effectiveness of IQ tests in predicting school achievement was recently evaluated by Dr. Leona Tyler, a University of Oregon professor. She reviewed a number of individual research projects that measured the relationship between intelligence test scores and scholastic accomplishment. In general, Dr. Tyler reported a definite but moderate relationship (.4 to .6) between intelligence tests scores and grades, promotions, teacher evaluations, etc. These studies point out that while it is more likely that those with higher IQ's will do better than those with lower scores, many high IQ children do poorly, and many low IQ children do well because of individual differences in motivation, work habits, and interests.

Intelligence test scores may also be helpful in predicting success in college and professional school. The average score of college students who complete all four years of their education has been found to be 120. Of course, this means that there are many college graduates with lower IQ's (and many with higher), since an average is the result of combining higher and lower scores. Intelligence can help predict college success, but again the student's motivation, work habits, and interests need to be considered. The lazy, procrastinating student who is bored and unchallenged by his curriculum will not survive college regardless of his IQ. Conversely, there are many relatively lower IQ students (IQ 100 to 115) who do very well in college. They make up by hard work, perseverance, and alertness what they lack in outstanding intellectual ability. Some characteristics usually associated with particular intelligence test scores are listed below.[1] Remember that these are averages and that the relationship between IQ and success is a moderate one.

130   Average score of persons receiving Ph.D. degree.
120   Average score of college graduates.
110   Average score of high-school graduates. Students with this score have about a 50-50 chance of graduating from college.

[1] Partly based on data reported in Cronbach, p. 174.

100 Average score for the entire population. Students with this score are usually able to finish high school, although they may find a precollege curriculum quite demanding.

90 Lower limit of normal IQ. Average score of children from low-income homes. Adults can perform most skilled and all semiskilled jobs.

75 Border line between dull normal intelligence and beginning of actual intellectual retardation. Students with this score have about a 50-50 chance of reaching high school. Adults can perform most semiskilled jobs, but feel most comfortable in occupations involving as little complexity as possible.

It is difficult to measure the degree to which intelligence is related to economic and occupational success. It is likely, however, that IQ is correlated with job success roughly to the same degree that it is related to academic accomplishment. Some idea as to the extent to which IQ and success in the world of work and money are related may be obtained from Table 8-3. It can be seen that the more rewarding occupations and higher IQ tend to go together.

Table 8-3 IQ AND OCCUPATION

Occupation	Approximate average IQ
Accountant	129
Medical student	127
Engineering student	125
Teacher	124
Pharmacist	121
Salesman	115
Store manager	115
Machinist	110
Policeman	109
Plumber	103
Automotive mechanic	100
Longshoreman	95
Barber	93
Farm worker	86

Source: Based partly on scores reported in Anastasi and Foley.

THE INTELLECTUALLY GIFTED AND RETARDED

The most thorough study of the intellectually gifted was carried out by Dr. Terman, compiler of the Stanford-Binet, and his associates. Terman selected 1,528 subjects with an IQ of 140 or better, from more than a quarter million who had been examined. The scholastic, personal, and social progress of these gifted persons was carefully recorded for more than twenty years, beginning in the 1920's.

The children selected on the basis of their high intelligence were found to be exceptional in almost all respects. They were healthier, both psychologically and physically, better looking, and taller; they were leaders, well-liked by their schoolmates, and socially and academically well advanced beyond their actual years. That the intellectually gifted were lonely bookworms or sickly sissies was shown to be foolish mythology. The intellectually gifted were superior not only in intelligence but in other areas of human ability such as health, leadership, and achievement.

When these same gifted children were studied twenty years later, were they still advanced or had their gifts disappeared? The nature of their achievements as adults demonstrates that with very few exceptions the gifted child grew to be a superior adult. The gifted adults had much higher incomes, occupations, and standards of living than those with normal intelligence. They were healthier, less likely to be insane, divorced, or alcoholics. In short, both as children and as adults the gifted were not only intellectually advanced but were significantly ahead of the rest of the population in personal happiness, health, and success.

The behavior of the gifted is in sharp contrast with those who are intellectually deficient. About 2 per cent of our population has an IQ of 70 or below, which is considered the beginning of mental deficiency. Most of the retarded have an IQ of about 50 to 70, which indicates they are mildly retarded. People at this level of intelligence may be expected to be able, superficially, to look like others but their capabilities are very limited. Most cannot go beyond the elementary-school level. But this group is in sharp contrast with the intellectual levels below the 50 IQ range. Mentalities between 30 and 50 are fairly rare; they are in great need of special help and care. They seldom are able to live even an outwardly normal life. Some of the characteristics of the retarded are described below, with IQ range indicated in parentheses after each category.

Mildly retarded, or educable, formerly called moron (IQ 50–70). These adults may learn the equivalent of fifth-grade arithmetic, reading, and writing. They can care for their physical needs, but are frequently lacking in social and financial judgment. They are capable of performing some semiskilled and most unskilled jobs. With special education and guidance, they can keep a job, marry, raise a family, and lead a "normal" life.

Moderately retarded, or trainable, formerly called imbecile (IQ 30–50). These people can usually learn to take care of personal hygiene but are incapable of any learned scholastic skills. They may do such things as shoveling, mowing, and laundry work if they are closely supervised. These mentally defective children and adults are frequently physically handicapped. Many are permanently institutionalized. Nearly all rely heavily on others for support and care.

Severely retarded, or dependent, formerly called idiot (IQ 30 or below). Most human beings with severe intellectual retardation are almost completely dependent, need to be protected and, frequently, to be hygienically cared for. They are almost always severely physically handicapped and typically have a short life span.

Man's superior intelligence is his chief distinctive characteristic. There are many animals that are swifter, more agile, more powerful, or more ancient inhabitants of earth. But none even approaches the intelligence of man. Although present intelligence test techniques can give only approximations of true intellectual ability, it seems that within the human race intelligence plays a crucial role in determining individual accomplishment. At the present time there is no conclusive evidence that either men or women, white, Negro, or any other group, is, in over-all terms, innately more intelligent than any other group. Within all groups, however, the gifted seem to be not only intellectually advanced but physically, socially, and economically far ahead of those with average IQ. Conversely, the few who are intellectually deficient seem to be deprived of many of the other assets enjoyed by average human beings. Intelligence has successfully set man apart from animals. Within mankind, intelligence sets man apart from man.

FOR REVIEW AND DISCUSSION

1. What is intelligence? Why may it be supposed that intelligence is hereditary? What are the differences between intelligence and IQ? Why can IQ be raised without affecting intelligence?

2. What are some differences between the Stanford-Binet and the Wechsler intelligence tests? Is IQ obtained by dividing mental age by chronological age? Is an IQ of 95 indicative of less intelligence than an IQ of 105? What percentage of all Americans have an IQ of about 90 to 110 (normal or average)?

3. Are there IQ differences among various ethnic groups in the United States? Has it been proved that the intelligence of various racial and religious groups is either similar or unequal? What factors may account for IQ differences among different American groups?

4. Can IQ scores be used to predict success in college, jobs, and other areas of life? What are some of the characteristics of the mildly retarded or educable person? What is the most common mental retardation? Are the intellectually gifted more or less likely than children of average intelligence to be physically and emotionally disturbed?

Abnormal

Processes

Is Anybody

Normal?

Ever since Freud and Menninger have become recognized names, we as individuals and as a society have been engaged in well-publicized examinations of our normality. Whether or not we are normal—and if not just what is wrong—is debated by experts in fields ranging from psychiatry to theology. The resulting assortment of opinions is not only confusing but frequently leads even the most stable to doubt their sanity. Is normality the same as adjustment, or are the standards for psychological health more demanding? Need an individual be completely free of behavioral defects to be considered normal or is being "average" the definitive criterion? Perhaps most puzzling of all are the questions that unite discussions of normality with inquiries concerning ethics and values and eventuate in considerations that go beyond psychology. In the following pages the dimensions of normality, many of which are subtle and elusive, are described.

PSYCHIATRIC DEFINITIONS

A simple way, seemingly, to determine who is normal is to examine and classify psychiatrically. The National Association for Mental Health, for example, estimates that one out of every ten Americans is in need of specialized care. About ten million are considered neurotic, two to three million psychotic, four million mentally defective and three to five million in other psychiatric categories. An even greater number were suggested psychiatrically unfit during World War II, when fifteen million men were examined by teams of medical experts. For every four inductees accepted into the service, one was rejected for neuropsychiatric reasons (USPHS). This would imply that more than twice as many Americans as were calculated by the mental health association are seriously disturbed. Yet these psychiatric evaluations contrast with the relatively few people (less than one in a hundred) who are so grossly afflicted that they require clinic or hospital care (see Table 9-1). The degree of psychopathology in the United States and other countries is doubtless very great, though few willingly recognize their own ill health.

Medical appraisers are able to label people who are brought to their attention as well or ill. But, important and indispensable as psychiatric practice is, its tools are not yet sufficient to determine the degree to which a specific person possesses the multiplicity of characteristics actually connoting psychological health. In order to understand the total meaning of normality, the definition needs to be approached from perspectives other than strictly psychodiagnostic ones.

Table 9-1 PATIENTS TREATED FOR PSYCHIATRIC DISTURBANCES
(IN THOUSANDS)

	Male	Female	Total
Clinic patients (1959)			
Under 18	138	70	208
18 and over	167	127	294
Resident patients in mental hospitals (1960)	250	285	535

Source: U.S. Public Health Service estimates.

ADJUSTMENT AND CONFORMITY

Partially to avoid the difficult scientific and philosophical problems inherent in any attempt to state what normality is, the notion of "adjustment" has been proposed. *Adjustment* is defined as the ability to get along with others. Psychological health is seen as consisting of the skills necessary to fit ourselves in with others and respond as desired by those with whom we associate. Psychologists have dubbed this an environment-centered approach to normality. Normality is viewed as the ability to adjust to our surroundings even when, at times, the environment is itself abnormal.

Many psychologists, such as Dr. Abraham Maslow of Brandeis University, are dissatisfied with definitions of normality that imply that man may retain his psychological well-being simply by fitting himself into a particular culture. The sadistic fanatic, it is pointed out, who slips comfortably into the role of party stalwart in an autocratic society is thus "well adjusted," but hardly normal in any ethical-psychological sense. An environment-centered definition of normality means that a particular culture or group, whether it be a settlement of religious idealists or a delinquent street gang, is the final arbiter of normality. The society that is itself sick therefore demands that all its members manifest a similar disorder. A person who is actually dangerously disturbed—a juvenile delinquent, for example—may be considered well adjusted by the disordered standards of his own social group.

Another critic of the emphasis on adjustment is Erik Fromm. In his quest for normalcy, i.e., adjustment, the individual in our culture is led to take on what Fromm has called a "marketing orientation." Personality is shaped to a considerable degree by the demands and expectations of our social equals—the so-called "market." The market-oriented personality develops those qualities that can best be sold. In his book *Man for Himself,* Fromm suggests that the basic characteristic of the "marketing orientation is emptiness . . . the lack of any specific quality which is not subject to change." Since any particular trait might someday conflict with the requirements of the market, the essence of this personality is that "no specific and permanent kind of relatedness is developed." The market-oriented personality confuses normality with the ability to blend in with the personal requirements of the society in which he lives and moves. He loses all sense of individuality and creativity.

To what extent, however, is adjusting to and conforming with the wishes of the groups in which we live a necessity? There is no answer equally applicable to all. Individuals continually find that they need to shape their own behavior to coincide with the inclinations of the majority. A businessman or professional may dislike suit and tie but wear them because they are a requisite indicator of his position. A PTA mother may not care for the superficial niceties that typify her contact with other members, but she conforms in order to enable herself to carry out her more valued functions. All of us must decide the degree to which we are willing to curb ourselves so that we may work in the ways most effective for us. The student or employee who consistently arrives late to class or job because, as he states, he cannot be bothered to conform to arbitrary deadlines is not expressing his individual creativity. He is permitting what may be relatively petty or immature motives to interfere with what should be more cherished goals. The ordinary and everyday discipline we exercise over ourselves, conforming to what is reasonable, is called by social scientists "respect for legitimate order." By subordinating some of our own wishes so that we may live and work together with other human beings, we recognize that society is legitimately entitled to some ordering of events and circumstances. Slavish conformity is not required. Illinois University Professor O. H. Mowrer has pointed out, "It seems empirically well established that, by and large, the good men in a society are the conforming and happy men. Only by making one's peace with one's society and 'playing the game' does one seem to achieve the kind of freedom and fulfilment that attend the good life."

That a measure of conformity is necessary does not mean society requires people to become empty, market-oriented shells and lose all feelings of personal worth. Probably too much emphasis is placed on adjustment in our own culture. It is only one ingredient of psychological health. The normal personality retains his identity and initiative even though he adjusts to the demands that his role imposes upon him. At the same time that he makes limited concessions so that he is enabled to live on a reasonably harmonious basis with those about him, he maintains the essential qualities that make him a unique human being. Furthermore, when conflict takes place, as it frequently does when one attempts to reconcile *ethically appropriate* individual needs with group demands, the normal person is likely to work through and incorporate social needs and follow through his own original satisfactions. As Professor Mowrer puts it,

> In my judgment the most effective kind of "radical" is a man (or woman) who has made all the renunciations that his society asks him to make, has accepted his full share of personal and social responsibility, and then steps forward to make his criticisms. The trouble with most self-styled radicals is that they are immature, irresponsible individuals who don't want to grow up and who cavil against society instead. Lenin obviously had this in mind when he said that the curse of a revolutionary movement is that it always attracts as followers a lot of people who are still adolescent in their mentality and social outlook. And I suspect that something of a similar nature might be said about neurotics. [Mowrer, p. 147.]

CULTURE AND ETHICS

Normality cannot be considered apart from ethical requirements. Every society defines normal behavior not only in psychological and emotional terms but also with respect to the degree to which the behavior is "good" or "bad." But the definitions of acceptable and unacceptable vary widely. American parents encourage a considerable amount of aggressiveness and achievement orientation in their children. What we consider ethically desirable and healthy competitiveness, the cooperation-centered Balinese might view as an unfortunate personality quirk. The degree to which normality is dependent upon cultural values and definitions is explained by Dr. Mowrer in the following terms:

> We find that, regardless of the way in which the details of approved action and attitude differ from one society to another, there is one thing common to life in all societies. Every human society is organized and conducted on the basis of certain principles—which are best described as social ethics. These principles have been worked out over a long period of time, with many mistakes and much suffering. Each individual born into a human society is under pressure to adopt the approved ways of that society, and each

individual experiences in the course of his own development some of the struggles, difficulties, and dilemmas which were involved in the evolution of his society. To the extent that an individual is able in his lifetime to assimilate the historically hard-won wisdom of society and to experience the fruits thereof, he may be said to be normal; to the extent that he fails, he is abnormal.

Since this is a struggle in which individuals in every society must engage, we arrive in this way at a conception of normality which is not culture-bound and yet which takes due account of the enormous importance of the culture-assimilation process. [Mowrer, p. 167.]

All societies are confronted with the problems of preserving life and property, protecting their young, and ensuring a certain degree of loyalty to their own codes. As a consequence, most cultures evolve ways to prohibit behavior they consider inimical to their well-being. Sociologists designate the degree to which behavior is regulated as mores, norms, and folkways. Figure 9-1 describes the regulatory struc-

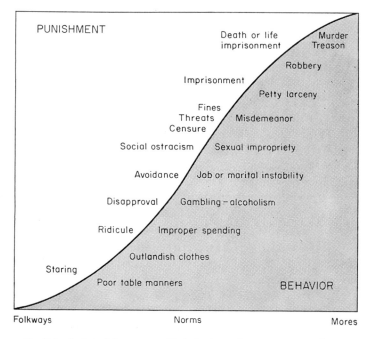

Fig. 9-1 Society defines acceptable behavior and appropriate punishment.

ture in our own culture and the types of sanctions applied. At the top, where absolute conformity is required, there are injunctions such as those against theft, murder, and treason. These morally sanctioned norms are called mores. Failure to conform is rare, and one who does not conform is severely punished. At the bottom of the list the nonmoral norms—social techniques and manners—appear. Deviation from these is considered poor taste, bad manners, or eccentricity.

RELATIVE, ABSOLUTE, AND DULL NORMALITY—
A NOTE OF CAUTION

The definition of particular behavior as normal or otherwise is to a large extent dependent upon the culture and setting in which it occurs. Whether a visual hallucination is regarded as evidence of mystical powers or psychosis depends upon whether the experience occurs among certain groups of Plains Indians or on Main Street U.S.A. It has become apparent that many human experiences and activities cannot be described as normal or abnormal on an absolute basis. Their status is *relative* to the society and setting in which they occur. But the recognition of relative definitions of normality has led to the erroneous conclusion that *all* conduct is relative to circumstances and that there are no absolute criteria for abnormality.

Overemphasis on the relative basis for assessing normality frequently results in the attitude that nobody knows what's normal anyway. Some social scientists have even supported this contention by writing that "We all need to define 'right' for ourselves" or "As long as two people agree, it's all right." What is considered normal, acceptable ethical conduct is thus left to the judgment of one or two individuals, and the ancient history and experience of the entire human race is disregarded. It is made to appear that all standards are relative, that whatever is not openly permitted or sanctioned in the United States is "all right anyway," since somewhere else it is bound to meet with approval. The view that all human activities are relative to their social context is not true. Just as an infected appendix or a broken leg is universally considered abnormal, so is a hostile mother who severely rejects her children. All parts of this earth believe sexual contact between close relatives and between mature members of the same sex abnormal. Every culture sets ethical standards governing property, propriety, and the relationship between individuals and groups. All societies regard unwarranted severance and disruption of family ties as an abnormality. In fact, the list of absolutes is endless. In his article "Society, Culture and the Human Organism," C. S. Ford lists over fifty specific acts that more than eight out of ten cultures throughout the world carefully regulate. There are absolute criteria of normality as well as merely relative ones.

Normal and ethical behavior join at the point where relative and absolute standards of behavior coincide. The universal patterns of behavior that men have lived by in every social setting have enabled them to distinguish themselves from unreasoning, unfeeling animals. These are the absolutes of conduct, the worldwide ethics, which are closely interwoven with all standards for normal behavior.

Equally as common as not understanding that there are absolute criteria for normality is the false belief that normality is synonymous with dullness and insipidity. To be identified as normal is, according to some, to be labeled an uninteresting bore. A typical instance of such confusion occurred in the pages of *The New York Times Magazine* in an article, "Close-up of the Normal Wife," by Rena Corman (September 8, 1963). Corman reported a long-range and valuable study of affectively healthy individuals conducted by a group of behavior scientists. Despite the fact that the normal families investigated were physically healthy, emotionally sound, and led deeply satisfying lives, the investigators, interjecting their own viewpoint, concluded that their subjects' normality made them mundane and dull.

What would you do if given $5,000,000? A 22-year-old (normal) woman, pregnant for the first time and living in a new home, gave a typical reply: "Well, we'd pay off this house and get all the furniture we need for it right away, instead of a piece at a time. Joe (her husband) would get a new car, too. . . . I guess we'd invest the rest. Maybe we'd need it for the future. . . . Of course, we'd give to charities, too, and our church. . . . And maybe Joe would retire and we'd travel some."

The investigators felt that much more imaginative responses came from some former juvenile delinquents, one of whom said, "Gosh, I'd never thought of more than one million. But I have plenty of things I'd like to do with it. First of all, I'd hire a French chef and get me a Rolls-Royce. And I'd hire a special attorney just to 'fix' my traffic tickets. I'd set up a public golf course, and endow a museum, and build a hospital for crippled children, and—say, Doc, do you think you could up the ante to 10 million?"

Not only were the normals alleged to have less fertile imaginations but their values and pastimes were made to seem ludicrous.

Reading opens no magic casements to delight for either of them. Nor does dining out or going to the theater. And they feel no passionate urge to join any particular organization. But he loves hunting and fishing, and spends about one weekend out of three in pursuit of these pleasures; and as a dutiful wife, she, often goes along. Then, when they visit their friends or their families, he can sit with the men and review their sportive accomplishments, while she, of course, sits with the women and confers about their children.[1]

We live in an age that extols the perverse. Yet this is not the entire reason why normality and insipid emptiness are erroneously confused. Dining out is apparently held to be a more enriching activity than participating in the spontaneous laughter of one's children. Indeed, the reverse could be true. It may well be that walking in the woods or weeding one's garden are recreations far more likely to contribute to the total well-being of self and others than discussing the drama of Williams or Albee. Whether a person reads Proust or attends the theater neither makes him normal nor abnormal. Whether a wife's aspirations are for a split-level suburban home or a New York penthouse well stocked with literati does not in and by itself indicate that she is or is not psychologically healthy. Further, the inverse relationship implied to exist between normality and creativity is simply untrue. It may well be that some modish theater and literature is produced by sources that are grossly abnormal. In fact, judging from the content of much contemporary work, there is little doubt of the pathology of the authors. But the vast majority of imaginative geniuses, ranging from the most eminent scientists now living to the brilliant minds of the past whose thoughts are still vital today, are and were and could not but have been sound, healthy, and extraordinarily intact human beings (Cox; McCurdy; Terman and Oden, 1959).

NORMALITY AND PERFECTION

Normality is frequently mistaken for perfection. The statement that no one is normal is correct if it means that everyone has at least some emotional or behavioral flaws. But it is, of course, just as unreasonable to expect everyone to be psychologically perfect as it is to hope that no one will have a cold or toothache next year. We all share a wide variety of minor physical pains and discomforts yet still consider ourselves healthy so long as our medical weaknesses are not threatening or incapacitating. Granted, it might be ideal to be free of all distress, psychological as well as physical. Since it is not a likely possibility, however, that all shortcomings can be eliminated, the

---

[1] "Close-up of the Normal Wife," *The New York Times Magazine,* September 8, 1963. © 1963 by The New York Times Company. Reprinted by permission.

normal personality permits experience to teach him to compromise with his psychological deficiencies just as he learns to adjust to his physical failings.

Lillian K., a recent nursing graduate, consulted a psychologist soon after beginning her first hospital job. She was twenty-four years of age, single, and an only child from a home broken by her father's death when she was fourteen. Although she and her mother got along well, Lillian wanted to feel independent after winning her R.N. and accepted a job in another city. Soon after her first job began, Lillian felt depressed, anxious, and incompetent. At first she attempted to rationalize her feelings as "homesickness," but since she did not seem to be recovering she became concerned about her "mental health."

Through her hospital contact Lillian was acquainted with the therapist and sought him out for help. A complete battery of psychodiagnostic tests was administered, and Lillian was also sent to a psychiatrist for an independent evaluation. The Rorschach, Minnesota Multiphasic Personality Inventory, and other tests revealed that Lillian was essentially within normal limits. She was intelligent, responded realistically and effectively to people, and seemed emotionally quite stable. All diagnostic indices pointed to a rather healthy personality. The separate psychiatric consultation independently confirmed that Lillian's personality was intact and healthy. No psychiatric problems were evident or believed imminent.

Lillian was essentially a healthy, emotionally normal person. Yet she was far from perfect. Her childhood with her prematurely widowed mother was filled with economic and social hazards that had left some scars on her personality. In addition, her fatherless upbringing made her relations with men somewhat strained and awkward. Throughout her life, in addition, when Lillian had faced periods of rapid change or stress, she was likely to act in a somewhat depressed and overly concerned manner. Yet, according to all evidence Lillian had overcome previous temporary adjustment problems in relatively rapid order and could be expected to meet the demands of her present situation with equal success.

Following her tests Lillian was seen by the therapist for four sessions. Her tests results were interpreted to her and she was informed that although there were no serious emotional problems a few "counseling" sessions might help her understand herself a little better and adjust more easily on this and other occasions. After four weeks of treatment Lillian's adjustment appeared highly improved, and therapy was terminated. Two years after the incident reported, Lillian was one of the most effective and pleasant nurses in the hospital. She was also engaged to a resident surgeon and reported that she felt "happier" than ever before.

Like Lillian, nearly everyone has some behavioral "problems" and difficulties and shortcomings that may eventuate in psychiatric contact. But an occasionally perplexing problem, or even a less than ideal upbringing or environment, does not automatically render a person abnormal.

Unfortunately, the fact that a certain degree of pathology is consistent with normality may be utilized to justify blatantly undesirable psychological traits and behavior. Violent outbursts of temper or aggressive displays of indifference to the feelings of others may be excused as normal minor shortcomings. Similarly, the disturbed mother who is rearing a troubled child may describe her offspring's emotional difficulties as just a normal developmental stage, and thereby hide her own responsibility. It is common that people seek to obscure their psychopathological behavior by arming themselves with popular but misleading mental health maxims such as "Everybody's got a few troubles and peculiarities" or "That's just a habit he'll grow out of." Such people, believing they know all there is to know about themselves and others, strongly resist any effort to seek aid, however much it is needed. Normality does not require psychological perfection, yet the imperfectibility of human beings should not serve as an excuse to resist personal change.

NORMALITY, TYPICALITY, AND MORALITY

Frequently, normality is defined in terms of statistical frequency or typicality. Most psychological traits are assumed to be evident in people along a continuum varying from the virtual absence of the trait at one extreme to its exaggerated presence at the other. Thus, the degree of anxiety experienced by most people, the middle of the continuum, is considered typical and assumed to be normal. The virtual absence of anxiety felt by the few people at the bottom of the continuum or the great degree of anxiety evident amongst the equally few individuals at the top is considered abnormal. The extremes, then, which constitute only a small percentage of the population, are designated abnormal, and the large proportion of the population clustering around the middle of the continuum is considered typical or normal (see Fig. 9-2).

The statistical approach is of great value and is frequently used by diagnosticians in order to reach a decision concerning normality. But the description of all that lies at the extremes as abnormal and everything that is in the middle as normal can be very misleading.

If all behavior that is in the majority were to be considered normal, then many types of conduct would have to be included that we personally may find morally objectionable or that a therapist might consider pathological. For example, in their studies of the sexual

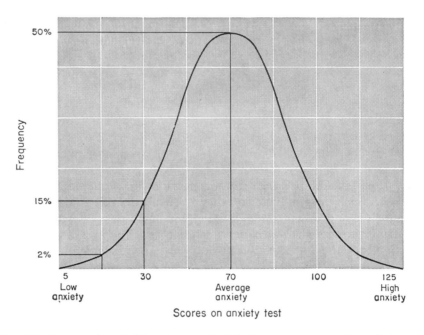

Fig. 9-2 The normal or bell-shaped curve. Psychological measurements often fall into a distribution shaped like the normal curve. The height of the curve at any point represents the relative frequency of measurement having the particular value indicated on the horizontal axis.

behavior of females Kinsey and his associates reported that over two-thirds of adolescent girls had experienced extensive sexual intimacies before marriage. That fact alone does not necessarily render such behavior proper or normal or abstention abnormal. Similarly, that an aspect of human behavior is statistically rare does not render it pathological. Less than two people out of every hundred, for example, have an IQ of 130 or more. But these intellectually gifted people are not only psychologically normal but likely to be far healthier, both physically and emotionally, than those in the majority. In their book *The Gifted Child Grows Up,* Stanford University psychologists Drs. Terman and Oden reported, after more than twenty years of study of hundreds of gifted children, that the bright child was in virtually all respects a healthy and normal individual. There is no "law of compensation," whereby the statistically rare child who is superior in intellect is inferior in any other way.

The statistical rule concerning normalcy—if it's frequent it's normal —often serves as a realistic and accurate guide. But it must be regarded with great care. Not *all* common behavior is normal and not *all* rare or extreme behavior is abnormal.

Closely related to the confusion of statistical frequency with normality is the attempt to define as moral all behavior that is in the majority. Dr. Norman Reider, a psychoanalyst, has pointed out that an individual may seek to justify undesirable behavior by alleging it is normal—meaning average. For such people, Dr. Reider suggests, the question "Is it normal or abnormal?" has replaced the real concern for "Is it morally right or wrong?" All too commonly, as a consequence, one encounters the excuse that some particularly unsavory aspect of human conduct is acceptable because it is typical. "After all, everyone cheats," the guilty student complains. "Why pick on me?" "Doesn't everyone lie on his income tax?" "Aren't all marriages spotted with infidelity?"

The delinquent, the callous violators of society's moral codes, unable to abandon their consciences altogether, attempt to assert the propriety of their behavior by displaying the supposed psychiatric ethic of statistical normality. But indecorous behavior, no matter how common, is not automatically rendered psychologically normal. Statistical compilation, as many a guilt-ridden neurotic discovers, cannot be made to serve as a substitute for conscience. Behavior is psychologically normal, regardless of whether it is rare or frequent, only to the degree to which it is in harmony with the valued needs of the individual and society.

PSYCHOLOGICAL DEFINITIONS OF NORMALITY

It is, in a way, simpler to detect psychological distress than normality. Psychiatrists, of course, are often compelled to make immediate and practical decisions. They may, because of circumstance, designate as normal even a rather disturbed person who continues to function only at some cost to himself and those about him. That is, a patient may be capable of continuing his life outside of a hospital and thus be considered psychiatrically normal, whatever his emotional deficiencies, as long as his disturbance is held in check and he is able to meet at least a minimum of his obligations.

For many, a strict psychiatric definition of normality is insufficient.

Dr. A. H. Maslow suggests that the psychologically healthy person is one who has "self-actualized"—that is, one who has satisfactorily met his fundamental needs for security, affection, sex, etc., and is therefore ready to develop his full potential as an individual. Conversely, those who have not satisfied their own basic requirements are believed too distorted by the resulting frustrations and conflicts to realize their own capacities. Although self-actualization does not guarantee freedom from anxiety or discomfort, according to Maslow, it does bring about a sense of meaningful accomplishment. For some, self-actualization may connote scientific or financial success, for others it may mean just living one's own life without being unduly influenced by current fads and social hypocrisies.

Another approach to defining normality is that of the psychoanalysts. According to L. S. Kubie, "Psychoanalysis has made it clear that behavior is normal precisely to the degree to which it is determined by conscious forces, and neurotic insofar as it is determined by unconscious forces. This holds true equally for individual acts and for personality traits as a whole." Whether behavior is normal, then, is determined not so much by whether it coincides with the behavior of other people, but by the nature of the forces that motivated it. The psychoanalyst would contend that loving one's child or mate is not necessarily normal although the act looks to be in harmony with the dictates of society. Similarly, refusing positions that promise great financial reward need not be regarded as abnormal. Behavior that is motivated by disturbed unconscious processes, regardless of the desirability of its results, is considered abnormal. To the degree that a person is aware of the needs that motivate his behavior he is said to be normal. The psychoanalysts might contend that the normal personality is one whose behavior is largely motivated by matured and conscious needs and drives.

It should be apparent that normality cannot be defined just in psychiatric terms, or only by statistical frequency or adjustment, although within the limits discussed all are necessary criteria of psychological health. Definitions of normality must also include room for the individualities of personality. The normal person does not merely fit in with others about him and conform. He has also learned satisfactorily to meet the requirements that his own character and universal human ethical values impose upon him. The normal individual is not without psychiatric flaws or even symptoms, as such, yet he is nevertheless able to mobilize his resources and, despite his limitations, work toward fulfilling himself and others.

FOR REVIEW AND DISCUSSION

1. What is meant by "respect for the legitimate order"? What are some differences between appropriate adjustment and overconformity?

2. Why is it necessary to include ethical concepts in definitions of normality? What kinds of behavior are commonly judged good and bad by all societies throughout the world?

3. Does being psychologically normal suggest that one is perfect? What are the differences between relative and absolute definitions of normality? Are "normal" people "squares"? Does normality require that individuals be dull and uninteresting?

4. Can normal behavior be statistically defined? Is all behavior that is typical necessarily desirable? Can a trait that is relatively uncommon still be "normal"?

5. Normality includes many different concepts and points of view. Evolve a satisfactory definition of normality including all the necessary qualifications and relevant factors. Is anybody normal?

Neurotic and

Psychophysiological

Disorders

T E N

170

Neurosis is a psychological disorder. It is not just a behavioral peculiarity or eccentricity. The word *neurosis* itself, like many other psychological terms, is often loosely used. Frequently even relatively informed professionals such as teachers, counselors, or physicians attach the label *neurotic* to someone who is suffering from another disturbance or may actually not be psychologically abnormal at all. In addition, there is an increasing tendency to call any person neurotic who does not meet some hypothetical criterion of sociability or conformity. Most commonly, those who have read a little about psychological maladjustments are the first to erroneously dub neurotic whatever they disapprove or do not fully understand. The classification *neurotic* is too serious to toss about lightly.

In this and other chapters some of the characteristics of mental disorders will be described. These general portrayals of pathological behavior cannot, and are not intended to, make amateur authorities of their readers. Ultimately only a skilled and specially qualified specialist is able to make valid diagnostic decisions.

Psychophysiological disorders, sometimes still referred to as *psychosomatic*, are emotional disturbances that lead to actual organic change or damage. Most people are well aware that under certain kinds of anxiety or stress they may develop physical symptoms such as diarrhea, nausea, or rapid heartbeat. Psychiatrists now believe that a large number of physical disturbances, ranging from certain kinds of ulcers to some allergies, may be initiated by chronic mental and emotional difficulties.

THE NEUROTIC REACTIONS

For diagnostic purposes neurosis is divided into several descriptive categories, or so-called reactions. The particular type of neurotic reaction is determined by the most prominent feature out of the total pattern of symptoms displayed. If the most noteworthy neurotic symptoms are severe, highly specific fears (heights, dirt, animals, etc.), the person is said to be suffering a phobic reaction. To bring order to what had been a confusion of labels and overlapping descriptions, the American Psychiatric Association agreed on the names of six broad neurotic reaction patterns:

Anxiety reaction. Diffuse, often vague anxiety and fear. Physical symptoms such as headaches and gastric upsets frequently accompany feelings of apprehension and helplessness.

Dissociative reaction. A reaction that may be characterized by a wide range of symptoms ranging from amnesias to feelings of depersonalization ("I don't feel like myself at all—I'm just watching myself act—as if from a distance"). May also be characterized by feelings of aimlessness, stupor, purposelessness.

Conversion reaction. Physical symptoms such as paralysis, loss of sight, hearing, plus various tics and tremors that are not caused by organic disorder.

Phobic reaction. Intense fear is focused on certain objects or circumstances. This may result in extreme aversion of things like closed places, heights, insects, dirt, disease.

Obsessive-compulsive reaction. Persistence of unwanted ideas and impulses to perform acts that may be considered silly or even morbid. Common compulsive rituals include touching, counting, verbalizing. Thoughts, such as those concerning sexual or aggressive impulses, may insistently intrude themselves.

Depressive reaction. Feelings of depression and unworthiness; frequently, worry over health, family, or security. Feelings of guilt over past misdeeds are often associated with the depression.

Although neurotic symptoms have been categorized, psychological diagnoses are not as meaningful as are specific disease labels in strictly medical practice. Pneumonia, diabetes, and angina pectoris involve highly distinct etiologic processes and are differently treated. But unlike physical disorders, differently diagnosed neuroses may stem from similar causes and be similarly treated. Conversely, the same set of neurotic symptoms may be provoked by different causative factors in different people. All neurotic patients, like all normal human beings, are highly individual, and their disorders can only be understood in relation to their total personality and functioning.

The following case history illustrates many of the features of a relatively severe neurosis. The condition has been diagnosed as displaying phobic and compulsive trends.

S. K. was admitted to a public mental hospital in 1949 at the age 29. The family history revealed no significant history. During the second and third grades of school "he was a problem to the nuns because of his stuttering. They would ask him to read a paragraph over two or three times." For a considerable period at this age "he felt he had to bless himself a certain number of times in the evening." When in the fourth grade and after an illness "he was afraid to go to sleep at night for fear he might die. He would call his mother two or three times before going to sleep. He would not go to sleep unless she reassured him that he would not die. This lasted for two or three months." He bit his nails until he was sixteen years of age.

At the time of his admission the patient's mother and wife were requested to describe his adult personality characteristics. He was, they reported, a quiet, serious, honest, thrifty, saving, stubborn and somewhat worrisome person. "He was ambitious. He wanted to go through college and be more than an ordinary working man. In college he studied very, very hard and was an honor student." When eighteen years of age the patient drank excessively for a period of several months. He then suddenly stopped and became so opposed to liquor that, to quote his wife, "He wouldn't touch a drop and I remember once when we were both young he walked out of a home where liquor was being served because he was so opposed to it."

In 1942 he enlisted in the Marine Corps. When, after his admission to the hospital, he was asked what prompted him to volunteer he replied, "Well, I felt uneasy a little bit with my scrupulosity. I wasn't too uneasy, but I thought somehow the service would take it away." What do you mean by 'scrupulosity'? "I was doubtful about my confessions." You were doubtful that you didn't confess enough? "That's right; I didn't have enough sorrow for my sins." When the admitting physician asked the patient about his duties in the military service he replied, "I had a job cleaning urinals. I probably was very good. I tried to do a thorough job. I saw cigarettes but I always kept on cleaning all the time. It could have been done in two or three hours but I worked eight or nine hours. I volunteered for the job." In April 1944 he wrote his fiancee that he wished to break his engagement as he was going to study for the priesthood after discharge from service. Six months later he wrote again saying he had decided not to become a priest and asked that their engagement be renewed.

After his discharge from military service in January 1946 the patient entered college from which he was graduated in June 1949 although by April 1949 his neurotic reaction had become so disabling that he was unable to continue his studies for the final two months of his senior year. In June 1946 he was married but had no sexual relations with his wife until seventeen months later.

Soon after the patient's admission to the hospital his wife was asked to give a history of the patient's illness. She reported that he had exhibited a compulsive handwashing for several months before November 1948 but that it became more serious at that time. "He used to wash his hands and keep the water running for fifteen minutes at a time. After he had washed them he would turn off the spigot with his elbow. He had to count and wash and rinse his hands a certain number of times. If he had touched the door or door knob he would go back and wash his hands again. One time he began to wash his hands at one o'clock in the morning. After we moved into our own house he refused to use the front door or to turn the knob on the door for fear there might be germs. He used to go to the back window and call me to go to the front door and open it for him. He reached the point where he would climb in and out of windows so he wouldn't have to enter the door at all." The wife described also the following compulsion: "He also had the idea that when he walked there was something under his shoe. He would stop and look on the sole of his shoe but there would be nothing there. He also worried as to whether or not his shoe laces were tied. He would pick up his foot and look to make sure. He had to do that a certain number of times before he was absolutely sure they were tied. When he walked down a street if he kicked a stone he felt that he should put it back in the same place. If he walked on a line then he would have to walk on all the cracks in the sidewalk."

On arrival at the hospital the patient frankly stated to the admitting physician, "I like to wash my hands many times a day in order to get them good and clean." While talking to the physician he stood with his arms folded in order to avoid touching anything. He readily acknowledged that he was worried about touching objects lest he give others disease. As he seemed somewhat depressed he was asked about suicidal thoughts. He replied that he felt he would be better off dead than be thinking of the things he did but added that he would "not really" commit suicide. He then added, "When I say things they have to be said a certain way. If I don't say them properly I must apologize. I do this all the time. This irritated my wife and was another reason why she couldn't live with me. I would leave my books to apologize to her. It was the apologizing that was bothering her—not being at peace. I thought if I rubbed my hands eighty-eight times, shut the water off and then went back again it would be all right. Then I thought maybe it hadn't been eighty-eight times."

A month after the patient's admission his ward physician entered the following note in the clinical record: "This patient has become extremely disturbed over his obsessive-compulsive ideation during recent days. He stops his physician at every opportunity and repeatedly asks the same questions, which include the following: "Should I wash my hands after I go to the bathroom and just do number one? Should I wash my hands when I go to the bathroom and have a bowel movement? My penis touches the toilet seat. Do you think I should wash it off with soap and water so there won't be a spread of disease? I wouldn't want anyone to get this disease. There's a rash there. Do you want to look at it? I think it is some sort of a disease. I'm afraid everybody will get it. I don't know, doctor, I'm afraid something is going to happen. I have a feeling that I might go crazy or something. Someone asked me if I thought these things were silly and I said 'yes,' but now that I think of it they don't seem silly. I just can't quite explain them. They must not really seem silly to me or I wouldn't have to do them like I do." The patient manifested an interesting inability to make any definite statement or to take any decisive action. When discussing a point he would say such things as the following: "Well, doctor, it's just like this. Well, no it isn't exactly like that. I should say rather that's a little on the order of—Well, that isn't quite right either. Perhaps I should put it this way. It's more of—uh—well, no that isn't it." [1]

[1] A. P. Noyes and L. C. Kolb, *Modern Clinical Psychiatry*, 5th ed. (Philadelphia: W. B. Saunders Company, 1958), pp. 523–25. Reprinted by permission.

This case illustrates a patient burdened with many obsessive-compulsive and phobic traits. But neuroses are not just characterized by specific symptoms leading to special diagnostic labels. All neurotic patients also share a large number of maladroit behavior patterns. Frequently, too, it is difficult to name a particular neurotic reaction, since patients tend to have the signs associated with several different types. Sometimes, because one feature predominates, the disturbance may appear to be an anxiety reaction, while at other times, when another symptom becomes prominent, it may seem best described as a depressive illness. On still other occasions a combination of neurotic traits may not be classifiable at all except as just a mixture of various disturbed patterns. Whatever the individual combination of symptoms, however, neurotics tend to have a common core of faulty adjustment patterns.

THE COMMON CORE OF NEUROSIS

Common to most neuroses is a lifelong pattern of periodic distress. The neurotic, when reporting his history, recalls long eras when he felt well and events seemed to be moving favorably. Interspersed with these relatively placid times, however, patients describe many episodes, sometimes lasting weeks or years, of personal discomfort and disorder. In fact, when helped to remember by the efforts of a therapist, the neurotic usually describes a continual lifelong pattern of maladjustment, varying only in the severity of symptoms. One patient put it this way:

When you get right down to it, I've never seemed to be all right, either to my own satisfaction or to anyone else's. As a kid I couldn't get myself to say I really liked my parents. I didn't fit in with my brothers either. And I was afraid—and hated the other kids. I don't know if I was more afraid—or hated them more. Anyway I had nothing to do with them—and got along with my own family by scrapping, sulking, lying, and threatening. The whole thing continued till I went into the army. For a while I thought I'd changed, but then it's just that things were different and it took me a while to learn to be miserable again. Right now it's the same all over again with my own wife and family—although I would have sworn when we were first married that I'd changed again and things would always be different. But I'm back to where I started—afraid, full of complaints myself, and making everyone around me either pity or hate me.

This patient's description not only illustrates a long history of neurotic disorder but also shows another aspect common to most neurosis. That is, neurosis is not limited to a single individual. It does not occur alone or in isolation. A person who is neurotic is disturbed primarily in terms of his *interaction* with other human beings. The neurotic is incapable of forming or maintaining any of the ordinary attachments to people. He is, for example, rarely comfortable with casual associates, since he is continually uncertain of their real feelings about him. Similarly, he is at odds with his friends and family members, since, consciously or otherwise, he manipulates them to fit in with his special neurotic needs. One neurotic person said, "I'd force my wife to give in, especially if my point was an idiotic one. That's just the way I used to do it with my parents. The more wrong I was the bigger a tantrum I'd have." The neurotic lives in a world populated by people to whom he is unable to relate with mutual satisfaction. He views the people closest to him as allies or enemies, depending upon the degree to which they are willing to erase their own personal selves and become virtually subservient to him.

A third characteristic of neuroses is fear. Despite the fact that the neurotic symptoms help discharge some anxiety, most sufferers are left with discomforting emotions. The neurotic is a "worrier," capable of developing extremes of concern over relatively minor or far-fetched circumstances. Sometimes, too, fear is symbolically represented by superficially rational trepidations concerning accidents, health, family matters, or financial security. In addition, a vicious cycle of fear, causing symptoms, causing more fear, may come about. Neurotic symptoms often represent the individual's attempt to minimize the anxiety he experiences. But symptoms may not only *not* reduce fear entirely but can themselves become a source of neurotic concern. A self-reinforcing cycle is thus produced, with anxiety stimulating symptoms and the symptoms feeding upon the discomfort they themselves engender. As a consequence, worry, apprehension, and multitudinous unpleasant emotional stresses are inseparably linked with all neuroses.

In one way or another I was always scared or worried. The main thing was I'd worry a lot about my health. Then having those dragged-out feelings and pains that the doctors didn't really do anything about made me feel that there was something really wrong. I had an obsession about cleanliness. If I could stay clean I could stay healthy. I couldn't eat anything in restaurants, or even in anyone else's home since there might be something dirty still on the plates or silver. Then the food might not have been washed the way I wanted it. At one time it got so bad that I couldn't talk to anyone because I might inhale some of their breath with all the germs. Sometimes I'd feel better. Especially when everything looked to be going my way. They all knuckled under. But most of the time all those precautions instead of making me feel better just made things worse. After a while all the senseless, frightening thoughts I had and the endless round of little rituals made me as depressed as hell. That's when I really started to get scared. I thought I was going crazy.

Another trait common to neurosis is what has been called the "neurotic's exquisite self-concern." The neurotic is chronically and painfully aware of himself. He feels that life is a burdensome struggle and that he is too inadequate and ill equipped to participate. In addition, the neurotic has little understanding of himself or those about him. He is rigid and lacking in insight. This is not to say that many disturbed persons are not expert in flinging about impressive terminology or psychiatric labels. Many neurotics, too, develop fanatic attachments to particular kinds of psychotherapy or marginal political or religious groups. They then attempt, however erroneously, to explain their own behavior and that of others in terms of their new-found allegiance.

The neurotic's continuing fear, his despondency, self-consciousness, and his nagging tensions combine to produce the fatigue and myriad physical complaints typical in neurosis. Neurotics are plagued by headaches, digestive disturbances, and a variety of vague aches and pains that upon medical examination are not found to have been produced by physical disorder. It is conservatively estimated that probably half of those visiting a physician's office with assorted complaints are more in need of psychiatric than physical treatment.

NEUROSES, NORMALITY, CLASS, AND CULTURE

Just as every neurotic person does not necessarily have all the symptoms common to most, normal people are not entirely free of neurotic reactions. Most people occasionally exhibit some neurotic behavior patterns when coping with the complex stresses of modern life. In fact, none of us can escape periods of tension and anxiety, since there are uncertainties, tragedies, and hazards in all our daily lives. But the difference between the neurotic and the normal person is that the healthy one is responding realistically to extreme peril, while the neurotic is fearfully anticipating events that may never occur. In wartime, for example, the neurotic soldier is liable to become distressed while still at home, in a training camp. A healthy soldier will not experience neurotic-like reactions, if he does so at all, until he is actually involved with the destructive dangers of combat. The neurotic chronically utilizes defenses and reactions that the normal person finds necessary only at very special or difficult times. The neurotic's behavior is elicited by his faulty perception of the environment and himself. The psychologically healthy respond to stress, sometimes with neurotic symptoms, but the reaction is appropriate and relatively temporary.

Although neurotic disorders are found in all segments of our own culture—in fact, in all societies in the world—certain types of disorders are more frequent in some groups than in others. In general, it has been observed that as the conditions of life become more complex and particularly as the family structure becomes more precarious, neurosis tends to increase. In their *Social Class and Mental Illness,* Hollingshead and Redlich pointed out that neurotic disorders were more common in the middle classes than in the lower classes. This should not be interpreted to mean that the lower classes were psychologically healthier, however, for it was also noted that psychoses were more common in the lower classes. The greater incidence of neurotic disorder in particular cultures and classes does suggest, however, that besides individual and family circumstances, there are societal pressures that may contribute to the development of neurotic adjustment patterns.

PSYCHOPHYSIOLOGICAL DISORDERS

The demands and stresses generated by both an unfortunate family milieu and the pressures inherent in our society may result in physical as well as psychological symptoms. The emotionally susceptible person, no longer able to maintain the delicate equilibrium he has precariously depended upon, may find his disordered feelings slowly bringing about undesirable physical changes or damage. Of course only a physician can determine whether an organic disorder such as colitis, for example, is primarily attributable to emotional or to other factors and how it may best be treated. It is now recognized, too, that many disease processes whose base is clearly understood to be physical may nevertheless have an important emotional component. A good pediatrician recognizes, for instance, that when he treats measles he must not only relieve a viral disease but also help ease some of the worries that plague both the sick child and his parents. Thus, nearly all sicknesses have some psychological factors. But only a relatively small group of maladies are today believed to be caused primarily by emotional disturbances. These are the psychophysiological disorders. They are listed here with the personality characteristics with which they may be associated.[2] Many of the symptoms may also owe their origin to purely physical processes.

Skin disorders (rashes, itching).   Immature persons, with ambivalent feelings toward those on whom they are dependent; repressed hostility. Frequently associated with feelings of helplessness, exhibitionistic tendencies, and sexual problems. Severe affectional conflicts.

Musculoskeletal (backaches, tension headaches).   Inhibited persons, unable to express feelings. Frequently come from mother-dominated homes. Highly dependent and tend to repress strong hostile and competitive feelings.

Respiratory (asthma).   Persons with repressed emotional tension resulting from overdependency on mother or substitute.

Cardiovascular (migraine, high blood pressure).   Persons with repressed hostility, difficulties in relating to people. Perfectionistic tendencies combined with high intelligence, and critical attitude toward others. If their plans are upset, these people react with intense but suppressed anger and anxiety.

Gastrointestinal (ulcers, colitis).   Highly anxious, striving, aggressive, and domineering persons. Usually with underlying feelings of inadequacy and dependence.

Genitourinary (menstrual and sexual difficulties).   Frequently, persons with hidden sexual fears and appetites; sometimes with faulty training or overly inhibited background.

The following case illustrates some of the factors underlying the development and many of the characteristics of a psychophysiological disorder.

The patient, a 46 year old retired policeman, was seen in September 1956 with the chief complaint of a skin rash. The onset of his dermatitis occurred 25 years previously when, shortly after his marriage, he noted the gradual appearance of a diffuse scaling eruption of the scalp. Some time later he developed redness and scaling in the groin, and a more or less generalized eruption, especially around the sides of his neck and in the creases of the knees and elbows. The rash was intensely pruritic and the patient frequently scratched until he bled. Two years prior to admission, the eruption became generalized. No relief was obtained from steroid therapy and a multitude of other medications. Because of a life-long history of emotional problems he was referred for psychiatric consultation.

The patient was the second of six children. His father was described as a strict disciplinarian who beat the children regularly with a cat-o'-nine-tails. Until 17 years of age the patient was not allowed to stay out in the evening without his father's permission and if he arrived home late he was beaten.

[2] The information is based partly on data reported by Coleman (1960), Noyes and Kolb, and Weiss and English.

The mother was described as a warm, understanding person who was affectionate with the children but showed little love toward her husband. The patient's older brother was a fireman who had retired ten years previously following an acute psychotic episode. The other four siblings appeared to be in good health. The patient explained their good fortune with the statement, "By the time they arrived my father had mellowed."

The patient's early development was unremarkable and his progress at school was average. He remembered that he was never able to express anger and never disobeyed his father's detailed instructions.

As an adolescent the patient was a shy, sensitive boy who was self-conscious and avoided social relationships with girls. There were exaggerated guilt feelings over masturbation. When confronted with social situations that were threatening he would turn to drinking. He stated, "I had a terrific inferiority complex and liquor helped me to overcome it."

Since a civil service position offered a secure position and pension he joined the police force at the suggestion of his father. When 20 years of age he married in the hope of getting away from home. From the first there was marital difficulty and he began to drink a quart of liquor daily.

Fourteen years before psychiatric consultation the patient, during a riot, was struck on the head and sustained a concussion necessitating a brief hospitalization. Following his discharge he became tremulous and complained of extreme nervousness. He believed he was losing his mind, had recurrent episodes of depersonalization and was unable to function at work. His alcoholic intake increased in an effort to alleviate the pruritus, his anxiety and the constant fear that he was about to die. He was discharged from the police force with a pension and the diagnosis of post-traumatic psychoneurosis.

During the subsequent two years he separated from his wife and child, lost contact with his family and lived with an alcoholic woman who was suffering from cirrhosis. There were several episodes of delirium tremens and he was hospitalized for alcoholic neuropathy, hepatic cirrhosis, and hematemesis.

Eight years prior to this consultation and following the death of his female companion he was warned by a physician that if he continued drinking he would probably not survive another year. He discontinued drinking, was reconciled with his wife and his dermatitis cleared, leaving only a few eczematous patches. He returned to work as a law clerk, attended church regularly and, in his own words, "became a model citizen." He maintained a rigid routine involving difficult hours of work. He dressed meticulously and attempted to do a perfect job at the office.

During the past two years his rash has again become generalized and intensely pruritic. His wife informed him that, while asleep, he scratched as if he were intent on killing himself. He was admitted to a hospital in the hope that separation from his family and job would help in the treatment of his skin condition.

When seen in psychiatric consultation he appeared as a well groomed, neatly attired, middle-aged man, alert and accurate, who spoke of his past experiences with obvious embarrassment. His memory was good and he was well oriented with an average intelligence and a normal fund of knowledge. He seemed anxious to please the interviewer and stated that he needed psychiatric help. During consultation he scratched freely. He volunteered that scratching usually brought him great relief and, at times, a satisfaction not unlike that of sexual pleasure. When psychotherapy was suggested he quickly agreed. It was explained that he would be seen once a week for a period of ten weeks by the psychiatrist in the outpatient department and that immediately preceding the interview he would be seen by the dermatologist for a brief examination.

During the first two interviews an anamnesis was obtained with particular emphasis on his current activity. He discussed the present fear of his father and the avoidance of situations which would bring him in contact with him. His wife frequently accused him of being a coward because of this but he could not admit his fear to her. He described his wife as a stubborn, outspoken woman who was usually the disciplinarian with his 17-year old boy. When he attempted to punish his son his wife became outraged and pointed out to him how good it was of both of them to accept him back eight years ago. He nevertheless denied that there was friction in the household and stated that, in many ways, they were an ideal family. His son had recently been arrested on a minor charge and it was suggested to the patient that perhaps he was failing as a father by not setting limits for the son.

During the third visit it was noted that the scratching had increased and there was no improvement in the skin condition. He stated early in the interview, "I followed your advice and asserted myself with the boy but was careful not to become angry." His wife had been angry with him but he pacified her by taking her out for a drive. He admitted that he dare not express anger toward her for fear she would leave him. Scratching was frequent, especially when his fear of expressing anger was discussed. His wife insisted upon knowing what was going on in therapy. He resented this, but felt he could not refuse to tell her. He was told that it was not necessary to tell her and he appeared to have considerable anxiety over this.

At work he was accused by a colleague of being a perfectionist; he admitted being angry at this criticism. When it was suggested that he deal more directly with the problems confronting him at work and at home, he scratched and talked of his extreme loneliness. When the patient attempted to discuss early experiences and relationships he was referred back to current areas of conflict.

At the fourth interview his skin condition was much worse and he was unable to attend work. He had purchased two suits of clothing without consulting his wife who usually accompanied him. He made some rather feeble attempts to tell his wife that he preferred shopping without her but felt that it was unsuccessful. He turned to the interviewer and asked, "Doc, tell me, what do you do when you become angry?" There was a fantasy of telling off a co-worker and he remarked that recently he felt resentful and angry, wondering if his increased scratching was related to this.

At the time of the sixth interview his skin remained unchanged. He expressed his fear of losing control of his anger and appeared more aware of his current problems. He talked of his helplessness and became angry with the interviewer for not being of more help to him.

With the seventh interview his skin looked considerably better. He had informed his wife that he was the boss around the house and, following a minor altercation with his son, had told him that he was "not yet dry around the ears." He appeared surprised that his wife was "snapping to," and that his son was spending more time around the house.

In the ninth week his skin improved remarkably. He related an incident with pride in which when his wife refused to prepare breakfast for him he had advised her that she had better behave herself, ordered her to the bedroom and had intercourse with her. That evening he took her to the movies and noted that she was affectionate.

He remarked that during the previous week he had been able to tell his employer that too much of the work fell on him and that this should be changed.

Treatment was terminated on December 31, 1956. The patient was seen in dermatology clinic two months later. His skin had cleared completely except for a small area of dermatitis behind the knees. He was feeling well, had no difficulty sleeping, required no medication and was much satisfied with the changes in his relations with his family and employers.[3]

THE ORIGINS OF DISORDER

Sigmund Freud, who remains the single most influential authority in any discussion of psychopathology, believed at first that neurotic conditions were caused by frustration of major "instinctual impulses." He suggested that during the process of growing up, human beings were compelled by society to restrain their native sexual, acquisitory, and biological inclinations. Emotionally based conditions were believed to result from the conflict between socially learned inhibitions

[3] A. P. Noyes and L. C. Kolb, *Modern Clinical Psychiatry*, 5th ed. (Philadelphia: W. B. Saunders Company, 1958), pp. 473–75. Reprinted by permission.

and these primary needs. In one form or another, this early version of Freud's work has become quite popular, so that parents frequently hear the erroneous notion that it is "bad to inhibit your child," and the misleading fable has sprung up that Freud said "everything is due to sex." In actuality, Freud, being a rather careful scientist, altered his earlier theoretical formulations as he became aware of new evidence. Eventually, Freud felt that disturbances were probably attributable to a wide variety of determinants. He believed that heredity, physical make-up, and many family and environmental factors combined to produce psychological disabilities (see Chapter Fifteen).

Today most authorities recognize that psychophysiological symptoms and neuroses owe their origin to a number of interacting factors. Undoubtedly both innate lack of structural resistance to stress and growing up in a family and social constellation filled with frustration, fear, and disordered affectional standards contribute to the development of psychiatric syndromes. Parents who are rejecting, no matter how much they may superficially indulge their children, tend to produce marked feelings of inadequacy and anxiety in their offspring. Social circumstances in which the child feels devalued because his own abilities or impulses are not realistically treated frequently produce severe conflicts that culminate in neurotic self-consciousness and paralyzing feelings of guilt. Faulty adjustment patterns leading to psychological sicknesses are partly learned, just as normal behavioral reactions are, through the example and psychological climate created by parents and family (see Chapter Two).

Sometimes neurotic and psychophysiological disturbances are said to be the end result of anxiety. *Anxiety* is a term used to describe the feelings of fear and uneasiness that result from a person's being confronted with stresses and pressures that he lacks the resources to handle successfully.

Frequently the disturbed person is not even aware of his anxieties or the nature of the conditions that are actually producing his uneasiness. Yet, though he is not fully cognizant of the interacting stresses and conflicts that make him distraught, he involuntarily tries to reduce his disturbed feelings. Psychological and physiological symptoms, therefore, are believed to represent the organism's attempt to alleviate anxiety. When the means employed to assuage anxiety result in observable symptoms and personality distortions, we say that neurosis results. But when relief from anxiety is not obtained from neurotic symptoms, the constellation of fear may attack, in a sense, the body's physical structure instead and eventuate in the production of psychophysiological symptoms.

Although a person is susceptible to neurotic disturbances because he has been reared in a relatively poor family climate, he will not necessarily develop difficulties. Whether symptoms clearly emerge is partly a function of the number of stresses that environment imposes. The soldier in the following description might never have produced hysterical manifestations had he not been put into a situation that provoked conflict and distress.

M., a young man who had been a dancer and acrobat in a circus, enlisted in the army long after World War I. Here he found the discipline rigid, his duties irksome and his experiences monotonous. He longed for travel, excitement, attention, and opportunity for exhibition enjoyed in his former life. The situation became quite intolerable, but to leave meant that he would be treated as a deserter. A hysterical conversion reaction, induced by two conflicting motives, the one to conform to the requirements of military life, the other to secure escape from a hated situation, provided a solution which permitted him to gain his own end, to obtain immunity from unpleasant experiences and tasks, and at the same time alleviated his anxiety and enabled him to maintain his self-respect. On arrival at the mental hospital to which he was transferred he could neither walk nor stand, and his legs were anesthetic to even vigorous pricking by a pin. At the same time he displayed a significant attitude of unconcern (la belle indifference) as to his disabilities although as far as he was consciously aware they were complete and incurable. His absence of concern is to be explained by the fact that the penalty was less than the gain, although one must not conclude that this weighing of advantages and disadvantages was at all a matter of conscious reflection. A few months later the man was discharged from the army on a surgeon's certificate of disability. Soon the suspended motor and sensory functions began to return. Persistent efforts to walk met gradually with success and in another three months he left the hospital practically well.[4]

Whether or not psychological ailments come about can be visualized in terms of a scale with one side carrying personal resources and the other balanced by stresses or demands (see Fig. 10-1). When a person's resources are low (little self-confidence, poor self-acceptance, unsound values) because of inadequate family and genetic background, stresses (guilt, sexual problems, money worries) may easily bring about the anxieties that result in neurotic or psychophysiological disorders. But when the person has an excellent physical and family heritage, then his resources are extremely good. He accepts himself, values his status, has a high tolerance for stress and a realistic way of looking at the world. Such a person is not likely to acquire symptoms unless the

[4] A. P. Noyes and L. C. Kolb, *Modern Clinical Psychiatry,* 5th ed. (Philadelphia: W. B. Saunders Company, 1958), p. 512. Reprinted by permission.

stresses are extremely severe or unusual. It is because individuals bring different degrees of strength and resistance with them that some do and some do not succumb to psychological disturbances. Just as a well-nourished, healthy person is less likely to develop pneumonia, the person who has been psychologically strengthened by a beneficent environment and background is less likely to become psychologically disordered.

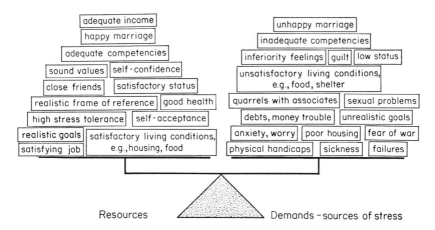

Fig. 10-1 Adjustive demands and resources. "Adjustive demands and our resources for meeting them can be conceived as weights on a scale. Moderate resources can balance light demands. Heavier demands call for more and better resources. If demands threaten to exceed resources, we focus on defensive measures; if they do exceed our resources, we become disorganized and perhaps mentally ill. Ability to handle stress always depends on the relation between the severity of the demand and one's resources for handling it, not on either factor alone." Redrawn from James C. Coleman, *Personality Dynamics and Effective Behavior* (Chicago: Scott, Foresman and Company, 1960), p. 183. Copyright © 1960 by Scott, Foresman and Company. Used by permission.

RECOVERY RATE

Unlike other varieties of mental and emotional disorder, neuroses are considered fairly responsive to treatment. Exact improvement and recovery rates are difficult to ascertain, because there are a wide variety of treatment procedures, and patients are not all equally cooperative in following through their therapist's recommendations. In addition, many psychotherapists have resisted collecting statistical data, for they have felt that the accumulation of mere numbers can be misleading. Psychoanalytically oriented therapists point out that when a neurotic patient is sufficiently motivated and continues to remain in treatment for the several years necessary, the chances for marked improvement are very good. They will attest that almost all patients who have not prematurely terminated treatment have been greatly helped.

One of the few attempts to collect statistical data concerning the effectiveness of psychotherapy is reported by Rogers in his *Client-Centered Therapy* and in subsequent work. On the basis of extensive studies and careful follow-up of patients, it was concluded that most clients who remain in therapy show marked improvement. In fact, even patients who prematurely terminated psychotherapy were helped considerably.

But neurotics themselves are frequently gloomy about their prospects. Often their despair causes them to end therapy before they should or unwisely "shop around" among professionals. There are some differences among psychotherapies, but most well-trained therapists, despite varying theoretical inclinations, achieve similar results (Wolpe). Coleman, after a survey of most treatment procedures and their effectiveness, believes that about 70 to 80 per cent of all psychoneurotics show improvement as a result of therapy. He notes also that, despite frequent skepticism, about half of all patients maintain a significant improvement for a sustained period. It should be noted, however, that the evidence for the effectiveness of psychotherapy is frequently far from reliable. As a consequence, some psychologists (e.g., Eysenck) have suggested that the incidence of recovery *with* psychotherapy may not be much higher than the improvements resulting from strictly medical treatment or even no therapy at all.

The recovery rate for psychophysiological disorders is extremely difficult to describe. In addition, treatment of psychophysiological disorders is nearly always primarily in the hands of skilled physicians. The well-trained dermatologist, for example, fully recognizes the important role that emotional factors may be playing in some of his patients' skin diseases. On occasion, physicians combine their medical treatment with psychiatric or psychological care. In general, it could be said that, like most essentially medical problems, psychophysiological disorders tend to respond well when recognized and treated early. In addition, the increasing practice of treating not just a part of a patient—that is, prescribing just for his disease symptoms—but taking care of the whole human being by giving him psychological as well as medical attention, portends well for the psychophysiological recovery rate.

FOR REVIEW AND DISCUSSION

1. What are some typical neurotic reactions? What is the common core of neurosis? What symptoms seem to be shared, to some degree, by nearly all neurotics?

2. S. K., the former marine, had several obvious compulsive symptoms. What were they? What background factors may have helped produce S. K.'s disorder? Which of the common core of neurotic symptoms did S. K. seem to have?

3. Are psychophysiological disorders "imaginary"? Are all cases of skin rash, headache, asthma, and ulcers psychophysiological disorders?

4. The retired policeman with a skin rash had a history of emotional problems. What characteristics evident during various periods in his life suggest that he may have been disturbed? Why did the skin condition improve during the course of psychiatric treatment?

5. What are the causes of neurotic and psychophysiological disorders? Describe adjustive demands and resources as they are illustrated in Fig. 10-1. Discuss the factors important in recovery or improvement.

Psychoses:

The Insanities

E L E V E N

188

We are not far removed from the time when instead of being hospitalized and treated, the insane were regarded as little different from criminals or pitiable unfortunates, and left to beg. Many of us still have little understanding of psychotic behavior. The popular notion is that mental patients spend their time posing as Napoleon, cutting out paper dolls, or indulging in "maniacal" outbursts of laughing and crying. To an extent, our lack of information is not our own fault. Only the bizarre and sensational is likely to become known through newspapers, magazines, and television, despite the fact that reality is frequently more interesting than fiction. For example, psychotic patients may be aware that they are hospitalized and can often discuss their own symptoms and condition. Psychoses today have the same status as all other physical and psychological disturbances. They are not a disgrace to the patient or his family. They can be treated, and often patients can look forward to remarkable improvement or recovery (see Fig. 11-1).

Psychosis is a term describing a number of mental disorders that only loosely resemble one another. The best synonym for psychosis

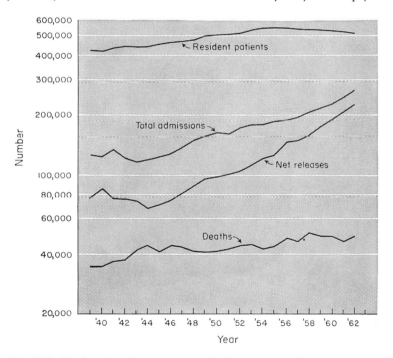

Fig. 11-1 Number of resident patients, total admissions, net releases and deaths in public mental hospitals in the United States, 1939–62. Redrawn from *Mental Health Statistics, Current Reports* (January, 1963), p. 4. Used by permission of the Public Health Service, National Institute of Mental Health, Bethesda, Maryland.

in everyday language is *insanity*. In the following pages, various schizophrenic, organic, and manic-depressive disorders are discussed. This is not by any means an inclusive or exhaustive description of these disorders or of all psychosis. And, of course, it should be unnecessary to caution against attempts at making amateur diagnoses on the basis of the few details presented.

THE SCHIZOPHRENIC REACTIONS

The schizophrenias are the most prevalent and common variety of psychotic disorder. A schizophrenic is typically unaware of the fact that his imaginary self, his own view of his personality and the world, may be radically different from the way things really are. The word *schizophrenia* is derived from Greek words for "cleavage" and "mind or heart." But the gap that the word implies is between a schizophrenic's perceptions of the world and the world as it really is. Schizophrenia does *not* mean "split personality" in the sense of a patient alternately assuming different identities.

Schizophrenic patients tend to be withdrawn, seclusive, and socially isolated. These symptoms may be hidden by gross distortions in the schizophrenics' conception of reality. *Hallucinations,* or false perceptions, and *delusions,* or false beliefs, may also be present. The following illustrates some of these characteristics.

Jim, twenty-four years old, was living with his parents before hospitalization. He was unemployed and had been unable to find another job. His parents described him as always tending to be very cold and aloof. He was sometimes observed to go for several days at a time without initiating a conversation. His hospitalization came about when his parents heard his voice in frequent loud arguments in his room. After a great deal of listening and questioning, Jim told them that a "blonde" came through the walls of his room to visit him and that they had been having an affair. The arguments concerned the fact that she had recently brought a red-headed girl friend along "through the wall," to share his attentions. When his parents ridiculed his story, Jim became upset but quickly recovered. He pointed to his own hair—actually quite black—which he said had now turned white because of his troubles. Further, he said he could hear the two women arguing over him since they "beamed" their dispute to him through a "radar-resonator" network, whose "vibrations" were relayed through the "hum" of the house wiring.

Schizophrenics may be "emotionally inappropriate." They may not seem to be feeling the way they should when they experience a particular event. One schizophrenic woman, for example, while relating the tragic death of her younger brother, giggled and exploded with mirth throughout her tale. Similarly, schizophrenics may readily reveal, without evident embarrassment or concern, details that to most people might be highly intimate or disturbing. When first admitted to the hospital, one patient loudly narrated to all within earshot of the admissions office in a visitor-thronged lobby the intimate details of her tempestuous two marriages and divorce.

The distortions of reality that typify much schizophrenic behavior are probably caused by schizophrenics' inability to think clearly and consistently in the way undisturbed people do. In fact, schizophrenia is called a *cognitive* or thought disorder. The schizophrenic finds it difficult to reason or control his thoughts. Random images and uncontrolled associations continually interrupt his rational processes. He slips into verbalisms that he himself has coined (neologisms) or tends to throw words helter-skelter into his conversation or writing (word-salad). The following is a letter by a hospitalized schizophrenic requesting a week-end pass.

> Dear Dr. Smith,
>   Herewith is presented my request for repass requass. I have long and faithfully been your faithful servant, though interfering balances have done in a pyromaniac display of passes in the nick of time which-since-it-too shall come to pass. Wordlings and pastlings, pastiching to our young and tender hearts. Lives there a man with a soul so dead. Whose dread had never been fed, or said.

Schizophrenia may take several forms. The American Psychiatric Association suggests they be thought of as consisting of the following nine types:

Residual. People who have had a schizophrenic disorder but are sufficiently improved to live in a community. Still show some signs of disturbed thought, emotion, and behavior.

Childhood. Schizophrenic reactions with special symptoms occuring before puberty.

Schizo-affective. A mixture of schizophrenic symptoms with extreme disturbance in emotion as seen in manic-depressive psychosis.

Acute undifferentiated. A reaction type frequently due to severe stress that mimics many schizophrenic symptoms but that tends to clear up in a few weeks or months.

Chronic undifferentiated. A combination of many schizophrenic symptoms that are longstanding and resistive to treatment.

Simple. Characterized chiefly by aloofness and withdrawal from human relationships, but rarely by hallucinations and delusions. These patients are frequently not hospitalized.

Hebephrenic. Shallow and inappropriate emotion, "silly" mannerisms, giggling, delusions, and hallucinations are common.

Catatonic. Many catatonics tend to withdraw to the point of vegetative existence. They frequently maintain rigid postures, or may on rare occasion exhibit extreme agitation and violence.

Paranoid. Delusions of persecution, feeling that everyone or everything is plotting against them. Many have ideas of grandeur, special eminence. Hostility and religiosity are common, as is an expansive delusional system.

THE MANIC-DEPRESSIVE REACTIONS

The manic-depressive disorders are but one variety of *affective* or emotional disorders. They are so called because the disturbance is characterized chiefly by an exaggeration of emotion. There is some disturbance of thought processes too, but it is not as extensive as in the schizophrenias. Whatever fallacies in reasoning are evident are usually in consonance with the distortion of mood.

Manic-depressive patients are commonly either of the manic or of the depressed variety. Some may have swings in mood and exhibit extreme elation alternating with deep fits of despondency.

Manic patients frequently appear to be the happiest people in the world. They wander up and down the hospital ward singing, making puns and jokes, and jabbing others in the ribs to cheer them up. They are highly elated and seem to have extraordinary amounts of energy. They may be so talkative, require so little sleep, and be so euphoric that other hospital patients complain it is impossible to put up with them. The following is part of the admissions history of a manic patient:

Miss R., an attractive thirty-eight-year-old single school teacher, lives in a large apartment house. She reported that she has been feeling "unusually peppy" and "inspired" for the past several weeks. Her hobby is painting. One week end, after finishing all the available canvases in her apartment, in a "fit of inspiration" she began on the walls. She ran out of materials and on Saturday afternoon dashed to a paint store and bought several gallons of house paint, large brushes, etc., and hauled them home in a taxi. By working more or less continually, Miss R. had painted murals on all the walls and ceilings of her apartment by late Sunday night. She then moved into the apartment house hallway. By Monday morning it was discovered that she had energetically covered several hundred square feet of walls and staircases with her unique abstract style. She resisted the janitor's admonitions, and the police were called. They took her to the hospital. Neighbors reported that they thought they had heard someone singing loudly and happily in her apartment and in the hallway for most of the week end.

Depressed patients are as troubled and as sad as manics are outwardly happy. The severely depressed person can be so distressed that he refuses to eat, sits in a helpless-looking stupor, and sometimes cries loudly, bewailing his lot. Depressives are often considered suicide risks; hospitals take unusual precautions to protect them from hurting themselves.

Mr. B., a fifty-seven-year-old machinist, was found in his garage with his car motor running. A clumsily constructed hood was fastened around his head to ensure his getting only the exhaust gases from the automobile engine. He was hospitalized and appeared in a dull stupor. He ate little, but was cooperative. He frequently sat on a bench with his elbows on his knees, resting his head on his hands and staring at the floor. An occasional tear and shrugging of the shoulders or shaking of the head were noticeable.

THE ORGANIC REACTIONS

Any disease or condition that temporarily or permanently involves the brain may produce psychotic symptoms. Many infectious diseases, including syphilis and encephalitis, may directly damage the brain. Other diseases like pneumonia and malaria can produce extremely high fevers that may provoke psychotic-like reactions. In addition, brain injuries, tumors, metabolic disturbances, and a number of chemicals ranging from improperly used medication to alcohol can also result in psychotic disturbances. Because so many different conditions can impair the normal functioning of the brain, the resulting psychological symptoms can be extremely varied. On occasion, organic psychoses may be mistaken for schizophrenic or manic-depressive reactions, since they often resemble them so closely. On the other hand, the symptoms of some organic psychoses are unlike those of any other reaction.

The psychotic symptoms following brain damage are usually influenced by the patient's previous personality and situation. A person who is somber and withdrawn even before he is ill is likely to become severely depressed when organic damage occurs. Another patient suffering the same organic disorder may become uncontrollably carefree and expansive as a result of his disease, since he was quite happy-go-lucky before his brain was damaged.

There are a few symptoms that tend to be shared by people whose psychotic reactions are initiated by brain damage. Such patients generally show a serious decline in their ability to think, reason, and remember. Judgment and the capacity to make logical decisions seem to be considerably weakened. Many patients also suffer from a distortion of their normal mood and feelings. They easily become overly happy or excited and may just as readily become morose and sullen to an exaggerated degree. In some cases too, hallucinations and delusions, just as in some schizophrenias, may be present. Often people whose damaged brains prevent them from answering questions reasonably or maintaining normal conversation may try to "cover up" their limitations by fabricating answers and events. These fabrications may emerge in continuing or wandering monologues and stories.

Senility

Some of the most common organically caused disorders are psychoses of the aged. Over 20 per cent of all first admissions in mental hospitals are for senile disorders (see Table 11-1, p. 198). Aging results in a wide variety of changes within the entire body and brain. Thus, slight declines in intellectual ability, memory, reasoning, and other faculties are common. Occasionally, however, the changes due to aging are far more extensive than usual. Much of the brain may be irrevocably injured by impaired circulation, hardening of cerebral arteries, strokes, and atrophy. With more extensive damage of this kind, many psychotic-like symptoms are common. The mental alertness and judgment of such patients decreases sharply. Many become extremely talkative, while their subject matter becomes irrelevant, disjointed, and nonconnected. Personal neatness and hygiene may also show a marked deterioration. Suspiciousness, jealousy, and even paranoid ideas are not uncommon. Frequently disturbing to relatives is the fact that many aged people seem to experience a revival of sexual interest that may take somewhat undesired forms. As the disorder progresses, disorientation and memory failures become very noticeable. The patient may not know where he is, forget the names of his relatives, and have little recollection of recent events. Typically, childhood experiences and incidents are recalled, and the senile patient may spend a considerable amount of time relating details that occurred fifty years ago as if they happened recently.

Mr. B. was seventy-eight years old when admitted to the hospital. During the past three years he has shown increasing memory losses and become extremely untidy and careless. He talked a great deal about his childhood and was confused as to when many of the events that he related actually occurred. He accused his wife and married daughter, who lived with him, of trying to "shake him down" for money by withholding certain "information" from him. His commitment was initiated when he made "vulgar" sexual remarks to his teen-age granddaughter's girl friends.

DR. How are you today, Mr. B.?

MR. B. So so. *(does not recognize doctor whom he saw for nearly two full days only one week ago.)*

DR. Do you know who I am?

MR. B. Sure. You're one of the K. boys. You can always spot that face. *(K. is a family the patient knew during his youth.)*

DR. Who is the President of the United States?

MR. B. I know! That's what they're trying to keep from me. Hoover, isn't it?

DR. Who is Kennedy?

MR. B. Yes, that's one of them too.

DR. One of who?

MR. B. *(looks at doctor curiously—pauses—does not answer question.)* Take my advice, Mister, don't you get married. You'll see where it gets you. It's a man's world. There's no work for women in it. I've done a good and respectable day's work in my life. You take the man over there, Mr. S. *(his hospital roommate)*. Hands soft as jelly. Never worked. Don't know the meaning of it. It keeps you fit. But if you don't eat right, nothing will help you. No coffee, nothing soft and mushy, anything that's cooked through.

Mr. B. has not answered the doctor's query. Instead, his conversation starts on a favored topic (women and marriage) but is quickly diverted by his own relatively uncontrolled thought processes.

Psychotic Stress Reactions

Psychotic reactions may follow any unusual stress or major change. The anxieties produced by accidents, major illness, death, or disaster may cause temporary mental aberrations. Sometimes childbirth or menopause initiates psychotic symptoms. Psychoses that are primarily the consequence of a particular stress or upsetting event tend to clear up fairly readily. On occasion, however, the symptoms that *seemed* to have been precipitated by stressful circumstances may actually have been lying dormant, developing slowly, and have been accelerated or brought into the open by the trying experience.

A psychosis that is perhaps precipitated by a change in living patterns —frequently a stressful change—and that has a partially organic basis, is *involutional melancholia*. Nearly all women tend to be a little upset during the menopausal years. A number of physically and psychologically rooted symptoms are common. Women may complain of headaches, dizziness, excessive perspiration, and nervousness. Feelings that life is over, aimlessness, and melancholy are typical. For most women these symptoms are mild or even unnoticeable. A very few, however, become so greatly disturbed that their reactions are called psychotic. The menopausal psychosis—involutional melancholia —derives its name from the fact that the female reproductive system undergoes changes medically described as involutional that culminate in the cessation of menses.

The woman with involutional melancholia is frequently described as an "agitated depressive." She is given to spells of weeping and noisy lamentation. She feels utterly worthless and frequently condemns herself in the strongest terms. She may believe that she is suffering from irremediable and bizarre physical symptoms such as a rotting-away stomach. Suicidal ideas and intentions are not infrequent.

Mrs. T. is a forty-nine-year-old mother and grandmother. She has been hospitalized for two weeks.

DR.   How are you feeling today?

MRS. T.   (*pathetic-looking, disheveled, untidy*) Miserable, just miserable. (*shakes head, weeps.*)

DR.   What's the trouble?

MRS. T.   (*crying into hands*) I don't know, doctor. That's the trouble. I'm not myself. It's all so useless. I'm such a miserable failure. What have I done to my husband, my children?

DR.   What do you feel you've done?

MRS. T.   Just look at me. Am I a mother? A wife or a grandmother? I'm miserable. (*wrings her hands and cries loudly.*) Doctor, what's going to become of me?

Women, because of the cessation of menstruation, experience a more dramatic physical change than men toward the end of their middle years of life. Yet men may also develop psychoses during their forties or fifties that seem to be related to physical innovations and changing life expectations. Sometimes the acute depressive disorders seen in middle-aged men are even called involutional reactions. They are not nearly so common as among women, however.

Table 11-1 lists the frequency of various mental disorders as indicated by first hopsital admission in representative states. These statistics can be somewhat misleading because the percentage in each diagnostic admission category is not the same as the actual number of patients in each classification residing in mental hospitals. Thus, while schizophrenia accounts for only about a fourth of all admissions, schizophrenics usually account for half or more of all hospitalized patients because they have a low discharge rate.

PSYCHOSIS IN CHILDHOOD

The psychiatric disturbances evident in adults may be seen even in the youngest children, though the symptoms that are apparent are often modified by the child's understanding and circumstances. In recent years, largely through the efforts of one psychiatrist—Dr. Leo Kanner—a severe though somewhat uncommon childhood malady has been identified. This psychosis, frequently called infantile or childhood autism, is similar to the schizophrenic reactions seen in adults. Although there are many kinds of youthful psychoses, autism has received closest study and thus will be the only children's disorder reported here.

Study of childhood psychoses can be particularly valuable, for it may yield clues concerning the genesis of these and related disturbances. Frequently, information is obtainable about a severely afflicted child that cannot possibly be gotten from adults who have left childhood far behind. The following case history of a young child, diagnosed as possibly evidencing early infantile autism, provides an excellent example of the symptoms found in many such children. It is also an instance of a superbly conducted psychotherapy and supplies a wealth of detailed background that suggests some of the factors that may have caused this and similar conditions. The case history is reported nearly in its entirety through the courtesy of the author, Dr. Herbert H. Eveloff, Los Angeles psychiatrist, and the *Archives of General Psychiatry*,[1] published by the American Medical Association.

As a clinic case, I was asked to see a $3\frac{1}{2}$-year-old white girl, Mary X., who was referred by her nursery school for psychiatric evaluation. Since her entrance into this school, just before the age of $2\frac{1}{2}$ years, she had been quite difficult to reach and unpredictable in her behavior. She was noted to be in a daze, content to sit in a corner in repetitive play. If interrupted, she would pinch herself and others, grimace, posture, and occasionally have a bowel movement. If not watched, she would wander off the grounds or nonchalantly walk across the blocks and toys of other children without realizing what she

1 *3* (July, 1963), 66–81.

Table 11-1   PER CENT DISTRIBUTION OF FIRST ADMISSIONS

Mental disorder	Arkansas	California	Illinois	Indiana
Number of patients	1,571	12,294	8,589	2,197
Total	100.0	100.0	100.0	100.0
Acute brain syndromes	2.4	3.2	5.1	1.7
Alcoholic intoxication	0.4	2.1	3.5	0.8
Other	2.0	1.1	1.6	0.9
Chronic brain syndromes	25.0	26.7	39.8	35.5
Alcoholic intoxication	0.2	3.9	5.4	3.0
Diseases of the senium	20.1	17.1	26.1	24.7
Other	4.7	5.7	8.3	7.8
Total psychotic disorders	35.7	35.4	26.6	34.0
Involutional psychotic reaction	5.8	5.8	3.5	4.6
Manic-depressive reaction	2.5	1.9	1.2	1.9
Schizophrenic reaction	24.1	26.3	20.2	26.0
Other	3.3	1.4	1.7	1.5
Psychoneurotic reaction	4.9	6.2	4.5	4.4
Total personality disorders	14.9	23.8	11.3	19.7
Alcoholic addiction	9.9	15.3	8.0	13.0
Other	5.0	8.5	3.3	6.7
Mental deficiency	4.2	1.0	1.7	3.3
All other	1.8	1.4	0.7	0.9
Mental disorder undiagnosed	5.4	1.8	9.0	0.3
Without mental disorder	5.7	0.5	0.4	0.2

Source: Public Health Service, NIMH, Patterns of Retention, Release, and Death of First Admissions to State Mental Hospitals, Monograph No. 58, 1959. Reprinted by permission.

was doing. The mother took the child for an evaluation, although neither she or her husband, or the grandparents saw anything really remarkably wrong with the child. They attributed the complaints of the nursery school to an accentuation of the child's tendency to be stubborn and spiteful, secondary to an adjustment reaction in the school. The parents concluded that the nursery school did not know how to handle Mary, since before her entrance she had been generally obedient. They took her out of school and brought her to the clinic, not for a psychiatric evaluation, but to have her hearing tested. When the parents were told that the child had a very serious emotional disorder, they were quite skeptical. However, after three independent clinic

TO STATE MENTAL HOSPITALS, BY MENTAL DISORDER.*

Louisiana	Minnesota	Nebraska †	New Jersey ‡	New York §	Oklahoma	Virginia
2,075	2,645	724	4,979	15,734	1,147	2,174
100.0	100.0	100.0	100.0	100.0	100.0	100.0
4.7	0.9	2.5	4.2	1.7	2.3	7.0
4.3	0.2	1.2	3.3	1.3	1.3	6.1
0.4	0.7	1.3	0.9	0.4	1.0	0.9
27.7	32.7	30.2	44.7	50.4	38.7	35.7
3.9	0.7	1.7	4.3	5.1	1.0	0.7
14.6	26.6	22.5	34.5	39.8	29.1	25.8
9.2	5.4	6.0	5.9	5.5	8.6	9.2
41.5	23.4	26.9	35.3	39.5	34.2	28.5
4.0	2.9	1.0	5.3	7.2	4.5	4.2
3.9	2.8	3.3	3.3	1.7	2.5	8.2
33.2	13.4	21.8	22.2	27.8	25.2	14.4
0.4	4.3	0.8	4.5	2.8	2.0	1.7
4.5	5.2	10.0	4.2	4.4	6.1	2.5
7.5	31.6	22.9	8.2	2.9	10.3	15.1
4.6	27.0	7.3	4.9	0.4	2.4	11.7
2.9	4.6	15.6	3.3	2.3	7.9	3.4
5.8	3.8	2.9	2.1	0.3	5.5	5.3
0.6	1.3	1.0	0.6	¶	0.9	1.2
7.6	0.8	3.2	0.6	0.5	1.0	0.6
0.1	0.3	0.3	0.1	0.3	1.0	4.1

* Selected model reporting states, 1954.
† Diagnostic detail does not add to 100 per cent because data are not available for certain categories
‡ Includes first admissions to county hospitals.
§ Includes civil state hospitals only.
¶ Less than 0.1.

observers and one private observer presented a uniform opinion to them, they agreed to treatment, but not without much anger toward the therapist and the clinic for bringing the psychiatric illness to light. The child was seen three times a week.

In order to understand this case X, I think it advantageous if we start with a condensed history of the mother. Joan X. is an attractive 21-year-old woman who is superficially charming but, by her own admission, inwardly detached, interested largely in herself, chronically angry and depressed. Mrs. X. was born in a Middle European country. Her mother and father separated upon her birth, and she went to live with her mother and maternal grandmother. She had almost no contact with her father, two brothers, or her father's family. Her mother was a business woman, who paid very little attention to her. Mrs. X. was left in the care of the more or less stern, distant grandmother. She was contented with living with her grandmother for the first five years of her life. At least she cannot remember any serious difficulties. At about 5 or 6 years of age she began to be lonely for her mother, who would visit her only between business trips. She also wished to have a father like other children. However, she hastened to assure the interviewer that she wasn't too distressed over her loneliness, because she alleged she distinctly remembered making a decision at that time that she would have to rely on herself and not expect love and attention from others. Consequently, she became an aloof, distant child who was no longer unhappy, and in fact was content, with her solitude. She did not remember playing much with toys. She had one expensive doll locked in a closet that she would go to look at every once in a while, but not play with. Although she had acquaintances among other children, she had her first friend at the age of 9, but was not too close even to this girl. Most of her day was spent either traveling to the homes of relatives and family friends or on long walks through surrounding neighborhoods. At about 12 years of age she and her mother left her native land because of political upheaval. Her mother went on to [the United States] and Mrs. X. remained in Europe with family friends until she rejoined her mother . . . at the age of 13. By this time the mother had suffered a second severe financial loss, which wiped out her remaining family fortune. Mrs. X. said that her mother changed remarkably at this time. Although she was cold and sophisticated before, she now became bitter and extremely frugal. This caused Mrs. X. great unhappiness, accentuated by the newly imposed material limitations.

When she was 15, the family moved. . . . While in high school, Mrs. X. met her future husband. . . . He was actually her first unchaperoned date. She was lonely, frightened, and very unhappy here in the United States and immediately accepted the attentions tendered by Mr. X. When she became pregnant, at the age of 16, she became even more frightened and depressed. Abortion was considered but rejected by her. She got married and did not tell her mother that she was pregnant. The couple had neither previously considered marriage or deeply loved each other at the time. The child was delivered without incident after a normal uncomplicated pregnancy. However, during the postpartum period she did suffer a kidney infection. Mrs. X. felt trapped by her responsibility and weakened by her poor health. She fell into a profound depression and became virtually uncommunicative for several months, suffering a weight loss of 30 lb. She felt overwhelmed, confused, and frightened by her role of mother, one she had learned nothing about in her early years of being jostled around Europe from one family friend to another. She tried to nurse the baby for the first three weeks. The child cried continually and did not gain weight. The mother finally went to a physician, who told her she was literally starving the baby to death because of a poor milk supply. A change to the bottle solved this particular problem.

Her subsequent method of feeding the child is significant. She rarely held the child to her body but sat it on her knee at arm's length and held the bottle in the child's mouth. Feeding was accomplished at four-hour intervals, according to the suggestions on a printed form. The child was never spoken to except to receive issued commands or to be chastised. She was rarely held or cuddled. From birth she was placed in her own room, and contact was limited to feeding. Crying was usually ignored but occasionally punished. Mrs. X. felt that even at 3 or 4 months of age the baby was crying to spite her and has admitted she expected Mary to be able to control herself much as one would expect it from an older child. At first, Mrs. X. told me she didn't know better, but later admitted that she and her husband agreed that they were too young to be robbed of their budding social life and decided that they would not let the baby interfere.

The child's development was retarded. Her father noted she would not grasp his finger, would not follow an object with her eyes even until the age of 4 months, and did not seem to recognize her parents up until treatment time. She did not play with toys or reach for them until the end of the first year and indeed rarely smiled or showed any kind of emotional response. Interestingly, this lack of smiling is substaniated by her baby album. Of the 30 odd pictures in it only one shows the child with a smile.

She did not crawl at all, but suddenly, at about 18 months of age, got up and walked. At this time she was put in a playpen. Most frequently this playpen would be placed in some secluded corner far enough away from the mother and other people so that any crying would not be too disturbing. In general the playpen and her own room made up the entire environment of the child until the age of $2\frac{1}{2}$, when she was enrolled in the nursery.

Speech also started precipitously. She said virtually nothing intelligible until about the age of 2 years, when she suddenly spoke in brief sentences. Bowel and bladder training was started at about 18 months and accomplished rapidly and easily for daytime control under very harsh conditions of threats and spankings. It was started under pressure of comments of friends and neighbors, and also to facilitate placing the child in a nursery. It was admittedly not starting earlier, as might have been expected from this compulsive mother, because of a lack of interest. Nighttime bladder control remained a problem up until five months after the start of therapy, handled by the parents by waking the child up routinely every night at

1:00 a.m. to visit the toilet. This practice was discontinued only after considerable discussion and suggestion, with the result that the child wet infrequently just one week after they stopped the mentioned activity.

Of equal importance to the direct traumata to the child was the atmosphere in the home. There was always extreme tension, while each parent vied for the dependent position, each one accusing the other of being a spoiled child. On the one hand, Mrs. X. frequently became angry and depressed because her husband did not help her in the house and wanted everything done for him. He seemed to pay more attention to his Service and later college work and his own affairs than to her. She felt and, indeed, he appeared clinically to be passive, immature, and chronically irritable. On the other hand, Mr. X. considered his wife's demands burdensome and unjustified.

There were many sexual problems. Mr. X. suspected his wife of dating other men that she met on her job as a model and movie extra. He also complained of her frigidity. Mrs. X. complained that her husband continually fondled her and made excessive sexual demands.

Absorbed in their own problems, Mary was frequently made the object of both the parents' anger but was oftener ignored. As soon as possible, the child was placed in a nursery at the age of 2 years 3 months. For the next nine months the increasing complaints made by the nursery were considered the result of adjustment to a new environment and went neglected. In the summer, when the child was 3 years old, the parents borrowed money from the senior Mr. X., a physician, withdrew the child from the nursery, placed her in the care of the maternal grandmother, and went on a trip to Europe in an effort to save the failing marriage, as had been suggested in a consultation by a psychologist. Upon their return in the fall the child was again placed in the nursery, and it was this institution that insisted on a psychiatric evaluation. As previously stated, the parents saw absolutely no basis for such a request, but conceded that something was wrong. They concluded it was her hearing and took her to the pediatric clinic. Of interest is the continuing opinion of the maternal grandmother that Mary is a perfectly normal child, not very different from the way she remembered her own daughter, Joan, at the same age. I first interviewed Mary when she was 3 years 9 months old, and the following is a report of this interview.

"The child and her father were greeted in the waiting room. The first thing that impressed me was the father's own lack of emotional tone and his rather abrupt, unfriendly manner. As for the child, she hardly seemed to notice me, even when the father called her attention to my presence. I took her hand, and she went with me without any complaints whatsoever and without looking up to see who was taking her where. By error I opened the wrong door leading into a small foyer containing a wash basin. She went up and looked into it, saying to herself, 'I can't wash my hands.' She repeated this several times, but the meaning of the communication could not be ascertained. We then found a playroom, and she expressed no emotion either of delight or unpleasantness upon entering the room. She first took up the doll and kept saying over and over again, 'Close your eyes.' I asked her whether or not the doll was sleepy, but she did not answer. She rapidly fingered several other objects, occasionally staring at one for several seconds in a somewhat manneristic way. Often she would look up at me without changing her distant expression and stare into my face for 15 or 20 seconds. She then discovered two holes in the floor and peered down through them to the ground below. She found a long piece of plastic that would pass through the hole but would not put it through herself and pulled me toward the hole, indicating to me by pointing that she wanted me to do it. I said, 'Oh, you want me to push it through,' and she repeated my words. When I did so, she quickly went to the hole, looked down at it, and stared into it, mumbling incoherently to herself for several minutes. She then found another object and asked me to push it through. Immediately after I did this, and while I still was stooped over, she put her hands on the back of my neck and with remarkable strength tried to push my head toward the hole. I complied, but later she would not let me up. I finally had to restrain her. After I did this, she came up to me and stared into my face. Suddenly she began slapping me violently saying, 'Cry; I want you to cry.' When I told her that I thought she might be angry with me, she slapped me again. She stopped for a few moments and then struck me, saying, 'Cry, bad Daddy; cry.' She stopped spontaneously. Before I could again restrain her, she went to the door, saying monotonously, 'I have to see Daddy.' I asked her to come back and continue playing, and she did. She pushed a toy steamroller around for awhile and then discovered a small closet. She got inside and asked me to close the door. As soon as I closed the door, she pushed it open, indicating to me that I should close it again. All the time she kept mumbling something. She then got out and began to sing a song in a remarkably melodic voice about a pussy cat. She did not change her facial expression. It was just as if someone was animating a wooden doll. I joined her in singing, and this possibly pleased her, although in keeping with the remarkably reduced affect of this child, this pleasure was barely perceptible. She went on to play with a little doll and kept telling it to shut its eyes and asked me to shut the doll's eyes. I again tried to engage her in play, but when I could not do as she asked (as the doll was broken) she ignored me. She played with this doll over and over again in a very repetitive way, trying to make the lids function. I put some clay over the doll's eyes to simulate lids, and she took this up and added more clay. Several of my verbalizations were echod verbatim by the child several times without her apparently understanding them. When I told her our time together was up and we had to go, she made no response but continued playing. When I took the toy from her, saying we would have to put it away, she became very angry—resisted and tried to pinch me. I put her hand in mind, and she suddenly stopped. It seemed that placing her hand in mine was a signal for her to obey any commands. In the hall she said, 'I want a drink,' but spent most of the time sucking at the stream and rolling her tongue around on it. She spashed some of the water on me in a disjointed way, without any obvious playful, or even angry, intentions. During none of these maneuvers did her facial expression change. When I brought her back to the waiting room, she did not appear to be particularly affected one way or the other by seeing her father. When he approached her, she said, 'No' and sat down on the bench. She then asked 'Where are we going?' He roughly picked her up, and for perhaps 30 seconds she stiffly retained her sitting posture. He then answered her question in a sarcastic manner by saying 'Maybe we'll go to the race track.' Again I was struck by the hostile, anxious manner of the father. He did not produce even the conventional smile when I offered to shake hands with him upon leaving."

Over the next few weeks I came to appreciate the marked autism of this child, which on the first interview was only suspected, since she did react somewhat to me. Her useful vocabulary was limited to perhaps 20 or 25 words, employed to order me around as though I were an automaton. There was little two-way communication via play or words. After several visits she allowed me to carry her, and she soon began rubbing her cheek and lips on my face. She seemed to be functioning on a gross body contact level, and I decided to invade her autistic world on this level. I noticed she liked the feel of water on her tongue, and I fed her from my fingers by letting the water drip off onto her tongue. This permitted the first real contact with the child. I noticed that she also liked to fly through the air into my arms from the bench top, and I permitted this also, although it was months before she recognized who was catching her. One time she jumped at me, even though I had my back turned. I carefully explained the front from the back of me, and she echoed my words for a few weeks each time that she would jump.

She was preoccupied with spinning objects, although she herself did not whirl. I had to keep a top going the entire hour, even though she was afraid of it. Later, when I repeated explanation and demonstrations of the innocuousness of the top, she conquered her fear and no longer insisted on this activity but replaced it with the revolving record turntable.

Her play was highly compulsive and repetitive. If I interrupted her, she would pinch herself and, later in therapy, the therapist. Often she would posture and grimace as a reaction to this interruption, although occasionally she did this spontaneously. Her poor delineation of her body awareness and boundaries was graphically demonstrated one day when she accidentally pinched her finger severely enough to leave a welt. She hardly seemed to feel it and told me, "You hurt yourself; cry." I pointed out directly to her that it was her finger that was hurt and not mine, but she monotonously repeated this request until I finally simulated crying, after telling her I would pretend because she wanted me to.

Her aggressive acts toward herself and the therapist presented a difficult problem. With a few exceptions, the early aggression was self-directed and appeared to be related to anger arising out of frustration of this or that wish. Apparently, she could select only herself as an object for this hostility, since from the history the parents severely punished her hostile acts toward adults. At first I encouraged her to direct her aggression outward, and it took the form of pinching, striking, and kicking the dolls. In an unwary moment the therapist became the target for these assaults but, fortunately, it was not difficult to direct it toward the life-sized dummies. Through constant verbal repetition of her actions, I tried to give her words for her feelings, such as "I made you angry, Mary, because I wouldn't let you break the toy." When I felt she mastered the concept (and this took months), I added, "You pinched me because you were angry with me," and even later I said, "That hurt, and you can tell me when you are angry." After several months the aggression became a minor problem. Now when she is angry she will say, "Go away," or she will announce her departure into another playroom.

The child reacted to my efforts to help her control her other impulsive behavior in an interesting way, exemplified by the following part of the 24th hour.

"I told her that we had to leave the xylophone in the room so that other little girls and boys could play with it. I said that it would be there if she wanted it the following day. She stood in the middle of the room with the toy clutched tightly in her hand. Her countenance suggested that she was working very hard at overwhelming her impulse to keep the toy (she had previously not been able to give a favorite object up). Then suddenly she ran over to the desk and put it down. This new control seemed to release a great deal of energy. As soon as she put the xylophone down, she dropped her tense expression and jumped up and down excitedly. I told her that I knew how difficult it was for her to give up things that she liked. I commended her by saying, 'My, you're getting to be a big girl now.' In the hall she had me hold her up to the fountain, and she rolled her tongue and face in the water. It seemed as if she needed this immediate gratification to make up for the deprivation of the previous incident. In the waiting room she hugged me and said goodbye."

As with any child, limit setting is a continuous process, and this is so with Mary too, but it has ceased to be a problem per se.

The child's grimacing and posturing was at first a complete enigma to me, but gradually I noticed she responded this way to any overwhelming emotion, even if it was a pleasurable one. Of perhaps greater significance was the suggestion that she also had this reaction to uncomfortable internal somatic stress, such as abdominal distress due to gas, but often not to external painful injury.

After failing in my attempts to understand the specific symbolic meaning of the various facial and body postures, I decided to approach it from a different point of view. I felt that if I could make the child aware of these movements and then bring them under her control, preferably in the form of words, she might be encouraged to give them up. This was done by a combination of techniques, exemplified by the following comments I made to the child in briefer sentences over several months. "My, Mary, you got real excited again"; then I imitated her gestures and tried to make a game out of it. When I made contact with her, I would usually say "That was a real funny face, wasn't it?" After about 50 such efforts, this behavior virtually disappeared. Recently the child aborted an attack herself, saying, "I'm making my funny faces again," followed by engaging me in a game of mutual imitation of the specific gesture.

Her difficulties in abstracting ideas and organizing thoughts have yielded steadily, though very slowly, to persistent verbalization of her actions and attempts at simple integration. An example of this defect and the child's reaction to my therapeutic efforts follows in this excerpt from her 32nd hour. "She asked me to play the record machine. The machine was in the playroom, but I could not find the records. I told her we had no records and therefore could not play the machine. She did not seem to comprehend that the records were needed to make the instrument function, even though she herself had put records on many times before. I told her that the records were needed to make music, and she kept saying, 'Let's go find the record machine' in a monotonous whine, even though it was directly in front of her and I had informed her of this. It seemed that her concept of the record machine was records plus the machine, and if one part was missing the entire thing was missing. I continued to explain to her what the situation was, over and over again. Eventually she began to show some sign of understanding when I discovered that holding her close and speaking softly in her ear seemed to reach her more effectively. When she finally comprehended what I was trying to tell her, she became elated, jumped up and down, and began kissing me. She repeated to me several times, 'We need the records to play the record machine!' "

This kind of rapid comprehension was somewhat unusual. More characteristically, she would at first merely echo my words of explanation or clarification concerning a particular concept without really understanding. Then gradually, after several weeks of repeating the same idea, she would come to have a useful, though stilted, verbal and intellectual grasp of that concept. However, even recently I failed in an attempt to convince her that the painted cane on a life-sized dummy could not be taken from the clown and given to her, even though I took her hand and ran it over the surface to show her that it was not three-dimensional.

Another area of severe pathology in which she has improved somewhat is that of her distorted, disjointed body image, as exemplified by the following excerpt: "She tried to dismember a doll. I told her the doll's arms did not come off. She then grasped her own head and said, 'It won't come off,' and I assured her that it wouldn't. She then grasped my head and said questioningly, 'It won't come off?' I said, 'No, it would not' and assured her that her neck or head would not come off either. She seemed very pleased and reassured." This behavior was common in the first 50 hours, but the following excerpt from the 56th hour further demonstrates her improvement.

"She engaged me in tracing out her hand, and then mine, on paper. At first this pleased her, but as she stared at it, she appeared worried. She looked first at the tracing and then at her hand and said, pointing to the outline, 'That's my hand.' I explained to her that it was only an outline and that she still had her hand. Later on, she said that her hand was hers, her eyes were hers, her hair was hers, and her body was hers. I agreed to all of these, and she again seemed pleased and said this over and over again. I gave her a piece of candy as a present to link the reconsolidation of body image with a gratifying experience. She then had me trace out my own hand and then her feet." Her father subsequently told me that he liked to play a game with her in which he would play at taking her nose. He wanted to know whether this was all right, since he noted that Mary would become extremely anxious and could not be convinced that her father really did not have her nose. He was asked not to engage her in such play, after explaining to him the reasons behind such a prohibition.

Building on this basic delineation of body image and body boundary, I taught her the idea of possession, of what was hers and what was someone else's. With this came an early stilted appreciation of the meaning of an exchange of gifts, a concept of differentiation from the environment that had been entirely absent before.

As the child has become increasingly more integrated, she has developed neurotic-like symptoms. In general, these are mild compulsions and phobias, which are clearly different from the stereotyped play and terror reactions related to her previous severe autistic state. I feel that now that some of the chaos is gone, her formerly vaguely perceived conflicts have begun to flow in more orderly and understandable channels. For instance, for months, with tense countenance, she would suddenly pinch the nipples and genital areas of the dolls or herself. After months of doing this without comment, she began saying along with this activity, "Pinch Mommie's titties," or "Pinch Mommie's potty," or "Mommie's potty hurts." Only recently, when she asked me to make the father doll do this to the mother doll did the meaning become clear. I told her that Daddy wasn't really pinching or hurting Mommie, he was just touching her because he loved her. The child responded to this interpretation, that is that the child misconstrued love play between the parents, by showing an initial elation, followed by gradual decrease of this activity. Interestingly, I obtained recent information that Mr. X. used to follow his wife around the house continually fondling her despite her angry complaints.

I wish to conclude the presentation of the clinical material with another example of the child's increasing abilities to express her problem in play. An example which I feel dramatically states what I consider a major, if not central area of frustration was taken from the 71st hour.

"The child said that she wanted to go into my office to feel the cool air, i.e., my air conditioner. I took her into the office and immediately she asked me to shut the lights off. Since my office windows are lined with aluminum foil, it was quite dark. She was not frightened but asked me to put the lights back on again. There then followed a period of having me put the lights on and off at her command. This really excited her and she began shouting the commands 'on' and 'off.' Then she finally asked me to keep the lights off, saying that she was going to sleep and she crept into my lap with her head on my chest. She asked me to cover her, and I did so with a large clinic coat. She lay in a prone position on my lap and moved her head from one side of my chest to the other, making sucking sounds. She then took my arm and put it around her as though she wanted me to hold her tight. She continued her apparent simulated nursing for a few minutes, then rested her head on my shoulder, and appeared to be relaxed. She said: 'Hi, Dr. Eveloff'; as I noted before, this was her way of getting re-assurance that she was not doing something wrong, and I said 'Hi, Mary.' She looked up at me, and her face reflected the very essence of satisfaction. She put her head on my chest and mumbled to herself. I was able to decipher 'Go to sleep, sun,' 'Go to sleep, grass,' 'Go to sleep, house,' from her continuous stream of softly spoken words. After 10 minutes of this activity she asked me to open and shut the door much as she had done with the closet door in the playroom. I could not help feeling that for the purpose of mastery the child was actively reenacting passively endured early frustrations centering about her oral deprivation and her isolation. The child's actions did not appear to have sexual significance, although this has to be considered a possibility. The father reported that at home the child appeared to him to be more human every day."

.   .   .   .   .

It is quite possible that Mary was born with a primordial ego defect, since her father noted that she had no grasp reflex, even in the first weeks of life. However, although he noticed it early, he cannot say whether she had the defect at birth. But perhaps we do not need to rely too heavily on inborn aberrations for an explanation of her difficulties. Her first experience with her mother was maximally traumatic. Even if we allow that the child could not appreciate Mrs. X.'s profound depression and admitted rejection of the child, we know that Mary at least sustained the important frustration of her oral needs. If you will remember, she was literally starved during her first three weeks of life. This kind of somatic insult is important for several reasons. When the baby's attention is constantly directed toward its body for reasons of illness, injury, or unsatisfied drives, little energy is left over for investment in recognizing or loving its mother or becoming familiar with the surroundings. Also, when the mother cannot or will not serve as an organizer or buffer against inner and outer tensions, the child is thrown by these tensions into an affectomotor rage, which, if not relieved, results in a stage of organismic stress and even stupor. We learn that this did happen to Mary, not only in her neonatal starvation period but even later, when she was put in her room and allowed to cry without the mother's ministrations. Therefore the normal autistic phase of infancy, which usually ends at 3 months, when the baby dimly begins to recognize the mother's breast, face, and hands, became permanent; i.e., the child's perceptual system, and hence the mother as an object, never fully became invested with mental energy. In short, this infant could not use the mother for normal symbiotic purposes and turned away from or ignored this first frustrating human being and all subsequent human beings. Coupled with the above traumata was the lack of opportunity to develop body boundaries. The development of a body image is more dependent on the early proprioceptive stimuli, such as deep pressure, warmth, and kinesthetic experience supplied by the environment, than it is on the function of the distance perceptors (i.e., eye, ear, nose) that the child is born with. As you recall, when Mrs. X. finally solved the feeding problem, instead of recouping these lost experiences for the baby, she then took the child from the breast and fed her on her knees. Rarely ever again was Mary held close to her body. This body image defect probably caused a poor concept of a sense of self. Briefly, a sense of self apparently depends a good deal on the integration of the body image with properly cathected, well-functioning distance receptors of sound, sight, and smell. This integration occurs at about the age of 3, when the child begins to refer to its mirror image as "That's me" or uses "I" in conversation. Mary lost out not only on these components of a sense of self but also on the necessary stable mental picture of a gratifying, consistent mother.

As if these psychological insults were not enough, the child was subjected to the equivalent of a sensory isolation experiment, even up to the age of $2\frac{1}{2}$ when she was placed in the nursery. If you remember, she was rarely spoken to except to be given orders or to be chastised. Little attempt was made, either in action or in words, to organize or explain even the restricted world around her. Until her nursery experience, she spent the majority of her early days surrounded by the four walls of her room or tucked away in the corner of the yard. Both these experiences yielded a limited amount of meaningful visual and auditory stimuli. If she came away from her infancy with any concept of the self apart from the world, it was lost, since this kind of isolation left only herself on which to discharge her few libidinal and many aggressive drives. Even the relatively intact adult can lose the organization of thought processes and appear schizophrenic if subjected to deprivation of meaningful sensory input.

And thus Mary came to the clinic relatively isolated from reality, existing almost totally in her own autistic world. The contact she did have served mainly to avoid intrusion by others into this world or to get her the things she needed to maintain it. . . .

If one inclusive statement concerning the early pathological relationships between mother and child can be made at all, it is this: Prior to treatment, Mrs. X. either did not know how to or was not able to communicate a feeling of love to her child.

And now permit me one final question; "What will happen to Mary?" . . . Mary has suffered greatly from the end-result of two or more generations of frozen existence in an emotional Antarctica. It is certainly impossible to accurately predict what the prognosis is for this particular child. There is no question that she has improved greatly, and there is considerable evidence to support the contention that this improvement is the result of psychiatric treatment both with the child and with her parents.

THE CAUSES OF PSYCHOSES

The causes of psychoses are complex and baffling. Some specific disorders, such as the rare Huntington's Chorea, are due primarily to genetic defect. But the simple notion that all psychoses are hereditary is probably inaccurate. Similarly inadequate, however, is the more recently accepted belief that all psychoses are caused exclusively by deficient child-rearing practices. In most instances components of both heredity and family milieu may jointly produce the personality structure that becomes psychotic.

The search for the causes of psychosis has frequently centered about schizophrenia, because it is one of the most prevalent of all disorders. Many researchers have demonstrated that schizophrenic patients tend to have parents who drastically neglected or rejected them as children. Schizophrenics typically come from homes where they have been painfully deprived of even the meagerest warmth, affection, and attention normally provided by mothers and fathers (Jackson, 1960), as is evident in the preceding case described by Dr. Eveloff. At the same time that evidence accumulates for the environmental basis of schizophrenia, however, a great deal of data suggests that the disorder is produced by a variety of chemical and hereditary factors. One investigator, Franz Kallman, has attempted to show that the chances of developing schizophrenia increase in direct proportion to the degree of blood relationship to a known schizophrenic. Data not yet complete enough to establish definitive relationships suggest that if one of a pair of identical twins has schizophrenia, the chances are 86 per cent that the other will also. Among fraternal twins, the likelihood of the second twin having schizophrenia drops to 15 per cent. Adding strength to the importance of hereditary factors, Kallman also reports that if one parent is schizophrenic, children have a probability of developing the disorder nineteen times greater than that of the general population.

There is growing belief, too, that schizophrenia as well as several other psychotic reactions may result from disturbances in the body's own production of certain chemical and regulatory hormones. In one recent compilation of research on the genesis of schizophrenia (Rinkel and Denber), several chemicals ranging from adrenaline-related substances to a compound named serotonin were identified as uniquely present in schizophrenics.

At the present time, the causes of schizophrenia and other psychoses are only beginning to be revealed. It is likely that schizophrenia may be shown to be due to some combination of faulty chemical and genetic factors as well as to a disturbed environment. Since schizophrenia actually describes many different, even distinct, disorders, it is possible that the various causes may be shown to play different roles in each type of reaction. Although no definitive answers are available yet, research is proceeding on all aspects of psychoses. The more that is learned about all the causes of psychoses, the more techniques to aid recovery will be uncovered.

THERAPY

Most patients with psychotic disorders are hospitalized. With few exceptions the hospital facilities provided for mental patients today, in contrast to former days, are humane and satisfactory (see Fig. 11-2). Of course, many mental hospitals do not have nearly so adequate a staff (see Table 11-2) or so up-to-date facilities as they should have, but in view of their limitations most hospitals do conscientious and worthwhile work.

The length of hospital stay, the duration of the psychosis, and the treatment administered vary considerably depending upon the specific disturbance. (For a description of the different types of therapy, see Chapters Fifteen and Sixteen.) Even the same disorder, because it

Fig. 11-2 Scene in a modern mental hospital's day room, with ample personnel, facilities, and activities for patients. Photo from NAMH film, *The Key*, 1957. Reproduced courtesy of the National Association for Mental Health, Inc., New York, N.Y.

affects individuals differently, may be treated in several ways and have many possible outcomes. Thus, while it is common that some kinds of schizophrenia are resistive to treatment and hospital stays are counted in periods of years, many patients diagnosed as schizophrenic respond very well to therapy and are ready for permanent discharge fairly rapidly.

The maladies that have the most favorable results are the stress psychoses. Equally good are the improvement rates for manic-depressive and involutional disorders. More than three-fourths of such patients are greatly helped by treatment, and most are able to resume normal lives after therapy. The schizophrenias are not so easily treated. But one investigator has reported that 78 per cent of his intensely treated patients showed marked improvement (Veit). In addition, most

Table 11-2 PERSONNEL EMPLOYED FULL AND PART TIME IN PUBLIC PROLONGED-CARE MENTAL HOSPITALS, BY OCCUPATION: UNITED STATES, 1960.

Occupation	Personnel Employed
Full-time employees	
Superintendents and physicians	
Superintendents and Assistant superintendents	405
Clinical directors	146
Psychiatrists	1,375
Other staff physicians	1,289
Psychiatric residents	915
Medical internes	42
Total	4,172
Dentists and dental assistants	668
Psychologists and psychometrists	850
Clinical assistants	324
Graduate nurses	8,423
Other Nurses and Attendants	89,700
Total	99,965
Therapists and assistants	
Occupational therapists and assistants	2,236
Hydrotherapists, physiotherapists and assistants	249
Other therapists and assistants	1,603
Total	4,088
Social workers	
Psychiatric social workers	1,424
Other social workers	467
Total	1,891
All other professionals	2,812
Business managers, stewards and assistants	548
Clerical employees	8,923
Other employees	42,095
Full-time employees reported	164,494
Part-time employees	
Consulting physicians	1,234
Other part time physicians	1,089
Other professionals	619
Other employees	639
Total part-time employees	3,581

Source: Public Health Service, NIMH, Patients in Mental Institutions, Publication 963, Part II, 1963. Reprinted by permission.

hospitals report that about 50 to 60 per cent of their first-admission schizophrenic patients improve sufficiently to be discharged (Public Health Service, 1962).

The organic disorders have a highly unpredictable prognosis. If brain damage is extensive, there is little likelihood of a significant degree of recovery, since once neural tissue is destroyed, it does not regenerate. On the other hand, many organic disorders produced by strokes, infectious diseases, or various chemical agents may evidence a high degree of recovery when the underlying organic processes have been alleviated. The senile organic psychoses, however, have a very low improvement rate. It is likely that less than a fifth of all senile patients can be restored to their normal lives and occupations to any significant degree (Public Health Service, 1962).

The psychoses have long been one of mankind's most puzzling and disheartening afflictions. Only recently have they even been admitted to be treatable disorders rather than the work of the devil or the result of moral sin. Although the work of the mental health professionals has really only begun, much is already known. In the not too distant future it is likely that our increasing understanding of many of the serious mental disorders will enable us to employ new therapies so that all of those who are mentally disabled may be helped.

FOR REVIEW AND DISCUSSION

1. What does *schizophrenia* mean? What are some common schizophrenic symptoms? What are some common types of schizophrenic reaction?
2. What are the manic-depressive psychoses? If manic patients smile and seem completely happy, why are they considered psychiatrically ill?
3. What are organic psychotic disorders? What are some common symptoms? What is senility and what are its usual symptoms? What are the causes of various psychoses?
4. How may stress precipitate temporary periods of psychosis? If stress produces a lifelong pattern of irreversible psychosis, is it correct to say the disorder was caused by the original stressful situation?
5. Mary X was suffering from a childhood psychosis. How may her parents have contributed to her disorder? What early clues suggested she was severely emotionally disturbed? What significance did the therapist discover in her grimacing and posturing? Was psychotherapy successful? Why? What will happen to Mary?

Personality Disorders:

Character and

Sexual Deviation

TWELVE

Distortions of Personality
Sexual Deviations: Homosexuality, Transvestism,
Fetishism, Exhibitionism, and Others
Origins and Treatment of Sexual Deviations

Neurotics are harassed by fearful symptoms and tensions. Psychotic patients seriously contort reality. But people with personality disorders neither suffer undue anxiety nor seriously misinterpret the real world. It has been argued, in fact, that personality disturbances, which include criminal behavior, sexual perversion, alcoholism, and other defects of character, should not be considered psychological maladies. People whose personality leads to unusual behavior—homosexuals, for example—may not really be sick in a strict psychiatric sense. They are ill solely in that their conduct is not in keeping with the prescriptions of normal society.

Personality disorder refers to lifelong patterns of deviant behavior that frequently conflicts with society. People with a *primary personality disorder* (formerly called character disorder) have none of the symptoms of a well-developed neurosis or psychosis. On the other hand, sometimes what appear to be symptoms of personality disorder are actually produced by underlying neurotic or psychotic disturbances. Thus, sexual deviation, alcoholism, and other common traits associated with personality disorder may be *secondary* symptoms of neurosis or psychosis.

It is important for diagnosticians and therapists to distinguish whether the behavior deviation (criminality, homosexuality, etc.) is primary or secondary. When the symptoms are a consequence of faulty development or any of the other multiple causes of personality disorder, they are said to be *primary*. But when the symptoms result from some neurotic or psychotic problem, they are *secondary*, and treatment is necessarily different from what it would be were the behavior deviations primary.

Personality disorders are commonly classified in three categories. The first two, personality pattern and personality trait disturbances, are partly distortions of normal functioning and partly almost minor varieties of some psychotic disturbances. When the entire personality is affected—that is, the totality of a person's behavior is slanted—then the disturbance is classified as a *pattern disorder*. But when only a particular trait, a fairly unitary aspect of behavior, is outside of normal limits (extreme aggressiveness, for example), the disorder is characterized as a *trait disturbance*.

The third category of personality disorder is labeled *sociopathic personality disturbance*. As the name indicates, persons so classified are "sick" in terms of their nonadherence to the expectations of society. By excessive drinking, stealing, or sexual escapades they violate the legal, ethical, and moral prescriptions that help bind people together.

In the following pages some of the major disorders of personality will be discussed. In this chapter, a brief discussion of pattern and trait disturbances is followed by a description of sexual deviations, which are sociopathic disturbances. In Chapter Thirteen criminal, alcoholic, and other sociopathic personalities are described.

DISTORTIONS IN PERSONALITY PATTERNS AND TRAITS

Several types of distortions in personality patterns and traits, as classified by the American Psychiatric Association, are described below.

Pattern Disturbances

Inadequate personality. The inadequate person is just what the name suggests: emotionally and socially inept. He shows poor judgment and is not resourceful.

Schizoid personality. This type is reclusive, avoids close relations with others, and seems cold, withdrawn, and distant. He may have highly peculiar preferences and habits. Many recluses and vagrants may be schizoid.

Cyclothymic personality. Zest, energy, and apparent warmth are the predominant traits of a cyclothymic personality. But his friendliness and outgoing behavior frequently alternates with periods of sadness and despondency.

Paranoid personality. The paranoid displays many traits similar to those of the schizoid. To these he adds a high sensitivity to interpersonal relations. He is envious, suspicious, and frequently hostile. Paranoid personalities tend to be drawn to extremist groups and causes.

Trait Disturbances

Emotionally unstable personality. Minor stresses will render this type of person excited and ineffective. He is often undependable and lacks good judgment. His relationships with others are fraught with continual crises.

Passive-Aggressive personality. There are many types of passive-aggressive personality. Primary characteristics may be passivity, dependence, helpless clinging, and stubborn procrastination. Or aggressiveness, destructiveness, and irritability may be stressed.

Compulsive personality. The compulsive person has chronic obsessive concern with conformity, neatness, and the standards set up by conscience. He will usually be over-inhibited, highly conscientious, and rather tense.

Schizoid, cyclothymic, and other distorted personalities result from the same processes that normally produce healthy and more typical individuals (see Chapter Two). The eccentric personality develops a pattern of existence in harmony with his needs and abilities, just as his more normal counterpart does. As a consequence, it is unlikely that those whose personalities are disturbed will ever seek, or come in contact with, psychotherapy. As long as they remain relatively free of stress, their personality patterns permit them to carry on more or less harmoniously with others in their environment. Under severe stress, however, the already distorted personality is more likely than a relatively normal character to quickly develop neurotic and psychotic symptoms.

SEXUAL DEVIATION

Sexual deviation is often a symptom—and an intricate part—of a neurosis or psychosis. Frequently, for example, paranoid psychotics have extensive homosexual histories. Neuroses are often accompanied by sexual irregularities. But sexual deviation may not only be symptomatic of more extensive psychological disorder; it may also represent a way of life. That is, just like any other personality disorder, sexual deviation can be a fully developed part of a person's behavior and character. The full-scale sexual deviate may not really be "psychologically" sick, since he has none of the harassing symptoms experienced by neurotics or psychotics. Like others with sociopathic personality disorders, he is ill in the sense that his conduct is contrary to the expectations of society.

It is not easy to define characterological sexual deviation. What may in our own day and age, in this country, be regarded as sexually perverted may be more or less accepted by some cultures or in special circumstances. Nor is it easy to agree about who is or will become a deviate. About a third of adolescent males have erotic contact with other boys while growing up, yet fewer than one in thirty men develop into true homosexuals (Kinsey, *et al.*, 1948). The diagnostician is always careful when asked to categorize what appears to be peculiar sexual behavior. What at first seems to be a deviation may be part of a neurosis or due to unusual conditions; or it may eventually simply develop into normal heterosexual activity.

Homosexuality

Sexual relationships between adult members of the same sex is the most common kind of deviation. About 2 or 3 per cent of the adult male population and less than 1 per cent of the adult female population are *true* homosexuals (Kinsey, *et al.*, 1948, 1953). It is necessary to distinguish the true homosexual from the situational deviate. Many people may have some homosexual experience while growing up, or under extraordinary conditions that deny them other outlets, such as confinement to a prison. The true homosexual is an *adult* who has clear and forcible need for sexual contact *only* with members of the same sex. Though they usually find heterosexual activity repugnant, even true homosexuals may, on occasion, marry and have children. Nevertheless, heterosexual family activity will be regarded as an unpleasant and necessary task to enable them to continue their homosexual relations.

George T., twenty-five years old, was brought to the clinic after having been arrested for attempting to "pick up" a detective used as a decoy by the police. George was eager for therapy at the clinic but suggested the therapist try to help him overcome his need to "cover up" his "real self." George was married and had two children but wanted to be able to carry out his homosexual activities without feeling the need to hide behind a normal-appearing family.

George first became aware of sexual interests before the age of six when he practiced mutual masturbation and oral contact with a slightly older male friend. This relationship continued sporadically until the boy moved away when George was ten. For several years George had no sexual contact other than masturbation. At about thirteen years of age George recalls becoming "excited" about a dark-skinned boy in his class and making efforts to befriend him. Although George and the boy became friends, he was not able to interest him in a sexual relationship. George traces his preferences for relationships with Negroes to this incident that "frustrated" him.

George has had numerous homosexual friends, "crushes," and "affairs" since becoming active at about fourteen years of age. He stated that he has never been apprehended—with the recent exception. At twenty-three he married a girl whom his mother had virtually selected for him. He had dated her on rare occasions during his college years when formality required it.

George's wife is apparently not aware of his homosexual predilections. Sexual contact betwen George and his wife is very infrequent, "once a month or so." George "puts up with it," since it is required. He believes his wife is happy that way, since she's supposedly "a prude" and would not care for an active heterosexual existence.

George is not overtly feminine, although he demonstrates in his dress and demeanor more care and consciousness than is typical for most males.

Many homosexuals, like George, take obvious pride in their deviation and will even attempt to persuade others of the moral and intellectual superiority of their way of life. Such homosexuals feel themselves slighted by society and in one way or another demand that their sexual preferences not be the object of ridicule or punishable by law.

Although homosexual males are often stereoptyed as squeaky voiced, swishing, and "arty," most are not immediately detectable by their manner or dress. Some male homosexuals, in fact, take great pride in their well-developed musculature, athletic abilities, and superficially vigorous masculinity. In the same way, few women deviates are mannish with short-cut hair or dressed in replicas of masculine clothes. Most women homosexuals maintain superficially sweet and feminine roles. Of course, some homosexuals attempt to absorb the role and characteristics of the opposite sex completely by dressing and acting like it. Some become quite adept. It may be difficult, for example, to recognize the true sex of a male homosexual dressed and acting like a woman. Many homosexuals make an effort to find one another, to establish clubs and entertainment centers, and to maintain a kind of communications network through abstruse channels. Homosexual newspapers and newsletters have even been reported.

Transvestism

A relatively rare deviation, transvestism is often related to homosexuality. The transvestite so closely identifies with the opposite sex that he literally tries to transform himself by wearing its clothing and adopting its habits. In some extreme instances transvestites even seek surgical intervention in an attempt to change the structure of their body and genital organs to conform to their wishes. Transvestism is frequently accompanied by homosexual activity, although possibly just as often it is correlated with other sexual practices and perversions. The following case of transvestism is not necessarily typical. A number of unique erotic interests were present as well as several neurotic symptoms and considerable anxiety. Nevertheless, it illustrates many of the features found in transvestism. The case is reproduced with the courtesy of its authors, R. E. McKenzie, Ph.D., and I. M. Schultz, M.D., and the *American Journal of Psychotherapy*.[1]

The patient was a 36-year-old, white male who had spent considerable time in the military service. Since about 1938, shortly after his enlistment, he had experienced the wish to wear women's clothing and this was was sexually stimulating. He realized the abnormality of these ideas, but could not dispel them. He had married in 1942, and had hoped that his marriage would in some way help him to conquer the obsessions regarding feminine clothing. However, he had found the impulses more difficult to control, and since his wife's clothing was available, had actually begun to wear female apparel. At first he wore it only in private or at costume parties. However, later he began to create occasions for donning the apparel and spent considerable money in the purchase of articles of feminine clothing when that of his wife was not

[1] "Study of a Transvestite," *15* (April, 1961), 267–80.

available. In addition to his fantasying and the wearing of women's clothing, he became concerned with ideas of being bound and gagged and other forms of what has been termed "bondage." In recent years he began to lose much of his interest in heterosexual activity. The transvestism became more pronounced, and he became progressively more concerned about the effect of this activity on his family life and the well-being of his children. During his most recent assignment he had difficulty relating to his immediate superior, and began to suffer heightened anxiety and periods of depression with some suicidal ideation. These factors induced him to seek medical attention.

On examination the patient appeared as a neat and courteous individual, with a normally masculine appearance. His affect was fairly appropriate, but he appeared mildly depressed. Although he spoke in a rather rigid, detached manner, with little variation in tone, he expressed concern and anxiety over his problems. His motivation appeared excellent. He was self-referred and had no ulterior motive in seeking help other than the solution of his problem. He voiced some concern for his job future in the light of a psychiatric history. However, he also noted that, in the past months, he had been ineffective in his work due to tension and increasing concern over his transvestism.

The patient brought to the hospital with him a 15-page typewritten account entitled, "The Saga of Gwendolyn Vera Sweet." This was the name he liked to fantasy for himself while dressed in female clothing In this "saga" he described the sexual thoughts and fantasies he had had for the major part of his adult life. He gave as his motive for writing the account the desire to achieve a more complete understanding of his problem, both by himself and those from whom he sought help and understanding, including his wife. In this document, he described the design and material of the women's clothing that he most liked to wear. He also described in great detail fantasies in which two women would dress him in a variety of women's clothing and then have contests to see which one could bind him most securely by means of handcuffs, straps, tight-fitting plastic bags, and other paraphernalia. In addition to the paper, the patient had a small collection of photographs made of himself with facial make-up, wearing articles of women's clothing and a blonde wig. There was also a collection of pictures which he had ordered through a commercial concern, showing women in various forms of tight fitting clothing being bound and gagged in different positions.

The patient's past history revealed a definitely traumatic early life. He was the youngest of five children and the only boy. His father died when he was six years old, and he spent many of his formative years surrounded only by women. His mother was a tense, dominating, and rejecting individual who was also rather prudish. The closest sibling in terms of age and relationship was a sister four years older than he was. The other sisters were all considerably older than the patient.

He recalled that as a child he had enjoyed wearing and handling women's clothing while playing with his next older sister. In addition, he had experienced the desire to be tightly bound up. He and his sister would tie each other up with clothesline and he would receive a great deal of satisfaction from this form of play, but without directly experiencing sexual pleasure. The home environment was, in general, a constricted one, with all of the children being forced to conform to the mother's wishes. There was no sexual instruction in the family and discussion of sexual topics was actively discouraged.

Gradually, all of the siblings revolted against the mother's domination and left home. The last to depart were the patient and his sister who left together for California. There his sister became involved in an unhappy love affair with an older man with whom they lived, an affair climaxed by an illegitimate pregnancy. Though he was only vaguely aware of the sexual aspects of this relationship, the sister's affair was upsetting to the patient and he recalled that at the time of this man's death in an automobile accident he had felt rather satisfied and even happy over it. A short time later he separated from his sister. He then got a job with an Army officer who persuaded him to join the service. He enlisted when he was 19 years old and has been on continuous active duty ever since.

He reported an episode that occurred during his adolescence, in which an aged homosexual attempted to perform sodomy with him, but this attempt was unsuccessful and the patient did not receive any satisfaction from the act. In one subsequent episode, he was approached by a homosexual and permitted an attempt at sodomy which was again unsuccessful and without gratification on his part. Prior to marriage he did not have heterosexual intercourse, and his main source of satisfaction had been masturbation and the fantasies about women's clothing. After his marriage he found that in heterosexual intercourse he was able both to achieve orgasm and to satisfy his wife. However, he did continue to masturbate after marriage and found that he had little interest in heterosexual activity unless his wife originated the act. . . .

Fetishism

Another variety of sexual deviation is fetishism. The fetishist derives heterosexual pleasure solely by fondling, mouthing, smelling, licking, or otherwise manipulating some desired object or a representation of it. The object may be something that most people would accord some sexual significance, such as hair, breasts, and lips, or some sexually associated article of feminine underclothing or adornment. But many things sexually arousing to fetishists have little or no erotic potential for normal people. Some fetishists fixate on high-heeled shoes, leather or woolen objects of clothing, straps, boots, fingers, or ankles.

The fetishist, like the homosexual, may attempt to obscure his preferences by marrying and even attempting to involve his wife in fetishistic
types of activities.

It needs to be pointed out that many healthy persons feel their
heterosexual pleasures heightened through certain physical manipulations, or by particular dress or scents. This is not unusual and is not
considered fetishistic. Fetishism refers to sexual satisfaction obtained
solely and exclusively through manipulation of specific objects which
does not serve as a preliminary to copulation.

The following report on a case of fetishism is reproduced here
through the courtesy of its author, Dr. Vernon W. Grant, psychologist,
and the *American Journal of Psychiatry.*[2]

The subject was a 35-year-old single white male of above-average intelligence who fully realized his abnormality, and fortunately was highly
articulate in describing it. His sexual interest centered around women's shoes,
ankles, and legs; he had little interest in the leg above knee. The interest in
feminine shoes was traceable, by clear recall, to the fourth year. He remembered playing with shoes stored in closets, having fantasies of shoes, and
was especially fascinated by those of slipper style with high heels. Shoe
fantasies accompanied masturbation, which began at age 9. He testifies, however, that his earliest interest in shoes, while strong and specialized as to
models, was free of sexual meaning. Later there were dreams in which shoes
figured prominently, accompanied by genital excitement. Following a period
of abeyance of fetish interest during late adolescence the urge reawakened in
his mid-twenties and became very strong. His method was to frequent public
places and search for a woman whose shoes and legs met the requirements of
his tastes (high-heeled pumps, gracefully formed ankles and legs); he then
achieved excitement to the point of orgasm simply by concentrating his attention. He describes the erotic effect of such concentration as not confined to
the genitals alone, but generally diffused and accompanied by sensations of
warmth.

A notable feature of fetish sensibility in this instance was its dependence
upon movement. Some degree of "gyration" of the foot was necessary to
progressive erotic excitement; for example, the rhythmic restless pendular
swinging of a crossed leg by a girl in a seated position. The motionless member, though erotically interesting, produced no cumulative effect or "build
up." The subject stressed, however, the great importance of his sexual
vitality at any given time, and states that at peak intensity of the urge his
excitability was such that even a window display of shoes modelled on a
mannequin was sufficient to arouse orgasm. (Once sufficiently excited, other

2 "A Problem in Sex Pathology," *110,* No. 8 (February, 1954), 589–93.

stimuli might acquire stimulus value; thus on one occasion he reached climax on watching the movements of a woman's hand. To this he was ordinarily indifferent though he might at times be aroused if the hand were long, well shaped, with slender fingers.) His requirements being rather highly specialized, pursuit of the fetish was often an excessively taxing ordeal. He often spent many hours before making a "sighting" that met his criteria, and he then was in constant anxiety lest his peculiar behavior—fixed scrutiny and expressions of emotion—attract attention in a public place.

The excessive strength of the deviant urge so often noted in the literature of fetishism is here impressively illustrated. At a time when he was unable to find employment the subject abandoned himself entirely to the urge, its power rendering him admittedly helpless. He recognized his sickness and termed it a "disease." Entire days were spent frequenting public places, from bus stations to churches, "any place where a woman wearing my fetish needs might be found seated long enough to make an ejaculation possible." Under protracted tension he suffered from intense headaches. So overmastering at times was the passion that despite a rather timid disposition he had once, in pursuit of the fetish under difficult conditions, reached orgasm while running at top speed, in a public place, with full realization that he faced imminent danger of arrest. At other times with sharpened sensitivity, his excitement rose to climax at the sound of the heel-taps of an unseen female.

Some unusual observations resulted from the subject's seemingly normal capacity for conventional love attachments, enabling him to compare amorous attraction with the fetish experience. The latter, he testifies, is more than a genital-sexual episode. It includes emotion of a different quality, which he states is closely similar to that of being "in love." While this nongenital effect of the fetish tends to envelop the personality as a whole, its focus continues to be the fetish members, and expresses itself in part, in a strong but non-sensual impulse toward caressing and kissing the shoes, ankles, and legs. This component of fetish behavior has been noted in other accounts. The subject felt certain that the basis of some of his normal love attachments was the "charm" of fetish traits that met his criteria.

A striking discovery was that motion picture films of feminine feet and legs in movement gave him fully adequate satisfaction. With a few short reels of material of this kind, obtained by employing models for the purpose, he was able to dispense altogether with the living stimulus.

Exhibitionism

During the childhood years sexual play with the same or opposite sex almost always begins with exhibition of the genitalia (Kinsey, *et al.,* 1948). As the child grows into adulthood, some exhibition and viewing of genitalia remains as an incidental part of mature sexual contact for both sexes. When displaying the genitals persists as the primary focus of sexual activity, the individual is considered sexually deviant.

Harry, a thirty-six-year-old mechanical engineer, was apprehended after a woman to whom he was exhibiting himself attracted police with her screams. Harry operated in several ways. He preferred to exhibit his genitals in darkened movies to fairly young women. He would sit next to them, attract their attention, and make masturbatory motions. He also parked his car near schools, exhibited himself to children, and then sped hastily away. On a few occasions he walked about the streets and displayed himself by opening and closing a raincoat.

Nearly all exhibitionists are men. Rarely, women may also have extreme exhibitionistic needs though they are not considered as such, since there are relatively acceptable avenues for them to satisfy themselves. The exhibitionistic male usually hopes for shock or consternation in his victim and may be disappointed when his victims act nonchalantly or advise him to seek psychiatric help.

Nine Major Sexual Deviations

Concise descriptions of nine significant sexual deviations, including those already discussed, and the relative incidence of each form of behavior for each sex are given below. It should be remembered that the distinction between normal erotic behavior and sexual deviation is often a matter of degree: deviation frequently stems from a fixation upon a single aspect of the normally diverse pleasures of sex. The information reported below is partly based on data compiled by Kinsey, et al., 1948, 1953.

Bestiality. The use of animals for sexual stimulation characterizes this deviation. It includes attempts at intercourse and oral or other contact. Bestiality is found almost exclusively in men.

Exhibitionism. Exposure of the genitals to members of the opposite sex is frequently attempted by exhibitionists in the streets, movies, dark parks, and other public places. This form of deviation is nearly exclusive to men.

Fetishism. The fetishist focuses sexual interest on a part of the body or on articles of clothing. He may derive satisfaction solely by looking at, fondling, or smelling whatever object he has fixated upon. Common fetish objects include underclothing, stockings, shoes, breasts, ears, and buttocks. This behavior is found only in men.

Homosexuality. Sexual contact with members of the same sex is known as homosexuality. This behavior is three to six times as common among men as among women.

Masochism-sadism.   The masochist obtains satisfaction only by suffering; the
   sadist obtains pleasure only by inflicting pain, but both tendencies may
   be present in a single person. Common techniques of inflicting or receiving pain include whipping, biting, beating, verbal abuse, binding, and
   trampling. Sadism is found primarily in men. Masochism is perhaps
   slightly more common in women than in men.

Pedophilia.   This form of behavior leads to sexual satisfaction through attempted intercourse with, or handling of, a child. Pedophilia is found
   almost exclusively in men.

Prostitution.   Sexual intercourse, usually adult and heterosexual, is called
   prostitution when it is an outright business transaction. Most prostitutes
   are female. Rarely, men are prostitutes to male homosexuals.

Transvestism.   The transvestite so closely identifies with the opposite sex that
   he makes every effort to transform himself. Adopting the clothing and
   habits of the opposite sex are transvestite characteristics. In extreme
   instances transvestites may seek surgical assistance in becoming more
   like the other sex. This is a relatively rare deviation, most often found in
   men.

Voyeurism.   "Peeping Tom" activities are the means to sexual satisfaction for
   the voyeur. Secretly observing women undressing and the erotic activity
   of others gives voyeurs pleasure. Most voyeurs are men.

Origins and Treatment

   Sexual deviations, particularly homosexuality, were once attributed
to physical defects. Homosexual males were believed, for example, to
have been born with structural and endocrinal inadequacies that
virtually forced them to assume feminine sexual interests. As a consequence, therapy was usually directed at redressing hormonal balances
and otherwise altering a supposedly defective physique.

   Most authorities today believe that while physical factors may on
occasion play a role in some forms of sexual deviation, perversion is
primarily the result of developmental abnormality. Sexual interests
exist from early childhood. They take many forms, such as mutual
genital exploration, masturbation, exposure, and other activities.
Several youthful sexual tendencies are such that if they continue into
adulthood they will be considered perverted. For the most part, however, children learn indirectly from their parents and through the
model presented them by society to guide their erotic interests into
socially acceptable channels. Even in normal adults, however, some
vestiges of childish sexual interest and activity can usually be found.

   If during the maturing of sexual drives the child is subjected to
undesirable parental controls, seduced by sexual deviates, or otherwise
diverted from a normal developmental path, he may fixate on unacceptable sexual techniques or objects. The relationship between the
potentially homosexual male and his mother seems to be particularly

crucial. It has been shown in several studies (e.g., D. J. West) that the mothers of male homosexuals tend to be overly intense, domineering, and controlling, and the fathers weak and passive. George, the homosexual mentioned earlier, described his parents as follows:

> Mother and I are very close. We understand each other. She's come to depend upon me, just like I used to depend upon her. There were times when we hated one another—deep down, I guess, you could always tell that we felt very deeply for one another. My father never amounted to much; I'm not really interested in him. He's good to mother, I'll say that—she knows how to handle him.

Psychoanalytically oriented writers have emphasized the essentially loving relationship that exists between male homosexuals and their mothers. They suggest that homosexuality, as well as other sexual deviations, is a result of the unsatisfactory resolution of childhood Oedipal feelings (wishing to possess the mother) and other failures in psychosexual development.

Psychotherapy is often attempted to treat sexual deviation. Some deviations, especially those that are likely to make their practitioners intensely uncomfortable and disgusted with themselves, seem to respond to therapy. Fixed patterns of sexual deviation, however, such as sustained exclusive homosexuality or fetishism, are not likely to be reversed by psychotherapy. In fact, most persistent deviates do not want to undergo therapy or to change their way of living.

When sexual perversions are accompanied by anxiety, conflict, and distress, they are considerably more amenable to successful treatment than when the deviant patterns are fully accepted as a way of life. The transvestite discussed earlier was reported by Drs. McKenzie and Schultz to have received a total of 154 treatment hours. Because their patient was essentially a neurotic in whom the transvestism, though well developed, was secondary, there was considerable hope for recovery. The following is the description by Drs. McKenzie and Schultz of psychotherapy with this patient.

> The patient was seen for a total of 154 treatment hours. Of these, 62 sessions were held daily, but the sessions were then decreased to a two to three times a week schedule. In this setting a therapy of fairly deep intensity developed. The approach was analytically oriented, largely directive; but on occasion, nondirective. With this pattern it was possible to deal with unconscious material and also to employ counseling and suggestion. During the probing work of therapy, the patient was remarkable in his ability to handle the anxiety and affect that resulted. He showed a marked ability to gain

insight and relate to the therapist. Thus early in the therapy a strong positive transference developed which figured prominently in the therapeutic
work.

Through the transference, it was possible to relieve the pressure of his
superego and aid him in discovering and accepting anxiety-laden id drives,
thus enabling his ego to regain some of its organizing and executive function.
The therapists examined the typewritten saga in detail, searching for significant
associations and symbolic meanings, just as one would a dream sequence. One
association, in connection with the head mask and gags mentioned previously,
was to a statuette of three monkeys that stood on the home mantle depicting
"see no evil, hear no evil, and speak no evil." In his childhood recollections
the patient reported many episodes of being fearful of his own sexuality. He
recognized early that as the only male (penis) in the family, he was feared
and made somewhat of an isolate . . . a role which he tried to continue in
later life. He recalled intense embarrassment over his erections and tried to
conceal them by wearing "jockey-type" shorts. He also recalled feeling guilty
and confused when a girl sitting on his lap during a hay ride stimulated
him sexually. He was able to work through his incestuous drives, with their
resulting guilt, toward his mother and youngest sister as substitute objects. In
associating to his desire for a black rustling dress, he recalled that his mother
favored dresses of such material. From this and other associated matter came
the insight that he equated this dress material with his mother and cathected
it with the same intensity . . . in turn attaching his forbidden sexual desires
to this symbolic substitute.

During therapy, the patient's attitude toward heterosexual activity
changed. He began to look upon his activity as a means of expression and a
method of establishing a relationship between himself and his wife. In discussing his wife, who was essentially a masculine type of woman in appearance
and attire, it was recognized that he had married such a woman largely as a
father-mother substitute. He was intensely dependent on her and wanted her
to play a masculine role, yet he resented this state of affairs. Thus, his wife em-
bodied some aspects of both his absent father and the mother he had come
to depend upon and yet fear. In this regard, he found that he experienced the
same feelings towards his wife as he had felt toward his mother and youngest
sister, namely, he feared that his sexuality, if openly expressed, would alienate
their love for him and destroy his dependent relationship.

The course of therapy was considerably aided when the patient's
wife came to the hospital in order to be interviewed and counseled by the
therapist and the supervising psychiatrist. She appeared to have a good deal
of insight and understanding in addition to a genuine love for the patient.
She recognized how she had, almost unconsciously, been forced into both a
pseudomasculine and maternal role in regard to her husband. She desired to
have a more feminine relationship with him and thus cooperated in establish-

ing a more realistic heterosexual pattern to the marriage. The couple were counseled on the techniques of heterosexual activity and subsequently began to seek a better sexual adjustment to each other. After a week of being together daily, the wife was again interviewed and related that the patient was greatly changed in his attitudes toward her and that he seemed much more relaxed and free in sexual intercourse. They had found new lines of mutual communication and their new sexual life was intensely pleasurable; they felt as if they were on a "second honeymoon."

As can be seen, the patient's improvement was rapid. For this reason, the therapist was cautious in evaluating his gains. However, the change was consistent and proved to be a measure of the patient's adjustment potential rather than a flight into health. He gave up much of his obsessive ideation and compulsive activity and appeared less tense and anxious. His depression and feelings of guilt subsided and he felt a great improvement in his affect and outlook on his problem. It was hard for him to believe that he could have despaired to the point of contemplating suicide and now he felt confident that he could handle his problems. His ward behavior also reflected his progress. Somewhat seclusive and reserved on admission, he gradually became more outgoing, socialized better, and took part in ward activities.

After 62 hours of therapy, the patient and his wife wanted to return to their home for a while with the idea of testing their adjustment and reuniting with their children. The authors agreed that this might benefit the patient and also serve as an aid in evaluating his progress. Consequently, a two-week leave was granted. During this period the patient maintained his therapeutic improvement and progressed in utilizing the insight and directive suggestions gained in his therapeutic sessions. He related that he and his wife had continued almost nightly intercourse and their sexual relations continued to show improvement. He also noticed that his relationship with his children, especially his son, had greatly improved. He discussed his problem, and the bearing it would have on his career, with his supervisor, and found an adequate understanding of his difficulties and the progress that he had made toward a solution. He also initiated action that would result in his following a different phase of his occupational field which would not take him away from his family for prolonged periods of time, as had happened previously.

Upon his return to the hospital, the patient was presented to the staff for re-evaluation and disposition. It was decided to continue treatment on a less intensive schedule and to work through the possible effect his psychiatric history might have on his work and social life outside of the hospital. As far as transvestism was concerned, the patient had gained sufficient insight to to be sure that the feminine clothing and the bondage pictures which he had acquired, no longer held an attraction for him. Secure in this conviction, he sold the clothing to a costumer and burned the pictures. He felt that these objects were part of his past and would no longer displace or substitute for his adult sexuality. Instead of symbols of his sexual fear, they now represented a conquest in which he was justly proud of his victory.

Follow-up

In order to evaluate both the therapeutic result and the dynamic formulation, the patient was contacted by letter six months after his release from the hospital and asked to aid in determining the state of his adjustment and his general situation. His written reply contained both subjective and objective evidence that his remission was substantial and that he was, in fact, improving.

From the subjective standpoint, he wrote he was feeling well, facing the reality of his situation, and working actively with himself and his environment. He was becoming much less repressive and compulsive, and relating in a more forthright and aggressive way to his wife and children, and to others. In the light of his previous pathology, it was felt that the progress in his sexual adjustment was the most significant indication of his psychotherapeutic gain. He had not engaged in further transvestism, which no longer held any significant attraction for him. In addition, he and his wife continued to have pleasurable and regular intercourse. His wife was much happier, and enjoying the role she had wanted to play throughout their married life—that of a woman. He pointed out that in the past his dependent traits had led him to permit others to make decisions for him, but that grappling with and surmounting his problems in therapy had given him added confidence, and a feeling he could now make his own decisions. He added that this transition to more mature behavior was not easy for him, and was, in fact, quite painful at times, but the knowledge that he was making steady progress was sustaining and satisfying to him.

The objective evidence was provided by a set of circumstances in connection with the patient's work. According to a suggestion of his employer, he referred himself for a psychiatric consultation about five months after having been discharged from the hospital. Since the patient forwarded a copy of this consultant's report with his reply, we had an opinion from another psychiatric source. In essence, the report stated that the patient had gained good insight into his problem, was able to cope with it, and that there did not appear to be any likelihood of his old symptoms recurring.

A Note of Caution

Exhibitionism, sadism, homosexuality, and other sexual disturbances may in psychiatric terms be either primary or secondary. If the sexual deviation represents a way of life, is as accepted a part of an individual's makeup as is heterosexuality among psychologically healthy people, then the perversion is considered the primary disturbance. If, however, the sexual misconduct arises from an underlying neurosis or psychosis or is a temporary reaction to growing up or unusual conditions, then it is a secondary result symptomatic of more extensive processes (e.g., the case of the transvestite just discussed). Most sexual behavior problems are probably a consequence of other pathologies. They are thus only secondary symptoms that may be alleviated when the basic malady is treated (East). When the sexual disorder is primary, it is extremely difficult to treat, a threat to the normal order of society, and like all deviations needs regulation by moral and legal codes.

FOR REVIEW AND DISCUSSION

1. What are some differences between personality disorder and neurosis? Why are those with personality disorders not considered psychiatrically sick in the same sense as neurotics?

2. Are all sexual deviations always personality disorders, or may they be associated with psychiatric illness? Why is it necessary to distinguish carefully between a true sexual deviation and one that develops under temporary circumstances?

3. What are the origins of sexual deviations? Do childhood experimentation and sexual excesses necessarily lead to adult disorder? The case history of the transvestite illustrates some factors important in the development of many sexual deviations. What are these? Why was treatment successful with this patient?

4. Is it fair to imprison and otherwise legally punish sexual offenders? Why does society feel it necessary to regulate and forbid certain sexual practices? Is legal restraint successful in helping curb the spread of sexual deviation?

Personality Disorders:

Criminality and

Addiction

T H I R T E E N

232

Personality disorders are characterized not by psychiatric symptoms but by a way of life that is out of harmony with the requirements of society. The criminal or addict may be literally as sane, as any normal human being. Yet his mode of living and unacceptable conduct demonstrate that something interfered with his healthy development. He has reached adulthood and has created a problem not only for himself but for the whole community and culture in which he lives.

CRIMINAL PERSONALITIES

In all walks of life, including professionals, laborers, businessmen, and civic leaders, there are a few people whose personalities appear to be lacking in moral and ethical development. Many of these improperly socialized people find their way into jail, and a few are mentally hospitalized. Though outwardly rational human beings, these criminal personalities often display emotional and thinking processes as distorted as those of a psychotic.

Psychiatrists distinguish two main kinds of criminal personality. The *asocial type,* also called *psychopathic,* refers to persons who are chronically in trouble but unable to learn from their experiences. They tend to be callous and pleasure-seeking, and have little allegiance to or feeling for any people or group. They tend to be "good talkers" and are usually able to arouse considerable sympathy and cleverly excuse their behavior. Frequently they convince legal officials or mental health workers of the injustices they have allegedly suffered and are thus able to absolve themselves of responsibility for their crimes.

Lou is a thirty-four-year-old jewelry store owner. He was convicted of selling worthless watches. He had put famous brand names on one- and two-dollar watches and sold them for as much as three hundred dollars. Lou gave his history readily to the hospital psychologist since he stated that he knew the material could not be used against him in court. Lou was affable, outwardly charming, and talked as if he were permitting the psychologist to share in some highly important secrets. Lou had begun stealing when a young child. He regularly visited a five-and-ten-cent store until he was apprehended. At that time he successfully "got away" because of his youth. Throughout the last twenty years he has been involved in countless varieties of crime, ranging from petty swindles to sales of worthless stock certificates. Despite several convictions Lou has managed to serve less than one year in prisons by enlisting sympathy for his supposed poor upbringing in a "broken" home and "bad" neighborhood.

The second criminal type is called *dyssocial reaction*. Lawbreakers who disregard ordinary ways of behaving because they have been reared in unconventional surroundings fall into this category. They look to their criminal friends for comfort and protection. They are usually strongly loyal to the code set by their group or gang. Many adolescent delinquent gangs depend upon and encourage such unswerving loyalty to their own criminal standards and activities.

Nick is a seventeen-year-old who was apprehended attempting to buy a gun from a man who was under police surveillance. Nick comes from a neighborhood in which a number of juvenile gangs and adult rackets flourish. Nick appears to have been involved in errands for bookmaking, policy betting, and selling marijuana and possibly addictive drugs. Nick would not discuss any of his friends or their activities. He seemed to feel great loyalty to his associates and appeared to be attempting to live up to the vow of silence prescribed by his criminal friends. Nick did indicate, indirectly, his ambition to be a noteworthy and valuable "operator," like Capone, whose name he mentioned frequently.

Not all criminals are asocial or dyssocial personality disorders. A small proportion of offenders are neurotic, psychotic, or mentally defective. A not insignificant group, too, apparently more or less voluntarily elect illegal careers. There are also some relatively normal people who are impulsively catapulted into committing a criminal act by circumstances or extreme provocation. This latter group, incidentally, because it has so little experience with courts and legal procedures, often suffers greater punishment for a single offense than do experienced violators for many felonies.

JUVENILE CRIME

Juvenile deliquency is a loosely used phrase that refers to any violation of law by a youngster, ranging from handling illegal fireworks on the Fourth of July to committing a gang murder. Accurately used, the term should refer to crimes committed by those adjudged juveniles by the court. This usually means that an offender must be under eighteen years of age, though different states have varying standards. In the past decade, according to records of the Federal Bureau of Investigation, juvenile crimes have increased each year. Nearly a half million juvenile cases are handled by the courts annually. In *A Look at Juvenile Delinquency*, the Children's Bureau of the Department of Health, Education, and Welfare made the following report.

Almost half of all delinquency cases referred to court are dismissed, adjusted, or held open without further hearings. In about a quarter of them, the child is placed on probation, and in about one-tenth the young offender is committed to an institution for delinquents.

Increases in both police arrests of juveniles and juvenile court delinquency cases have far outstripped increases in the population of children age 10 through 17 over the past 5–10 years. . . . A sizeable increase is predicted in the 10–17 age group in the years ahead.

Boys outnumber girls by a ratio of 4 to 1 in court delinquency cases, excluding traffic cases. The most frequent offenses of boys are stealing and malicious mischief, like window breaking and other damage to property. Girls get into court most frequently for being ungovernable, running away, and sexual promiscuity.

Rates of delinquency court cases in urban areas are about $3\frac{1}{2}$ times higher than in rural areas. More and more of the population is centering in metropolitan areas, where 60 percent of all people now live. Recent rate of delinquency growth in these areas has been four times as great as in nonmetropolitan areas. [Pp. 3–4.]

It is not known exactly what proportion of juvenile crimes are committed by asocial and dyssocial personality types. According to psychological evaluations conducted at one installation, the Child Study Institute of the Family Court in Toledo, Ohio, probably about half of the delinquent children seen were psychologically disturbed. Of this number half again were afflicted with disorders in personality and outlook that made their adherence to the rules of society difficult. It may be said of this sample, then, and probably of most delinquents throughout the country, that only a minority are suffering from extreme disturbances in personality that make their criminal behavior difficult to remedy.

Checklist for Predicting Delinquency

Delinquency in adolescence or early adulthood may be forecast by certain behavior at a younger age. Any child who fits a large number of the eighteen characteristics listed here might be a potential problem at a later age.[1]

Shows marked dislike for school.
Resents school routine and restriction.
Is disinterested in school program.

[1] Data reported in Calvin, *et al.* Based on W. C. Kvaraceus, *Juvenile Delinquency* (Washington, D. C.: American Educational Research Association, 1958).

Is failing in a number of subjects.

Has repeated one or more grades.

Attends special class for retarded pupils.

Has attended many different schools.

Intends to leave school as soon as the law allows.

Has only vague academic or vocational plans.

Has limited academic ability.

Is a child who seriously or persistently misbehaves.

Destroys school materials or property.

Is cruel and bullying on the playground.

Has temper tantrums in the classroom.

Wants to stop schooling at once.

Truants from school.

Does not participate in organized extracurricular programs.

Feels he does not "belong" in the classroom.

ORIGINS AND TREATMENT OF CRIMINAL DISORDERS

A great deal of scholarly effort has been expended on understanding and treating the inadequately socialized or psychopathic personality. People who are seemingly entirely without conscience challenge many of the developmental theories of psychologists. Some have suggested that asocial types are structurally defective and have noted that their EEG (electro-encephalograph or "brain wave") patterns are distinctly different from those of normal people. But despite attempts to define the physical and psychological patterns of psychopathic criminal personalities, it has not proven possible to diagnose them medically with any precision (Toby).

Criminal behavior—like all conduct, whether normal or abnormal—is undoubtedly a joint product of many personal, social, and environmental elements interacting. For some criminals the fact that they are of a certain body type, muscular and aggressive by nature, may well be an important though not determining factor. For others, an inadequate family, corrupt friends, or neighborhood may be critical. In many instances lawbreakers have come from homes that imparted defective values, lacked standards and ethical orientation. For all potential offenders, however, many individual social influences and circumstances combine to produce criminal behavior. No single causative agent, such as slums, minority status, or lack of parks and playgrounds, can be blamed. The efforts to reduce criminality are often directed at such alleged single causes as poor neighborhoods, inadequate jobs, or other inequities. But since none of these in and of itself produces criminals, much of the effort to provide better living conditions or planned recreational facilities, laudable as it is, has only minor impact on the curtailment of crime (Steiner).

Traditional psychotherapeutic approaches toward criminal behavior have also been discouraging. Asocial criminals are particularly difficult to involve in therapy since they are so grossly lacking in personal feelings to begin with. (See Chapter Sixteen for a case history of psychotherapy with a juvenile delinquent.) In many prisons group therapy has been attempted, but it, like other therapeutic approaches, seems to be of limited value. Although experimentation is continuing and many interesting, often encouraging, results are reported, psychotherapeutic techniques have not yet made any large-scale contributions to the rehabilitation of criminals (Empey and Rabow).

It is important to attempt to change the personality structure that led to criminality through therapy. But this does not mean that punishment for wrongdoing is excluded. The erroneous notion has gotten about that crime should be rewarded with psychotherapy, rather than punished by jail sentences, fines, or other limitations. All criminals and all illegal acts must be judged, tried, and dealt with as courts of law, judges, and juries see fit. The psychotherapist does not displace the legal processes. He offers his service to help rehabilitate the offender while he is undergoing the punishment decreed by society.

ALCOHOLISM

People use *alcoholism* to mean different things. Some would include all those who are frequently intoxicated, go on "benders," and look forward to the next "binge." According to the Public Health Service four million Americans belong to this group. A somewhat smaller group of perhaps 800,000 feel themselves unable to live without alcohol. They need a morning "pick-me-up" and continue drinking throughout most of the day, every day, without let up. They are virtually inebriated continually with few periods of intervening sobriety.

The incidence of alcoholism, as revealed by a number of studies conducted at the Alcohol Research Centers at Yale and Rutgers Universities, varies with ethnoid and national background. People of English, Irish, Germanic, and Scandinavian heritage are more likely to produce alcoholics than are Jewish or Italian groups. Alcoholism is also much more common among men. There are three or four male to every female alcoholic. In addition, most alcoholics are over thirty-five, since ten to twenty years of increasingly hard drinking are necessary to build a true alcoholism (McCord and McCord).

Intoxication affects individuals differently, but nearly all share disharmonies in motor coordination, slowing of reaction time, visual difficulties, and digestive upsets. While some become excited and combative under alcohol, others tend to be mournful and soul-searching. And although since antiquity alcohol has been believed to be a sexual exciter, it actually tends to lower erotic physical capabilities.

Attempts have been made to demonstrate that alcoholics have similar personality characteristics that lead them to excessive drinking. By and large, however, a clear alcoholic-prone personality has not been substantiated, although alcoholics are usually quite poorly adjusted (Gerard, *et al.*). It is most likely that several cultural, developmental, and personal factors combine with accidental circumstances to produce alcoholism (McCord and McCord).

Consequences of Alcoholism

Continued alcoholism leads to physical and psychological symptoms and may eventuate in death. Some of the characteristics and consequences associated with chronic drinking are described below.

Chronic alcoholism. Physical symptoms of chronic alcoholism include the following: bloated appearance of the face and other areas; tremors of the hands and tongue; dilated capillaries in face (reddish nose and cheeks); loss of muscular power; gastrointestinal and digestive disturbances. (See Fig. 13-1.)

Cirrhosis of the liver. This is a serious disorder of the liver found in about 10 per cent of all alcoholics, probably the result of nutritional deficiencies.

Delirium tremens. Popularly known as the D.T.'s or "the shakes," delirium tremens constitutes an acute psychotic episode characterized by delirium, confusion, and frightening hallucinations. This disorder is brought on by several years of intensive drinking; episodes may last two to ten days.

Korsakoff's syndrome. Delirium tremens frequently precedes the onset of this psychosis. Korsakoff's syndrome describes memory loss, confusion, disorientation, disturbances of mood, and confabulation or falsification of memory. Patients may recover in one or two months, or the condition may persist indefinitely.

Some Warning Signs of Possible Alcoholism

Anyone who recognizes himself in any *one* of the descriptions below should seriously examine his drinking habits and perhaps seek professional help to prevent impending alcoholism.

Fig. 13.1 "Sleeping it off." Continued, severe alcohol addiction may result in a downward spiral culminating in loss of job, friends, and family. The alcoholic without ties soon finds himself drifting toward the status of a derelict. Photo courtesy of NaCamU Studio.

Drinking before or instead of breakfast.

Drinking in secret.

Cacheing drinks (hiding alcohol to ensure adequate future supplies).

Gulping (gulping the first two or three drinks hurriedly to get in the proper mood).

Threat of loss of wife or job, or other social punishment, because of drunkenness.

Carrying alcohol and frequently gulping.

Several alcoholic blackouts (loss of consciousness or memory loss due to intoxication).

Binges or benders (sprees of excessive drinking lasting several days or weeks).

Therapy

One of the most successful approaches to helping alcoholics stop drinking has been through Alcoholics Anonymous. AA, as Alcoholics

Anonymous is called, consists mainly of former heavy drinkers who are interested in helping rehabilitate fellow sufferers. They hold meetings and discuss their joint problems over cordial cups of coffee. In a sense AA sessions are not unlike group therapy. AA also stresses spiritual help, and many groups depend heavily upon prayer and religious belief. Though AA is fairly effective in helping alcoholics recover, it should be pointed out that only those already well on the way toward restricting their drinking are likely to go to meetings.

Another method for combating alcoholism is through medication. One popular drug with the trade name Antabuse is supposed to teach the patient not to drink by associating extreme discomfort with imbibing alcohol. Drinking up to several hours after Antabuse has been swallowed causes painful and severe gastric upset. The theory is that alcoholics will learn that drinking has unpleasant physical effects. Unfortunately, this kind of conditioning therapy, which dates back to early Greece where noxious herbs were put in the wines of the intemperate, is not very effective. Often it merely teaches the alcoholic to avoid taking his medication. Research for other medical aids to help alleviate alcoholism nevertheless seems to be promising. Recently, LSD-25 in combination with psychiatric treatment has been reported fairly useful (MacLean, *et al.*). It is important to remember, however, that what is true with all human disorders is especially true with alcoholism: not much progress can be made unless the patient himself is highly motivated to change his habits.

DRUG ADDICTION

There are relatively few drug addicts in the United States. The Public Health Service estimates that there are about sixty thousand addicts, mainly men, half of whom are known to the authorities. But despite their small number, addicts continually come into prominence because considerable criminal activity is stimulated by their dependence on narcotics. An addict may require from twenty to one hundred or more dollars per day to supply himself. As a consequence, many turn to illegal activities to obtain sufficient money. In addition, elaborate smuggling and clandestine distribution arrangements need to be made to get the illegal drugs to their users. The buying, selling, and consumption of narcotics has engendered an elaborate criminal network that even occasionally corrupts high officials or law enforcement personnel.

Addicts may come from all classes of society and all walks of life, though at the present time in some places, like New York City, nearly all addiction is limited to a few ethnoid groups. Not infrequently, however, particular occupational groups, such as physicians, that have special access to drugs, produce some addicts. Similarly, professions in which addiction seems to be considered less intolerable, as in the entertainment industry or among jazz musicians (Winick and Nyswander) may tend to have a larger than average share of addicts. Most commonly, however, addicts originate among adolescent groups from slum environments (Ausubel). These teen-agers, especially in large metropolitan areas like Chicago, New York, and Los Angeles, typically begin by smoking marijuana. For most, experimentation with narcotics will not progress beyond marijuana cigarettes (popularly known as weeds or reefers) and will end when the novelty fades. Some teen-agers, however, will be enticed into or deliberately seek further "thrills" by toying with truly addictive drugs. In short order they are "hooked" by a habituating narcotic like heroin ("horse").

Heroin is one of the most addictive drugs. In order to experience its effects the user is forced to take larger and larger quantities, usually by injection directly into the veins. Heroin is said to have a very heavy *tolerance effect* because it is required in increasingly large quantities to bring satisfaction. If the heroin addict stops, there are serious effects, since the drug is physiologically as well as psychologically addictive. Withdrawal of the drug results in extreme muscular pain, twitching, and many gastrointestinal symptoms (see Table 13-1). Not all drugs

Table 13-1 SOME COMMON DRUGS AND THEIR EFFECTS IN ADDICTION

Drug	Physical effects	Tolerance effect	Withdrawal effects
Opiates Morphine Heroin	Sleepiness, pleasant reverie, relief of pain, carefreeness.	Heavy	Restlessness, perspiration, crying, muscle twitches, vomiting diarrhea, pains
Cocaine Amphetamine	Brief feeling of ecstasy, hallucinations, and excitement that may make the user dangerous	Little or none	No physical symptoms
Peyote Mescaline LSD-25	Visual hallucinations, sometimes excitement or relaxation	Little or none	No physical symptoms
Marijuana	Mild intoxication, giggling, talkativeness, sometimes recklessness	None	No physical symptoms
Barbiturates (sleeping pills, etc.)	Confusion, drowsiness, mild intoxication	Some	For severe addicts, seizures, convulsions, delirium

are physically addictive in the sense that heroin is. Marijuana does not have any notable tolerance effects—does not require ever increasing doses for its effects to be felt. Nor does it stimulate organic *withdrawal reaction,* although there may be intense psychological craving for it when it is withheld.

"Just what is so satisfying about narcotics?" many people wonder. For users, the satisfactions obtained from drugs are similar to those some obtain from alcohol. Narcotics permit the users to feel giddy, gay, and relaxed. People who usually are timid and feel inadequate can believe themselves unusually capable and daring, when drugged. Some of the more potent drugs, such as cocaine, lead addicts to feel a kind of euphoria that they describe in glowing terms as comparable to the sensations experienced during sexual contact.

The following is a report of a case of heroin addiction in a male adolescent. As is true in many histories of addiction, the use of drugs is not necessarily the primary problem. The patient in this instance was treated not only for his addiction but for some of the psychotic symptoms that were evident as well. The report is reproduced with the courtesy of its author, Dr. J. B. Rioux, psychiatrist, and the *American Journal of Psychotherapy.*[2]

In the case about to be reported, less emphasis was placed on the short-ness of the withdrawal period than on the establishment of a personal relation-ship with the patient. . . . Although initially it seemed that the patient would respond to treatment, three main complications interfered with his psycho-therapy: a full-blown psychotic episode, the emergence of a dormant idiopathic epilepsy, and the unprepared transfer of the patient by the father to another hospital.

The patient is a twenty year old, single, white male, the only child of a couple who were divorced ten years prior to the patient's admission to [the hospital]. Up to the age of ten he remained constantly in the company of his domineering, scrupulously concerned mother. He was considered a "good" boy because he was docile and obedient. The divorce of his parents changed his life radically, [and] also his attitude. His father remarried and did not con-tact him during four years. His mother, with whom he lived, became a chronic alcoholic, had promiscuous sexual affairs, and neglected him. The patient responded early with a reaction-formation. He brooked no discipline and avoided all maternal care.

He associated with the arrogant and rebellious boys in school and sur-passed them in rebellion. He "played hooky" often. He was smart enough to remain in high school for almost two years without opening a book. His parents were oblivious to his associations and activities. The positive part of

2 "Heroin Addiction in a Male Adolescent," *10*, No. 2 (April, 1956), 296–321.

his behavior received no recognition from them, as, for instance, when he excelled in sports and won many awards.

By the age of fifteen he was mixed up with delinquents. Unknown to his mother, he made friends with an older boy, a gun collector, and learned how to fabricate a gun of his own. He practiced a secret game of skill with this gun. He would keep it with him all the time while taking pains to conceal it from his mother and from the police. Gradually he grew bolder and began exposing the gun more and more. Thus he would leave it on his bed openly at certain times. On election day he carried it on the street in a paper bag with the handle exposed. He was apprehended by a detective, arrested, and brought to trial. His father was called to help him, marking the first contact between them since the divorce. The father persuaded the judge to give the patient a chance at [a school] instead of a sentence at a reformatory.

He remained at [school] but three months and was dismissed for drunkenness. It has not been possible to determine any more facts surrounding this episode. Thus it is not known how much drinking he did, or if it was his first contact with alcohol; it is not known what his behavior or life was like at the academy. This much is known: when the patient got drunk he phoned his mother. She rushed to the school and strongly reprimanded the authorities for permitting this conduct. They, in turn, told her to take the patient out. The dismissal was apparently a response of the school authorities to the mother's behavior rather than to the patient's.

During the next two years or so, the father made efforts to get the patient jobs and to help him make a work adjustment. The patient never remained on these jobs more than a week or two at a time. The paternal assistance probably had serious limitations. For one thing, the placements were usually with firms from whom the father purchased materials. The patient was hired purely to please a customer and without concern for his relationship to the job. Secondly, on some jobs, the boy, slight in build, was asked to lift packages beyond his physical capacity. The father apparently did not concern himself with such details.

At the age of seventeen, the patient readily persuaded his parents to give their signatures for his enlistment in the Air Force. His desire to enlist was due to peculiar reasons. He had been consorting with a girl whose mother presumably knew something of his activities and tried to keep him out of her home. One day she predicted that he would die in the electric chair by the time he was twenty-one years of age. He took this threat literally and was haunted by the fear that the prediction would be fulfilled. Certain as he was of his doom, he was bent on calculating an escape from it. The Air Force seemed to offer him that means.

With the same kind of reasoning he concealed his identity by changing the first letter of his first name, as one might change one's name from Donald Jones to Ronald Jones. In fact, he planned to enjoy a wild time

while in service as a "last fling" before his expected electrocution. By changing his name his true self would not be responsible for the activity of his alias.

According to his own description in therapy sessions, the patient's military service was rich in delinquent adventures. He went AWOL numerous
times, usually with another soldier, and, as a result, spent a total of nine
months in the stockade.

This is the story he gave of one of his escapades. He picked up a girl,
the teen-age daughter of a local police chief, and took her to a hotel room.
He also invited a number of friends to join him. The group remained
together for a few days. Although the patient announced that the girl was
his partner, only the others had intercourse with her. The group was apprehended by the local police, but the patient escaped. He returned to his
post, was put in the stockade, and eventually faced with indictment for statutory rape, speeding, and an attempt to elude the police. The whole case was
ultimately dropped, but the patient went through severe anxiety, although
he "would not show it." On the contrary, he became provocative with prison
guards and attempted to escape under fire from the guards who pursued him.

During another AWOL he became very destructive at home. He had
come all the way from Texas to see his mother. When he arrived she was
in the midst of a drinking spree and paid no attention to him. He took a
few drinks himself and started to break glasses and tear up his mother's
clothes. His uncle (his mother's brother) was present and punched him in
the nose. The patient looked calmly in the mirror, examined his swollen
nose, and said matter-of-factly: "I like my nose better this way!" This
incident was verified by the uncle, a man who is divorced, drinks heavily,
and fights, but who, in his own way, tried to help the patient through the
years.

During another AWOL the patient suffered a left tibial fracture which
required seven months hospitalization. It could not be ascertained whether
some of this hospitalization was devoted to psychiatric diagnosis or treatment. After two years (with sixteen months out of duty) the patient was
offered a Discharge Without Honor. He considered this offer a disgrace, a
reflection on his character, and he refused to accept it. Finally he was given
a Dishonorable Discharge—in military terms a more severe indictment—and
of this he was proud. During his entire military career he had received one
legitimate leave, and, as a reward, his father had bought him a car.

Returning home in October 1953 he quickly established himself in the
company of heroin addicts and in the ensuing months became a heroin addict himself. How the habit originated is not too clear. As he relates it,
he was asked to smoke a marijuana cigarette, "just to see the effects." After
all, he reasoned, a man must find out by himself. Supposedly out of curiosity
he also began using heroin a few weeks later. He soon discovered that "horse
was boss" (the best drug and the best thing there is, "because it is really boss

of your mind.") He said: "I dreamed and forgot the world and its atrocities."

Rapidly heroin took precedence over anything else in life. He pressed his parents for money and obtained it; he sold his valuables and attempted to sell his mother's. He developed the ability of "burning other junkies," that is, depriving other addicts of some of their own drugs by verbal manipulations. This last aptitude was recognized by the gang leader who treated him as his buddy. He was pleased with this special status and very careful to preserve it. Others could make mistakes which led to their arrest, but not he. He laughed at the stupidity of some addicts; their inability to sense the presence of the police in a given situation. He grew steadily more brazen.

One day he left some of his hypodermic equipment in his bathroom where his uncle found it. The following was noteworthy. This uncle did not live in the household but visited there very often. He had worked in state hospitals and was acquainted with the ways of addicts. He had even talked of these things at times to the patient. At any rate, the uncle called in the father who arranged for the patient's hospitalization. . . .

It should be mentioned that during his cooperative moments in the Air Force, the patient had passed a vocational test which established that he had mechanical abilities. He despised mechanics and then chose to be a cook. After discharge, he was offered various mechanical jobs by his father. He never expressed objection to them; he simply quit each of them within two or three weeks. In one instance, and to his father's pleasure, he did surprisingly well as a photographer's helper. He said that it was only because he needed the money to buy heroin which he was taking in heavy doses at that time. He commented sarcastically: "After all, who wants to work?"

The patient's parents were able to provide very little information about their son's history inasmuch as they knew relatively little about him. They had no knowledge of the fact that he had been an addict for ten months, until two days before his admission to the hospital. They were ignorant of much of his other activities. They were evidently ignorant of, or oblivious to, all that was going on within their son emotionally and psychologically. The data already mentioned and other information to be reported later were largely provided by the patient himself.

The patient's father is a forty year old business man. He has an attractive wife and two younger sons, four and two years old (the latter adopted), whom he considers definite social assets. With his second marriage he rapidly ascended the social scale. According to the uncle, people in general find him warm and likeable. He does favors for them.

He presumably divorced his first wife and remarried when he became aware of his own business and social potentialities. This second wedding was rapidly followed by a depression. He also appeared depressed and expressed personal guilt when his son had to be admitted to the hospital.

At first, he seemed genuinely concerned about his son's condition and ready to follow any recommendation which the hospital made. Neverthe-less, from the very beginning he also appeared guarded and somewhat se-cretive. As the treatment progressed, his attitude of concern appeared to shift more and more to the effects of his son's illness on himself. Once, while being told that the patient was a possible epileptic, he wept and dis-played resentment that this was happening to him. Later he began to com-plain about the hospital expenses, although a few weeks before he would have paid $450.00 for three tickets to the World Series. Ultimately he stopped visiting the patient, and a month later he had him transferred to another hospital.

While the patient maintains that his father is "a snob," he believes his mother is a social outcast. Many years of alcoholism and of all sorts of common-law relationships which came in the wake of her divorce, made her look older than her years. . . . She is jobless and constantly fears the loss of her alimony. She has retained her ex-husband's name and emphasizes her rights still to be called "Mrs. R.," though there is a second "Mrs. R." She sees her ex-husband and the divorce as the only causes for the patient's illness and is unaware of her own role in it. She expresses contempt for her ex-husband's social ambitions.

Her inability to help her son was illustrated at the hospital under strik-ing circumstances. Upon her first visit she left him rather embarrassed because she made no move to greet him in front of other visitors. She postponed seeing the therapist in spite of his repeated requests that she see him. Toward the end she believed that her ex-husband was wrong in contemplating a change of hospital, but she could not oppose him.

His uncle once made the remark: "Between his father and his mother, the patient is at a loss." Both actually rejected him.

Upon admission to [the] hospital the patient could not specify the amount of drug he had been using. He was taken off heroin entirely and given demerol instead. . . . He was not informed of the substitution. He accepted his hospitalization as a just punishment. He voiced no complaints in spite of manifest withdrawal symptoms, i.e., marked tremors, perspiration, dilated pupils. Only after persistent questioning did he admit having head-ache, backache, nausea and muscular cramps. He asked for no additional medication, however. During the first twelve hours, the therapist, observing the obvious withdrawal symptoms, gave the patient two additional injections. The administration of demerol was progressively decreased until it was com-pletely discontinued at the end of one month.

In appearance this patient was short (5'2"), slight, quite young looking, and with an unassuming demeanor. To the personnel he was "just a kid." His zoot-suit and duck-tail haircut were out of keeping with his general slight physique. One was even astonished to find on his right arm the fol-lowing tattoo: a stalking panther moving toward the inscription MOM.

Psychological testing revealed the following: "Although the scores achieved on the Bellevue-Wechsler (Form I) were representative of low average intelligence,

Verbal I.Q.   95

Performance I.Q.   93

Full Scale I.Q.   94

it was obvious from the quality and range of various individual responses on both the intelligence and projective test data that the patient is of inherently superior intelligence.

The patient's psychosexual and social development is viewed as amorphous and infantile and is consistent with his self-picture which is confused. . . .

The projective techniques give the impression of a depressed, guilty and anxious young man who gives indications of being subject to ruminative phantasies of a destructive and threatening nature. His method of relieving his unbearable tension was primarily through impulsive acting out than by introspective thinking.

.   .   .   .   .

At the time of testing the patient did not show evidence of any psychotic thinking. However, his withdrawal and isolation, and his inability to relate meaningfully to others were extreme enough to classify him. . . .

Other patients remarked on the politeness of this newcomer who was shy but inviting. In sessions he spoke in a low and unassertive tone of voice, as if ashamed of himself. He appeared mainly concerned with the wrong he had done. He was sorry for having used heroin during the last ten months and wanted to break the habit. He regretted entertaining doubts in regard to his family's intentions, having suspected that they would send him to jail and not to a hospital. He appeared glad to have the opportunity for treatment. He added that he had tried to help himself, but withdrawal symptoms prevented him from overcoming the habit. He admitted being unhappy and indirectly indicated that it was so since the divorce of his parents.

At that point, it appeared that the patient would respond to psychotherapy. The father was told of the necessity of a long term treatment. The patient was told that he had a serious emotional illness but that he could be helped if he cooperated. His therapy would emphasize insight and he would receive a minimum of three sessions a week.

The patient responded in a positive manner. He answered questions freely and volunteered to talk about the last few years of his life. With time he grew more confident and more assertive with patients, personnel, and therapist. Soon he described with relish the adventures and the mores of drug addicts. The more he talked about them the more fascinated he appeared to become by the various adventures he was describing and, in turn, the more assertive and boastful he became. His shameful feelings fell away, and he narrated with growing pride the various manipulations necessary to maintain the status of a drug addict.

Taking heroin, he said, gave him at last a goal in life and confidence in himself. He considered himself an expert in persuading his parents to lend him money and in outsmarting other addicts. He boasted that he would not hesitate to enter sexual activity with rich older women and homosexuals, whom he despised, to extract money from them to buy heroin. He regarded such actions as the essence of being a man. He emphasized that his and his friends' great concern was to preserve a status of "supermen." Consequently, they went to great length to show that they avoided "dependency on women." They did not care for female companions or, if they did, it was merely to use them as servants. The girl who accompanied one of them to the theater or restaurant had to pay, while the addict ostentatiously stepped back to indicate his importance to his friends, as well as to the rest of the world. A woman could not speak up in front of his companions lest she be slapped by her "escort" or by another addict. If a woman was promiscuous with one of them, they would insist that she be with the whole gang.

As these things emerged in sessions, the therapist noted the following: The patient would answer specific questions only to a point. Beyond that he would reveal only what he, the patient, wanted the therapist to hear. Hence, he prevented the therapist from exploring the patient's narration in fullest details and from determining what was fact and what might have been fancy.

After one month the patient began to yield material relative not only to his grandiosity, but also to certain of his weaknesses. One day he entered the session brooding. Upon inquiry it developed that he had been turning his attention toward certain situations in which he felt he had been exploited by others. He was really angry at himself for getting "burned" (deprived of his own drug by other addicts). The incident occurred when he had felt sorry for them and believed their stories. He went on to admit that only a "softie" could have been deceived by these lies. Then he complained of tension and nausea.

During this period the therapist had suggested to the father that he do something more for his son. As a result, the patient was taken to the World Series and he responded enthusiastically. It was the first time in ten years, he said, that he went out with his father. He described him as a patient man whom he liked more than his mother. He could not think now of leaving the hospital as he had before, because he would not "be doing right by his father." Instead of bragging about his previous misbehavior, he repeated: "I am sorry for what I did *to my father*."

So much for what he said. But what was going on in the patient's unconscious in regards to his father's intentions is essentially a matter of speculation. As it were, one might suspect that he sensed some deceit in the making. In fact, two days after the last baseball game, the patient developed a severe anxiety reaction with all the manifestations of a catatonic excitement. He became restless, wandered about, and refused to see anybody. On his aimless walks he would come to a sudden stop, assuming fixed positions. At other times, he would hold on to the bed frame for fear, as he confessed later, of losing control of his mounting rage. He verbalized a high degree of ambivalence in his will and emotion. Should he think of his father as a nice man, or as someone he wanted to kill? On second thought, and as he wanted to kill at any rate, it would be better to start with himself, so disgusted was he with his life. A whole month elapsed before he was able to verbalize some of the underlying fantasies; they will be described later.

In the meantime, it should be indicated how treatment proceeded under the circumstances. Whatever insight the patient was gaining was accompanied by such a negative reaction that it was decided to introduce adjunctive therapies. A modified form of sleep-therapy was initially used to fight his homicidal and suicidal tendencies. It was abandoned a few days later in favor of insulin-coma therapy, because the administration of high doses of barbiturates required more personnel and presented a danger of addiction. Insulin produced an amelioration of his anxiety. He appreciated the greater attention he received by the nurses who supervised his treatments. He began teasing young women and finally cut his own hair, eliminating the duck tail hair style. The compliments he then received from nurses and from female patients brought on a more apparent than true resentment, although for his embarrassment he wore a hat even when going to bed.

.   .   .   .   .

The patient remained less anxious after insulin was interrupted. The personnel noted his improvement and responded by a greater acceptance of his behavior, which now and then was still marked by a spurious defiance. He accepted restrictions and postponements. Occupational therapy started to interest him and he mingled with all groups, including the "intellectual elite." It was obvious that the patient had developed a feeling of belonging to the hospital. He even confessed to one patient that he was grateful for the opportunity of being treated.

Around the beginning of the third month, the patient reported about "the two most unhappy weeks of his life," connected with the statutory rape indictment. This prompted the therapist to remark: "You seem to get into most trouble when you are most unhappy."

Shortly afterwards the patient requested a special interview at 10:30 p.m. He stated, for the first time, that during the last four years he had lived with the fear that he would die in the electric chair on his twenty-first birthday. He was preoccupied with preparing himself for this event. His friends would read in the papers how cool and collected he had been in the face of death. When he sat down he often tried to compose himself in order to reach a posture indicative of great cold-bloodedness. His conviction that he was heading for the electric chair had engendered a chain of antisocial behavior. This conviction in turn, had been reinforced by his parents' repeated warnings whenever they came to his rescue: "Wait until you are twenty-one; we will not bother with you!"

For a short while the patient appeared helpless, without the resource of his usual defenses. However, when the therapist made a statement of fact in regards to his unhappiness, he looked up with a fleeting air of bravado and, as if answering primarily his inner thoughts, he said: "There is the consolation that I will have killed at least two men. I know it. The first one because the time will come soon when I won't be able to control my anger. The other will be purely for gain. Every man possessing a certain amount of money (let us say $10,000), is worth killing, and I will take his money."

A short description of his interpersonal relationships as they were observed in the hospital will be introduced now. His associations with patients presented definite patterns. He avoided male company by and large. One boy with a passive-dependent personality irritated him greatly, supposedly because of "the way the 'creep' combed his hair." Another, who was aggressive, won the patient's admiration but left him fearful.

With women he felt more at ease. He had a way of provoking their motherly interest. They treated him more as a protector than as a protected, which he really was. They listened to his adventures and praised his strength. They encouraged him to work by trading stockings and sweaters for other objects that he would try to make for them. Whatever little he accomplished was highly complimented. He observed with humor: "These women throw me rocks!" but he continued, nevertheless, to provoke their flatteries and he enjoyed them.

Toward the most disturbed female patients he showed sympathy. Once when a catatonic girl hit him on the head with her shoe, he simply walked away. The following Sunday he told the story to his uncle, but with the distortion that he had inflicted a retaliatory beating upon the patient. There were many other instances of similar falsification, because he apparently did not want to show that he could be kind.

Of course, the situation had to be different with the hospital personnel and, in particular, with his therapist. Toward them, exception being made for his initial submission, he assumed a definite demanding, trying-to-scare attitude. When requesting, for instance, that his night sedative be given earlier, he threatened: "If I don't get it now I will burn down this joint!" Very often it was noted that he could not actually formulate a request. His needs were probably so great that he had to hide them. When given attention, he responded to it as if it were his due. When refused, he felt hurt like a child, but he acted "tough."

His problem with toughness was finally tackled therapeutically. After the discontinuation of insulin therapy, his attention turned toward wanting to be a strong man. The importance of strength was supported by the therapist, but with the idea that psychotherapy was his real key to strength. Appropriate examples were extracted from his previous recitations of adventures. The patient was reminded that in one instance he had showed ingenuity, in another power of persuasion, in still another manual dexterity. Above all, he had manifested kindliness. He was shown, in brief, that he had real assets from which he could draw strength. Perhaps he would not need to rely on bravado alone.

Kindliness, it was indicated, can go with strength and need not be confused with softness. Thus if he were kind it could be because he was strong enough to afford to be. In the past he had brought into conflict these tendencies: strength versus kindness (social respect)—creating a dilemma, and he had sought to solve the problem by erroneously deriding himself for his tendencies toward kindness.

To the above statements the patient showed the following reaction. He confided to a female patient that his antisocial behavior was a result of his unhappiness and he was wondering if he could not do better than he had. At the same time, he became more resistant in his therapeutic sessions. Upon receiving an appointment for the second day in a row, he commented sarcastically: "didn't I see you yesterday?" During this and the following sessions he kept his hat on and made imperative demands. He wanted to be placed in a better group (Group III) right away, or else. The therapist said: "Patients who want to be in Group III remove their hats when sitting in a treatment session." This firm statement had a good effect on the patient and he responded with a more cooperative attitude.

It is worth noting that this patient reported no dreams during his three months of therapy.

Suddenly, at the end of the third month, his father, without warning, decided to take him out of the hospital. When the therapist notified the patient, the patient's eyes teared visibly. The reaction passed, however. Within a few minutes he resumed a "tough-guy" attitude and reestablished his old delinquent-type mode of behavior. He walked around the ward boasting of the "good news." He called his therapist by his last name without a title, adding that he was only a simple intern. He was provocative toward the therapist and personnel. At the same time, he manifested almost complete relief from the tension, anxiety and agitation that had characterized him during the entire period of his positive response in the hospital. Evidently his father's reversal made both the world and the father understandable once more to the patient. Once more he could feel in his own distorted way that he knew what things were all about and knew how to handle them.

The father was told of the serious implications of his decision. He was told that the patient at the time equated his desire to get well with his being in the hospital. If removed abruptly he could lose this desire to get well altogether. This made no impression on the father, however, and the patient was transferred.

Therapy

Confirmed addicts are extremely resistive to treatment. Through special hospitals, such as the one at Lexington, Kentucky, considerable money and professional effort has been aimed at rehabilitating narcotic users. Although recovery rates are improving, the proportion of treated addicts who discontinue drugs permanently is probably less than one out of four or five (Noyes and Kolb). In special instances, when working with unusually motivated addicts, recovery rates may be higher. Winick and Nyswander report that their treatment of fifteen addicted jazz musicians was highly successful.

Great Britain has a controversial approach to addiction that many contend is extremely successful. Addicts who register and come to clinics may get narcotics free or at nominal costs. This system is believed to have almost eliminated the criminal network of drug peddlers, since it is impossible to sell narcotics to those who can get them free. Moreover, it does not pay to "hook" adolescents since after they are addicts they can go to clinics for their supply. Little or no drug-connected crime is reported in Great Britain.

In our own country the therapeutic effects of police efforts should not be overlooked. Rigorous law enforcement, meaningful penalties, and incorruptible officials can be extremely effective in curtailing traffic in drugs and addiction.

SUMMARY OF PERSONALITY DISORDERS

In Chapters Twelve and Thirteen we have discussed various personality disorders. By way of summary and review, they are listed here.

    Personality Pattern Disturbances
        Inadequate personality
        Schizoid personality
        Cyclothymic personality
        Paranoid personality
    Personality Trait Disturbances
        Emotionally unstable personality
        Passive-aggressive personality
        Compulsive personality

Sociopathic Personality Disturbances
    Asocial (antisocial, psychopathic) reactions
    Dyssocial reactions
    Sexual deviations
    Addictions
      Alcoholism
      Drug

Deviation: Causation and Responsibility

Criminal and all deviant behavior can often be explained. In specific cases of sexual perversion, dope addiction, or crime it is frequently possible to trace back and uncover the elements that led to the condition. Further, in some instances, when the offender is particularly well motivated and otherwise favorably disposed, psychotherapeutic techniques may aid in rehabilitation. Because the causes of deviant behavior are sometimes apparent and since therapy is occasionally successful, confusion about the meaning of criminal responsibility has developed.

Too often criminal and other undesirable behavior, which is properly the concern of courts of law, is relegated to mental health facilities. Too often also, "insanity" or "mental or environmental stress" is held to excuse violations of society's rules. In actual fact it is quite improbable that an offender, despite the pleas of attorneys, is so confused or his concept of reality so distorted that he is unaware of the socially disapproved nature of his conduct. That the reasons for deviant actions can be explained in terms of the offender's background and development does not pardon him from the crimes he has committed. All social deviates, from sex offenders to armed criminals, live in our own culture and must conform to its standards. Those who deviate, fully aware of the consequences, need to be prepared to be chastised for their nonconformity.

People whose behavior is detrimental to society should be treated as humanely as possible. All efforts, including psychotherapy and imprisonment, need to be directed not only to punish but also to rehabilitate. Deprivation of personal liberty through imprisonment is probably not the most effective or commendable type of chastisement, but until a system is devised that is demonstrably superior, there is no reason why it should be abandoned. Punishment can be an effective treatment technique in and of itself.

There has been a progressive weakening of our system of rewards and punishments. Criminals and other offenders against society's moral and legal codes increasingly find their conduct excused on the basis of faulty home or environmental background. This kind of reasoning is hardly likely to act as a deterrent to other potential violators.

The facts concerning lawbreakers are continually distorted. We are presented glamorized pictures of unjustly mistreated homosexuals or dope addicts. We are persuaded that these are "harmless" people persecuted by society, who practice their vices in the quiet seclusion of their homes and should therefore not be harassed. They too, it is argued, are entitled to their own style of life. Whatever the popular charitable view may be, it turns out that the peaceful homosexual and addict are fables. Nearly all addicts are involved in one way or another in inducing others to join them in their craving for narcotics. Similarly, many investigators (e.g., East; Greenspan and Campbell) have noted that seduction by older homosexuals may well be the single most common environmental factor in leading to homosexuality. The conduct of nearly all deviates is such that in pursuit of their particular distorted need they adversely affect the innocent healthy majority among whom they live.

Our social structure seeks to maximize the opportunity for all people to grow into healthy and mature human beings. Unquestionably, our society is not doing as well as it could or should. There are serious deficiencies that need to be corrected. But we are not helping to provide the kind of healthy surroundings we want for ourselves and for those for whom we care when we excuse, or our entertainment media glamorize, all kinds of crimes against the legitimate order. Those who deviate because of disordered personality and circumstance need to be given every opportunity for psychiatric treatment. But the well-being of our social structure also demands that all be held responsible for their actions and subjected to the ethical and legal restraints necessary to maintain the intactness of our culture.

FOR REVIEW AND DISCUSSION

1. What are the differences between asocial and dyssocial criminal personalities? What are some causes of criminal behavior? Why is legal restraint and punishment initially more important, than psychiatric treatment?

2. Is there such a thing as an alcoholic personality? Are dope addicts characterized by a single clear personality pattern?
   Define delirium tremens, Korsakoff's syndrome, tolerance effect, and withdrawal.

3. The case report of the twenty-year-old male heroin addict details symptoms suggestive of a wide variety of psychiatric disorders. What disorders might the subject have? What were some possible causes of the

patient's symptoms? What needs did the heroin addiction satisfy? Discuss the signs that seemed to indicate the therapist was making progress.

4. Do you think that someone who commits a criminal act and is diagnosed as having a personality disorder should be allowed to plead that he was "insane" and did not "know" what he was doing? Should criminals, sexual deviates, and other offenders be held responsible for their actions? Why?

Disorders of

Speech and

Habit

F O U R T E E N

The Development of Language
Parental Role in Speech Development
Identifying the Speech Handicapped
Defects of Articulation, Voice, and Rhythm
Speech Therapies
Habit Disorders: Nail Biting, Enuresis,
Tics, Twitches, and Spasms

*The material in this chapter was prepared by
Adelaide N. Haas, M.A., speech and hearing therapist.*

Few disturbances focus attention upon themselves or upset people as much as disorders of speech and habit. For many people, severe stuttering, enuresis, tics, or other behavioral aberrations are deeply rooted patterns that are difficult to modify. Others similarly afflicted may be greatly relieved by competent treatment. In the following pages some of the major varieties of speech and habit difficulties, their origins, and outcome are detailed.

THE DEVELOPMENT OF LANGUAGE

Man is a talking animal. By expressing feelings and thoughts orally, by a continuous process of speaking, listening, and analyzing, human beings develop as individuals.

Language as we know it is not inborn. The physical vocal apparatus is present at birth, but it is many years before the mechanism can be put to full use in communication. Throughout a person's lifetime, the language he has learned and the way in which he speaks both reflect and affect his total adjustment to the world about him.

Language does not come by itself; it is learned. Children deprived of an opportunity to hear the spoken word, such as those born deaf or reared in isolated circumstances, can utter sounds but have tremendous difficulty learning to speak. Similarly, youngsters reputedly raised by animals, such as Lucas the baboon boy of Africa and Victor the wild boy of Aveyon, were able only to grunt and make noises when brought back to human company. The spoken word does not emerge unless a child is enabled to function in an optimum communicating human environment (Van Riper).

Learning to talk begins with the birth cry. During the first few months of life, crying, gurgling, grunting, sighing, and other vocal play exercise the speech apparatus and prepare the child to form meaningful sounds. During these early months the infant babbles freely and is in the main uninfluenced by the language or dialect spoken in his home. Yet though beginning sounds are fairly free of the influences of milieu, it has been found that if a young child is in hostile or tense surroundings during his first six months of life, babbling may not emerge. The child appears to be disinterested in vocalizations. (See the case of Mary in Chapter Eleven.)

During the second half of the first year the developing infant shows he is aware of the speech of others by repeating sounds in the process known as *echolalia*. Eventually these random repetitions shape themselves so that by about a year of age phonetic combinations, "mama," "dada," "bye-bye," and similar "words" emerge. After the first year additional words are added slowly so that by two years of age most children have about three hundred words that they are able to hook together into two- or three-word sentences.

The growth of language is not a smooth or orderly process. Periods of rapid growth are interspersed with lapses during which not much seems to be happening. These speech lulls often coincide with the learning of a new motor skill such as walking or eating from a spoon. Accompanying the growth and intelligent use of words is a continuation of jargon, a "senseless" chattering and playing with words, sounds, and noise (often directed to toys) that is preparatory for further linguistic development.

While most children reach certain levels of proficiency at particular ages, many perfectly normal, intelligent, and healthy youngsters deviate considerably from average rates of progress. That an otherwise normal and healthy child does not use three hundred words at age two is likely to be due simply to the fact that he is developing at his own pace; he is probably neither more nor less able than children who know more words than he does (see Table 14-1). If, however, a child has not yet begun to speak any recognizable words by age two, professional consultation should be considered (Darley and Winitz).

Table 14-1 NORMAL SPEECH DEVELOPMENT

Age (years)	Patterns	Words in vocabulary	Sentences	Sound stabilization
½	Babbling, vocal play			Range unrestricted
1	Babbling, echolalia	1		Range narrows
1½	Jargon, often to toys	10–20	One word long	
2	Pitch and rhythm inconsistent	300	2–3 words long	Pronunciation erratic
2½	Repetition of phrases often at a peak	500–600		Articulation still not stable
3		900	Approximation of adult sentence structure	Speech is 90 per cent intelligible

Source: Based on data reported by Van Riper; Berry and Eisenson.

By the third birthday most children have about nine hundred words available. More and more phrases and expressions are added rapidly until the age of six, when the verbal skills, as well as other capacities, decelerate. There is great individual variation in speech development, but girls in general develop more rapidly than boys. Parents who are more than ordinarily warm and attentive, are employed in the professions, or have high intelligence are conducive to the relatively quick growth of speech. Children from families characterized by low ability levels, neglect, or disinterest generally tend to speak later than those from more usual backgrounds (Berry and Eisenson).

Parental Role in Speech Development

Since speech is largely learned, there needs to be a teacher as well as a pupil. Whether they are aware of it or not, parents serve as the main instructors of language. In addition, of course, the child learns to speak from friends, school teachers, television, and all other sources of communications. Just as the mother is not conscious that she is teaching her child, the learner is not cognizant of the sources of his instruction. Children do not deliberately set out to emulate the speech of any particular person, although it is by *imitation* that they chiefly learn to talk. Does the fact that parents serve as teachers indicate they need to set about deliberately to instruct their children? Although some experts recommend special techniques, the greatest contribution to salubrious speech development is probably made by the parent who himself speaks simply and clearly, with a healthy lack of anxiety and pressure directed at his own or his child's communicative abilities.

If children learn by imitation, then they will emulate not only desirable speech patterns, but also undesirable ones. If parents use "baby talk," for example, does it not assure that their youngster's speech will be burdened with infantile phrases and pronunciations? Popular advice has it that using phrases like "Es go dinky milky-wilky" is poor parental policy. It may well be so, since the child is likely to copy the phrase, assuming this kind of distortion is proper language. Eventually his speech may become so disabled that it can only be corrected therapeutically. The temptation to use and embellish their own young child's mispronounced words is very great among many affectionate parents. But all such usage is not potentially damaging. Parents who limit baby talk to a few pet phrases such as "nighty-night" but otherwise speak simply and correctly are not likely to engender speech difficulties.

In view of the immense amount of material a child needs to learn and the complexity of the subtle motor skills needed to perform, it is to be expected that hesitancies and other speech inadequacies occur.

But for the overwhelming majority of youngsters the early difficulties that sound like lisps, stutters, stammers, and other handicaps are wholly temporary. Left to their own devices and provided with normal models to imitate, nearly all children gain fluency as they grow older. A sure way for parents to ensure the continuation of nonfluency and the growth of impaired speech, however, is to belabor their offspring's temporary difficulties. If children are punished, chastised, or continually corrected, the imperfect habits are likely to continue and even grow worse.

Mrs. L. married quite late and was forty-two when her first child was born. She was an unusually conscientious mother, doubtless more concerned and anxious than she needed be. When her daughter was three years and five months old, she was brought to a clinic by her mother who stated that the child had a "severe speech problem." Actually the girl had only a few hesitancies and misarticulations, characteristic for her age. Nevertheless the mother was worried and admitted she had been "tutoring" and "correcting" her child, but that her efforts "only seem to make things worse."

The child was examined by a speech therapist, and it was recommended that, although the child did not require therapy, the mother needed some counseling sessions in order to prevent her from seriously impairing the child's speech.

The mother was seen for nine therapeutic counseling sessions, during which time it was explained that her child's speech was acceptably normal, but might become handicapped by overattention. Some of the mother's anxiety and overconcern about her child were explored, and significant progress was made so that after two months of treatment the parent was discharged and a noticeable relaxation in her attitude was noted. Follow-up one year after contact showed that the child's speech was normal and that the mother was continuing to treat her child with less extreme concern.

IDENTIFYING THE SPEECH HANDICAPPED

Disorders of speech are usually described and categorized in terms of the specific difficulties interfering with normal sound production. Yet speech impairments are seldom simply mechanical problems involving pronunciation, clarity, rhythm, or any other of the components of talking. In nearly all cases personality, attitude, behavior, and the total mental well-being of the individual are involved in the discernible handicap. For this reason speech problems are best treated by clinical teams consisting of physicians, speech and hearing therapists, psychologists, and other specialists. It must be kept in mind, therefore, that though a particular patient is labeled, say, a stutterer, his entire being is ultimately the source of difficulty and the focus of treatment.

The precise incidence of speech impairment is difficult to determine. Extensive population surveys and studies of school children suggest that about five out of every hundred Americans have some degree of handicap (see Table 14-2).

Table 14-2 APPROXIMATE INCIDENCE OF SPEECH DISORDERS

Type of defect	Number in population (based on 1960 census)	Estimated percentage
Functional articulatory	5,400,000	3.0
Stuttering	1,260,000	.7
Voice	360,000	.2
Cleft palate speech	180,000	.1
Cerebral palsy speech	360,000	.2
Delayed speech development	540,000	.3
Impaired hearing with speech defect	900,000	.5
Total	7,500,000	5.0

Source: Based on data of W. Johnson, et al.

DEFECTS OF ARTICULATION

Roughly 3 per cent of the nation's children incorrectly use speech sounds although they are not hindered by any physical abnormality. The person with an articulatory disorder says "Bwing me tome pains" when he means "Bring me some paints." In this example several sounds are substituted and distorted. The w sound is used for the r in bring and the t for an s in some. Distortion occurs in the unacceptable production of the s sound in paints. In an articulatory disorder the speaker may also omit sounds. " 'and me the 'at" is accepted Cockney English for "Hand me the hat," but it is inappropriate in most other English-speaking environments.

False labeling of articulatory disorders occurs frequently during the period a child is learning to speak. Adults are ready to accept the limited vocabulary of the preschooler, but expect the words to be perfectly pronounced. In investigations by Poole and others the age at which the physically and mentally normal child regularly pronounces all English sounds correctly was found to be six and a half years for girls and about seven and a half for boys.

There are also *physical reasons for faulty articulation*. Most common, and quite transitory, is missing or abnormal teeth. The toothlessness of a six-year-old, for example, may partially account for his inability to correctly say such sounds as *f, v, th, s,* and *z* (Snow). There is generally no need for correction in such cases, since the growth of adult teeth should remedy the situation.

A more serious cause of articulatory disorder is a *cleft palate*. This is an opening (cleft) in the roof of the mouth (palate). It may range from a congenitally short palate to a complete hole extending from the uvula (the small flap of tissue descending from the roof of the mouth) through the palate and upper lip, ending at the nostrils or a cheek. Because of this space the person is unable to prevent air from escaping through the nose each time he opens his mouth to speak. This imparts a nasal quality to most sounds. In addition, there may be sound substitutions such as the glottal plosive (a coughlike explosion) for *k, t,* or *p.* These sounds require air pressure in the mouth for correct production—which the patient with a severe cleft cannot provide. Sound distortions also occur in cleft palate speech because of tongue inflexibility. The sounds *l, t, d, s,* and *sh* are most frequently involved. Most of the 180,000 Americans with cleft palate speech were born with the defect, though a few instances are the result of accident or imitation of a person with this type of speech.

Impaired hearing accounts for speech impediments in about one in two hundred people. Since we learn to talk by listening, the articulatory effects of hearing loss depend on the type and degree of auditory impediment and when it occurred. Severe hearing damage before the child learns to talk usually means complete speech inability without extensive training. But *conductive deafness* caused by abnormality in the outer or middle ear need not result in articulatory disorder. People afflicted in this way generally hear all speech sounds in an undistorted manner if they are said loudly enough. In *perceptive* or *nerve deafness* the person typically is unable to hear high frequencies or tones found in sounds like *f, v, s, z, sh,* and *th.* Because the perceptively hard of hearing miss these sounds, they fail to articulate them appropriately.

Cerebral palsy affects more than a quarter of a million Americans. Most people with this condition have some speech defects, since cerebral palsy is characterized by paralysis, weakness, incoordination, and other motor losses due to pathology within the brain itself. The extent to which speech is disturbed depends mainly on the degree to which the neural and mechanical components of voice and articulation are incapacitated.

DEFECTS OF VOICE

Identifying a voice defect and agreeing upon who has one is more difficult than determining articulatory problems. Most listeners understand what the person with a "voice defect" is saying, so why should such conditions be considered speech problems? One reason is that a speaker's pitch, loudness, and quality give his voice the unique quality that permits listeners to say "That's Joe next door; I recognize his voice." The voice that is too high pitched, rasping, or otherwise unpleasant or irritating puts the speaker at a distinct disadvantage. It may even produce or reflect a real psychological handicap.

Dr. W. E. Moore studied a group of 119 students at Colorado State College and Kent State University who had voice-quality deficiencies of various types. He found that breathy voices tended to be associated with students high in neurotic tendencies and introversion. Those who whined appeared somewhat emotionally unstable and submissive. Students whose voices were harsh and metallic were generally dominant in personality and emotionally stable. The results of this study tentatively suggested the kinds of relationship between voice and personality that many had long suspected.

Pat, a twenty-year-old, attractive coed, was told she would not be granted an elementary school teaching certificate unless her voice was freed of speech defect. Though Pat's voice was adequate in most situations, she failed a speaking course because her extremely high pitch and whine made listeners uncomfortable. An initial interview revealed that in quiet conversation her voice quality was near normal, but when addressing a group it went up in pitch and nasality, since she feared public speaking. She said that she always had the feeling students in the class were laughing at her behind her back.

Psychotherapeutic sessions at a clinic helped Pat obtain a better understanding of herself and reduce her anxieties. It was brought out that Pat's father was the principal of her high school and that he and her classmates expected extraordinary performance from her. In order to hide her average abilities Pat learned to make herself very unobstrusive and retiring.

Counseling combined with lessons in physical relaxation and conscious pitch control from a speech therapist soon evidenced a marked improvement in Pat's speech, attitude, and conduct.

Disorders of Rhythm (Stuttering)

There are three types of nonfluent, dysrhythmic speech. The first is *normal nonfluency,* apparent in many children around four years of age. This is merely a stage in learning to talk and should not be labeled stuttering any more than inability at this age to pronounce a word such as "flower" correctly should be called a disorder of articulation.

The second type, called *primary stuttering,* consists of repetitions or blocks that occur so frequently that they hamper communication and attract more attention than the message itself. These nonfluencies occur in situations where most children are fluent. A primary stutterer is not self-conscious about his speech nor does he attempt to conceal it. Stuttering can often be stopped at this point by counseling the parents.

Once a child becomes aware of and is alarmed by his stuttering, the most resistive type of nonfluency, called *secondary stuttering,* develops. It is characterized by symptoms intended to conceal defective speech. The prognosis for primary stutterers referred for help is excellent. In a secondary stutterer, therapy is more involved and much more difficult. A secondary stutterer has learned to fear words and situations that cause nonfluency. In an attempt to escape the impending stutter he develops avoidance techniques and mannerisms, so-called secondary symptoms. He may substitute a synonym for the word originally intended, blink his eyes, stamp his feet, or click his tongue in an attempt to utter the sound correctly. These tricks soon develop into habits and patterns that can become more handicapping than the original nonfluencies.

Stutterers are not equally nonfluent in all situations. Many can act, sing, recite, talk to certain people, and speak another language flawlessly. With patient care and careful therapeutic efforts, most, too, can regain considerable competence in usual encounters.

Stuttering remains something of an enigma. Theories of the cause of stuttering and recommendations for treatment are numerous. Some are convinced that stuttering is an inherited disorder. It is known, for example, that there is a tendency for stuttering to run in families. In one study of 204 families containing a stuttering member, more than 50 per cent of the families showed stuttering in the kinship group for several generations (West, *et al.*). Other investigators have found stutterers to be poorer in motor coordination and other physical skills than normal speakers. This tends to confirm the possible genetic base of rhythm speech disorders.

On the other hand, there are authorities who feel that stuttering is a learned phenomenon independent of any physiological or hereditary factors. Wendell Johnson, speech therapist, psychologist, and semantician, claims that stuttering is the result of falsely labeling normal childhood nonfluency as stuttering. Just as children do not begin by perfectly pronouncing all the sounds in all words, they do not speak fluently at all times. Johnson contends that stutterers become what they are because their once normal nonfluencies have been labeled and traumatically brought to their attention over and over again. Evidence such as that uncovered by Bloodstein showed that parents of stutterers are more likely to falsely identify common nonfluencies as stuttering than are mothers of normal speakers.

Change of handedness has been blamed for stuttering. The theory was based on the idea of cerebral dominance of one brain hemisphere over the other. Normally, it was believed, cortical control of speech is located in the left cerebral hemisphere for right-handed people and in the right cerebral hemisphere for left-handed individuals. Failure to establish dominance was said to cause conflicting neural impulses to the speech mechanism and so result in the hesitations and repetitions associated with stuttering. This point of view is not accepted today. Even one of the earliest advocates of this theory, Lee E. Travis, has in recent years modified his initial position.

Stuttering may actually be due to a multiplicity of causes. Parental overconcern may contribute to speech pathology, but physical impediments not now discernible may be responsible also. It should be recalled that not all people are innately equally fluent. Like other human attributes, fluency may be statistically distributed in a curve that ranges from virtually undisturbable fluency in some to easily provoked failures in rhythm in others. Stuttering may eventually be shown to be caused in somewhat different ways, involving an interaction between physical and environmental factors, for different individuals.

THERAPY

Before effective therapy can be initiated, the background and circumstances of the disorder must be investigated. When a person comes to a speech therapist or a clinic, he is interviewed, and as complete a case history as feasible is obtained. In learning about the person's birth, family, education, and environment, insight is obtained into the possible roots of the speech handicap.

Present linguistic functioning is determined by a phonetic analysis of the patient's articulation, and by an estimation of over-all intelligibility. A variety of hearing tests are also performed to check whether audition or sound discrimination ability are possible causes of the speech impairment. Physical checks for organic abnormalities or motor incoordinations of the musculature essential for speech are routine. Finally, psychological and intellectual assessments may be indicated to determine whether or not counseling might be a useful adjunct of treatment. The information obtained through examination and interview are studied, and tentative therapeutic recommendations are made.

Therapy for voice and articulation disorders often begins by making the patient cognizant of the exact nature of his disturbance. This is not so unnecessary as it might seem: it is a highly unusual person who recognizes and accepts his voice the first time he hears it on a tape recorder. By carefully listening to his own sounds, the speech-handicapped person becomes able to acknowledge his problem and to recognize how he may overcome it if he cooperates fully in the treatment process.

Correction is a gradual process. Voice and articulation are slowly reshaped to approximate acceptable patterns. Someone who lisps, for example, first may learn to say the *s* sound by itself, then in words, in simple sentences, and finally in conversation. The person with a high-pitched, thin voice begins by learning how to relax and control the vocal mechanism. Then single acceptable sounds are produced and used in words, then in sentences, until the new patterns become habitual. The last step of transferring what has been learned in therapy to everyday life is often the most difficult and typically involves periodic checkups after formal therapy has been completed.

Therapy for young or primary stutterers is commonly indirect. The child may receive little or no speech treatment as such. Instead, effort is directed at alleviating home pressures and making his daily environment more conducive to fluent speech. Sometimes psychotherapy is suggested to help the child build up his resistance or to desensitize him to many of the difficulties he must face daily. Outright efforts to instruct the youngsters to speak without stuttering tend to be ineffective and are avoided.

The older stutterer who has learned to accompany his dysrhythmic speech with compensatory or secondary symptoms such as eye blinks, head jerking, and the like, is helped to face his problem squarely. He is taught to accept his nonfluent speech and to do away with the false crutches that his physical symptoms provide. He begins to be able to look directly at his conversation partners without turning away in shame. Gradually, as he develops confidence, the patient gains control over his stuttering symptoms by the use of a variety of techniques. This is limited at first to simple sheltered exposures, such as talking with the therapist, but is slowly expanded to spontaneous natural situations.

There are many varieties of treatment, just as there are important differences in each speech problem that requires care. The nature of speech therapy and its probable outcome depend largely on the handicap treated, its duration, and the goals of therapist and patient. Generally, however, most serious speech difficulties, not complicated by physical limitations, respond well in the course of about a year of once- or twice-weekly treatment. Frequently, too, a less serious problem is helped after only several months or even weeks of effort. Speech disturbances that are severe, have a long history, or are complicated by intellectual or organic damage may require several years of carefully managed therapeutic effort.

Speech therapy is most readily obtainable through clinics associated with colleges, hospitals, and other health services. Very few speech therapists are in private practice. Before electing an independent therapist, the patient should assure himself that the practitioner's training and background qualify him and that he is professionally certified. The American Speech and Hearing Association, 1001 Connecticut Avenue, N.W., Washington, D.C., may be contacted for further information. In Chapter Sixteen an extended discussion of psychotherapeutic procedures and information and addresses concerning competent psychological assistance are provided.

HABIT DISORDERS

Habit disorder describes conditions as mild as nail biting, as embarrassing as bedwetting, or as serious as uncontrollable motor compulsions, twitches and tics. Though these disorders are loosely grouped together, their etiologies and significance may be vastly different.

Nail biting. At one time or another nearly all children bite their nails. The habit disappears as most of them mature and become concerned about their appearance and conduct. In some instances nail biting remains into adulthood though all discernible causes for its presence have long been left behind. Psychoanalytic and other dynamically oriented writers report many kinds of deeply significant motives behind nail biting and may even counsel extensive psychotherapy for the habit. More modest approaches, however, are probably indicated, since the habit may be annoying and unsightly but is not commonly handicapping or symptomatic of any serious adjustment problem (Pennington). In nearly all cases, when nail biting persists into adulthood it does so largely against the person's own conscious wishes. Typically, biters report they find themselves chewing on their nails during periods of stress, without their volitional participation. Habitual nail biting—without thinking and under tension—is a response that has been well learned and will take considerable effort and self-discipline to unlearn.

Enuresis.   Habitual bedwetting after childhood may be both physical and psychological in origin. Whenever the involuntary discharge of urine persists beyond three or four years of age, complete medical examination is called for. In most cases enuresis is found to be of psychological origin and can be remedied only by altering the emotional circumstances associated with it. The incidence of enuresis is fairly high. About one in ten children continue frequent bedwetting after age five, and nearly 2 per cent do not gain adequate control until they reach age eighteen (Thorne).

Enuresis in children and teen-agers is often associated with anxieties arising out of sibling and parental relationships or tensions attributable to difficult social and scholastic adjustments. As in most habit disorders, symptoms may persist after the original underlying causes have been alleviated. When nocturnal wetting does not stop, though underlying fears and stresses have been substantially relieved, reconditioning procedures intended to teach urinary control may be very effective (see case described in Chapter Sixteen). For some patients, however, bedwetting may be just one external symptom of a complex emotional and adjustive disorder requiring extensive psychotherapy involving the child and members of the family.

Tics, Twitches, Spasms.   Tics and related involuntary motions may involve only a few muscles, such as those in eye blinks and lip twitches, or they may consist of gross movements in which the arms, shoulders, trunk, and other parts of the body are shaken, jerked, and twisted. In addition, tics may be verbal, involving tongue clicks, barking, and rasping sounds as well as words uttered with varying degrees of discernibility. Tics can also look like voluntary exertions and may only be noted as compulsive habits because of their frequency. One patient patted his pants and jacket pockets as if looking for a package of cigarettes. Only after he did this every two or three minutes while being interviewed could it be seen this was a tic rather than simple searching for cigarettes.

Tics, like other habit disorders, may originate in childhood and may be attributable to any of the situations that give rise to anxieties and malappropriate responses during the period of growing up. In many instances the tics are a form of neurotic compulsive ritual, the meanings of which are hidden in the dynamics and history of the individual. In other cases tics represent unpleasant habits no more significant than nail biting. Very rarely, what seem like common childhood tics develop into an infrequent disorder first described in 1885, Gilles de la Tourette's disease (*maladie des tics*). Tourette's Disease is characterized by the appearance of tics, grimaces, and spasms during childhood, eventually followed by abnormalities of speech. Soon after the head, limbs, and body become involved in jerking movements, patients begin to emit sounds such as squeaks, barks, and shouts. After some time certain phrases and words are fixated on, continuously repeated, and new phrases compulsively echoed. Particularly diagnostic of the later stages of the disturbance is the emergence of corprolalia, the repetition of vulgarities and profanities.

The following case is reported by James R. Dunlap, M.D. It demonstrates some of the early signs of Tourette's Disease. The whispered, occasionally shouted, compulsively repeated profanities and curses marking later stages of the disorder are not yet evident in Peter's case.

Peter G. L., a 12-year-old boy, was referred for psychiatric evaluation as a differential diagnostic problem. The initial pediatric impression had been Sydenham's chorea. However, lack of a typical recent streptococcal infection had raised doubts about this possible diagnosis. The presenting complaints were marked facial grimacing, blinking, and twisting movements of the face and neck. This was associated with paroxysms of guttural noises. Peter would whistle, grunt, bark, or repeat phrases such as "ha-ha-ha," and these would break into his normal stream of conversation. It was noted that he tended to repeat statements over and over. . . .

Because of the uncontrollable nature of Peter's noise-making he became an object of ridicule among his classmates, and one of concern and vexation to his teachers. Two weeks later, Peter was taken out of school and remained at home until seen in this clinic. On the day that he first began to make the "ha-ha-ha" noises, he was slapped by his father each time this occurred. When the father realized that Peter could not control the noises, he felt extremely guilty and bought Peter a toy gun. . . .

The treatment of simple tics, like that of other habit disorders, is complicated by the fact that the symptoms seem to obtain their own momentum. Though underlying dynamic factors may be assuaged by psychotherapy or the passage of time, tics can persist. Eventually the tics themselves may become the focus of concern because they handicap the patient in everyday social and vocational contact. Nevertheless, many simple tics are ameliorated so that as the individual matures they disappear or are converted into habits or symptoms that are not too obvious or grossly disconcerting. Psychotherapy is not always necessary, since tics and other habit disorders treated through medical and psy-chopharmacological techniques sometimes respond favorably.

Gilles de la Tourette's disease, the etiology of which may not be entirely psychogenic, has been resistive to medical and psychothera-peutic treatment. But a team of Johns Hopkins University specialists (Eisenberg, *et al.*) has reported that in instances when psychiatric intervention occurred in favorable circumstances and complete patient and family cooperation was obtained, the prognosis for the disorder was very good.

Speech and habit disorders have much in common. While it is likely that the disturbing symptoms arise in organically susceptible individ-uals, because of psychologic stress the symptoms themselves soon prove so handicapping that they in turn engender further tensions and anxieties and thus feed on themselves. Yet many children who start with what seem to be potential speech or habit disturbances lose their symptoms if attention is not unduly riveted on them and they are provided with healthy and beneficent environments. Others learn to modify their symptoms so that they are minimally interfering. A few eventually require medical, psychotherapeutic, or other specialized intervention in order to achieve freedom from long established handi-caps. The most severe forms of speech and habit disorders are resistive to treatment, but present evidence suggests that serious and highly motivated patients who obtain expert, often prolonged, help obtain significant benefits and show marked improvement.

FOR REVIEW AND DISCUSSION

1. What does a delay in language development for several months or even a year indicate? What words tend to appear first for most children? Why? How can parents help or hinder the development of speech?

2. Define articulation defects, stuttering, and defects of voice and rhythm. What are some of the possible causes of stuttering and other speech disorders? What role may psychological factors play in speech disorders? Why does the speech therapist attempt to work both with the mechanical process of speech itself and with the emotions and feelings of his patient?

3. What are habit disorders? Can enuresis, tics, and nail biting be merely superficial annoyances? Why is it difficult to distinguish whether a habit is only a minor unpleasantness or an outward sign of a more seri-ous disturbance?

4. What are some of the causes of habit disorders? How may simple habit disturbances frequently be alleviated or eliminated? Why is it inadvisable to treat the habit or speech symptom directly if it is the result of a more extensive underlying disturbance?

Techniques

of

Treatment

What

Psychoanalysis Is

In the 1880's Joseph Breuer, a physician practicing in Vienna, found a curiously afflicted twenty-year-old girl in his care. The patient, bedridden for months, seemed to have paralyzed legs and arms and found it difficult to speak and hear. Yet no physical reasons could be found for her disorder. Experimenting with a number of techniques to relieve his patient, Breuer noted that when the girl was permitted to talk freely about herself (by being put into an hypnotic trance), she seemed to get better. Breuer was eventually joined by a young Viennese physician named Sigmund Freud. Together they deduced from their experiences with patients like the disabled girl that just letting patients talk could have therapeutic effect.

Dr. Breuer soon discontinued his experimentation with the radical new "talking cure," partially because the novel technique attracted so many women who seemed, as a result of his therapy, to become personally interested in him. But Freud devoted the rest of his brilliant life (he died in London in 1938) to the development and extension of psychoanalysis.

Freud came to believe that psychological disturbances were the result of painful feelings and incidents that were deeply buried. It seemed clear, therefore, that the way to cure disorders was to try to uncover their obscured roots. The process of recalling past incidents and thereby ridding oneself of long stifled feelings was called *abreaction* or *catharsis*. By telling the therapist everything without inhibition or hesitation, patients unburdened themselves of the forgotten past which supposedly caused their neurotic symptoms.

Freud tried to encourage his patients to talk without restraint in a number of ways. Like Breuer, he tried hypnosis at first, but soon found that too few clients could be successfully put into a trance. Eventually he hit upon the technique he called *free association*. The patient was instructed to relax on a couch and let his thoughts roam freely. He was to report whatever came into his head, regardless of logic or decency.

Using the tool of free association, Freud rapidly came upon the next step in his quickly maturing therapy. He found that the material revealed through free association not only helped his patients recover but gave an understanding of the origin and growth of personality and mental disorders. Freud used the details his patients related to him to construct a complex theory of the nature of human behavior and the development of abnormality. Since the information was derived through analyzing the products of the *psyche* (mind), Freud called both his theory and his type of treatment *psychoanalysis* (E. Jones).

PSYCHOANALYSIS—THEORY AND THERAPY

Psychoanalysis is both a theory that attempts to explain human behavior and a method of psychotherapy. As a theory of personality development and structure it has not only shaped a great deal of contemporary psychology but has had substantial influence upon literature, education, history, and all of the social sciences. Psychoanalysis as a therapeutic technique has laid the groundwork for and determined the structure of all other psychotherapies. The conversational interaction between patient and therapist and much of what transpires during the treatment hour in any kind of psychotherapy owe their origin to Freud and psychoanalysis.

THEORY

It is difficult to condense into a few pages all of the main trends, contributions, and theoretical components of psychoanalysis. Freud was a prolific writer, though his frequent lack of systematization makes much of his work seem disjointed. He was also a careful observer of even the most minute human behavior and a fairly self-critical scientist. He admitted that large portions of his work were tentative and speculative. In reporting some of the fundamentals of his thinking it must be stressed, therefore, that Freud himself did not believe his descriptions of the roots of human conduct to be irrevocable. Unfortunately, many who have attempted to express what Freud wrote have given his thinking a rigidity that it never possessed. By condensing the important tenets of psychoanalysis and skipping many of the modifying details, some publicists have made Freud's work seem dogmatic. In Freud's hands, psychoanalysis was a growing, open-minded system to explore, explain, and direct the actions of men.

Unconscious Determinism and Repression

The pillar upon which the edifice of psychoanalysis rests, Freud wrote, is repression. *Repression* refers to the fact that disturbing memories and experiences are forced out of awareness. They become unconscious. Nevertheless, though man is not aware of them, Freud believed that the repressed, the assumed unconscious motives and experiences, can direct behavior. Thus, only by probing the "unconscious reservoir" can the therapist determine all the events and desires that motivate human conduct.

Freud believed that neurotic symptoms are attributable to repressed unconscious feelings and experiences. The partially paralyzed girl originally treated by Dr. Breuer was thought to owe her physical disabilities to experiences that she could no longer recall. Thus if she were allowed diligently to trace back the origins of her neurosis, bring into consciousness important hidden feelings and events, she should be able to rid herself of her symptoms.

Breuer's young female patient had attempted to nurse her father during a lingering, eventually fatal illness. On one occasion while sitting by her father's bedside supposedly watching over him, she fell asleep. While sleeping she dreamt that a monstrous dark snake was about to attack her father. She tried to fend it off, using her right arm, but was not successful. The frightening dream woke her up feeling terrified. She noticed too that her right arm, carelessly flung while she was dozing, seemed to be asleep. The young woman, feeling guilty at having slept while her father was so critically ill, tried to recover herself so that her father would not notice her lapse of attention or her dream-induced terror.

After this experience at her father's deathbed, the girl's guilt feelings mingled with other hidden feelings and were unconsciously converted into physical symptoms suggested by the arm that had fallen asleep. The entire experience was then blocked from conscious awareness as the girl lapsed into the condition in which Dr. Breuer first observed her. When the distressing memories were slowly brought back and relived through the "talking cure," many of the neurotic symptoms disappeared.

Dream Theory

Unconscious, repressed feelings and strivings reveal themselves at unexpected moments. Dreams, as well as other seemingly nonmotivated, even trivial, acts, are largely the result of hidden needs. Slips of the tongue, seemingly accidental mistakes of omission, forgetting names, and many other everyday occurrences could be carefully analyzed and their unconscious roots revealed. Dreams were of special interest to Freud, for he believed that by carefully dissecting the contents, hidden wishes and desires could be revealed. Of course, Freud pointed out, dreams are themselves disguised. Much of what is presented in a dream or recalled upon waking is symbolic, distorted, or otherwise out of focus. The real meaning of dreams has to be carefully pursued by analysis of the superficial content. The following is an example of a psychoanalytic-type dream interpretation. It is reprinted by courtesy of its authors, Drs. E. Earl Baughman and George Schlager Welsh.

The dream that we shall consider was written down by the dreamer immediately after he had awakened. He had not been in the habit of recording his dreams in writing, but this particular one made such a deep impression on him he wanted to preserve it. He was afraid that he would forget either the whole dream or parts of it, or that he would distort it in other ways if he did not make an immediate written record of it.

The dreamer, whom we shall call MK, was a 25-year-old single white male. Both his parents were living as were two sisters, one four years younger and the other six years older than he. He had been in treatment with a psychoanalyst for almost two years when this particular dream occurred. His therapy had made him sensitive to the importance of dreams, and, in addition, he was acquainted with Freud's basic writings on the subject. He had entered treatment after graduation from college because he was unable to adjust to the business career he had selected.

First, we shall present the dream as MK recorded it. The reader may find it valuable to study the dream and to formulate his own impressions before proceeding to the discussion that follows. Remember, this dream is being scrutinized to shed light on the personality characteristics of the dreamer. To facilitate reference in the later discussion each line of the dream is numbered.

A Dream

Scene 1

1. I am at the surface of the water; I start to sink.
2. I keep going down farther and farther; it seems that I will never stop.
3. It gets darker as more and more water pushes on top of me.
4. Then I stop and then I begin to rise.
5. Suddenly I am once again at the surface, out in the light.
6. I am on the edge of the water, people are around me.
7. I am the center of things.
8. And then from the outside my sister enters the group.
9. People turn towards her.

Scene 2

10. The scene has changed; I am in a room that appears to be part of a house.
11. The room is remarkably like my analyst's office, but the room is larger.
12. I am on the couch, across the room is my dog.
13. Dr. B. is seated in his chair; I believe that he is smoking but I am not sure.
14. I do not and cannot seem to look at him.
15. I am most miserable, extremely unhappy.

16. I weep, I am so full of emotion that I can do nothing but cry and that comes only in sobs.
17. I see a clock, it reads 5:33.
18. I begin to draw myself up, to see whether or not I can leave.
19. Dr. B goes toward what seems like the kitchen and returns with a bowl.
20. It has several kinds of candy in it, the bowl is full.
21. I reach for a colored one, but he points to another kind.
22. I take the clear kind, the kind that reminds me of rock sugar candy.
23. Dr. B leaves again to return in a few minutes.
24. This time he brings a cup and saucer filled with something hot.
25. I cannot be sure whether it be tea or coffee.
26. During all of this time Dr. B has not uttered a word, he has remained calm and matter-of-fact.
27. Suddenly I am awakened by our dog barking at what turns out to be the milk man.

Interpreting a dream like this is a laborious process if we follow Freud's classical technique of asking the dreamer to associate to each part of the dream before interpreting it. For example, what does a clock make him think of? What about the numbers 5:33? And so on for the other parts of the dream. Freud's basic hypothesis is that the dreamer, during the course of giving such associations, will reveal the hidden, or latent, meaning behind the manifest symbols in the dream. (In our language, of course, the dreamer's associations provide us with the basis for inferring relevant constructs.) When the analyst has uncovered these hidden meanings he can substitute them for the manifest symbols and, thus, can determine the meaning of the dream. To Freud, the procedure in the end is not unlike deciphering a message written in code—as the true referent for each of the symbols in the message is determined, it is substituted into the original message and gradually the total communication is understood.*

With the accumulation of experience in dream interpretation since Freud, many analysts are now able to shorten this process, in part because many symbols seem to be used repetitively so that lengthy associations by a patient can be dispensed with. Besides, few analysts attempt to do a complete

---

* This summary interpretation of Freud's interpretive technique may leave the reader with a false sense of its objectivity. When, for example, a dreamer gives several associations to a manifest symbol it is not easy to specify criteria by means of which the decision regarding the "true" referent is made. Moreover, even well-trained analysts frequently disagree on the significance of a particular dream. All of which is to say that dream interpretation is still a pretty subjective business, highly influenced by mental processes in the analyst that are difficult to describe or teach. We are interpreting a dream, then, not because we can defend our interpretation as *the* truth but because we think the reader should be familiar with the technique. Hopefully, future discoveries will bring greater objectivity to this area of personality.

interpretation of each dream; instead, most focus on major themes. These major themes often become more readily apparent, too, when an analyst is able to examine a series of dreams (which is usually possible in practice) rather than a single, isolated dream. Thus, central themes may stand out in sharp relief when a series of dreams is studied, whereas a single dream may lack clarity and require lengthy associations before it can be interpreted.

Space clearly does not permit us to report the lengthy associations of MK to each element of his dream. So we shall concentrate on the end results of this associative process. By so doing we hope to highlight the chief themes expressed in the dream so that the reader can see how dream interpretation might increase his psychological understanding of MK.

MK's dream has two distinct parts, labelled Scenes 1 and 2. The impression the report gives is that these two parts are so different that they hardly seem to be related. As a working hypothesis, however, let's assume that, since they are continuous parts of one dream sequence reported by a single dreamer, the parts must be meaningfully related. What we need in order to establish unity in this dream is the correct connecting link between these two scenes. As we noted earlier, many such connections cannot be rendered in the visual imagery of dreams but must be established by the associations of the dreamer and the total context of the dream. In this instance the most probable connecting link is the word "because"—that is, the second scene of the dream has occurred because of something that happened in Scene 1. To put it more simply, the events referred to in Scene 1 are the reasons for the dreamer's predicament in Scene 2.

After we have dealt separately with the two scenes, the reader will see more clearly why "because" is a reasonable connecting link in this dream. If we accept the "because" link, the whole fantasy falls into place as an insight dream. That is, during sleep the dreamer is able to formulate a basic reason why he needs psychoanalytical treatment, something he has not been able to do when awake. If our interpretation is correct, then, the dreamer is more insightful, at this point, asleep than awake.

All of MK's associations to the water and his movements in it (lines 1-5) suggested that water is the dream's symbol for MK's birth. It is as if MK were reliving his birth experience in the dream: The sudden appearance in the light after being immersed in water is the dream's concrete reference through visual and kinesthetic imagery to that experience. A good many analysts have suggested that immersion in and expulsion from water is a common dream symbol to connote birth.

Lines 6 and 7 reveal rather directly that MK was the center of attention after his birth, the usual experience for a newly born child. His associations to this part of the dream suggested, too, that he had continued to want to be at the center of things and that he was easily "hurt" when people ignored him or directed their attentions to others. It developed further that

MK was currently quite angry with his analyst because the latter's recent behavior made MK feel that he was not receiving his share of Dr. B's attention. Here then was the current experience, related to a childhood experience (suggested by lines 8 and 9), that provided the basis for the dream. It is apparent in lines 8 and 9 that MK blames a sister for the diminished attention given him in childhood. Furthermore, MK's associations hinted that this must have been his younger sister, the one who pre-empted the center of the stage after he had been there for four years.

In summary, then, we can infer from the description of Scene 1 that MK felt himself to be the center of attention until his younger sister came along and disrupted things. Consciously, MK was unable to recall the birth of this sister, and he was aware only of predominantly tender feelings toward her. But when MK asked his parents about his reaction to her birth, they reported that he had been very jealous of her and that it had been difficult for them to get him to accept her.

Actually, the idea that the sister is responsible for the withdrawal of the spotlight from MK is expressed quite directly in Scene 1. No far-fetched interpretation of symbols is required in order to reach this conclusion. Interpreting the immersion in and expulsion from water as a symbolic reference to birth simply rounds out the interpretation without being the cornerstone of it. In Scene 2 there are also symbols that can be interpreted only tentatively, but again, the basic theme is reasonably apparent.

Scene 2 exhibits that irregular relationship to reality we spoke about earlier. The analyst in the dream is MK's analyst, and certain other aspects of the dream seem to be direct copies of real-life experiences, such as the calm and matter-of-fact behavior of the analyst. But other aspects of the dream, such as Dr. B's serving candy and liquid, had no counterpart in MK's experience with Dr. B. There are several points in Scene 2 where it is especially easy to infer wish-fulfillment.

In line 11, while describing the office in the dream and comparing it with Dr. B's, MK adds, almost as an afterthought, "but the room is larger." The reader may have paid this remark little attention when he read the narrative, but MK's associations revealed that it was noteworthy. Dr. B's real office was small, and in this remark MK is expressing his wish that it were more spacious. At this point in his analysis he was quite hostile to, and disparaging of, Dr. B, and he is saying here, in effect, that if Dr. B were more adequate and successful his office would not be so tiny, that he would have an office consistent with this greater competence. Although this is an essential component of MK's relationship with Dr. B, it is represented in the dream by a seemingly inconsequential remark.

In line 12 the presence of the dog presents an interesting interpretive problem, especially since patients do not really bring their dogs to analytic sessions. MK's associations to the dog suggested that in relationships with these animals he feels the loyal, devoted attention he is unable to enjoy in his relationships with human beings. People cannot be trusted, for sooner or later they will direct their affections elsewhere, as was suggested in Scene 1. The dog symbolizes the kind of trust and devotion that MK wants but cannot achieve, even with Dr. B. The presence of the dog in the dream, then, is in part an indictment of Dr. B for not giving MK what he wants.

Line 13 was never clarified by MK's associations. In talking about the dream he could not be certain whether Dr. B was smoking. Perhaps this is merely a trivial failure of recollection, but the very reverse may be true. We may speculate that smoking has some deeply disturbing erotic connotations for MK and that his failure to deal adequately with this part of the dream in his associations serves as a protective device against uncovering the truth about this reference. Such an interpretation would be pure speculation, however, since MK's associations do not document it.*

Lines 14-16 suggest that MK feels guilty because of his hostility to Dr. B; he should not feel angry with a man who is trying to help him. The crying in this part of the dream reflected what had actually occurred during two analytic treatment sessions. MK's associations at this point indicated that crying was an unconscious means of securing greater attention and affection from Dr. B, a wish or goal actually achieved later in the dream when Dr. B brings him candy and liquid.

In line 17 we are confronted with a particularly interesting interpretive problem. Although in reality Dr. B had no clock in his office, there was no doubt that a clock was in the dream and that it read precisely 5:33. What could this image refer to? MK's associations provide one interesting possibility, although we cannot be certain that it is the correct one. Recall that MK is an only male child with both an older and a younger sister. This actual situation might have been represented in the dream if the numbers were ordered 3:53, with the unlike number being bracketed by two like numbers. So the ordering in the dream—5:33—might represent MK's wish to be the oldest, strongest, and most prominent of the siblings rather than be hemmed in by two females. At least such an interpretation is hinted at by MK's associations. Of course, since this motivation might have been expressed by other numbers—say, 7:22—why the numbers 5:33 were chosen remains obscure.

In lines 18-20, just as time is about to run out, Dr. B begins to come through with a "full bowl" and to feed MK in the motherly way he has been waiting for—the doctor begins to satisfy MK's dependency needs that have been frustrated for such a long time. Here is another example of wish-fulfillment expressed by concrete visual imagery.

* Interestingly enough, though, MK, at another point in his analysis, did recall how violently he had objected to his mother's attempts to begin smoking. In fact, his reaction had been so intense that his mother dropped her plan.

Lines 21 and 22 are also interesting when considered in the light of MK's associations, for the idea of moving away from the impure (colored) to the pure (clear) under Dr. B's direction is implied. It is as if MK recognizes the base nature of his impulses, but sees also that he can move toward purer and clearer objectives by following Dr. B's guidance. Finally, there is the hint that if he follows Dr. B's counsel, additional rewards will be forthcoming, for does not Dr. B go away only to return with further nourishment (lines 23-25)? Throughout all these deeply felt moments, Dr. B remains the model of calmness (line 26), the kind of person that MK's associations suggest he himself would like to be.

In summary, Scene 2 presents a number of important clues to the type of person that MK is, and when these inferences are combined with those drawn from Scene 1, we can glimpse quite a comprehensive picture. Scene 1 suggests that MK felt displaced when his younger sister was born and attention was shifted from him to her. Scene 2 goes further and indicates MK's desire to reorganize his sibling relationships so that he would be the oldest and strongest. This is an interesting reorganization in fantasy, especially since he might have chosen to reorganize the sibling structure to put himself in the position of the youngest. That position would be more likely to secure for him the babying that his strong dependency needs might lead us to suspect would be a determining factor in his fantasy life. We are led to conclude, therefore, that MK suffers from a basic conflict between dependence and independence—although he wants to assume the dominant, masculine position, he also wants to receive the maternal ministrations that come with being in the dependent position.

The dream in addition gives an inkling that a complex relationship exists between MK and Dr. B. MK is hostile to Dr. B for not giving him what he wants, but he also feels guilty for having such attitudes. At the same time he has not given up hope that Dr. B will come through and guide and tend to him as he desires.

Finally, the two scenes together suggest that MK is beginning to recognize, if ever so slightly, that a fundamental reason for his current psychological difficulty (as depicted in Scene 2) can be found in the intrusion of the younger sister into the family (as depicted in Scene 1). Additional information indicates that MK repressed the hostile feelings he developed toward the sister, that he feels guilty for being so hostile, and that he blames himself for being unable to cope with the situation. In Dr. B he hopes to find a person who will purge him of his evil impulses and show him a path to a clear and pure future.[1]

[1] E. Earl Baughman and George Schlager Welsh, *Personality: A Behavioral Science* (Englewood Cliffs, N. J.: Prentice-Hall, Inc., 1962), pp. 402–8.

THE STRUCTURE OF PERSONALITY

Personality, Freud contended, may be conceived as consisting of three parts: id, ego, and superego. They are not structural entities, but serve as explanatory devices to help describe the functioning of individuals.

Id describes the primitive, inborn needs and desires. Motives such as thirst, sex, aggression, and acquisition—unmodified and unchecked by social restraints—are called id. An infant only a few months old is "all id," so to speak, since it possesses only needs and wants as yet unrestrained by any socializing force.

As an infant grows, raw, untrained id impulses are blocked by the demands of reality. When a child wants something, his id may dictate that he grab for it. But he quickly learns that grabbing may result in punishment or other delay in gratification. The confrontation of the id by reality produces what Freud called ego. *Ego* refers to the ways of thinking and planning that we have learned in order that we may effectively deal with the world. Ego devises the means through which id needs may be satisfied. The ego was described by Freud as being in the service of "the reality principle," since it "serves no other master but expediency."

Finally, there develop in most people feelings of right and wrong, morality and immorality. The ego is not concerned with whether an id impulse is good or evil; the function of the ego is solely to see to it that ways are devised in which the impulse may find satisfaction. But feelings of "conscience" develop at the "mother's knee." Some things are felt to be evil, immoral, unethical; others, to be virtuous or at least acceptable. The combination of personal morality and restraint, Freud called *superego*. In addition, Freud believed that within the superego was a picture of the self which he called the ego ideal. The *ego ideal* is our own picture of how we would like to be. We are always judging ourselves in relation to the degree to which we live up to our own imagined standard.

The following is an illustration of how Freud's description of personality may be useful. The final behavior is the result of a complicated interaction of id, ego, superego, and ego ideal.

A thirty-seven-year-old married patient reported that working in the same office with him was an unusually attractive girl of another racial background. Although the girl was not aware of it, the patient was sexually excited by her presence. On one occasion when the patient was walking down a relatively deserted part of the building in which he worked, he saw her just ahead, carrying some wastepaper baskets. "I felt, right then and there, like knocking her over and mauling her—raping her." *(Id)*

"I might have done it too. I couldn't shake that feeling for a minute. But then what stopped me was I knew I couldn't get away with it. It's just not realistic; there must be other ways of getting her, I figured." *(Ego)*

"Then I said to myself, you can't go around trying to make other women. You're a married man. It's not right." *(Superego)*

"Anyway, why would I want to have anything to do with someone like that—I'm a white man, and a white man has no business having anything to do with them." *(Ego ideal)*

A person who is unscrupulous and attempts whatever he believes he can get away with may be described as lacking superego. The overly inhibited, unspontaneous, and constricted person, on the other hand, is likely to be burdened with too domineering a superego structure. And the individual who seems to have a poor grasp of reality, who really does not seem to understand what is expected of him, may be said to have a poor ego.

Freud and Sex

Popular belief has it that Freud said "Everything has to do with sex." In a sense this is an accurate statement, albeit a misleading one. Freud pointed out that sexual motives were part of the broader concept called *libido,* and as such were involved in most significant human behavior. Since libido describes all the psychic energy that people possess, sexual needs, which are part of it, are involved to some degree in all motivated behavior.

Freud further modified his references to sex by pointing out that sexual needs are not necessarily synonymous with adult genital motives. *Sex* refers to a comprehensive physical function that strives for affection, interaction, and pleasure in general. A fair equivalent for the way in which Freud used the word *sex* might be our common word *love.* When he stated that sex underlies some human activities, Freud was suggesting that a fundamental stimulant of human conduct is the need to interact with others and experience acceptance, pleasure, warmth, and affection.

When Freud wrote about infantile and childhood sexuality, many authorities objected that his theories had "gone too far," because they did not understand the psychoanalytic reference to sex. They emphatically denied that children had sexual interests. But Freud, of course, was not asserting that children had adult physical desires. For children, sexual stirring takes specifically childish forms. Children, just as adults, need love and affection. When a child becomes ill because of being separated from his mother, the analyst could say that his sexual life—meaning his need for affection—has been disturbed.

The Defense Mechanisms

Everyone, whether normal or abnormal, continually battles within himself, largely on an unconscious level. Nearly all behavior is the result of a dynamic interaction between various forms of libido, and the compromises of id, ego, and superego. For nearly everyone these internal struggles produce tensions and anxieties. To relieve uneasiness and to placate some of the unconscious needs that ask to be fulfilled, certain techniques called *defense mechanisms* are employed. Repression, the blocking from memory of particular motives or experiences, was held by Freud to be a central and commonly used defense mechanism. Some other mechanisms that Freud recognized and described are given below. It is important to note that all normal individuals use these techniques. The mentally disturbed, however, are believed to overuse and exaggerate defense mechanisms.

Displacement. Shifting of needs to an object less threatening, or more accessible. For example, a child who is hostile to his mother "takes it out" by mutilating dolls and toys.

Fantasy. Achieving suppressed or frustrated wishes in reverie and daydreaming. For example, imagining oneself handsome, rich, capable, and powerful.

Projection. Ascribing to others one's own unacceptable motives and needs. For example, the latent homosexual male accusing others of trying to seduce him.

Reaction formation. Repression of one's actual wishes and substitution of their exact opposite. For example, a person unconsciously obsessed with sexual cravings takes a strong stand against immorality in films, books, and other material.

Regression. Retreating to less mature or demanding levels of behavior. For example, the wife who does not receive the affection and attention she craves from her husband acts sullen and pouts as she did when she was a child.

Sublimation. Substitution of socially approved goals for sexual and related needs. For example, a spinster schoolteacher, frustrated in her needs for a normal marital relationship, channels her energy instead into being an affectionate, understanding, and exemplary schoolteacher.

The Development of Personality

Freud believed that personality unfolds in several critical stages. These developmental levels are biologically determined. Each stage is characterized by certain sexual (in the broad Freudian sense) pleasures. A person's successes and failures in achieving these pleasures could have special psychological consequences. The earliest psychosexual stage, present during the first year of life, is called the *oral stage*. During this period all libidinous activity centers about chewing, eating, sucking, and other ingestive and mouth pleasures. This stage, like all others, if successfully transpired has little impact on personality. But if the child's oral needs are thwarted, if stress develops about them, or if they are overindulged, *oral fixation* may occur. This means that the damaged infant even as an adult will carry with him certain immature oral needs, as well as character distortions that are oral in origin. A psychoanalyst might contend that being overly dependent, smoking, talking excessively, practicing certain sexual deviations, and overeating are evidences of early oral difficulties. Listed below are some of the stages that Freud suggested help determine personality.

Oral stage (first year of life).   Interest centers on pleasures derived through chewing, biting, sucking, and other mouth activities. May leave individual dependent, aggressive, overtalkative.

Anal stage (ages 2 to 3).   Interest centers on pleasures derived from excretory activities. May leave individual stubborn, possessive, stingy.

Phallic stage (ages 3 to 5).   Interest centers on pleasure to be derived from autoerotic genital stimulation. Sexual-affectional love for opposite-sexed parent, called *Oedipus complex*, begins. If this stage is not adequately passed through, many kinds of neurotic, specifically sexual disorders may result.

Latency stage (ages 6 to 12).   Interest becomes centered on peers of same sex. Sexual urges are repressed. (Boys "hate" girls and vice versa.) May lead to various personal and social inadequacies.

Genital stage (puberty onward).   Sexual interest reawakened and centered on opposite sex. A mature person who has successfully passed through all the preceding stages finds his pleasures in adult heterosexual, affectional love.

An interesting example of how a contemporary psychologist uses psychoanalytic development concepts to help understand the behavior of a patient is illustrated below. The case study is reproduced with the permission of the author, Bertram P. Karon, Ph.D., and the *Journal of Abnormal and Social Psychology*.[2]

The term "orality" is used in psychoanalysis to refer to the mouth and its functions—especially eating, drinking, sucking, and biting—to the dynamic characteristics connected with these (e.g., dependency is seen as being connected with the experience of being fed), and to the first psychosexual "stage" of early infancy, when these functions of the mouth are

[2] "A Clinical Note on the Specific Nature of an 'Oral' Trauma," *61* (1960), 480–81.

assumed to be the most important activities in the life of the child. The term is thus used to refer both to problems which originate in this early period of life and to problems having to do with mouth functions. According to Fenichel, one would expect oral pathology to be prominent in the symptoms of someone who had been excessively deprived of oral gratification, excessively indulged in the oral period, or excessively indulged in the oral period and excessively frustrated in the succeeding stage.

Both in theoretical discussions and in attempts to investigate the importance of "oral" experiences, attention has frequently been focused upon whether or not a child was breast-fed or how early he was weaned. More recently, it has been realized that an abrupt weaning at any age is more traumatic than a gradual one, no matter when it takes place.

Destructive oral experiences have been said many times to play an essential role in the development of schizophrenia. A thirty-two-year-old male chronic paranoid schizophrenic patient . . . illustrates this contention. . . .

This patient's delusions were such that any psychoanalytically oriented psychotherapist would have concluded that he suffered severe problems of an obviously oral nature and that he must have undergone an oral trauma of considerable impact. For example, the patient was afraid of being poisoned. He would not drink milk at the beginning of the therapy and confided that: "The Athenian girls are laughing at me. They say their breasts are poisoned."

One day a woman with a rather well-endowed bosom walked by him. He made frantic wiping gestures from his side. Afterwards he said: "She approached me with her breast, and I got a pain in my side."

Despite these symptoms, it was possible to verify that this patient had been breast-fed for a full year and had been gradually weaned. Where, then, could there have been an oral trauma?

On one occasion, his mother (who had read some of the literature of psychoanalysis) said to him: "Didn't I give you enough milk? Didn't I give you enough to drink?" The patient stared into space and replied: "The cow gave her calf milk and then kicked it. She shouldn't do that. It's something that happened hundreds of times in the history of the world."

In this delusion of the cow who kicked her calf (the patient, of course, denied that it had anything to do with him) is the key to the oral trauma. It did not consist of being deprived of the breast or of being weaned too early or too abruptly. The oral trauma consisted of a sequence of interactions: The child got fed and then got hurt. The "poisoned" milk seems not to be due to any characteristic of the milk itself, but to the fact that the mother resented any demand upon her to feed the child so that immediately after feeding him, she got angry. The child then felt the impact of her hostility and was hurt. "Poison" is simply something you eat, and you get hurt afterwards.

This sequence—child eats, mother gets angry, child feels hurt—was not something which happened once or twice in the patient's life. It was not something that happened to him only during a specific period of childhood. It was something that started when he was an infant and continued all his life. Even at the age of 32, it was observable. The mother took care of the treatment home * for a period of time so as to save expenses. She seemed to be making every conscious effort to help her son. The therapist was startled to notice after every meal she cooked for her son, she had an argument with him. If she did not cook the meal, there was no argument. Thus, it was not merely a single childhood experience, but the continuous re-enactment of the trauma that prevented it from ever being overcome.

It must not be supposed that this was in any way a conscious process for the mother. Consciously, she was doing everything she could for her son. She was unaware of her constant pattern—feed, get mad—which seemed obvious to an observer. Each evening the content of the argument dealt with something else.

Her emotional inability to feed is exemplified by the fact that after raising two children and after many years of married life, her cooking was barely palatable, not only according to the patient but according to the therapist's judgment as well. Her needs were exemplified in the very beginning of the treatment when she complained of her obviously sick son: "He always took and never gave; it's about time he gave a little." Actually, the patient had been forced to give in a number of different ways—his gifts to his mother, his writings, his paintings, etc. . . .

Since it is typical of the schizophrenogenic mother that she cannot tolerate the demand to feed, to take care of, to nuture, it is likely that this repeated pattern of activity—feed, get mad—is frequently present in such cases. The important point is that the oral trauma is not merely a single childhood event, but the continuous re-enactment of the traumatic sequence.

Without being aware of it, the mother continuously imprinted the notion that after eating comes the pain. Is it any wonder then that the patient is afraid of being poisoned?

. . . The apparent discrepancy between clinical case studies and experimental findings seems to be due to the fact that "oral trauma" has been interpreted as referring to a single specific event—usually weaning. This is not entirely the fault of the investigators since psychoanalytic theory is usually presented as if the key to symptom and character formation lies in such isolated events. The present case suggests that the important "oral" variables are the persisting patterns of interactions, including the mother's involuntary and unconscious reaction to the demand for nurturance. Isolated events, like weaning, are easily influenced by "enlightened" child care education or by conscious good intentions without removing the destructive character of the total relationship.

* The patient, while under therapy, lived in a private house with treatment personnel and with his mother.

THERAPY

Today psychoanalysis is but one method of psychotherapy—and it is one of the least common. In the entire United States there are only about eight hundred fully accredited psychoanalysts, members of the American Psychoanalytic Association. The small proportion of psychoanalysts is best seen when contrasted with the fact that there are over thirty thousand other specialists, including psychiatrists, clinical psychologists, and other trained professionals equipped to do psychotherapy. Even those who call themselves analysts do not necessarily follow the teachings of Freud. Rank, Horney, Adler, and others have substantially modified and revised Freud's hypotheses. Yet, though there are theoretical differences among them, psychoanalysts continue to use techniques that have not been drastically altered since Sigmund Freud first suggested them half a century ago.

Psychoanalytically trained therapists believe that repressed or unconscious childhood experiences may be responsible for adult disorders. In order to uncover these hidden events and memories, therapists instruct their patients to *free-associate*. The *analysand* (one who undergoes psychoanalysis) is asked to put into words whatever he is thinking no matter how indecent or illogical it may seem. In this way the doctor hopes to obtain clues concerning the long obscured recollections that still affect his patient. He may also try to uncover unconscious material by examining his client's dreams, since the innermost and deepest motives may be symbolically expressed during sleep.

Not all therapeutic effort is devoted to searching for unconscious remnants. The therapist also establishes a *transference relationship* with his patient. This means that the client is encouraged to feel and act toward the doctor the way he does to others. Though he may not be aware of it, the analysand eventually responds to the therapist the way he used to react toward his father, mother, wife, or other significant person in his life. The transference relationship is doubly useful. It permits the analyst to understand the patient's feelings toward others. It also enables the client to re-examine his interpersonal reactions and to experiment in the secure, protected therapeutic surroundings with responses that he may have previously feared.

Throughout the treatment the analyst *interprets* for the patient. This means he shows the client how his early experiences and unremembered needs have shaped and distorted his life. He helps the patient understand how many of the reasons he has given for his way of life are just rationalizations since the roots of his behavior lie in feelings and situations of which he is no longer aware.

Mrs. P. is a thirty-two-year-old mother of two girls who has been married for eleven years. She has been, in her own words, "nervous, high-strung, and sensitive" for most of her life. Presently she is very anxious, easily irritated, and as she states, "impossible to live with." She is a "perfec-tionist," continually "picking on" her two girls and her husband. She de-mands that their manners, dress, and conduct be impeccable and makes no allowances for youthful spontaneity or adult male casualness. She and her husband have rarely been comfortable together, but during the last several years their relationship seems to have deteriorated completely. They con-tinually bicker and frequently shout at each other. Mrs. P. believes her husband is "involved with a girl friend," since they have little or no sexual contact. Mrs. P. has been free-associating and has paused for a while.

MRS. P. *(smiling)* Doctor, may I ask you something? Personal?

ANALYST.   Please go ahead.

MRS. P.   I've been meaning to ask you this but I've wondered whether I should.

ANALYST.   Yes. *(nods encouragement.)*

MRS. P.   Well *(smiling broadly)*, you do seem to have such a, well . . . used-looking?—is that the word?—shabby, office? I mean you expect someone like you to have modern pieces in here—walnut desk. You know. What I really mean is . . . it couldn't be money—could it? You do have a lot of patients coming to see you, so you must have some reason for having such a very modest looking office. What's the reason?

ANALYST.   It was difficult for you to say that because you don't wish to be critical of me, just . . .

MRS. P. *(interrupting)* Yes! But it's important; you'd do so much better, you know, if you had a more impressive office.

ANALYST.   Let's pause a moment and ask what you are really saying—and doing—by pointing to my office furnishings and suggesting—both that I have enough money to equip myself better and that I would make more money with nicer surroundings.

Those few remarks by Mrs. P. enable the analyst to point out that she is now using a pattern of behavior with him that she uses with her husband. She is criticizing him, but allegedly doing so for his own good. The doctor makes use of this transference of feeling. He wants his patient to understand clearly the significance of her criticism of him and how it demonstrates a personality pattern that is inimical to her.

An excerpt from another session suggests how the analyst employs the patient's own fragmented recollections to help her understand some of the origins of her feelings. Mrs. P. has been talking about her fifth birthday and some of the presents that she had received.

MRS. P.   I keep thinking of that set of crayons that I got. I remember it was my fifth birthday and I think my father or older brother gave them to me. They were expensive looking . . . and I didn't think I deserved them. *(seems disturbed, even angry.)*

ANALYST.   There is something about the crayons, their expense, perhaps, that might have some meaning for you. Why do you look so disturbed?

MRS. P.   Yes, that's it. My mother, I think, was jealous; no, I don't want to say that—I mean she didn't want him to spend so much money on something like that, on something for me. It makes me sad to think of it.

ANALYST.   You may have put your finger on an underlying feeling there when you said your mother was jealous.

MRS. P.   Well, she probably was. And the way she made me distrustful of my own father, the way I am of my own husband, was probably because she hated the closeness I must have had with him rather than with her. *(Mrs. P. is close to tears.)*

ANALYST.   You're still acting like a good little girl, aren't you? Although you're a grown woman, you follow your mother's example and try to destroy your own husband.

(Mrs. P. nods tearful consent.)

Insightful moments like the one evidenced above establish the foundation on which a successful analysis builds. To complete the process, the patient has to *work through* her disturbed needs and feelings. She has to learn to see her life and her interactions with others in a new light and respond to them in more mature, realistic ways. By continual effort she is expected to be able eventually to modify her personality sufficiently to be no longer disturbed and distorted by emotions that have long resided within her.

Not all analyzed patients continue treatment to the point where their personality is virtually reconstructed. Some stop after obtaining a slightly better understanding of themselves and their motives, feeling this suffices to make living a little easier and more enjoyable. The majority of other patients eventually settle for secondary goals, too. When they are relieved of a particular distressing symptom, or are a little better enabled to cope with their lives, they terminate treatment.

Freud on Freudians

Freud's brilliant and prolific writings quickly attracted many admirers, students, and disciples. Some, like Dr. Ernest Jones from England and the American Dr. A. A. Brill, remained trusted friends and themselves contributed to the development of psychoanalysis. Others, particularly Alfred Adler and C. G. Jung, soon disagreed with Freud and acrimoniously ended their relationship with their teacher. Freud was not averse to letting others know his opinion of errant students. He suggested, for example, that Jung's attempted modification of psychoanalysis was incomprehensible and muddled.

Freud was fairly firm with himself also. He did not claim that his theories were unmodifiable and fixed for all time. In fact, during his own lifetime he changed his mind about important facets of his thinking. Quite late in his career he was disposed to reject the hypothesis that neurosis is attributable to anxiety engendered by conflict within the personality. He thought that perhaps neurosis might be explicable in terms of constitutional, genetic, or other physical factors. He also revised his concept of personality structure. Instead of emphasizing ego, libido, and so on, he suggested that dual forces determine behavior. *Eros* impelled man to live, love, build, plan, and hope for the future. Balanced against this, Freud believed, were the forces of death, destruction, and violence that he called *thanatos*. Human motives and actions, Freud suggested, could be thought of as the outcome of the struggle between these opposing innate energies.

An Assessment of Psychoanalysis

There has been much criticism of psychoanalysis but little effort to investigate its worth scientifically. The complex, often disjointed theory developed by Freud and his disciples is so vast and sprawling that it does not lend itself to simple confirmation or refutation (Hook). Moreover, too much partisanship has developed about psychoanalysis. For the faithful, Freud, or another analyst, is a kind of demigod whose sayings are pondered, expostulated, and interpreted, but never empirically evaluated. At the other extreme are those who regard the entire analytic enterprise as so much "errant nonsense."

Occasional attempts are made to validate particular parts of Freud's thinking. Thus, a psychologist may evaluate whether one of Freud's defense mechanisms, say reaction formation, actually works as it is supposed to. As might be anticipated the results are usually highly variable. As often as special aspects of the theory are supported, others are denied. Frequently, as Dr. Bellak has suggested in his extensive review, "Research in Psychoanalysis," studies are poorly designed or else do not really even test what Freud actually said. In any case, Freud's theoretical structure does not allow an over-all experimental evaluation.

At present, psychoanalysis must be judged specifically in terms of its usefulness and results. Some analytic hypotheses, such as those concerning psychosexual development and sex-like motives, are descriptions that do not meaningfully apply to the information about human behavior we now possess. Many other specifics of Freud's thinking, such as the Oedipus complex, are phenomena limited to particular cultures and times, if they are applicable at all (Heilbrunn). On the other hand, psychoanalysis has helped teach all behavior scientists that much of personality and motivation lies beneath the surface and that a good deal of adult conduct is explicable by understanding the circumstances of childhood. Most important of all, perhaps, is that psychoanalysis has provided a technique for psychotherapy. No matter how individual therapists or orientations may differ, the basis for all psychotherapy remains as Freud first described it.

Recognizing many of the inadequacies and erroneous assumptions of Freud, current analytically directed therapists and theoreticians have attempted to update the hypotheses Freud propounded. Neo-analysts such as Karen Horney, Harry Stack Sullivan, and Erich Fromm have been leaders in the effort to understand human behavior and think in terms more harmonious with contemporary behavior science and American culture. These writers have data available to them that Freud could only guess about. Working within the framework that psychoanalysis provides and using the information uncovered by countless scientists in the past fifty years, contemporary analysts have often been able to contribute to our understanding of normality and psychological disorder (Harper).

Psychoanalysis was a new and radical attempt to understand, correct, and guide human behavior. Its explanations and its therapy have met with only modest success. But it has stimulated new outlooks in psychiatry, psychology, and many other disciplines. This was one of Freud's primary objectives. As such his goal has been realized.

QUESTIONS FOR REVIEW AND DISCUSSION

1. Psychoanalysis is both a theory of personality formation and disorder, and a form of therapy. Explain.
   Discuss unconscious determinism, repression, id, and superego.
2. Why was psychoanalysis called the talking cure? What are defense mechanisms? Why does the analyst ask his patient to recall dreams? What kind of information can be obtained from dreams by analysts?

3. According to psychoanalysts, what are some of the steps in personality development? What is the meaning and significance of the Oedipus complex? What is an oral personality?

4. Define free association, transference, and interpretation. Why is transference essential to successful psychotherapy? How successful is psychoanalytic treatment? How do most psychologists today evaluate Freud's contribution and the validity of psychoanalysis as explanation and as treatment technique?

Psychotherapy

295

Psychotherapy refers to the techniques used to help rehabilitate mentally distressed patients. Today, therapeutic methods include medication and insulin coma treatment as well as procedures in which patients recline on a couch and talk freely to a therapist who records their remarks in a notebook. Physical remedies such as electric and insulin treatment are called medical psychotherapies, while the "conversational" techniques are simply called psychotherapy.

Variations in "conversational" psychotherapies will become clear in the following pages. Some psychotherapists stress techniques that other therapists may not use at all. While many psychiatrists specifically advise their patients, nondirective practitioners conscientiously avoid giving directions. Even the objectives of therapy may differ. Analysts frequently aim toward a complete resynthesis of personality, whereas most specialists tend to limit themselves to helping patients overcome specific difficulties. The treatments of psychological disorders are not so uniform as the methods used to alleviate physical incapacity. Significant variations in psychotherapy are brought about by the practitioner's training and background, as well as his own interests and temperament.

Psychoanalytic Roots

The foundation of all extended psychotherapeutic efforts was provided by psychoanalysis. The analyst, in attempting to produce major changes in his patient's way of life, relies heavily on the interaction between himself and his client to bring about new behavior. This patient-doctor relationship, called transference, is now part of all psychotherapies. Even advice-oriented therapists depend on patient's feelings toward them to some extent. The analysts, however, probably have made the transference relationship a more intimate part of therapy than have most other therapists.

Analysis involves many different techniques and procedures that grow out of the particular analytic orientation of the therapist. The extent to which dreams, free association, questions, and interpretations are used varies from one analyst to another. Those who adhere to Freud's fundamental approach stress methods and determinants somewhat different from those advocated by Adlerians. Nevertheless, fundamental to all analysis are the procedures and guiding principles discussed for psychoanalysis in Chapter Fifteen. The present chapter describes *nonanalytic treatment* techniques.

APPROACHES

Advice, Relearning, Insight, and Ventilation

Less than a few decades ago, psychotherapeutic techniques were still mainly limited to advice and persuasion. The therapist was an authoritative expert who prescribed how to behave, much the way a physician writes an order for medication. Often, patients were counseled to seek a change in environment, move to another job, or even marry or divorce. Frequently too, rest or hobbies were generously recommended. One well-known American psychiatrist, Austin Riggs, usually suggested that patients leave their homes, because he believed that it was there that the origins of most disturbances lay. Customarily, Riggs planned a comprehensive schedule of activities designed to help his patients re-educate themselves in the techniques of successful adjustment.

Advice by experts is still a frequently encountered type of therapy. It should not be entirely viewed with suspicion, since it may often prove valuable. Stanford University psychologist Dr. Albert Bandura suggests, in fact, that many contemporary psychotherapists are too antiadvice oriented. In child therapy, for instance, parents frequently need to be given directions concerning how they can help alleviate their children's disturbances. Dr. Bandura points out that since most human acts and feelings are learned, they can also be unlearned. The psychologist who fully understands the learning processes may be able to teach parents methods to overcome specific behavior difficulties.

The way in which a specific psychogenic problem may be relieved by advice and learning can be illustrated by a case of enuresis brought to the attention of a practicing psychologist. The child, eleven years old, had been a bedwetter for most of his life, though there was no discernible physical cause. During the last two years the condition had become severe. The family and child were interviewed and psychodiagnostically evaluated. No pathological trends were evident, although there was some anxiety and conflict about the bedwetting and about the pressure the child felt to achieve in school. As a result of the examinations the parents were informed that their son had strong needs to achieve scholastically and that any additional pressure exerted by them made him feel anxious and might contribute to his almost nightly enuresis. In addition, the parents and child were both informed of a device that has been demonstrated to curb bedwetting successfully. The apparatus, attributed to Dr. O. H. Mowrer and marketed by one firm as "Wee Alert," is a kind of pad that slips between mattress and bed sheet. It is electrically wired so that as soon as the first drops of urine moisten it, a sharp alarm bell is activated. The child who wets is thus taught, by conditioning, to anticipate the awakening bell as soon as he feels the first urinary urges. Eventually, to avoid the unpleasant loud awakening, the child wakes up before wetting so he can go to the bathroom. In this instance, through a combination of advice to parents, the learning device, and some informative discussion with the child and family, the condition was completely relieved.

Many psychiatrists make maximum use of the fact that just allowing patients to *ventilate* or "get it off their chest" helps them to feel better. Freud himself noted that encouraging his patients to talk freely about their problems and emotions invariably permitted them to feel unburdened and encouraged. Coupled with expert advice, *catharsis* or talking-it-out often is sufficient to enable a distressed patient to function adequately again.

Another tool used by many therapists is *insight*. Patients are helped to understand some of the reasons for their difficulties and confusions. The therapist explains to his client how his faulty perceptions and attitudes have led to distorted reactions and undesirable habits. He is encouraged to criticize himself and try to change his style of living. Sometimes the patient's "reason" is appealed to—he is instructed in the ways in which he may work out better solutions to his situation.

The following excerpt illustrates the approach of an insight-advice oriented therapist. The patient, a forty-eight-year-old woman, complained of feeling depressed, lonely, and useless. She had been frequently ill, and had worried about becoming seriously sick both mentally and physically. Here is what the doctor told her.

Now, I want you to remember three things when you leave here today. First, physically and mentally you're in very good health. We've examined you thoroughly and there is nothing wrong with you, outside of some aches and pains that are perfectly normal and all right when you get past thirty-five or so. You're in good health, so stop worrying about it. Second, you've got a lot to look forward to. You'll be a grandmother before too long. Your children and husband aren't perfect—granted—but they need your love and attention. You can learn to be very helpful to them, so long as you're careful not to get in their way too much. You know how to do it. You've done it before. You are needed and can be very helpful. Third, your life is not over. Many of the feelings and symptoms you've had are typical and perfectly normal, as you now realize, during menopause. You're now beginning a new part of your life, which can be very exciting for you if you just give it a chance.

Expert guidance, if it is well thought out and *based on a substantive understanding of human behavior,* can be an effective therapeutic technique in particular instances. But it can be worthless and even harmful when teachers, ministers, and other intelligent but therapeutically untrained professionals imagine themselves psychotherapists. One patient humorously related during his first interview in a mental health clinic his experience with a well-intentioned but untrained clergyman.

> I told him about my mother, how she was in and out of the [mental] hospitals and how it worried me. I felt sort of scared when I got them feelings she had, like everything was going to bust wide open. I didn't want to see nobody and just wanted to stay home.
>
> He told me to move. He said that I'd have more chances in my trade out West. He said I ought to have a hobby to keep my mind off myself.
>
> You could say I did what he said. I moved to the bar, almost, and started to drink—that was my hobby.

Rogers and Client-centered Therapies

Dr. Carl Rogers, for many years a professor at the University of Wisconsin, has devised an interesting new approach to psychotherapy that has been very influential among psychologists. Rogers calls his orientation client-centered or nondirective to demonstrate that the essence of treatment lies within the patient himself. The nondirective therapist does not interpret unconscious materials or dreams, or make suggestions to the patient concerning the significance of childhood experiences. Instead the Rogerian therapist attempts to guide his client to a reasonably accurate understanding of himself. He strives to make the patient accept the responsibility for the direction of the therapy hour and for any insights that may occur. The therapist tries to see the world the way the patient does and to help the patient understand his own existence by *reflecting* his own feelings.

Contrary to older techniques, client-centered therapists will not attempt to advise, persuade, or reason with their patients. Rogers has described the role of the nondirective therapist as follows.

> When the counselor perceives and accepts the client as he is, when he lays aside all evaluation and enters into the perceptional frame of reference of the client, he frees the client to explore his life and experience anew, frees him to perceive in the experience new meanings and new goals. But is the therapist willing to give the client full freedom as to outcomes? Is he genuinely willing for the client to organize and direct his life? Is he willing for him to choose goals that are social or antisocial, moral or immoral? If not, it seems doubtful that therapy will be a profound experience for the

client. . . . To me it appears that only as the therapist is completely willing that any outcome, any direction, may be chosen—only then does he realize the vital strength of the capacity and potentiality of the individual for constructive action. [Rogers, 1951, pp. 48–49.]

The client-centered approach to therapy relies heavily on a single technique called *recognition of feeling*. The therapist restates what the client has said, but instead of simply parroting the patient's words, he points out the emotions underlying them. If the patient says that he and his wife are mad at each other because "She doesn't like what I do," the therapist would not ask what the patient had done. Instead, he would focus on the feeling and probably respond, "You are angry with your wife." The purpose of the pointing out of feeling is based on Rogers' hypothesis that human beings possess self-correcting growth tendencies. Rogers believes that when a person is given a chance to explore his emotions in a safe therapeutic environment he will eventually rid himself of destructive emotions and give his positive impulses a chance to take over and guide his life.

The process of client-centered counseling can be described in the following sequence. First the counselor establishes an outflow of feeling by continually reiterating the emotional content of his client's descriptions. This leads the client to give vent to the negative feelings that Rogers asserts have impaired his continued growth. When the negative feelings have been disposed of, "one of the most certain and predictable aspects of the whole process"—the emergence of positive impulses—begins. Now the mature, positive feelings such as love, faith, and acceptance are liberated. These guide everyone to psychological health, according to Rogers. The released healthy emotions more and more dominate the treatment hour and let the client see himself in a new light. He achieves new insight into his behavior and sees fresh possibilities for action. The emerging behavior, at first gradual and sometimes disappointing, soon culminates in a rewarding and salubrious set of standards and style of life.

The following excerpt features a client-centered therapist who refuses to make a decision for his patient. Instead, by reflecting his feelings, he helps the client reach his own conclusions. The patient is a forty-six-year-old salesman who suffers from ulcers and has not been able to maintain himself in any employment for more than relatively short periods.

PATIENT. I can't figure it out. Why would he want me to be section head? If I took it, I'd get a raise, and have more than twenty men and a couple gals working under me. I mean he knows my record. Still, this could be my break. My wife, of course, says take it. She don't have much business sense. How about my ulcer? What would you do? I mean I know you don't like to tell me what to do, but do you think I should take it or shouldn't I?

THERAPIST.   You're expressing a number of feelings. You wonder why you merit the confidence of your boss so that he would want you to be head. You doubt your wife's advice and you wonder how well you are able to decide for yourself.

PATIENT.   Well, that's right. Nobody has ever had any confidence in me before. Why should he?

THERAPIST.   You haven't given him any reason to put his faith in you.

PATIENT.   I wouldn't put it just like that. This time I really have tried to make good and all. I never worked as hard. I can see why he trusts me. I think this is my big opportunity. I tried hard and now I can feel that it's been recognized. I'm going to take it. And I'll give it my damndest.

The methods described by Rogers have gained wide acceptance among nonmedically trained therapists. Although most psychiatrists have not been receptive to client-centered procedures, Rogers' writings have had an interesting and useful variety of effects. Strange as it may sound, Rogerian theory has taught therapists to listen carefully to what their patients are telling them and not to interrupt them with extraneous questions. The technique of reflection, if it does nothing else, does not divert the patient from what he is saying but rather makes it easier for him to tell what is really uppermost in his thoughts. Teachers, interviewers, and others who need to communicate have also learned to listen and respond more effectively as a result of Rogers' work.

Client-centered approaches are not believed to be applicable to severe emotional disturbances. It is likely that only a relatively narrow range of well-motivated and intelligent individuals can benefit from the treatment procedure. Psychoanalytic writers have been particularly critical of client-centered techniques, since, unlike the analyst, the client-centered therapist does not "intervene" in his patient's life by directly cultivating a transference relationship or making interpretations. Still other critics have pointed out the almost religious belief in the body's positive growth tendencies and the oversimplified notions of human dynamics and conduct. However, Rogers' point of view has won many adherents and has influenced many areas where the processes of learning, teaching, and investigation are important.

Group Therapies and Hypnosis

Group therapy.   Psychotherapy need not be limited to an interaction between a single adult patient and a therapist. There are many forms of therapy in which several patients meet together with one, two, or even more therapists. Commonly, group treatment involves five to eight patients in conference with one or two therapists (see Fig. 16-1).

Fig. 16-1 Group therapy in a mental hospital. Photo courtesy of the National Association for Mental Health, Inc., New York, N.Y.

The range of discussion during this kind of treatment depends largely on the orientation of the practitioner and the difficulties and interests of the patients. Analysts who conduct group therapy rely on free association, transference, interpretation, and other standard Freudian techniques. Of course, many of the tools they work with are modified by the group situation. Patients in joint therapy, for example, may have a transference relationship not only with the psychoanalyst but also with others in the group; they may interpret each other's comments and in general behave not only as clients but as doctors toward one another. Nondirective group therapists also adjust their special techniques for group treatment. Generally, since group treatment is an outgrowth of individual therapy, it reflects the orientation and training of the therapist. Group therapy is useful in helping to treat a wide variety of disorders; by itself it may help achieve limited therapeutic goals.

Play therapy.   Special adjustments in psychotherapy are made when children are clients. A nine-year-old cannot be expected to sit quietly in the doctor's office, free-associate, and clearly narrate the details of his conduct and feelings. In order to facilitate communication of children's difficulties, therapists frequently engage their young clients in play. Meeting with one or more children several times a week, the therapist himself may play with the child, or provide dolls, paints, and games to occupy him. The therapist can use the child's play both to help understand the child's feelings and to direct new and better adjusted behavior. (See the account of Dr. Eveloff's therapy with Mary in Chapter Eleven.) The exact nature of play therapy varies, like all treatment, with the training and background of the therapist and the nature of the child's disorder. In well-trained hands, this has been found an effective type of treatment for children not too severely disturbed.

Psychodrama and role playing. Two highly interesting forms of therapy of which there are many varieties are psychodrama and role playing. These techniques consist essentially in having patients participate by acting out various assigned parts, in order that they might better comprehend their own positions. Useful as an aid to other therapies, psychodrama and role playing by themselves have limited applications.

Hypnosis. Another frequently used device for special therapeutic ends is hypnosis. Essentially, a patient is hypnotized in order to secure hidden information and/or to enable the therapist to suggest that undesired symptoms disappear. The usefulness of hypnosis is limited, although when used in combination with other psychotherapy, it may be quite effective. The whole of Chapter Seventeen is devoted to a discussion of hypnosis.

Medical Psychotherapies

More patients are treated by some form of medical psychotherapy than by any other treatment technique. Shock therapies and tranquilizing medication are probably the most commonly used, not only in mental hospitals for the severely disturbed but also with those whose afflictions are relatively minor. Frequently, medical techniques help prepare a patient for individual psychotherapy, or they may be used jointly with group or other treatment processes. A wide range of medical psychotherapies now available, listed below, have had a dramatic effect on reducing the length of hospitalization and relieving many kinds of distress. Medical psychotherapies promise to make even greater contributions than they already have in combating mental disorders.

Insulin shock. Insulin is administered to the patient to produce a coma lasting from half an hour to a full hour or more. Five or six treatments are given per week until the total reaches about fifty. Insulin shock is of limited effectiveness with some schizophrenic patients. Research sug-

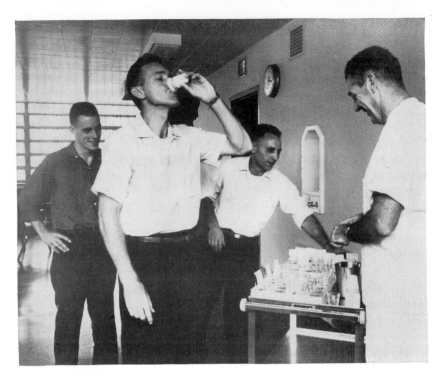

Fig. 16-2 Drug therapy in a mental hospital. Photo courtesy of the National Association for Mental Health, Inc., New York, N. Y.

gests that it may also help some other conditions, but the technique is no longer in common use.

Electric shock.   An electric current of from 70 to 130 volts is applied to the patient's head for a fraction of a second, and the patient loses consciousness immediately. A common procedure is to use three treatments a week to a total of twenty-five to thirty. The technique seems to help patients overcome stressful emotions, partially by blocking disturbing memories, and has been found very useful in treating depressive disorders.

Psychosurgery, lobotomy, leukotomy.   These words refer to surgical separation of the frontal lobe from the rest of the brain. The technique is rarely used today, since the severe, intractable conditions that it relieves are now treated with medication.

Medication, pharmacological chemotherapy.   Specific medications (drugs commercially known as Sparine, Trilafon, Serpasil, Miltown, Equinal, etc.) are useful in many disorders and, by reducing the severity of symptoms, help prepare patients for other forms of therapy (see Fig. 16-2).

Narcosynthesis, narcoanalysis.   Drugs are administered until the patient is semiconscious. The technique permits patients to talk and express hidden feelings more freely, but its uses are highly limited. It is of value in some conditions brought on by severe and acute stress, such as wartime, accidents, disasters.

THE FUNDAMENTALS OF PSYCHOTHERAPY

Client-centered psychotherapy, standard psychoanalysis, and other verbal techniques each have their philosophy of treatment as well as their specific techniques. While the theoretical orientations differ, the basic therapeutic techniques and fundamental processes at work share several necessary principles. In his book *The Abnormal Personality*,[1] Harvard professor Dr. Robert W. White has outlined the five essentials of all contemporary psychotherapy paraphrased below.

1. Initial therapeutic relationship. The therapist establishes a unique personal relationship with his patient. He is an expert, since he possesses special training, experience, and knowledge about maladjusted and disordered behavior and can help show his patient the way to recovery. The therapist is interested, permissive, and friendly, and communicates in this way full acceptance of his patient and a warmth that makes the relationship more personal than is ordinarily the case in a professional consultation. The doctor avoids all false reassurance, but the effect of his presence is to increase his patient's courage. "The patients dares to express feelings and relax defenses because of his strengthening alliances with the therapist. It is within the shelter of this relationship that corrective emotional experience begins to take place."

2. Expression of feelings. The therapist encourages the patient to express his feelings by asking questions and allowing the patient to give his own story. In nondirective counseling, therapists believe that feelings come to expression more readily when the patient rather than the therapist leads the way in the conversation. Free association is another technique intended to remove resistances and encourage the uninhibited flow of conversation. Both methods result in bringing into prominence the emotional patterns that stand in need of correction.

3. Pointing out of feelings. A therapist points out the feelings that his patient expresses so that the patient becomes more fully aware of his emotions, develops insight, and is better able to profit by further experiences in which he is moved by the same feelings. Nondirective therapists call this "recognition of feeling." They paraphrase what the patient says in such a way as to emphasize its emotional implications. The continual emphasis on feeling brings about a greater and greater expression of feeling. Rogerian therapists believe the very process of expressing feelings, as well as recognizing them, constitutes a corrective emotional experience.

Interpretation used by psychoanalysts is not very different from the recognition of feelings. "Interpretation may be regarded as a more active form of recognition. Instead of recognizing the patient's feelings as they are expressed, the therapist recognizes feelings before they are expressed or when they are still being expressed in disguised ways—at all events, before the patient himself has recognized them. When suitably timed, this procedure also results in corrective emotional experience."

4. Transference.   During the course of treatment patients tend to develop the same emotional conflicts with the therapist that they had with parental and other important figures in early life. This is useful in therapy because it allows the patient to realize the inappropriate character of his feelings and reappraise the forgotten dangers from which they spring.

5. New behavior.   As treatment progresses, the patient begins to behave in new ways outside the therapeutic relationship. He replaces his maladjustive patterns with better adjusted forms of behavior. Increasingly his new actions are successful and prove rewarding. Therapists then usually reinforce the healthier attitudes, feelings, and conduct by simple recognition, encouragement, direction, or even praise.

The Language of Psychotherapy

Here are summarized some terms used by psychotherapists to describe the fundamental processes and basic therapeutic techniques:

Advice, persuasion, reasoning.   Used by many psychiatrists and psychologists, these may, in some instances, be effective procedures.

Ventilation, abreaction, catharsis.   These words refer to the process of relieving one's feelings by talking about them. All methods of psychotherapy encourage patients to "get it off their chest."

Free association.   The patient is instructed to talk freely without inhibition or restraint about whatever occurs to him. The associations supposedly bring to light repressed thoughts and memories and hidden conflicts. This technique is used primarily in psychoanalytic therapies.

Questions, repetition of the patient's statements.   In order to explore a particular area further or to call a patient's attention to a statement of possible significance, nearly all psychotherapists use interrogation or repeat particular phrases the patient has uttered.

Reflection or recognition of feeling.   Used mainly by nondirective therapists, this technique is found among other therapies also. It consists essentially of the therapist's restating the feelings, rather than the content, inherent in the patient's statement.

Structuring. At the outset and during treatment, all therapists define for patients what the course of therapy will be like. The term *structuring* is used mainly by nondirective therapists, but the process is a part of all therapies.

SPECIAL CONSIDERATIONS

A Patient's Willingness to Be Treated

Like many physical illnesses, mental disorders are most responsive to therapy when the patient is young, the disturbance not yet severe, and the treatment timely. Unlike physical maladies, however, psychological ills necessitate that the patient be cooperative and at least minimally motivated to recover. A patient suffering from pneumonia and uninterested in whether he gets better can be physically rehabilitated with the help of medication. This is not the case with mentally disturbed persons. In order to change their malfunctioning way of living, they must be actively interested in participating with a therapist in efforts to bring about changes within themselves. One of the major problems of psychotherapy is that frequently those most in need of therapeutic help are least interested in obtaining it.

In order for psychotherapy to be successful, the active cooperation of the patient is essential. A dramatic instance of where therapy achieved limited success against the will of the patient is reported by Washington, D.C., psychiatrist Robert P. Odenwald. Through the insightful and patient efforts of the therapist, one emotionally confused adolescent may have actually been helped despite his resistance. The history is reproduced in its entirety through the courtesy of the author and the *American Journal of Psychotherapy*.[2]

Should a patient receive psychiatric treatment against his will, and should a judge grant probation only under the condition that he receive such treatment? How effectual will such treatment be and is the judge justified in making such demands?

This problem confronted us in a seventeen-year-old boy, a senior in high school, who was in difficulty with the police authorities. It was his second offense. Both times he had stolen an automobile. The first time he was put on probation, but on this, his second offense, no decision had been reached by the Juvenile Court. However, on his eighteenth birthday he was referred to the Probation Court where he was put on probation for one year with the strict warning that he must undergo psychotherapy.

He was 5 feet 10 inches tall, a boy unpleasant in appearance, morose,

---

[2] "Psychotherapy Against the Will of the Patient," *6*, No. 2 (April, 1952), 274–79.

sullen, negativistic and having a definite lack of emotions. Though at first appearance he was properly dressed, afterwards he usually looked as if he had slept in his clothes, his hair uncombed, his shoes not shined, his shoe laces often untied and his hands and fingernails dirty.

He told me that he came to me on the suggestion of his father and the Probation Court because he had stolen a jeep. He said that he had not intended to steal it; he had only wanted to drive around and bring it back. He said the owner of the car was the one who was really guilty because he left the keys of the car inside. Otherwise he would not have used the car.

He stated that he lived with his father and paternal grandmother, that his mother was an alcoholic who was divorced from his father since the patient was seven or eight. He definitely showed that he did not come of his own free will but only to escape punishment. However, he added that he was still wetting the bed and he thought that as long as he was here, that something might be done about that.

His behavior was hostile, one of accusation against the present-day cultural and social conditions. He complained of his "bad luck." He stole his first car and was caught immediately, yet he had a friend who stole a car, had it licensed and nobody noticed anything.

He visited his mother in Milwaukee last year, but she was always drunk and he was glad when he got back home. His childhood memories dwelt on this unnatural mother. One day while sitting with his sister in the bathtub, but not hurrying to wash himself, his mother ordered them to lie down and turned the water on them as if she wanted to drown them. Another time he came in dirty from playing in the street and he was put under the shower with his clothes on and was not allowed to change them later. And another time his mother was "mad" and ran the water in the bathtub so hot that he was afraid he was going to be burned. His mother had been drunk as long as he could remember. Often on coming home from school at 3 o'clock he had to hunt in all the bars to find her and often saw her in intimate positions with some strange men. At one time, he remembered, she brought a man home and had intercourse with him.

He complained that he was taunted about his mother's drinking. He had guilty feelings because his mother had been drinking long before he was born. "Sure, my mother was no saint, but my father and my grandmother are enough to drive anyone to drink. My father was a coward and when my mother was in a temper he took his hat and stayed away for hours."

He said he didn't understand his father and didn't care to understand him. "One day he is mad and the next day nearly like a human being." He described him as a selfish person who couldn't get along with anyone. "He drinks a lot too and sometimes brings cheap blonds home with him."

"I don't know much about my grandmother but I know my mother hated her and that she is probably the cause of the drinking. Grandmother thinks she knows all the tricks, but I know as much as she does. I had sex relations when I was 16 years old. Grandmother goes to church all the time; she thinks she's a saint. She forgets that she married twice, that she sent all her children away to be educated in strange surroundings."

The boy had a warm feeling toward his brother and sister, but especially the brother with whom he had lived in an institution after the divorce of his parents. He related the following dream:

His mother was chasing him and his brother but didn't catch them. They went for a swim on a high cliff. His brother was caught under the cliff. He tried to free him but couldn't. When the water was drained out of the cliff he found his brother dead.

He was worried about this dream, for he likes his brother. "I was always close to him in boarding school and I knew my brother better than anyone else."

The general outlook on life of the boy was that no likeable people exist in the world; he did not like anyone. He never met any person who did not think only of himself. Sure, the church has easy lines like "Love your neighbor like yourself," but nobody does. He should like to analyze the probation officer and tell him what is wrong with him. The probation officer thinks he is a "big shot" but he has no education; he has political connections, and that's more important. Any person can be bought with money, the judge, the police, the probation officer "You can't get happiness except with money." He wanted to have lots of money, to get revenge. Perhaps some kind of dictatorship, perhaps communism, would be the right thing. He would like to be a dictator and he would tell people what to do; if they didn't obey, he would kill them.

I had 36 sessions with the boy in 15 months. In the beginning he was unable to relax. He was tense, hostile, negativistic and unwilling to relate his story. He mentioned his fear of water; he would swim only where his feet would touch ground. He declared he had no friends and didn't want any. He said he had flunked his test for a driver's license, but after his father bribed the examiner he got his license anyway. After one month of treatment, two weeks before the final examinations, he was "kicked out" of high school for truancy. He was absent from school thirteen times without reason. He did not worry about it because he knew his father would take care of the school situation. He was ordered to report regularly to the probation office, but he did not do so. He knew that his father, as always, would take care of it for him.

He did not like to talk to people, because "there is nothing in the world to talk about except politics." He mentioned again that he wanted to go out and make a lot of money, but that he was not going to pay taxes. He knew all the tricks. "Farmers don't pay taxes," he said, "and the big shots give parties and take it off their income taxes." With a superior air he stated, "My father pays taxes out of his salary, he doesn't know any better."

After two months he told me that he had "taken" some cars for a ride and had not been caught. In the eleventh interview he was exceedingly hostile. Though he came against his free will, he realized in his therapist, for the first time, a person to whom he could relate his thoughts, his accusations and even aggressions, and who listened to him. Part of his hostility was directed against the therapist and often after a barrage of accusations against him he was able to relate his experiences. He showed an extreme dependency toward his father, such a dependency that he thought his father would omnipotently be able to straighten out all of his difficulties. Yet, at the same time, he revealed a tremendous fear and anxiety. He displayed the air of a "smart Alec" trying not to betray his fears.

In the first eleven interviews he was testing how much the therapist was able to take and tried in every way to upset him emotionally. The patient's desire to impress his superiority on the authorities and the therapist was apparent. Meanwhile he tried to attend summer school, but was not accepted; he blamed his father for this failure.

In his eleventh interview he exhibited an unusual amount of anxiety, but he continued to put up his strong defenses against it. In the next few interviews he changed, however. He cried, wet his pants and behaved like a baby. At this time he came unshaven, unwashed, his hair uncombed, finger-nails dirty; he also had a bad odor. He complained of lonesomeness, of his inability to make friends and that he did not know what to do on his day off. He accused his father of coming to the Clinic not in his behalf, but for his own selfish purpose. He was now eighteen and he told his father that according to the ruling of the Clinic he was now an adult and could come on his own. At times he was able to talk of his mother. He wondered if she were alive or dead, for after the way she had been drinking she could hardly be still alive. In relating this, he cried and mumbled, "I really think I love her and would have liked her to be different."

This behavior may be regarded not only as a regression but as an evidence of a closer relationship to the therapist. He relived the time of the most satisfying period in his life. This may be regarded as abreaction. However, after every emotional outbreak he would shut up and no inter-pretation of his feeling at such time was possible. Not until three or four interviews later was he able to relate to his therapist again.

After about twenty interviews his behavior changed. He also became cleaner and took better care of himself. He was able to smile and, under certain conditions, had a sympathetic attitude. He was able to discuss his fear of failure and his fear of dying. He mentioned that he had heard the world may be doomed and added that when the end of the world did come he would say his prayers, but it wouldn't help him because he would go to hell anyhow. He admitted that there were some "good guys" in this world, after all, and wondered why he was so different from the others that he would wet his bed, for example.

The boy now showed some insight into his condition and he was over-joyed when his father dissolved his connection with the Clinic to seek private psychiatric help. At that time he was still on probation but, unfortunately, only under the conditions that he receive psychiatric care. He counted how long he would have to continue psychiatric treatment. He stated that nobody could be close to his father, that it was impossible to talk to him. He felt that his father could have arranged for him to finish school and study journalism. Very often the patient defended himself and claimed that he had been forced to come to me, but when he was told that he could terminate his visits at any time, he replied, "I don't want to stop now."

After leaving school, he tried to earn money in four or five jobs but was discharged either for coming irregularly or for being disobedient. How-ever, for one half year he was able to keep a job on the railroad.

One month before the end of his probation time he stopped coming to me and did not answer any letters written to him. One half year later, the father called up and told me of the improvement in his son; he had finished high school and kept his job now for over a year.

In recapitulating the whole treatment process it may be said that, as far as psychotherapy is concerned, the results were unsatisfactory. Though the father mentioned some improvement, it must be stated that the only positive result achieved in this case was the patient's enhanced ability to relate freely his feelings of hostility, antagonism and delinquency.

I regard the thirty-six interviews the patient had with me as a prepara-tion for intensive therapy. Recently the boy applied for psychiatric help of his own free will; he brings along sufficient insight into the therapeutic process to participate in the future treatment.

When I saw him last, he seemed a different person. His anxieties came to the fore. He now was afraid to walk on the street alone or to ride in a car, perhaps he was also fearful that he would be tempted to steal another car. His agoraphobia made him seek help urgently.

Judging from this case, it appears that psychotherapy even if it is at first conducted against the will of the patient, can turn out to be successful because it may motivate the patient through the medium of catharsis to deal more efficiently with his anxieties. The decision of the judge that such treatment should be given, rather than punishment, appears, therefore, justified.

Effectiveness

When asked to describe the effectiveness of their treatment, psycho-therapists are cautious men. To an extent they are justifiably so, since,

after all, there is no single method of treatment described by the term
psychotherapy. Not only are there vast differences in the forms of
therapy practiced, but even legitimate therapists differ in the kinds of
training and understanding they bring to their task. In addition, many
different types of disorders are treated with psychotherapy, and it is
difficult to evaluate the effectiveness of treatment without knowing
what is being treated. Some of the caution of therapists is, however,
likely to be due to the fact that psychotherapy is still largely an un-
tested procedure. Even the most sincere and well-motivated practitioners have not put their methods and theories to definitive tests. The
few instances in which there has been research to determine the prac-
ticality of various types of therapy have frequently been disappointing.

One iconoclastic psychologist, Hans J. Eysenck of London, is very
doubtful of the value of all nonmedical psychotherapies. Dr. Eysenck
has made a number of studies comparing thousands of patients with
similar disorders who sought either psychotherapy or routine medical
treatment. Eysenck reported that the rate of improvement for both
types of patients was about the same. He believes that psychotherapy
did not contribute anything uniquely useful. He put it, "We thus
find that among neurotic patients being treated by psychoanalytic or
[other] psychotherapy, about two out of three recover. Similarly, among
neurotics treated by [an ordinary physician] along non-psychothera-
peutic lines, or obtaining simple custodial care, again two out of three
improve. It is difficult to interpret these results as supporting in any
way the hypothesis that psychotherapy has a beneficial effect." Eysenck
himself warns against using the evidence he has adduced to conclude
that therapy is of no value. But it should serve to caution those who
are overly enthusiastic about its results.

Eysenck's work has been criticized as being deficient in experimental
design and biased against psychoanalytic therapies. Some authors have
demonstrated that therapy can be quite useful. In their 1959 *Research
in Psychotherapy*, Rubinstein and Parloff cite a number of studies that
attest to the effectiveness of treatment. Most recently the famous Menninger Clinic has been the source for a comparison of patients treated
in a variety of ways. Hall and Wallerstein, conducting the experiments,
suggest that, when judiciously used, psychotherapy can be a meaningful
rehabilitative method.

The evaluation of legitimate psychotherapies is made more difficult
by the fact that it is bedeviled with all kinds of pretentious treatment
claims that are of little value. Just as medicine was confronted with
glittering nostrums several decades ago, psychotherapy is surrounded
by elaborate but inadequate systems that unfortunately, by their very
existence, make even authentic therapies appear suspicious. One of

the best examples is the "orgone" treatment of Dr. Reich. Reich had his patients sit in a special metal-lined box about the size of a telephone booth while they were in analysis. This was to help control the flow of "orgones," supposed invisible vital forces that determine health or illness. Dr. Reich was eventually convicted of a federal offense in connection with claims made concerning the healing potential of certain orgone apparatus and sent to the Federal Penitentiary in Lewisburg, Pennsylvania. Most bizarre therapeutic claims do not result in jail terms for their authors. Sadly, on occasion even the most vacant therapeutic notions become momentarily popular through a best-selling book or an eloquent exponent. The fame of a therapeutic claim and its mystical or incomprehensible style are seldom a guarantee of value.

Medical therapies appear to be fairly effective, but this may well be because the goals for shock or tranquilizers are quite modest. Psychotherapies that hope to bring about significant personality changes are far more grandiose in their ambitions, and consequently it is more difficult to assess their worth. The present state of uncertainty concerning the usefulness of psychotherapy can probably be summed up by saying that while no general condemnation of therapy is justified, it cannot be hailed as a contemporary miracle. In skilled hands, in particular instances, psychotherapy is a valid, important healing technique (Masserman).

Time and Cost

All psychotherapies are time-consuming procedures. Analytically trained therapists may meet their patients three or more times per week for an hour on each occasion. Client-centered therapists usually have only one or two hourly sessions per week. A complete course of analysis is typically two, three, or more years in length. Nondirective therapists meet patients for a shorter period of time. Psychotherapists who rely heavily on techniques like advice and understanding may have only one or two and seldom more than a half dozen sessions altogether.

The length of therapy is not an indication of the effectiveness of treatment. The amount of time required to aid a patient depends on both the severity of his disorder and his own decision concerning how extensively and deeply he wants to explore and reconstruct his personality. It is also partially dependent upon the background and treatment preferences of the therapist.

Like many professionals in the service of the public, therapists adjust their fees to the patient's ability to pay. Nearly all active practitioners occasionally treat patients who contribute little or even nothing. More commonly, however, patients pay from ten up to more than thirty or forty dollars per consultation or treatment hour. It should be noted that more than with any other professional specialty, a great deal of psychotherapy is available free or at nominal cost. Many cities and towns have low-cost mental health clinics or psychiatric treatment facilities supplied by religious or charitable groups. All states have state and Veterans' Hospital systems that provide psychiatric care for those eligible and in need. The names of appropriate treatment facilities may be obtained by writing to the addresses supplied at the end of the chapter.

Mental Health Professionals

Several different specialties contribute to the diagnosis and therapy of mental health problems. Each profession shares a number of tasks but also has particular duties and abilities. In Table 16-1 some of the characteristics and contributions of several mental health specialties are described.

Table 16-1 MENTAL HEALTH PROFESSIONALS

Training	Psychotherapy	Special Contribution
Psychiatrist		
M.D. degree plus specialized psychiatric training	May use all kinds of medical techniques and psychotherapy	Frequently heads a mental health treatment "team" that includes psychologists and social workers
Clinical psychologist		
Ph.D. degree earned after about four years of schooling beyond B.A.	May use several kinds of psychotherapy	Administers special tests diagnosing personality, intelligence, and emotional well-being
Psychiatric social worker		
Master's degree (M.A. or M.S.W.)	If trained, occasionally may do psychotherapy	Obtains patient's complete history, may prepare patient and family for hospital discharge
Psychoanalyst		
Usually an M.D. degree plus specialized psychiatric and psychoanalytic training	Usually limits himself to psychoanalytic therapies	Treats disorders that are specially amenable to analytic therapy

Finding Therapeutic Help

Because of the many different techniques and treatment orientations, many people wonder what kind of psychotherapist is best suited for them. Actually, this is a problem that need not concern one. The only question that a potential patient should ask is whether the therapist he chooses is a legitimately trained practitioner. No ethical therapist will hesitate to detail the nature of his education and experience, when asked. The person who feels in need of treatment need not concern himself with whether a Horney analyst or Rogerian client-centered doctor is more likely to succeed in helping him. Although treatment procedures differ, competent therapists are about equally successful regardless of their particular philosophies.

People seeking help for personal distress are often puzzled where to begin. They may not know the name of a psychiatrist or how to locate one. Or if there is a practicing psychologist, they wonder whether he is well trained and qualified to help them. One way to begin to look for treatment is to consult a physician in general practice and discuss one's personal problem with him. From him the name of a qualified psychiatrist may possibly be obtained.

There are several other ways in which help—sometimes at little or no cost—may be obtained. Many universities and colleges maintain clinics and treatment centers as part of their educational facilities. Inquiries directed to such institutions may result in obtaining treatment. In many areas, community agencies such as Red Feather, Association for Mental Health, Community Chest, and the Red Cross may list the names of mental health facilities and can be called upon for information. If none of these possibilities appear promising, then the following sources may supply the information described.

Veterans may inquire about treatment by writing to
  Veterans Administration
  Washington, D.C.
The names and addresses of qualified area psychiatrists can be obtained from
  American Psychiatric Association
  1785 Massachusetts Avenue, N.W.
  Washington 6, D.C.
The names and addresses of some qualified clinical psychologists can be obtained from
  American Psychological Association
  1333 Sixteenth Street, N.W.
  Washington 6, D.C.
The names and addresses of qualified area psychoanalysts can be obtained from
  American Psychoanalytic Association
  36 West 44th Street
  New York 16, New York
Literature and additional direction concerning some public treatment facilities may be obtained by writing to
  The National Association for Mental Health, Inc.
  10 Columbus Circle
  New York, New York

FOR REVIEW AND DISCUSSION

1. What are advice, persuasion, insight, and ventilation? Are they effective therapeutic techniques? Why are amateurs frequently tempted to use therapeutic techniques like advice and insight? Why are their attempts commonly unsuccessful?

2. What is client-centered therapy? What assumptions do client-centered therapists make about their patients and human beings in general? Do you think that client-centered treatment techniques could be used to help psychotics?

3. Discuss hypnosis, group therapy, play therapy, and other special techniques. When is each form most likely to be useful? What are some common medical therapies and their applications? Why are medical therapies for use by physicians and psychiatrists only?

4. What techniques are used by nearly all therapies?

5. Discuss some therapeutic techniques apparently used in the case history of therapy against a patient's will. Why was therapy apparently successful? How did the patient's background contribute to this apparent success?

6. How effective are the various psychotherapies? Describe the mental health professionals. What are the best steps to take in finding competent psychotherapeutic help?

Hypnosis

SEVENTEEN

317

Through the ages hypnosis has baffled and fascinated people. More than four thousand years ago the Egyptians undoubtedly relied on it to bring about a "sacred sleep" that eased the pains of surgery and disease. Since antiquity too, mystics have claimed extraordinary powers through hypnotic trance. But more in keeping with the scientific spirit of our own age is the use of hypnosis by practitioners and researchers to help correct and to explore human behavior. Some dentists employ hypnosis to relieve the pain of drilling and extraction. Obstetricians may depend on it to alleviate the discomforts of childbirth. And psychotherapists have found hypnosis practical in a great variety of diagnostic and therapeutic ways. In the hands of trained specialists, hypnotism has become a valuable scientific tool.

THE ANTECEDENTS OF MODERN HYPNOTISM

Though the potentials of hypnosis have long been recognized, it was not until the late 1700's that it was brought once more to popular attention. In France, the immensely persuasive Franz Anton Mesmer hit upon a new method to relieve psychological and physical distress. Essentially Mesmer's therapy rested on reiterated suggestion, but Mesmer himself believed his "cures" attributable to a kind of magnetism. Throughout much of the eighteenth and nineteenth centuries, *mesmerism,* as it was called after its popularizer, made startling claims that were rarely substantiated. In 1841 an English physician, James Braid, attended a demonstration of mesmerism, prepared to expose it for the fraud he felt sure it was. To his chagrin, however, the changes produced by hypnotic trance were visibly effective. Braid interested himself in the new method and quickly saw that it had nothing to do with magnetism, but resembled the normal processes of sleep. He thus coined the word *hypnosis* from the Greek meaning "sleep," and added scientific respectability to what had till then been regarded as merely a kind of charlatanism.

Sigmund Freud also became involved with hypnosis. In 1885, after losing his job at the University of Vienna because of a wrong diagnosis, Freud journeyed to Paris to study the now medically accepted hypnotic techniques. Working at the Salpêtrière Hospital with Charcot, Freud first conceived his ideas concerning how hypnosis could uncover the unconscious forces he believed capable of producing mental disturbances. Eventually, however, Freud discontinued using hypnosis. He found, as most psychologists and therapists soon discover, that many patients are not easily hypnotized, and some not at all. On occasion, when Freud wished his patients to be fully alert and independent, hypnosis seemed only to dull their thinking and make them highly passive. Once more toward the end of the 1800's hypnosis slipped into disuse.

For many years during the early part of our century hypnosis remained neglected. Its scientific and therapeutic contributions were minimized. The chief function of hypnosis may well have been entertainment. During the primacy of vaudeville in the early decades of the twentieth century, the bill of fare frequently included a hypnotism act. Subjects were called on stage and made to behave like barking dogs, to shiver and shake with cold, and to demonstrate countless other absurdities to the delight of the audience. In this atmosphere it is little wonder that hypnotism for professional purposes was regarded with great suspicion.

It is possible that the work of the English physician Grantly Dick Read, the advocate of "natural childbirth" in the 1930's, helped revive serious interest in hypnosis. Dr. Read believed that if he could sufficiently remove unwarranted fears and tensions, mothers could give birth with relatively little discomfort. To induce his patients to overcome their anxieties, Dr. Read instituted a number of procedures among which hypnotic-like suggestions were very important. Read and his followers, interestingly, have avoided stating that their methods involve hypnosis. This may be just as well, since it assures readier acceptance of their approach. Though it is now rapidly gaining a place in medicine, psychology, and research, many laymen and professionals still look askance at hypnotism and question the propriety of its practice.

WHO CAN BE HYPNOTIZED AND HOW DEEPLY

Only about 15 per cent of the population is insusceptible to hypnosis.[1] But hypnosis varies in depth, and not everyone can be brought to the same degree of hypnotic trance. Frequently three stages of hypnosis are distinguished. The first, here designated *light* hypnosis, brings about a form of physical relaxation and simple cooperation. Light subjects may be induced to stiffen limbs or to feel that their eyelids are firmly fastened shut. Most can also be put to sleep and might, if the hypnosis is taking place at night, progress from the hypnotic trance into a normal eight- to ten-hour slumber. About six out of ten people can reach this stage of hypnosis.

About 20 per cent of the population can reach a *moderate* hypnotic

[1] Figures used in this discussion are based on data reported by Weitzenhoffer and by Wolberg.

level. These subjects can commonly speak with the hypnotist although they remain in the trance. They may perform simple motor tasks like writing, and can be relieved of sensation to a modest degree. Their arms, legs, back, and other parts may be rendered unresponsive to pin-pricks, and a small amount of medical and dental work may be done with a minimum of discomfort to them. Posthypnotic suggestion, to be discussed later, is possible with these subjects.

The deepest hypnotic stage is reached only by about one American in twenty. In the *deep* stage the subject is capable of acting as if he were fully awake while he is completely hypnotized. *Negative* and *positive hallucinations* can be induced. This means subjects can be made *not* to see things that are there, or to see things that are not actually present. Many of the deeply hypnotized can undergo quite extensive surgery without reporting pain or discomfort (Rosen).

There are differences between those readily hypnotizable and those who are somewhat resistive. But hypnosis has nothing to do with "will power." It is *not* a matter of "stronger will" dominating a "weaker will." Quite the contrary is true in a way. Good trance subjects tend to be bright, mature, deferential, and extraverted (Lang and Lazovik). People with low intelligence or serious maladjustments are not easily hypnotized (Faw and Wilcox).

Another common question is whether one can be hypnotized involuntarily or "against his will." It is not likely that anyone is ever hypnotized without his fullest cooperation. It is technically possible for a physician to administer medication that might make a resistive subject more amenable to suggestion. In fact, this may be done on request when medical necessity dictates. But most people need not fear that they will be put into a trance as they innocently walk along the street or sit in someone's living room. Hypnosis is a difficult procedure requiring that the subject be actively involved. In fact, even the slightest hesitancies or anxieties about hypnosis on the part of a subject are enough to prevent the induction of a trance. People cannot be hypnotized without their full consent.

HYPNOSIS AND SUGGESTIBILITY

We do not know what hypnosis really is. Some believe a trance explicable in terms of learning: the hypnotized subject is said to learn to be more and more cooperative while being trained to become progressively less critical of the directions given him. Others have attempted to explain hypnosis in physiological terms, contending that, perhaps like sleep, trance results from the inhibition-activation of certain areas within the brain (Weitzenhoffer). In contrast with the special explanations offered by most writers, some authors (Barber, Leuba) have suggested that perhaps no extraordinary condition is actually involved when a subject is in a trance. They suggest that it is possible to produce most, if not all, hypnotic behavior voluntarily with a fully awake subject. Wherever the explanation of hypnotism lies, it will have to account also for the closely related phenomenon of suggestibility.

Ordinary suggestion subtly merges into hypnosis. When a dentist says to a patient, "Relax, this will sting just a little," many patients literally feel less pain than they otherwise would. Similar processes are operative when a physician gives a patient an inert sugar pill and successfully combats wakefulness by stating that it will help him sleep. It is known that people differ in degree of suggestibility. Some are so highly suggestible that just telling them they look ill makes them feel incapacitated. On the other hand, some are very unsuggestible. In fact, they may even be rather negativistic, so that when told one thing, they do another. The 5 per cent of subjects who can enter the deepest hypnotic trance have been found among the most suggestible group. The 15 per cent, approximately, who are insusceptible to hypnosis are mainly those who are unsuggestible.

Hypnotists recognize that suggestibility and hypnotic susceptibility are closely related. For this reason many experts, particularly entertainers who need to be sure that they have a few good subjects, use tests of suggestibility to select volunteers. The stage hypnotist may begin by asking the entire audience of several hundred to participate in the initial tests of suggestibility and choose the very best from among them. The entertainer is thus assured of ferreting out the critical 5 per cent of the population who are easily hypnotized, enter deep stages, and in general make excellent subjects. The following are some typical suggestibility tests.

The sway test. Subjects are asked to stand erect, eyes closed and feet together. The hypnotist, standing ready to catch them, then suggests they are swaying further and further back and forward. Usually the most susceptible subjects sway furthest.

Handclasp test. There are many different ways in which this test is conducted. Some techniques have the subject clasp his hands firmly together in back of his neck or resting in his lap. The hypnotist then suggests, "Your hands are locked together, they're tightly locked, stuck, you can't pull them apart." The most suggestible patients are likely to find their hands immovably locked together.

These tests of suggestibility have a rather dramatic quality that is not always appropriate for therapeutic hypnosis. Many clinical hypnotists therefore do not use suggestibility tests. But they may use other techniques that evaluate relaxation and cooperation to find the best method for inducing hypnosis.

METHODS OF INDUCING HYPNOSIS

Hypnosis is a valuable research tool and worthwhile therapeutic method. In trained, specialized hands, it is a safe, ethical procedure. Attempts at hypnosis by untrained nonprofessionals for entertainment or other nonscientific purposes can be harmful. Deep hypnosis induced by novices may provoke actions and feelings that are potentially deleterious. Hypnosis is not for those who are not specifically qualified to use it. Further, everyone should strenuously resist submitting to hypnosis in any but a serious professional setting. Stage and party hypnotists would soon be without subjects if those who foolishly volunteer were fully aware of the potential dangers of hypnosis in unskilled hands.

The following brief descriptions of methods of hypnotic induction are incomplete and sketchy, and are not intended to teach hypnosis. Their purpose, instead, is to give some understanding of the procedure used by medical and psychological experts.

Qualified hypnotists induce trance in a number of ways. Most begin by describing hypnosis and frankly discussing it with their patient. Then they ask him to sit comfortably in a chair or relax lying down on a couch. Some hypnotists require their patients to stare at a spot on the wall or fixate on an object. Others may request that the subject imagine some peaceful, calming scene such as clouds drifting through a warm, lazy, summer sky. The hypnotist, as he will explain, uses these concentration techniques to help the patient put himself into a receptive mood. All along, the hypnotist is highly dependent on his subject's strong motivation to cooperate. After the patient relaxes, the hypnotist points out his feelings of ease and rest. "You feel comfortable, warm. You're relaxing and slowly drifting to sleep." Eventually, when the specialist judges that his subject is asleep, he starts to deepen the trance state. "Your eyelids are tightly closed; they're fastened very tightly— you can't open them."

Throughout the trance session the doctor assesses the depth of hypnosis by testing for catalepsy (muscular rigidity), arm levitation (involuntary raising of arm), induction of numbness in certain superficial skin areas, and other simple challenges. When the subject appears to have reached an hypnotic plateau, the session is terminated. Awakening may take place as follows: "I'm going to count backwards from five. When I reach one you will be fully awake and refreshed. Five, you're getting ready to wake up. Four, you're awakening. . . ." When the subject is fully awake, the hypnotic session may be jointly discussed and evaluated by doctor and client.

The number of hypnotic sessions that a therapist has depends on the goals of therapy. Some conditions respond to just a very few hypnotic sessions, whereas other psychological disturbances are relieved only after months of hypnotic treatment.

THE USES OF HYPNOSIS

Hypnoanalysis. Hypnoanalysis is a technique used in psychotherapy to help the patient recall long-buried, unconscious memories. It is not really a form of treatment but a supplement to more standard kinds of analysis. Freud originally used hypnosis to help his patients talk freely and thus uncover some of the roots of their disorders. Hypnotic age regression, which is described later in this chapter, is sometimes also applied to uncover and air unconscious feelings and memories.

Habit disorders. Hypnotic suggestion is occasionally employed to help relieve patients of undesirable symptoms such as tics, twitches, nail biting, and cigarette smoking. It is difficult to describe the effectiveness of hypnosis with these kinds of conditions. Some therapists select their patients carefully and use not only hypnotic suggestion but more intensive and prolonged psychotherapy as well. Such treatment combinations can be fairly successful. Occasionally a nonscientifically trained hypnotist—frequently an outright charlatan—advertises that he can "cure" various "bad habits" by hypnosis. Though these unqualified practitioners are sometimes able to render what looks like relief temporarily, nonprofessionals should be diligently avoided because of the danger of meddling with symptoms.

The relief of pain. Hypnosis may relieve the pain engendered in many medical procedures. It has been most extensively used, probably, by obstetricians for childbirth and by dentists for oral procedures. Hypnosis has also removed the pain of "phantom" limbs. After amputation, some patients feel discomfort in a leg that is no longer there. This is a very real phenomenon and can result in severe intractable distress. Hypnosis can successfully relieve such phantom pains.

Obesity and alcoholism. There have been attempts to assuage addictions such as alcoholism or overeating through hypnosis. Generally the results have not been encouraging, but with carefully selected, well-motivated patients, in skilled hands, some disorders have responded well to hypnotic therapy. Dr. Herbert Mann of San Jose, California, psychiatrist and clinical hypnotist, has reported good results with hypnosis in helping a patient who both drank and ate improperly.

The case of Mrs. M. D., aged 42 years, illustrates a logical, realistic application of hypnotic techniques. The patient verbalized her complaint as one of obesity and could not account for the excess weight of many years duration. She steadfastly maintained that she ate nothing other than a small meal in the evening, which amounted to about 400 calories. She was an intelligent woman, neatly and expensively attired, apparently co-operative, but was adroit in evading questions directed toward consumption of alcoholic beverages. Hypnosis was suggested in order to create for the patient a more protected situation, in which she could feel free to express herself. In the very lightest trance, with eyes closed, the patient readily revealed a long history of alcholism culminating in her present routine of starting the day off with a bourbon highball, then drinking vodka martinis throughout the day. . . . In therapy, no attempt was made to precipitously remove the habit disorder, not because of any fantasied danger in such an approach, but because a direct attack is almost invariably ineffective. A suggestion was offered that perhaps, upon awakening in the morning, a cup of hot coffee or tea might be substituted for the bourbon highball and that the patient might experience the same stimulating, eye-opening effect from coffee or tea that she had been obtaining from bourbon. Such substitution would also aid her in reducing excess weight by eliminating one source of her obesity. It was also suggested that at noon she might enjoy the stimulating effect of another hot drink, perhaps a cup of bouillon, soup, coffee, or tea.

.   .   .   .   .

No further suggestions were directed at the problem of alcoholism. Over a period of three months, during which time the patient was seen weekly, proper eating habits became well established, while the consumption of alcohol rapidly decreased and was entirely and spontaneously eliminated within the first five weeks. During therapy, it was repeatedly emphasized that the goal was not loss of weight per se, but the acceptance of ideas and suggestions that help in developing eating habits which are effective in removing excess weight and in maintaining optimum weight when that level has been reached. The patient has maintained her optimum weight over a year, has had no desire to indulge in alcoholic beverages.[2]

2 Herbert Mann, "Hypnotherapy in Habit Disorders," *Am. J. Clin. Hypnosis, 3* (1961), 125–26.

Psychiatric and physical disorders. Attempts have been made to use hypnosis with severe psychiatric disorders such as schizophrenia and with certain physical conditions such as asthma and allergies. These efforts are highly experimental and results have not been favorable (Wolberg). As with any other therapy, some clinical hypnotists occasionally report encouraging results using hypnotism for a wide variety of physical and psychiatric disorders. This does not imply, however, that hypnotism is readily available for the relief of all disturbances.

Learning. It is claimed that hypnosis can help people learn. It may be that when a tense person is relaxed by hypnotic suggestion he can study more effectively. Or perhaps suggestion can help people concentrate a little more diligently. Typically, however, when hypnosis is attempted in order to help students learn more quickly and easily, few real benefits emerge. In nearly all cases most benefit derives solely from the fact that students believe that they are being helped. This in and of itself increases motivation and may temporarily facilitate learning. Generally, however, there is little probability that hypnosis leads to lasting, significant improvements in study or learning (Fowler).

Posthypnotic Suggestion

During hypnosis in moderate and deep stages, the hypnotist may give directions that are to be carried out after the subject awakes. Instructions given during hypnosis but completed after awakening are called posthypnotic suggestions. Sometimes posthypnotic suggestions can be dramatically helpful.

A young actor was giving his first "live" television performance and was extremely frightened that he would be so nervous that he would forget his lines or badly jumble them. Several sessions were held; he was brought to a moderate hypnotic depth and the television debut was vicariously rehearsed. Shortly before his performance, it was suggested that when he was in front of the cameras he would feel a new surge of confidence and challenge that would make him act surely and with professional ease, as he usually did. Subsequently, the actor reported that he was nervous and doubtful about the effectiveness of hypnosis as the time for his appearance approached. But when he stood before the "live" cameras he felt as if the entire scene was intimately familiar to him and confidently gave what he believes to be one of his better performances.

Posthypnotic suggestions usually do not last more than several hours or a few days. There are some instances where they have reputedly lasted for months or longer. But if a hypnotist suggests something ludicrous, as stage hypnotists frequently do, like "When anyone says 'Hello,' you will shout 'Whoopee,' " the suggestion is likely to last only a very short time.

Hypnotic Age Regression

In order to restore memory for long forgotten events, hypnotists may try age regression. The subject is told that he is back at a designated age level and that he will act and feel exactly as he did at that time. One way in which this is done is gradually to induce the patient to forget where he really is and slowly to revive scenes at a particular age. Thus a subject might be asked to forget today's date, week, month, season, and year. He would be disoriented as to place—told he was not in the doctor's office, not in this building, city, and so on. Eventually the hypnotist builds the memories for the period he wants. "You are in Chicago. It is cold and wintry. You are with your mother. You're going Christmas shopping. This year you will buy a present for your new baby brother. You're four years old."

Age regression can be of assistance in hypnoanalytic psychotherapies. It can help patients recall distant, disturbing parts of childhood and narrate long buried events which, once talked about with the therapist, may lose their damaging effects. Some subjects not only vividly remember forgotten experiences but seem to act as if they were again at the level to which they have hypnotically returned. They speak, write, and act like a child. The emotions that were originally experienced at an earlier age are literally relived. Through age regression an adult recalling a frightening experience he had at the age of four may actually cry and carry on as if he were that young again (Yates).

Control of Physical Processes

Some involuntary bodily processes, such as heartbeat, gastrointestinal activity and cutaneous functions, may be altered by hypnosis. Heartbeat can be speeded up or a full stomach made to act like an empty one. Even blisters have reputedly been produced simply by suggestion. Before marveling at these phenomena, we should remember that many autonomic processes can be influenced "voluntarily" while fully awake. Heartbeat may be accelerated, for example, by vividly imagining oneself in a very exciting or frightening situation. Similarly, digestive changes can be consciously brought about by hungrily describing in juicy detail a thick, sizzling steak, french fried potatoes, or some other favored food. The fact that hypnotized subjects can slightly alter autonomic functions does not appear remarkable when we realize the extent to which all of us can deliberately influence many involuntary bodily activities (Barber, "Physiological Effects," 1961).

It is sometimes reported that subjects have demonstrated extraordinary physical capabilities while hypnotized. Some assert they have seen a person whose body was rendered so rigid by trance that he could be laid across two chairs, stiff as a board, with only head and ankles resting on each chair. Even more dramatic exhibitions of strength and unusual physical prowess under hypnosis are reputed to take place in India and elsewhere in the Orient. In nearly all cases, however, as Arthur Koestler noted after extensive observation in the Far East in the late 1950's, such peculiar feats of strength and endurance are the results of diligent physical discipline and practice rather than attributable to mystical hypnotic phenomena.

The degree to which hypnosis might be of assistance in improving physical performance has actually been experimentally tested. W. R. Johnson and G. F. Kramer of the University of Maryland evaluated the effects of hypnosis on athletic strength, power, and endurance. Ten young male athletes were put into a trance, and their jumping, reaching, lifting, and other strengths were compared to their nonhypnotized performance. None of the athletic abilities improved significantly under hypnosis—with one exception: for some athletes endurance did increase under hypnosis. Apparently some normal reactions may be slightly exaggerated in a trance just as they would be under certain emotional circumstances. In times of stress or need, or when hypnotized, many subjects sharpen their ordinary abilities by calling upon the reserves of energy made available by the human endocrine system.

Self-Hypnosis

Self-hypnosis is sometimes taught patients by their hypnotists. It is frequently used to relieve conditions like insomnia, where the patient's ability to induce his own trance is especially convenient. The hypnotherapist has already successfully hypnotized his subject several times and tells his hypnotized patient, "You are capable of putting yourself to sleep. I don't really do anything to you; you do it all yourself by cooperating with me. I'm going to help you learn a way that you can hypnotize yourself." The patient who has learned auto- or self-hypnosis is usually safeguarded so that he will employ his technique only in appropriate circumstances. For example, if he has learned to put himself to sleep, it would be unsafe to begin to think about the procedure while driving an automobile. Therapists look after their patients by using a technique like the following. "Everything has to be prepared and in order before you will go to sleep yourself. You'll pull the shades, darken the room, and when you feel your head resting on the pillow you'll begin counting backward from twenty-five. . . ."

It is not likely that a person can learn to hypnotize himself entirely

without assistance. It is possible, however, that one can teach himself
to relax sufficiently to overcome mild insomnia or facilitate dental
work. One person who entirely by himself induced sleep at night used
the following technique. He concentrated on all parts of his body,
beginning with his toes, working up to his legs, knees, on to his head,
and consciously observed all of them till they were fully relaxed. "I'd
concentrate on my toes, wiggle them and just try to feel they were fully
relaxed and going to sleep. After I have them taken care of, I'd concentrate on my ankles. I could feel them relaxing also. It would take
me about ten minutes to get every muscle in my body to relax. Before
I knew it I was usually asleep. At first I had to go over my whole body
sometimes twice or three times. Eventually, like now, by the time
I'm up to my legs, or sometimes arms, I'm fast asleep." Another method
of self-hypnosis is reported in Fig. 17-1.

Fig. 17-1 Self-hypnosis. An insomniac patient reported being able to induce sleep by imagining
himself all alone in a huge stadium watching a slow-
motion football game. In a few instances, patients
can be taught self-suggestive techniques to aid in
the relief of minor difficulties.

Antisocial Behavior

If we were to believe what motion pictures and other fiction present, then we would have to believe that normal human beings will commit all sorts of villainies while in a trance. According to story, hypnotists can seduce innocent maidens, provoke loyal citizens to treason, and make criminal monsters out of law-abiding citizens. The extent to which such falsehoods are believed is evidenced by the occasional thief or lawbreaker who attempts to avoid responsibility by asserting he was forced to commit crimes through hypnosis. As far as can be determined, however, there are no instances of illegal activity motivated by hypnosis. Careful investigation of some crimes claimed to have been committed under hypnosis have demonstrated that hypnotism was not responsible (Barber, "Antisocial and Criminal Acts," 1961).

In order to evaluate whether harmful conduct could actually be instigated, hypnotized subjects have been ordered to shoot, rob, forge, poison, strangle, and commit all sorts of dangerous acts and crimes. All of these violent activities have been carried out under carefully controlled experimental conditions, of course. But the utmost efforts were made to make the "crimes" and prospects of "apprehension" seem real to the subjects. Frequently, deeply hypnotized people commit the experimental crimes or willingly expose themselves to danger. In one series of investigations, subjects were instructed to reach for a deadly rattlesnake or to throw a powerful acid into another's face. Hypnotized individuals both reached for the snake and threw the acid. Of course, in both cases the people involved in the experiment were protected. "Invisible" glass prevented the hand from reaching the snake and acid from reaching the face. The question may well be raised, then, whether the hypnotized subjects were truly behaving dangerously. Could they not have seen the supposedly invisible protective shields?

In his review of antisocial and criminal acts during trance, Dr. Barber of Boston University points out that hypnotized subjects have deep trust, faith, and respect for the hypnotist. They are as incapable of believing that he would order them to act harmfully as any normal person would be to believe that a trusted doctor would deliberately advise him to commit a felony. In addition, subjects appear to believe that, whatever seems to be happening, the hypnotist has arranged events so that no truly antisocial consequence occurs. Finally, many hypnotized subjects feel that they themselves are not personally involved and impute all responsibility to the hypnotist.

It seems impossible to make a true test in a laboratory setting of whether antisocial behavior can be produced through hypnosis. While a few subjects in deep trance follow the directions of the hypnotist in a laboratory situation, not all people are readily compliant. Even in a research setting many people given a destructive or improper order become so unsettled that they resist the command or break the trance. It is not an easy or simple matter to obtain the cooperation of most people in violations of law or morality, even in contrived, artificial situations.

The question of whether a subject can be induced to act in unethical, illegal ways in the real world has not been definitively answered by laboratory investigation. Perhaps a few rare individuals might actually commit almost any illegality the hypnotist suggests. But before one concludes that criminal and immoral behavior is likely to be motivated by hypnosis, one should remember that it is not easy to attain the extreme depth of trance that would probably be required to promote illegal activity. Subjects would have to be in a trance stage where they could walk, talk, and act as if fully awake while hypnotized. This profound hypnotic level can be reached only by about one of twenty people. In addition, a great deal of effort and specialized professional competence is necessary in order to induce a subject to reach the greatest depth of hypnosis. In general, then, while it might be possible to command a very few hypnotized subjects to expose themselves to danger or to act illegally or against their best interests—which they might do anyway, while awake—it is highly unlikely that this has actually happened.

Hypnosis is increasingly accepted as a legitimate and often worthwhile treatment and research technique. Although, like all newly acquired methods, its value is sometimes exaggerated, many patients burdened with undesirable symptoms or habits have in highly skilled hands been relieved of distress. A few others undergoing the discomforts of childbirth, surgery, or dental work have in select instances also been assisted by hypnosis. Hypnosis may be of aid too in helping patients relive and recall memories of which they are not ordinarily aware. Hypnotism has already contributed to our understanding of behavior, and we may expect it to play an increasing role in the advancement of human welfare.

FOR REVIEW AND DISCUSSION

1. Can everyone be hypnotized? How are hypnotic depth and hypnotic suggestibility related? What proportion of the population can probably be put into the deepest hypnotic trance?

2. What are some explanations of hypnosis? Why do stage hypnotists—and some others—use tests of suggestibility? What are some common ways of inducing hypnosis?

3. How is hypnosis useful for psychotherapy? How can hypnosis be used to aid in relieving undesirable habits such as overeating? Can hypnosis enhance learning, athletic feats, and other ordinary abilities?

4. Discuss posthypnotic suggestion, age regression, and self-hypnosis. Can hypnotized subjects be compelled to act in ways that might ordinarily be objectionable to them? Why is it difficult to obtain experimental evidence about antisocial acts under hypnosis?

An

Approach

to

Mental

Hygiene

Understanding

Ourselves and

Others

E I G H T E E N

Man lives in an uncertain, sometimes rewarding, often unjust world. That is not to say as some do, romantically, that there ever was a time anywhere when men were free of the hazards of living. Since their emergence as intelligent animals, men have puzzled over the seeming contradictions inherent in the splendor that life promises and the misery that so frequently results. For Macbeth, life was

> . . . a tale
> Told by an idiot, full of sound and fury,
> Signifying nothing.

The twentieth century may well be a time of anxiety and may seem to have made life meaningless by its excesses. Yet it is doubtful that the immediate psychological character of life in ancient Persia or Rennaisance Europe was fundamentally different. The problematic questions of existence have not been greatly altered, though from century to century and place to place the sources of concern may have shifted. While infectious plagues now hold little terror, wars, which were once confrontations between armed individuals, today threaten to annihilate entire cities or nations.

Throughout his history, man has pitted his wisdom, tolerance, and energy against the world in his struggle to survive, and if possible to give meaning to his short stay on earth. The continuing demands imposed upon them forces human beings to *adjust* if they are to prevail. But man is not endowed with many reflexive adjustive capabilities. He cannot like a chameleon change his coloring or like a bear slow down his metabolism for a food-scarce winter. Man is, however, gifted with a splendid mental capacity that permits him, unlike any other animal, to reason, learn, plan, and choose.

Can our abilities to think and understand enable us to avert or remedy psychological aberrations? Physically disabling afflictions ranging from smallpox to diabetes can be prevented or modified. Although there are medications to guard against polio or whooping cough, nothing is available to protect against hostile parents who by their punitiveness deprive children of the strenths they need for normal emotional development. Because many of the factors that contribute to mental well-being—such as the milieu provided by family and the stresses imposed by environment—are not within our command, the extent to which we can practice successful mental hygiene is limited.

Though the degree to which we may consciously help ourselves adjust is modest, there are still worthwhile mental hygiene practices. Proper physical hygiene, regular tooth brushing, and sensible eating habits do not eliminate tooth decay or other organic disturbances. But such careful self-regulation may make a difference. Similarly, it has been demonstrated that coronary difficulties are related to a wide variety of factors (heredity and height, for instance), many not within our control. But by manipulating the few variables that are in reach (diet and exercise) the likelihood of heart and related disorders can be reduced (Cady, *et al.*). So too, informed and rational patterns of living may help modify our own possible psychological disturbances or at least increase the effectiveness of our adjustive capacities.

It is tempting to suggest rules conducive to good mental hygiene; but it is difficult to benefit from such homiletic advice. "Don't save up your irritations. Let people know where you stand." The trusting listener who follows these recommendations and discharges himself of his feelings with his teachers, employer, friends, or relatives may soon find himself out of school, fired, or a social leper. Mental hygiene is not advanced by an easy-sounding set of rules, but by an informed and receptive attitude and goal-directed expectations toward one's own life and world. Appropriate mental health practices cannot be put on like a suit of clothes. The thinking and emotional patterns of many are already so distorted that a rational reorientation of their living habits is nearly impossible. Like the 315-pound habitual overeater, they may not be able to change their familiar, deeply engraved responses even if their accustomed ways threaten their very existence. In addition, those already grossly mentally disturbed should not look to themselves but to psychiatric help—and the sooner the better. Nevertheless, some people not entirely free of emotional flaws but generally healthy can increase their human effectiveness by learning more about themselves and others and seeking meaningful values to guide their lives.

THE LIBERATING EFFECTS OF INTELLIGENCE AND PERSONAL VALUES

For most of the last fifty years the increasing understanding of the causes of behavior has encouraged the belief that all human activities are mechanically determined by circumstances beyond our control. Without discussing "free choice" as a philosophical problem, we can certainly state that too much emphasis has been given the notion that human lives are inalterable products of specific environments and inherited characteristics (Immergluck). Even children from apparently disruptive homes are capable of applying their own abilities and making reasoned choices to emerge as well-balanced human beings (Senn; Rogers, 1961).

We are gifted with superb intellectual skills that constitute one of our strongest mental health assets. If our intelligence is nourished by a healthy and receptive inquisitiveness about ourselves and the world, it may free us from many of the shortcomings imposed by our physical and psychological background.

Conscious recognition of worthwhile human values may also help liberate us from some undesirable handicaps. Of the nine out of ten Americans (see Table 18-1) who identify with some religion, many derive confidence, security, and responsibility from the beliefs they cherish and practice. Others are liberated and turned toward lifelong goals by ethical codes originating from nonreligious, social, or philosophical affiliations. In one way or another those who seek to strengthen themselves have developed a set of values, a philosophy that enables them to meet future difficulties with a sense of individuality, direction, and perspective.

Table 18-1   RELIGIOUS AFFILIATION OF AMERICANS FOURTEEN YEARS OF AGE AND OLDER

Religion	Number	Per cent Total
Protestant	79.0 million	66.2
Roman Catholic	30.6 million	25.7
Jewish	3.8 million	3.2
Other religions	1.5 million	1.3
No religion	3.2 million	2.7
Religion not reported	1.1 million	0.9

Source: Based on Broom and Selznick, p. 441.

Jane, a eighteen-year-old college sophomore, came to see her psychology instructor with what she described as a "new kind of problem." Jane was enrolled in an abnormal psychology course and had become concerned about some of the material discussed. She revealed that her family background was quite disturbed. She characterized her mother as a "negativistic" woman who seldom praised or encouraged anyone. He brother had left home when he was only fourteen (and she was ten) and had since written only rarely. Jane's father began drinking shortly after the parents were married, and she could remember serious fights about his drinking and periodic desertions while she was growing up. After her brother had left, Jane and her mother moved away from her father and into the home of the maternal grandparents. Jane occasionally receives letters, gifts, and visits from her father. She visited him about a year ago, found him apparently satisfactorily remarried, and believes that while he still drinks he is not an alcoholic. Her brother has joined the armed service as a career. Jane confided to her instructor her concern that her disturbing background would eventually result in a "neurosis or psychosis." From what she had learned in the course, it seemed to her that it was inevitable that her own personality would be seriously distorted and her chances for a satisfactory marriage and family gravely impaired. At the same time Jane recognized that her family situation had resolved itself and that she "felt normal" and had a "happy outlook." She was active in several campus groups and was a well-liked, successful student.

Jane's *background* suggested to her, as it would to many professionals, that she was inalterably headed for psychological disorder. Nevertheless in Jane's case it was apparent that despite the trauma of her first ten years she was a healthy, poised, and talented person. She was attractive, intelligent, and perceptive about her own strengths as well as the weaknesses partly imposed by her insecure unbringing. She had an independent and confident approach to life and was prepared to meet its problems. In this instance, as is frequently the case, Jane's searching intelligence and her developing goals permitted her to compensate for her family limitations and approach her existence with zest and fruitful expectations.

CHOICE AND CONFLICT

The greater a person's understanding about himself and the more information he has obtained about the world in which he lives, the more capable he is of making sound and worthwhile decisions. But motives and choices do not arise one at a time. Often we are driven toward two or more conflicting goals (see Chapter Three). Moreover, the information we have about the alternatives we face is often incomplete.

Whenever someone is faced with incompatible decisions, his selections are no longer simple choices but rather conflicting goals. Adolescents' sexual inclinations are often in conflict with moral standards, fear of pregnancy, and other inhibiting factors. Similarly, a choice of job, neighborhood, or even husband or wife may produce serious conflict when choosing one alternative results in giving up other attractive choices. The girl who states she likes two boyfriends equally has a real, if not very traumatic conflict. If she decides to encourage Bill more than John, she may win him as a husband but lose not only John but also the moneyed background he represents. Conversely, by favoring John she gives up Bill as a husband and also loses his youthful, lusty enthusiasm for life.

Psychologists have been able to characterize four primary types of conflicts. These experimentally based descriptions cannot be regarded as complete or inclusive, since human conflicts typically involve multiple motives and decisions many of which are relatively below awareness. The four primary types of conflict can be used, however, to help illustrate the nature of some of the more intricate forms of choice and indecision that occur in human beings.

Approach-approach conflict. As the name suggests, approach-approach conflict is a conflict between two or more equally attractive goals. The applicant offered similarly appealing jobs is faced with the task of deciding between seemingly equivalent alternatives. C. I. Hovland and R. R. Sears demonstrated the effects of this type of conflict in human motoric behavior. They seated subjects with a six-inch-square piece of paper before them and trained them to draw a line toward one or another corner of the paper depending upon where a green light flashed. After subjects had learned to respond quickly to lights flashed randomly in one or another corner, the experimenter simultaneously flashed green lights in both corners. Subjects now had to choose between two opposite goals. Nearly two-thirds quickly resolved the approach-approach conflict by drawing a line to one corner and ignoring the other goal. This is very much like the behavior of the man who quickly chooses between dating blonde Jo Anne or equally appealing, vivacious Vivian. He recognizes that both are attractive, but once he makes his choice has no regrets about not dating the girl who once looked equally appealing.

But not all subjects resolved the approach-approach conflict so easily. About a fifth of the experimental subjects *alternated*. They drew a line toward one green light, then the other, then the first, and back again. Another tenth of the subjects sought a *compromise* by drawing a line to neither corner but straight up the page between the lights. Still another tenth were *immobilized* by the two approach goals. They were unable to draw any line at all.

Many of us have already found that the choice between two positive goals is often not a simple one. Like the experimental subjects, we alternately choose first one goal and then another. The closer we get to the one we have chosen, the more attractive the other seems, forcing us to backtrack and try the alternate once more. Equally attractive goals often result in attempted compromises that sometimes are not available. In the long run, many of us faced with two attractive alternatives, like the experimentally immobilized subjects, do absolutely nothing. A student anxious to attend a leading Ivy League college had appealing offers from Princeton and Yale. He reported that both looked so good that he kept changing his mind which to choose. He vacillated so long between them that eventually his deadline for acceptance passed and he was unable to have either.

Avoidance-avoidance conflict. To illustrate avoidance-avoidance conflict, Sears and Hovland trained their subjects to draw lines *away* from a red light appearing at either one or another corner of their work sheet. When lights at two corners of the page were flashed red simultaneously, subjects had to respond to two negative goals. In this situation nearly half of the subjects reacted ineffectively. Instead of reacting quickly to one or another negative goal, they either found themselves frozen and incapacitated or tried to avoid both alternatives at the same time. Similarly, when we are faced with real-life unpleasant alternatives our behavior may, instead of being mobilized to meet the situation, deteriorate and leave us virtually paralyzed. Upon graduation, a student was faced with either taking a relatively unpleasant job with a chemical company (which would have made him draft exempt) or being inducted into the army. Like the experimental subjects, the student felt unable to act and sought to withdraw from the situation by feigning illness that he thought would save him from both work and the service.

Approach-avoidance conflict. To assess the effects of this type of conflict, subjects who had been trained to draw a line toward a green light and away from a red light were flashed red and green lights at the same time in the same corner. Subjects were now caught in the classic conflict situation. They were both attracted and repelled at the same time. A frequent result of this type of conflict is *vacillation.* The subject moves toward the goal because of its positive aspects. But the closer he gets the more prominent the negative ones appear and the stronger becomes the tendency to move back. In actual experimentation with animals, rats can be seen literally running back and forth in front of an approach-avoidance object. The girl who has serious reservations about the man she wants to marry typifies human approach-avoidance conflict. Her love for her financé and her urge to marry impel her to set a wedding date. But as the ceremony nears, her serious doubts and anxieties force her to postpone the marriage and set it further in the future.

Double approach-avoidance conflict. The most common variety of conflicts are those that involve several alternatives, each possessing both negative and positive elements. In the drawing experiment, double approach-avoidance choices were simulated by lighting both red and green signals at two corners of the paper. Subjects were now compelled to choose between drawing a line toward or away from two goals at the same time. In this experimental situation nearly three out of every four participants reacted ineffectively or irrationally.

A twenty-two-year-old college senior deeply interested in world affairs was strongly motivated to accept a two-year Peace Corps assignment abroad. At the same time, he was very fond of a girl he had known since high school and had considered marrying her. Both choices, remaining at home and marrying, or going overseas with the Peace Corps, were strongly attractive, but both also contained negative elements. The puzzled senior was apprehensive about the hardships, discomforts, loneliness, and illness that might await him in his foreign assignment. At the same time he was unsure that he should marry, since he did not know whether the girl was really suitable or whether he was ready for the responsibilities of family life. Interestingly, the student slipped between the ambivalent horns of the dilemma by deciding neither to marry nor to go with the Peace Corps. He resolved instead to remain single, stay in the United States, and continue his schooling for a graduate degree.

Table 18-2 summarizes the four primary types of conflict.

Table 18-2   FOUR TYPES OF CONFLICT

Type	Description	Outcomes
Approach-approach	Two equally attractive goals	Usually easily resolved, but may sometimes result in ineffective vacillation
Avoidance-avoidance	Two equally unpleasant goals	Frequently results in "freezing"; may cause subject to attempt to run away from both goals
Approach-avoidance	One goal contains both attractive and undesirable elements	Commonly results in vacillation, inability to make up one's mind
Double approach-avoidance (type most commonly encountered by human beings)	Two or more goals each contain attractive and repulsive elements	Causes indecision; produces tensions, uncertainty, and anxiety

The Resolution of Conflict

Good mental health practice suggests that conflicts be recognized and appropriately resolved. The ways in which conflict is frequently alleviated have been partially explained. Research with animals (Miller) has suggested a number of postulates that may account for the ways in which conflicts are resolved. Two such postulates are given here.

1. The strength of the tendency to approach or avoid a goal may be increased or decreased by strengthening or weakening the motives to achieve the goal.

2. The tendency to approach or avoid an alternative is stronger the closer an individual comes to the alternative and weaker the further he is away.

When confronted with seemingly deadlocked alternatives, the first postulate suggests that if we fathom our own motives more clearly, we may be able to solve our dilemma. Careful examination of our needs is likely to lead to a strengthening or weakening of our drives and should thus eventuate in some solution. Similarly, the second postulate suggests a sensible way to reach a decision about an ambiguous goal. Instead of speculating about alternative actions from a distance, we should move toward the situation in order to strengthen avoidance or approach feelings. Instead of looking at the water and speculating how cold it is from up on the beach, it is often best to go close and stick in an inquisitive toe.

ADJUSTMENT AND CHANGING LIFE EXPECTATONS

Conflict is universal. All men sooner or later reach an impasse they feel incapable of solving. But by learning about both the nature of conflict and our own motives we may facilitate appropriate solutions. So too, we can contribute to our own effective adjustment by learning more about the points in our lives that will require new decisions and directions as our expectations change. For those well prepared, the new responsibilities and opportunities inherent in getting married or beginning a first job are met with an attitude characterized more by a sense of challenge than of foreboding.

School and Job Adjustment

One of the most exciting and frequently frightening events in a young child's life is the beginning of school. During his fourth or fifth year, a child prepares himself for nursery school, kindergarten, or the first grade. Most children who have already developed effective adjustment techniques and come from warm and healthy parental backgrounds have little or no difficulty responding appropriately to the new demands imposed by school. This is not invariably the case, however. Even children from the most desirable homes, particularly if they are only children or are separated by many years from their siblings, may have some troublesome anxieties when school time starts. Children from over-protective homes or hostile and rejecting environments or who have been otherwise weakened in their self-appraisal and ability to deal with others may find the beginning school experience a very hazardous one.

Most children respond to the teacher in almost the same way as to their parents. Attitudes of acceptance, suspicion, trust, or dislike toward parents are transferred to the teacher. Frequently too, the child expects to be able to manipulate his teachers, by cajoling, whining, or pouting, just as he has kept his mother or father in line. It may well be at the point that the child realizes his teacher possesses her own personality and must be responded to differently from his own parents that he makes a significant step forward in his perception of the needs and character of other people.

Education occupies more than half of the child's active day from the time he is five or six until well into his late teens or early twenties. During the school years, attitudes toward self and one's capabilities are set in motion that may influence aspirations and achievements throughout life. In school many of the all-important social skills that teach a child to live with and be considerate of others are initiated. Throughout the time he is learning, the child's achievement needs are reinforced or handicapped by being satisfied or frustrated. Ultimately, the child's *level of aspiration,* the goals toward which he steers himself realistically or foolishly, are determined during the school years.

Level of Aspiration

The goals we set for ourselves and the steps we make to attain them define our level of aspiration. Ideally we should aspire to that for which we are best equipped. A teen-ager with outstanding intellectual and scholastic abilities who thinks of himself only as a future factory worker may have a grossly lowered and distorted level of aspiration. Similarly unrealistic are the daydreams of adolescents (nearly a third of all high school students in a study conducted by E. S. Jones), who aspire to be physicians, lawyers, and other professionals but lack the intelligence or have not made sufficient academic preparation to realize their plans.

Laboratory investigation of level of aspiration has shown that there is a tendency in most children to increase their aspiration slightly with success and lower it when confronted with failure. Most important, however, are studies such as those of I. L. Child and J. W. M. Whiting, suggesting that continual failure seriously damages aspirational level. People with intelligence on the low end of the normal scale (about one-fourth have an IQ below 90) if continually confronted with difficult material may have one failure experience after another. The definitely retarded child (about 5 per cent have an IQ below 75) may be so harassed by failure that the little ability he has may be further eroded by destroying his need to achieve.

More than half of all children today complete high school, and more than half of these begin college (see Table 18-3). And besides all the

Table 18-3 RETENTION RATE PER 1,000 STUDENTS FROM FIFTH GRADE
THROUGH COLLEGE (1951–59)

Elementary	
Fifth	1,000
Sixth	981
Seventh	968
Eighth	921
High school	
Freshman	886
Sophomore	809
Junior	709
Graduated	582
Entered college	308

Source: U.S. Bureau of the Census, Statistical Abstract, 1961.

other reasons for staying in school, there are sound economic ones for their doing so (see Table 18-4). But after a dozen or at most sixteen years, for the great majority the relatively sheltered and well-regulated environment of school must be left behind and job responsibilities assumed. It is little wonder that perhaps even greater than the anxiety upon entering school are the intense apprehensions upon leaving. There are few jobs, if any, in which one can depend upon indulgent supervisors to overlook laziness and errors in the same way that sympathetic teachers did. And while academic curriculums are nicely scheduled, assuming work responsibilities means working and planning a great deal on one's own. We may never have had to compete with our peers in the classroom, but when we look for work and seek to maintain a job we quickly learn that we are in a race with many others—some of whom are far more skilled and motivated than we are.

Table 18-4 YEARLY INCOME FOR MALES 25 YEARS OR OLDER
BY YEARS OF SCHOOL COMPLETED

	1949	1959	1965 *
Elementary			
Less than 8 years	$2,026	$2,551	$2,800
8 years	2,829	3,769	4,100
High School			
1 to 3 years	3,226	4,618	5,100
4 years	3,784	5,567	6,200
College			
1 to 3 years	4,423	6,966	7,800
4 or more years	6,179	9,206	10,200

Source: U.S. Bureau of the Census, Statistical Abstract, 1961.
* Projected.

On the job itself many new conditions face the recent graduate. For the first time in his life he finds himself concerned with being able to continue to hold a job, earn more money, obtain promotions, and feel secure and important. Perhaps even more surprising may be the fact that although the student may have eagerly prepared himself for a career or profession and spent long years in its anticipated pursuit, once he begins his career it may not turn out to be so satisfying as he expected. About one-fourth of all college graduates wish they had chosen a profession other than the one in which they find themselves (see Fig. 18-1). The extent of dissatisfaction with the actual choice

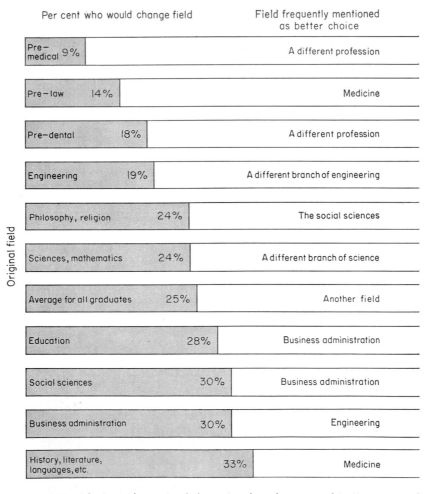

Fig. 18-1   Dissatisfaction with vocational choice. Based on data reported in Havemann and West, p. 149.

may sometimes be strong enough to actuate a professional to return to school and completely retrain himself.

> Gilbert W. had obtained a Ph.D. in sociology at the age of twenty-four and was regarded by his teachers as one of their brightest students. During his last few years of graduate work, however, Gilbert had become increasingly disenchanted with his field. He began to feel sociology was a "pedantic translation into cliquish jargon of commonly recognized phenomena." He felt that he was really of little use to fellow human beings and was serving neither himself nor others by doing research and teaching in a discipline that "substituted imaginative, usually fictitious, concepts and quantities for hard fact." After some exploratory discussion with a counseling psychologist, Gilbert began to turn his attention toward medicine. He felt it could provide him with the kind of challenge and the satisfaction he sought. Although becoming a physician meant that he would have to spend six more years in school, Gilbert enthusiastically began his new career.

The working force is not composed exclusively of men, of course. In the early 1960's about one of every three *married* women was employed (Broom & Selznick, p. 393). The wife who works is subject not only to the same concerns about security and advancement that face her husband but must also deal with many nagging doubts she may have about her own role. Is she shirking her responsibilities as a wife or mother by having a job? How shall she deal with the men with whom she works? Some of them regard her with envy and others with suspicion. Whether it is justified or not, the employed married woman may be confroned with the fact that solcly because she is not a male, she is denied a raise, a position of higher responsibility, or even a permanent position.

Youth, Marriage, and Old Age

Along with the transition from family to school to job are the accompanying aging processes that change one from child to adolescent to elder. During each developmental stage new problems, conflicts, and decisions can be anticipated, as described in earlier chapters. The relatively carefree environment of the child in a healthy home quickly gives way to the adjustments called for by the demands of the peer group. At about six years of age, the beginning of the gang age (see Chapter Two), the child gradually shifts his dependence from parents and siblings to friends and aquaintances his own age. Parental attitudes, whether permissive, rejecting, warm, or unaffectionate, have already shaped the child's attitude and provided him with a set of expectations that become part of him. But his next experience among his childhood and adolescent peers permits him more and more to feel his own potentials and frequently helps him liberate himself from some of the liabilities imposed by short-comings in his family situation.

A college student who contributed an essay, "What I Am," for a mental hygiene course described early independence from his family in the following way.

> For as long as I can remember I would watch the other kids in the neighborhood playing without a care in the world. I was three or four when I started to watch them out of our window or from the front steps of our house. I knew that if I could be with them I would be helped to get rid of the overpowering influence of my parents.
>
> I knew, very early, that there was a lot wrong with my family. I could see it whenever we visited with my aunt or cousins. Not only did they seem so extra kind to me but they whispered and acted as if they were amazed at my being able to look as normal as I suppose I did.
>
> During the summer when I was about five I began to fall in with the other kids. I remember how important it was to me when I found myself really taking part in their games. After that I needed by own family less and less and got whatever satisfactions I needed in the way of attention and friendship from my buddies. I think that being able to stand on my own with the help of the other kids took me out of the neurotic surroundings of my home and made me the fairly healthy person I think I am.

The adjustive challenges of adolescence, marriage, and family responsibilities are much discussed in all media and are the subject of Chapters Three, Four, and Five of this book. But since our culture values youth, little real concern is focused on maturity and old age. Adults in their forties already find their problems (unemployment, physical failings) ignored, if not the butt of jokes.

It is possibly an inevitable ingredient of our youthful pioneer-descendant society that so little is accorded the mature and aging. In many European cultures wisdom and kindliness are attributed to those who are older. Though the aged represent a growing portion of the population in our contemporary setting, nothing is felt to be more hopelessly inadequate than being "old-fashioned."

Just as with any other age group, older people cannot be characterized as a uniform group. There are those whose lives flow from youth to middle years to older age with smoothness and continuity. Others may almost literally "fall apart" when asked to retire. Still others become morbidly concerned with their health as some of their aged friends and relatives become ill or die. Though all older people respond uniquely to the new conditions and challenges of aging with whatever skills they have always had, there are some characteristics shared by most aging people.

Along with age there is a consequent decrease in physical capacity and ability. Not only is there a decline in the ability to take part in demanding recreations; many subtler skills are hampered. But there is *no over-all decline in intellectual ability.* Some of the components of intelligence as measured by tests do decrease, however. The capacity to learn new motor skills, to remember quickly, and to perform tasks requiring speed may be lowered somewhat (Wechsler). Physical disabilities, never completely absent, become more prominent during aging. Table 18-5 reports some of the chronic conditions that are present at particular ages.

Table 18-5 AVERAGE PREVALENCE PER 1,000 PERSONS OF SELECTED CHRONIC CONDITIONS BY AGE, SEX, AND RESIDENCE (1957–59)

Chronic conditions	Total	Age		
		0 to 44 years	45 to 64 years	65 and over
Heart conditions	29.5	8.0	53.6	148.8
High blood pressure	30.8	8.5	66.7	129.1
Diabetes	9.0	2.2	19.3	40.4
Peptic ulcer	14.4	9.6	27.6	22.3
Arthritis and rheumatism	63.9	16.9	144.5	265.8
Hernia	14.9	7.3	24.7	54.6
Chronic bronchitis	11.7	10.0	14.5	18.9
Visual impairments	17.9	5.8	24.1	103.2
Deafness and other hearing impairments	34.1	12.7	50.3	171.8
Paralysis of major extremities and/or trunk	5.5	2.7	8.2	22.4

Source: U.S. Bureau of the Census, Statistical Abstract, 1961.

ADJUSTMENT AND MENTAL HYGIENE

No period of life is free of hazard or change. Our resources are strained from earliest childhood to extreme old age. Continually we are called upon to learn a vast array of skills—like reading—or make major readjustments—as when in our later years we suddenly face the death of family and friends or having to live on a small pension. We can call all these encounters the *adjustive challenges* of life. The major ones are summarized here, grouped by the age at which they are presented us.

Childhood
1.   Develop feelings of self-worth and acceptance.
2.   Socialization—learn expected skills and standards.
3.   Learn physical tasks, language, and other "tools."

Early School Years (The Gang Age)
1.   Acquire scholastic abilities.
2.   Set achievement needs and level of aspiration appropriate to our capabilities and intelligence.
3.   Slowly become less dependent on parents and increasingly value experience with age-mates.
4.   Obtain appropriate sexual identity.

Adolescence
1.   Adjust to invigorated physical and sexual demands.
2.   Grow dependent on self and independent of others.
3.   Prepare for marriage, occupation, or further schooling.
4.   View "self" as a distinct, capable human being.

Adulthood
1.   Assume full responsibilities of maintaining a home; set an example for children; raise a family; be an effective spouse; pursue a career.
2.   Develop a sense of direction and personal values.
3.   Participate and assist in the development of self, faith, and community.

Middle and Later Years
1.   Ensure financial ability to educate children, provide for self and other dependents.
2.   Adjust to decreasing physical and intellectual abilities.
3.   Prepare for decrease in size of family unit, retirement, and other changes in the direction of life.

In addition, throughout our existence we are faced with conflicts and blocks that give rise to tensions and anxieties. Caught on the horns of a dilemma, we ineffectively and fearfully wander from one alternative to another and yet another. Or perhaps we are frustrated and angered because unrealistic levels of aspiration impel us to reach for objectives that are unattainable. We may respond to conflict and frustration in many ways: with indecision, apathy, or vacillation; with anxiety and worry; with resort to fantasy, rationalization, projection, repression, or other defense mechanisms.

But these self-defeating reactions need not be our responses. We are not helpless in the face of all the impediments that threaten to arouse negative emotions within us. To the extent that we can *recognize* and *prepare* for the inevitable and *re-evaluate* our *choices* and *motivations,* we can hope to modify them. There are no specific rules; but certain attitudes toward life and its challenges will function as invaluable *adjustive aids*. Someone who is well prepared for life's challenges will have first an *attitude* characterized by *willingness to understand* himself and others, and by a *realistic assessment* of his own choices, motives, and environment. Second, he will have developed a *realistic set of expectations* about life based on *information* about its changing demands. Third, and finally, he will have achieved *meaningful values* to help direct his existence. Thus, effective mental hygiene consists not in memorizing specific laws but rather in cultivating an informed and receptive attitude and a set of directed and sustaining expectations toward one's own life and the world in which he lives.

Our intelligent anticipation, guided by developing personal standards, can help us to meet the challenges of life and to maximize the opportunities they offer. But nearly all of us, at one time or another, and a very few of us nearly from the start of our lives will require professional assistance. When we are deeply distressed, gravely out of harmony with others, and confronted by challenges and situations with which we are unable to cope, we are wise in seeking immediate specialized guidance. If the family physician, college, or other established medical or counseling office is not available or useful, other contacts may have to be made. The list at the end of Chapter Sixteen may prove useful.

All men who wish to be born must know that they will die, according to a centuries-old folk saying. To this might be added that nearly all who live must know that they will pass quickly from childhood to adulthood and into old age. They will be husbands or wives and parents and grandparents. And in one way or another their existence will be filled with days of work, for some of which they have little appetite. How then may we help ourselves? By encouraging attitudes that both prepare us to learn all we reasonably can and lead us to important values through which we may help guide ourselves and those dependent on us.

FOR REVIEW AND DISCUSSION

1. Can our abilities to think, learn, and understand help us to avoid or modify psychological disorder? Discuss what is meant by the "liberating effects of intelligence and personal values."
2. What are some varieties of conflict that psychologists have identified? How can these identifications be applied to human situations? How may conflict sometimes be resolved?
3. What are the major transitions and changes in life that require impor-

tant adjustment? What is "level of aspiration"? How does it help determine life goals and expectations?

4. Discuss the adjustive challenges in life and how best to prepare to
   meet them effectively. Why are there no simple mental hygiene rules?
   Discuss the following: "We can aid ourselves by encouraging attitudes
   that both prepare us to learn all we reasonably can and lead to important values through which we may help guide ourselves and those
   dependent on us."

References

and

Index

References

Allport, G. W., and L. Postman, *The Psychology of Rumor*. New York: Holt, Rinehart & Winston, Inc., 1947.

Alonso, A. M., "Who Is Mentally Healthy?" *World Mental Health, 13,* (1961), 21–25.

American Psychiatric Association, *Diagnostic and Statistical Manual: Mental Disorders*. Washington, D.C.: American Psychiatric Association Mental Hospital Service, 1952.

Anastasi, A., and J. P. Foley, Jr., *Differential Psychology*. New York: The Macmillan Company, 1958.

Ausubel, D. P., "Causes and Types of Narcotic Addiction: A Psychosocial View," *Psychiat. Quart., 38,* (1961), 523–31.

Bandura, A., "Punishment Revisited," *J. Consult. Psychol., 26,* (1962), 298–301.

Barber, T. X., "Antisocial and Criminal Acts Induced by Hypnosis: A Review of Experimental and Clinical Findings," *Arch. Gen. Psychiat., 5,* (1961), 301–12.

———, "Physiological Effects of Hypnosis," *Psychol. Bull., 58,* (1961), 390–419.

———, "Towards a Theory of Hypnosis: Posthypnotic Behavior," *Arch. Gen. Psychiat., 7,* (1962), 321–42.

Baughman, E. E., and G. S. Welsh, *Personality: A Behavioral Science*. Englewood Cliffs, N.J.: Prentice-Hall, Inc., 1962.

Bellak, L., "Research in Psychoanalysis," *Psychoanalyt. Quart., 30,* (1961), 519–48.

Bergeer, E., and W. S. Kroger, *Kinsey's Myth of Female Sexuality: The Medical Facts*. New York: Grune & Stratton, Inc., 1954.

Berry, Mildred F., and Jon Eisenson, *Speech Disorders—Principles and Practices of Therapy*. New York: Appleton-Century-Crofts, 1956.

Bloodstein, O., W. Jaeger, and J. Tween, "A Study of the Diagnosis of Stuttering by Parents of Stutterers and Non-Stutterers," *J. Speech Hearing Disorders, 17,* (1952), 308–15.

Bradway, K. P., and C. W. Thompson, "Intelligence at Adulthood: A Twenty-five Year Follow-up," *J. Educ. Psychol., 53,* (1962), 1–14.

Britton, E. C., and J. M. Winans, *Growing from Infancy to Adulthood*. New York: Appleton-Century-Crofts, 1958.

Bronfenbrenner, Urie, "The Changing American Child: A Speculative Analysis," *J. Soc. Issues,* 17, (1961), 6–17.

Broom, L., and P. Selznick, *Sociology* (3rd ed.). New York: Harper & Row, Publishers, 1963.

Burt, C., and M. Howard, "The Multiple Factorial Theory of Inheritance and Its Application to Intelligence," *Brit. J. Statist. Psychol., 9,* (1956), 95–131.

Cady, L .D., Jr., M. M. Gertler, L. G. Gottsch, and M. A. Woodbury, "The Factor Structure of Variables Concerned with Coronary Artery Disease," *Behavioral Sci., 6,* (1961), 37–41.

Calvin, A. P., M. Scriven, *et al., Psychology*. Boston: Allyn and Bacon, Inc., 1961.

Cattell, R. B., *Personality and Motivational Structure*. New York: Harcourt, Brace, and World, Inc., 1957.

Child, I. L., and J. W. M. Whiting, "Determinants of Level of Aspiration: Evidence from Everyday Life," *J. Abnorm. Soc. Psychol., 44,* (1949), 303–14.

Children's Bureau, Department of Health, Education, and Welfare, *A Look at Juvenile Delinquency*, Publication No. 380. Washington, D.C.: Government Printing Office, 1960.

———, *The Adolescent in Your Family*, Publication No. 347. Washington, D.C.: Government Printing Office, 1955.

Cloward, R. A., and L. E. Ohlin, *Delinquency and Opportunity: A Theory of Delinquent Gangs*. New York: Free Press of Glencoe, Inc., 1960.

Coleman, James C., *Abnormal Psychology and Modern Life*. Chicago: Scott, Foresman & Company, 1956.

———, *Personality Dynamics and Effective Behavior*. Chicago: Scott, Foresman & Company, 1960.

Cox, C. M., *The Early Mental Traits of Three Hundred Geniuses*. Stanford: Stanford University Press, 1926.

Cronbach, L. J., *Essentials of Psychological Testing*. New York: Harper & Row, Publishers, 1960.

Darley, Fredric L., and Harris Winitz, "Age of First Word: Review of Research," *J. Speech Hearing Disorders, 26,* (1961), 272–90.

Davis, A., and R. J. Havighurst, "Social Class and Color Differences in Child Rearing," *Am. Sociol. Rev., 11,* (1946), 698–710.

Davis, C. M., "Self-Selection of Diet by Newly Weaned Infants," *Am. J. Diseases Children, 36,* (1928), 651–79.

Dunlap, T. R., "A Case of Gilles de la Tourette's Disease (Maladie Des Tics): A Study of the Intrafamily Dynamics," *J. Nervous Mental Disease, 130,* (1960), 340–44.

East, W. N., "Sexual Offenders," *J. Nervous Mental Disease, 103,* (1946), 626–66.

Eisenberg, L., E. Ascher, and L. Kanner, "A Clinical Study of Gilles de la Tourette's Disease in Children," *Am. J. Psychiat., 115,* (1959), 715–23.

Empey, L. T., and J. Rabow, "The Provo Experiment in Delinquency Rehabilitation," *Am. Sociol. Rev., 26,* (1961), 679–95.

Escalona, S., and G. M. Heider, *Prediction and Outcome: A Study in Child Development.* New York: Basic Books, Inc., 1959.

Eysenck, H. J., *Uses and Abuses of Psychology.* Baltimore: Penguin Books, Inc., 1953.

Faw, V., and W. W. Wilcox, "Personality Characteristics of Susceptible and Unsusceptible Hypnotic Subjects," *J. Clin. Exptl. Hypnosis, 6,* (1958), 83–94.

Ford, C .S., "Society, Culture and the Human Organism," *J. Gen. Psychol., 20,* (1939), 135–79.

Ford, D. H., and H. B. Urban, *Systems of Psychotherapy.* New York: John Wiley & Sons, Inc., 1963.

Fowler, W. L., "Hypnosis and Learning," *Int. J. Clin. Exptl. Hypnosis, 9,* (1961), 223–32.

Fromm, E., *Man For Himself: An Inquiry into the Psychology of Ethics.* New York: Holt, Rinehart & Winston, Inc., 1947.

Gerard, D. L., G. Saenger, and R. Wile, "The Abstinent Alcoholic," *Arch. Gen. Psychiat., 6,* (1962), 83–95.

Goddard, H. H., *The Kallikak Family.* New York: The Macmillan Company, 1912.

Goode, J., *After Divorce.* New York: Free Press of Glencoe, Inc., 1955.

Greenspan, H., and J. D. Campbell, "The Homosexual as a Personality Type," *Am. J. Psychiat., 101,* (1945), 628–89.

Gurin, G., J. Veroff, and S. Feld, *Americans View Their Mental Health.* New York: Basic Books, Inc., 1960.

Haas, K., "Conditioning of Affective Verbal Responses," *J. Gen. Psychol., 67,* (1962), 319–22.

Hahn, E. F., *Stuttering: Significant Theories and Therapies.* Stanford: Stanford University Press, 1943.

Hall, B. H., and R. S. Wallerstein, "Operational Problems of Psychotherapy Research. II. Termination Studies," *Bull. Menninger Clinic, 24,* (1960), 190–216.

Harms, Irene E., and Charles C. Spiker, "Factors Associated with the Performance of Young Children on Intelligence Scales and Tests of Speech Development," *J. Genet. Psychol., 94,* (1959), 3–22.

Harper, R. A., *Psychoanalysis and Psychotherapy: Thirty-six Systems.* Englewood Cliffs, N.J.: Prentice-Hall, Inc., 1959.

Havemann, E., and P. S. West, *They Went to College.* New York: Harcourt, Brace, and World, Inc., 1952.

Hayakawa, S. I., *Our Language and Our World.* New York: Harper & Row, Publishers, 1959.

Hebb, D. O., "The Role of Neurological Ideas in Psychology," *J. Personality, 20,* (1951), 39–55.

Heilbrunn, G., "Psychoanalysis of Yesterday, Today and Tomorrow," *Arch. Gen. Psychiat., 4,* (1961), 321–30.

Hollingshead, A. B., and F. C. Redlich, *Social Class and Mental Illness.* New York: John Wiley & Sons, Inc., 1958.

Hook, S., *Psychoanalysis, Scientific Method and Philosophy.* New York: New York University Press, 1959.

Horney, K., *The Neurotic Personality of Our Time.* New York: W. W. Norton & Company, Inc., 1937.

Hovland, C. I., and R. R. Sears, "Experiments on Motor Conflict. I. Types of Conflict and Their Modes of Resolution," *J. Exptl. Psychol., 23,* (1938), 477–93.

Hurlock, Elizabeth B., *Developmental Psychology.* New York: McGraw-Hill Book Company, 1953.

Ilg, F. L., and L. B. Ames, *The Gesell Institutes Child Behavior.* New York: Dell Publishing Co., Inc., 1960.

Immergluck, L., "Determinism-Freedom in Contemporary Psychology: An Ancient Problem Revisited," *Am. Psychologist, 19,* (1964), 270–81.

Jackson, D. O., ed., *The Etiology of Schizophrenia.* New York: Basic Books, Inc., 1960.

Jacobson, P. H., "Differentials in Divorce in Duration of Marriage and Size of Family," *Am. Sociol. Rev., 18,* (1953), 235–44.

Johnson, W., *People in Quandries: The Semantics of Personal Adjustment.* New York: Harper & Row, Publishers, 1946.

———, V. Anderson, G. Kopp, D. Mase, H. Schuell, J. Shover, and W. Wolfe, "ASHA Committee on the Midcentury White House Conference, Speech Disorders and Speech Correction," *J. Speech Hearing Disorders, 17,* (1952), 129–37.

Johnson, W. R., and G. F. Kramer, "Effects of Stereotyped Non-Hypnotic, Hypnotic and Posthypnotic Suggestions Upon Strength, Power and Endurance," *J. Am. Assoc. Health Phys. Educ. Rev., 32,* (1961), 522–29.

Jones, E., *The Life and Work of Sigmund Freud,* ed. Lionel Trilling and Steven Marcus. New York: Doubleday & Company, Inc., 1963.

Jones, E. S., *College Graduates and Their Later Success.* Buffalo: University of Buffalo Studies, 1956.

Kallman, F., "Modern Concepts of Genetics in Relation to Mental Health and Abnormal Personality Development," *Psychiat. Quart., 21,* (1947), 535–53.

Kerckhoff, A. C. and K. E. Davis, "Value Consensus and Need Complementarity in Mate Selection," *Am. Sociol. Rev., 27,* (1962), 295–303.

Kinsey, A. C., W. B. Pomeroy, and C. E. Martin, *Sexual Behavior in the Human Female.* Philadelphia: W. B. Saunders Co., 1953.

———, *Sexual Behavior in the Human Male,* Philadelphia: W. B. Saunders Co., 1948.

Kirkpatrick, C., and T. Caplow, "Emotional Trends in the Courtship Experience of College Students as Expressed by Graphs with Some Observations on Methodological Implications," *Am. Sociol. Rev., 10,* (1945), 619–26.

Klineberg, O., *Negro Intelligence and Selective Migration.* New York: Columbia University Press, 1935.

———, "Negro-White Differences in Intelligence Test Performance: A New Look at an Old Problem," *Am. Psychologist, 18,* (1963), 198–203.

Klopfer, B., M. D. Ainsworth, W. G. Klopper, and R. R. Holt, *Developments in the Rorschach Technique.* New York: Harcourt, Brace, and World, Inc., 1954.

Koestler, A., *The Lotus and the Robot.* New York: The Macmillan Company, 1961.

Koppitz, E. M., "Diagnosing Brain Damage in Young Children with the Bender-Gestalt," *J. Consult. Psychol., 26,* (1962), 541–46.

Korzybski, A., *Science and Sanity.* Lakeville, Conn.: Institute of General Semantics, 1948.

Kubie, L. S., *Practical and Theoretical Aspects of Psychoanalysis.* New York: International Universities Press, Inc., 1951.

Landis, J. T., "Marriages of Mixed and Non-Mixed Religious Faith," *Am. Sociol. Rev., 14,* (1949), 401–7.

———, "The Trauma of Children When Parents Divorce," *Marriage and Family Living, 22,* (1960), 7–13.

Lang, P. J., and A. D. Lazovik, "Personality and Hypnotic Susceptibility," *J. Consult. Psychol., 26,* (1962), 317–22.

Leuba, C., "Theories of Hypnosis: A Critique and Proposal," *Am. J. Clin. Hypnosis, 3,* (1960), 43–48.

Lion, E. G., H. M. Jambor, H. G. Corrigan, and K. P. Bradway, *An Experiment in the Treatment of Promiscuous Girls.* San Francisco: Department of Public Health, 1945.

MacClean, J. R., D. C. MacDonald, U. E. Byrne, and A. M. Hubbard, "The Use of LSD-25 in the Treatment of Alcoholism and Other Psychiatric Problems," *Quart. J. Studies Alc., 22,* (1961), 24–45.

Maier, N. R. F., *Frustration.* New York: McGraw-Hill Book Company, 1949.

Mann, H., "Hypnotherapy in Habit Disorders," *Am. J. Clin. Hypnosis, 3,* (1961), 123–26.

Maslow, A. H., *Motivation and Personality.* New York: Harper & Row, Publishers, 1954.

Masserman, J. H., ed., *Current Psychiatric Therapies.* New York: Grune and Stratton, Inc., 1963.

McCord, W., and J. McCord, *Origins of Alcoholism.* Stanford: Stanford University Press, 1960.

McCurdy, H. G., "The Childhood Patterns of Genius," *J. Elisha Mitchell Sci. Soc., 73,* (1957), 448–62.

McGurk, F. C. J., *Comparison of the Performance of Negro and White High High School Seniors on Cultural and Non-Cultural Psychological Test Questions.* Washington, D.C.: The Catholic University of America Press, 1951.

McNemar, Q., *The Revision of the Stanford-Binet Scale.* Boston: Houghton Mifflin Company, 1942.

Miller, N. E., "Liberalization of Basic S-R Concepts: Extensions to Conflict Behavior, Motivation, and Social Learning," in *Psychology: A Study of a Science,* Vol. 2, ed. S. Koch. New York: McGraw-Hill Book Company, 1959.

Miner, J. B., *Intelligence in the United States.* New York: Springer Publishing Company, Inc., 1957.

Moore, W. E., "Personality Traits and Voice Quality Deficiencies," *J. Speech Disorders, 4,* (1939), 33–36.

Morgan, C. R., *Introduction to Psychology.* New York: McGraw-Hill Book Company, 1961.

Mowrer, O. H., "What is Normal Behavior?" in Arthur Weider, ed., *Contributions Toward Medical Psychology,* Vol. 1. New York: The Ronald Press Company, 1953.

Neilon, P., "Shirley's Babies After Fifteen Years: A Personality Study," *J. Genet. Psychol., 73,* (1948), 175–86.

Newby, Hayes A., *Audiology, Principles and Practice.* New York: Appleton-Century-Crofts, 1958.

Newman, H. H., F. N. Freeman, and K. J. Holzinger, *Twins: A Study of Heredity and Environment.* Chicago: University of Chicago Press, 1937.

Noyes, A. P., and L. C. Kolb, *Modern Clinical Psychiatry* (5th ed.). Philadelphia: W. B. Saunders Co., 1958.

Pennington, L. A., "The Incidence of Nail Biting Among Adults," *Am. J. Psychiat., 102,* (1945), 241–44.

Poole, Irene, "Genetic Development of Articulation of Consonant Sounds in Speech," *Elementary English Reviews, 11,* (1934), 159–61.

Pressey, S. L., and R. G. Kuhlen, *Psychological Development Through the Life Span.* New York: Harper & Row, Publishers, 1957.

Public Health Service, *Alcoholism,* Publication No. 730. Washington, D.C.: Government Printing Office, 1961.

———, *Facts on Mental Health and Mental Illness,* Publication No. 543. Washington, D.C.: Government Printing Office, 1962.

Reider, N., "The Concept of Normality," *Psychoanalyt. Quart., 51,* (1943), 138–39.

Renner, K. E., B. A. Maher, and D. T. Campbell, "The Validity of a Method for Scoring Sentence Completion Responses for Anxiety Dependency and Hostility," *J. Appl. Psychol., 467,* (1962), 285–90.

Riesman, D., N. Glazer, and R. Denney, *The Lonely Crowd.* New Haven: Yale University Press, 1961.

Riggs, A. F., *On Intelligent Living.* New York: Doubleday & Company, Inc., 1929.

Rinkel, M., and H. C. B. Denber, *Chemical Concepts of Psychosis*. New York: Ivan Obolensky, Inc., 1958.

Rogers, C. R., *Client-Centered Therapy*. Boston: Houghton Mifflin Company, 1951.

————, "Cultural Evolution as Viewed by Psychologists," *Daedalus, 90,* (1961), 574–75.

Rosen, H., "The Hypnotic and Hypnotherapeutic Control of Severe Pain," *Am. J. Psychiat., 107,* (1951), 917–25.

Rubinstein, E. A., and M. B. Parloff, eds., *Research in Psychotherapy*. Washington, D.C.: American Psychological Association, 1959.

Ruch, F. L., *Psychology and Life* (6th ed.). Chicago: Scott, Foresman and Company, 1963.

Rutgers Center of Alcohol Studies. Various pamphlets. New Brunswick, N.J.: The State University.

Sears, Robert, Eleanor Maccoby, and Harry Levin, *Patterns of Child Rearing*. New York: Harper & Row, Publishers, 1957.

Senn, M. J. E., "Problems of Infancy and Childhood," *Symposium on the Healthy Personality,* Supplement II. New York: Josiah Macy, Jr. Foundation, 1950.

Sheldon, W. H., and S. S. Stevens, *The Varieties of Temperament*. New York: Harper & Row, Publishers, 1942.

Sherif, M., *The Psychology of Social Norms*. New York: Harper & Row, Publishers, 1936.

Shirley, M., *The First Two Years: A Study of Twenty-five Babies*. Vol. 3, "Personality Manifestations." Minneapolis: The University of Minnesota Press, 1933.

Simon, C. W., and W. H. Emmons, "Responses to Material Presented During Various Levels of Sleep," *J. Exptl. Psychol., 51,* (1956), 89–97.

Spock, B. E., *Baby and Child Care* (rev. ed.). New York: Pocket Books, Inc., 1957.

Steiner, L. R., *Understanding Juvenile Delinquency*. Philadelphia: Chilton Books, 1960.

Stern, C., *Principles of Human Genetics* (2nd ed.). San Francisco: W. H. Freeman & Co., Publishers, 1960.

Stuart, I. R., "Complementary vs. Homogeneous Needs in Mate Selection: A Television Program Situation," *J. Soc. Psychol., 56,* (1962), 291–300.

Tanser, H. A., *The Settlement of Negroes in Kent County, Ontario, and a Study of the Mental Capacity of Their Descendents*. Chatham, Ont.: Shepherd, 1939.

Terman, L. M., *Psychological Factors in Marital Happiness*. New York: McGraw-Hill Book Company, 1938.

————, and M. A. Merrill, *Stanford-Binet Intelligence Scale*. Boston: Houghton Mifflin Company, 1960.

————, and M. H. Oden, *The Gifted Child Grows Up*. Stanford: Stanford University Press, 1947.

————, *The Gifted Group at Mid-Life*. Stanford: Stanford University Press, 1959.

Thorne, F. C. "The Incidence of Nocturnal Eneuresis After Age Five," *Am. J. Psychiat., 100,* (1944), 686–89.

Titchener, E. B., *Experimental Psychology.* New York: The Macmillan Company, 1905.

Toby, J., "Early Identification and Intensive Treatment of Pre-Delinquents: A Negative View," *Social Work, 6,* 3, (1961), 3–13.

Travis, Lee E., "My Present Thinking on Stuttering," *Western Speech, 10,* (1946), 3–5.

Tyler, L. E., *The Psychology of Human Difference.* New York: Appleton-Century-Crofts, 1956.

United States Bureau of the Census, *Statistical Abstract of the United States* (82nd ed.). Washington, D.C.: Government Printing Office, 1961.

Van Riper, Charles, *Teaching Your Child to Talk.* New York: Harper & Row, Publishers, 1950.

——, *Speech Correction: Principles and Methods* (4th ed.). Englewood Cliffs, N.J.: Prentice-Hall, Inc., 1963.

Veit, H., "Insulin Therapy at Colorado Psychopathic Hospital," *Diseases Nervous System, 8,* (1947), 320–23.

Watson, Goodwin, "Some Personality Differences in Children Related to Strict or Permissive Parental Discipline," in M. L. Haimowitz and N. R. Haimowitz, *Human Development—Selected Readings.* New York: Thomas Y. Crowell Co., 1960.

Wechsler, D., *The Measurement and Appraisal of Adult Intelligence* (4th ed.). Baltimore: The Williams & Wilkins Co., 1958.

Weis, E., and O. S. English, *Psychosomatic Medicine.* Philadelphia: W. B. Saunders Co., 1957.

Weitzenhoffer, A. M., *Hypnotism.* New York: John Wiley & Sons, Inc., 1953.

——, *Hypnotism: An Objective Study of Suggestibility.* New York: John Wiley & Sons, Inc., 1957.

West, D. J., "Parental Figures in the Genesis of Male Homosexuality," *Int. J. Psychiat., 5,* (1959), 85–97.

West, R., S. Nelson, and Mildred F. Berry, "The Heredity of Stuttering," *Quart. J. Speech, 25,* (1939), 23–30.

White, R. W., *The Abnormal Personality* (2nd ed.). New York: The Ronald Press Company, 1956.

Winick, C., and M. Nyswander, "Psychotherapy of Successful Musicians Who Are Drug Addicts," *Am. J. Orthopsychiat., 31,* (1961), 622–36.

Wolberg, L. R., *Medical Hypnosis.* New York: Grune & Stratton, Inc., 1948. 2 Vols.

Wolpe, J., "The Prognosis in Unpsychoanalyzed Recovery from Neurosis," *Am. J. Psychiat., 118,* (1961), 35–39.

Yates, A. J., "Hypnotic Age Regression," *Psychol. Bull., 58,* (1961), 429–40.

Index